IRREPARABLE HARM

FRANK SNEPP

IRREPARABLE HARM

A Firsthand Account
of How One Agent
Took On the CIA in an
Epic Battle Over Secrecy
and Free Speech

RANDOM HOUSE
NEW YORK

All rights reserved under International and Pan-American Copyright Conventions.
Published in the United States by Random House, Inc., New York, and simultaneously
in Canada by Random House of Canada Limited, Toronto.

RANDOM HOUSE and colophon are registered trademarks of
Random House, Inc.

Library of Congress Cataloging-in-Publication Data
Snepp, Frank.
Irreparable harm : a firsthand account of how one agent
took on the CIA in an epic battle over secrecy
and free speech / by Frank Snepp.
p.   cm.
Includes index.
ISBN 0-394-50503-4 (hc)
1. Snepp, Frank—Trials, litigation, etc. 2. Snepp, Frank.
Decent interval. 3. United States. Central Intelligence Agency—
Officials and employees. 4. Prior restraint—United States.
5. Freedom of the press—United States. 6. National security—
United States. I. Title.
KF228.S559S65   1999
342.73′0853—dc21   98-53462

Random House website address: www.atrandom.com

Printed in the United States of America on acid-free paper

24689753

FIRST EDITION

To my beloved sisters and brother,
Candy, Frances, and David,
for whom this book became
a passage of reconciliation
in more ways than one

ACKNOWLEDGMENTS

Any book nearly twenty years in the making has many midwives. Some of those who labored and sacrificed in service to my obsession have become the actual heroes of this narrative, with their names and exploits celebrated here. But countless others are due both recognition and apology.

First among them: Meg Bennett, who in the final eight years of my journey to this watershed supported and succored me beyond all measure and endured my excesses with love and truly saintly forbearance. Without her I would surely have become a casualty along the way.

Earlier, the J. Roderick MacArthur Foundation, then under the directorship of Lance Lindblom, threw me a desperately needed fiscal lifeline in the form of a grant just as I was about to go under. I can never repay their generosity.

My brother-in-law, Richard Friedman, and my niece and nephew, David and Katie, offered love and encouragement. My friend and erstwhile journalistic colleague John Drimmer and his brilliant wife, Barbara Bliss Osborn, hacked their way through early versions of this text and furnished invaluable insights and suggestions. Constitutional scholar John Sims, about whom you will read more within, checked legal details and bucked up my spirits. Television journalist Bob Long forced me to keep a sense of humor. Jacqueline Melchiade challenged me to stay calm and compassionate, and Wendi Gomez kept me mindful of the positive side of my Southern heritage, the darker side of which figures so importantly in this story. F. Peter Model, who contributed valiantly to the success of my first book, provided food and shelter at various critical junctures in the writing of this one when I might otherwise have been on the streets. To him and many others I owe much more than thanks—in fact, my very survival.

— —

A brief word about sourcing: In the course of the litigation that is part of this story, the CIA and the Justice Department declassified and turned over to me many confidential documents that revealed how they viewed me and my transgressions. In addition, both defense and prosecution elicited hours of sworn testimony from principals within the Agency and elsewhere who would not otherwise have waxed so candidly about me or themselves. In documenting this book I have drawn extensively on these sources and have also interviewed many minor and major players.

Court battles, like actual combat, defy easy recapitulation in print. Condensation and elision are inevitable, and often one is forced to isolate a theme simply for clarity's sake that is merely one of many important threads in the tapestry. I have tried to wrestle the complexities of this story into intelligible form with as little distortion and prejudice as possible, despite the fact that many to whom I give voice here were clearly out to destroy me.

— —

Personal note: In an earlier book I told a story that is recounted here, concerning a woman I call Mai Ly, but did not provide precise details of her life and passing out of a sense of guilt that has taken years to overcome. Also, I remained hopeful that she might still be alive in Vietnam, and fearful that any highly specific reference to her might expose her to official retribution there. Circumstances no longer require such circumspection.

FRANK SNEPP
Marina del Rey, California
June 1999

CONTENTS

PROLOGUE:
FATHERS, SONS, AND SPIES

The little boy's head seems tilted at a painful angle under the crooked elbow of the man with the Errol Flynn mustache and the look of pained forbearance. It is a feigned embrace like all the others, father and son seated arm in arm on a granite outcropping in the Carolina Blue Ridge, the boy twisting away yet reluctant to make a display, the plump little cheeks frozen into a rictus that is neither smile nor grimace but a compromise of both.

Nearly fifty years later, I can still affect that same neutral expression, even though the jaw has tightened and the sandy curls have turned ashen. For if living with my father taught me anything, it was the spy's best lesson: how to bury your feelings so deep no one will ever find them.

My father had not wanted to come home after V-J Day, not after the Marine command offered him a coveted staff job with the American postwar administration in Japan. But I was the complication, the last-minute love child of a last-minute marriage consummated just before his departure for the Pacific three years before, and he could not wish me away. So he declined the assignment and the chance of a lifetime and came home—and never forgave me or my mother for it.

The melancholy he felt is preserved in that photo of the two of us in the Carolina mountains, in the tight-lipped stoicism that would become a model for my own, though by then he'd given himself over to it so completely he probably no longer realized how wretched he was.

Beyond that moment in the photograph, I can clearly remember only one other childhood encounter with my father, so protective has memory become. I'd been playing in my grandmother's pantry and apparently had left some spilt milk behind. My father found it, and though I honestly couldn't recall having made the mess, he beat me until I confessed I had. It was a defining moment, one from which I never quite recovered—and I vowed never to be broken again.

If the CIA's recruiters had known of this episode, they might have thought twice about plucking me out of Columbia's School of International Affairs in 1968 and signing me on. An unyielding spirit does not well become any bureaucrat, even a covert one.

But I had compensating virtues: Aryan blood, a country-club mentality, and an immense capacity for dissembling.

That I was a Southerner merely burnished the appeal. Growing up in a culture that can blithely portray a war to preserve slavery as a crusade to protect states' rights is wonderful preparation for a career of endless charade.

— —

I did not join the CIA to escape my father or to replace him, but in the course of my two tours in Vietnam as a spy I did both. Not once during those turbulent five years did he communicate with me, for reasons you will soon understand. But the man who presided over the final American mission in Saigon and the last CIA station chief there both adopted me as their own.

Ambassador Graham Martin had lost a son to combat in Vietnam, and as a fellow North Carolinian he recognized something achingly familiar in my own soft Southern drawl and filial deference. In due course, he embraced me, encouraged me to romance his daughter, and made me his principal military briefer. A man of towering ego and commensurate paranoia, he also used me to spy on my own CIA colleagues to ensure their fealty. Among his targets: my own boss, CIA station chief Tom Polgar, who, no mean conspirator himself, relied on me to keep him abreast of the ambassador's machinations.

A heavily accented Hungarian Jew whose like seldom flourished in the Agency's WASPish fraternity, Polgar saw me as the perfect straight arrow to his own complex persona and granted me favors seldom accorded any young spy of my decidedly modest skills. After I returned to CIA headquarters for a brief sabbatical in 1971, he brought me back to interrogate our most important Communist prisoner, and following the 1973 cease-fire and the withdrawal of the last American forces, he allowed me to establish and maintain contact with our most productive sources behind enemy lines.

With his patronage, and the ambassador's, I had nowhere to go but up. The forgotten son had found two attentive surrogates in lieu of the absentee.

— —

It was in the summer of 1969 that I first stepped into the steaming chaos of wartime Saigon, and though I'd come fearing the worst, I quickly discovered that my premonitions were overdrawn. The CIA obligingly insulated its cadre by keeping us as far from the carnage as possible and by swathing our consciences in a rationale that made even our worst excesses seem, well, conscionable. As long as we were getting the truth out, I was told over and over, the worst we did was redeemed. For a Southerner nurtured as I was on the incongruous fruits of chivalry and racism, such cynical pap went down easily.

So did the illusory sense of relevance that came with the posting, the sheer fascination of being at what seemed the center of things. One blistering morning two weeks into my first tour, as I was winging my way toward a firefight at the tip of the delta, I realized in a flush of exhilaration that nothing would ever matter so much as what I did here, and I heard myself murmuring over the roar of the engines, "I love it! My God, I love it."

And so I did, with such unfathomable passion that I was eventually striking one compromise after another simply to stay on. Early in my second tour, for instance, I discovered we were deluding ourselves about the viability of the South Vietnamese military. But instead of protesting the self-deception, I became an accomplice to it, sloughing over the truth in the analyses I wrote for Polgar, garnering such credit with him that he soon had me drafting all the strategic appraisals he sent to Washington.

Whatever scruples I brought to the task quickly disintegrated against the grindstone of expediency that passed for protocol in that embassy. It isn't hard to describe the process, only to forgive it. One morning you walk into your office and discover that some small achievement has won praise in high places. Next thing you know, your superior rewards you with a larger piece of the action—a new source to interrogate, a fresh prisoner to break—just enough to tempt you with the prospect of more, and from then on it becomes oh so easy to fold the vocabulary of the "System" into your own. If you're idealistic (the worst affliction of all), the short dizzying slide into virtual lockstep feels preordained, for having committed the original sin, the first compromise itself, you've nothing to hold on to.

For those overburdened with a sense of "mission," there's always the comforting illusion that a larger purpose is being served. Give in on this small point, compromise on that one—you assure yourself—and soon you'll earn enough credit to wage a fight on truly important issues. The hook, of course, is that the important ones quickly recede into something you'll always defend tomorrow.

Over time, by just such degrees, my own conformity won me plaudits, promotions, and all the top-secret clearances. I became Polgar's mouthpiece, the ambassador's shadow, the man in the embassy with more "access" than anybody. But inevitably, the expansion of my pretensions forced character flaws to the surface, and by the summer of 1974, midway through my second tour, my fitness reports were sprinkled with red flags: "Sometimes impatient with the bureaucracy . . . not a compromiser . . . more idealistic and 'involved' than most . . . a somewhat intense individual who works best when left to his own devices . . . stubborn at times, especially on points of conviction."

Not exactly rave notices, especially in an organization like the CIA, where team play is everything. But ultimately my blemishes were forgiven because Martin and Polgar protected me, and because when I did their bidding I did so with the dedication of the true disciple.

"Mr. Snepp quickly adapts to each audience," Polgar once wrote of my briefings. "He is careful never to overstep proper bounds; he is perceptive of nuances. He defers to his superiors when appropriate."

With such kudos the scales were balanced, the negative impressions outweighed, and I might have ridden the slipstream of approval all the way to a glorious third tour and a sycophant's just reward—total moral decrepitude—except for the intervention of the North Vietnamese army. But as Hanoi's forces closed round us in early 1975, the illusions that had sustained me and my masters collapsed in on us and the "peace" Henry Kissinger had negotiated two years before was exposed for what it was, merely a decent interval before the inevitable Communist takeover.

Martin and Polgar, hard-liners both, were slow to grasp this fact. Till the bitter end, they trusted in the duplicitous optimism of the French ambassador to Saigon and other local diplomats and remained convinced that the Saigon government could be held together long enough for a face-saving negotiated settlement. Believing this, they let our evacuation planning stagger along, so that on the day of the pullout itself there wasn't even a master list in the embassy of the Vietnamese spies, collaborators, and employees who were counting on us to deliver them from Hanoi's vengeance.

During the war's terrible last days, I recognized what I'd become and what we were facing. The agents and informers I'd been assigned to interrogate left me no choice. Time and again they warned that Hanoi would stop at nothing short of total military victory. Terrified, I tried to impress this on Martin and Polgar, timidly at first, then more boldly, and finally, when that didn't work, I began leaking my fears to journalists with their own back channels to Washington.

Too late. The president and his men had been seduced too. And when the end came and the helicopters rushed to the rescue, the evacuation degenerated quickly into an improvised experiment in racism: only those with white skin were assured a way out.

Choppered off the embassy roof with the last CIA contingent on the night of April 29, 1975, I could see from the porthole thousands of Vietnamese jammed in the streets below, gazing skyward for the help that would never come. Till then, the war had been a B-52 strike from sixty thousand feet up, the consequences of my actions often only barely visible through the haze of euphemism I'd conjured to shield my conscience. But that last day, there were no euphemisms for what we'd done. We'd betrayed the Vietnamese who'd depended on us, and those of us who'd worked most closely with them—the young CIA and State Department officers from the trenches—now had blood on our hands, for it was we who in our daily contacts had convinced them to trust us.

PART I

SEARCH FOR REDEMPTION

CHAPTER 1

Ghosts

Ｓo, how *do* you crawl out of a country standing up!"

Offering this judgment with a finality that defied argument, Bill Johnson shoved himself away from the ship's rail and turned his back on the reporter with whom he'd been sharing confidences. His eyes glittered like splintered mica under the flop-brimmed fishing hat he'd worn throughout the evacuation. He'd just run out of rationalizations for the debacle we'd been through. But maybe this last one said it all.

Gazing beyond him at the mist-shrouded bleakness of the South China Sea, I marveled at his capacity to rationalize at all. I felt dazed, disembodied, incapable of much more than self-recrimination. But he, a twenty-year veteran of the espionage wars, seemed to have lost none of his typical sangfroid. Perhaps it was experience that made the difference. Or perhaps simply Vietnam. Vietnam had always been an old man's war and a young man's tragedy. The old men had rationalized their way in and had almost as deftly rationalized their way out, and the young men had been left to bury the bodies and ideals and bear the shame of America's first lost cause without the soothing panaceas of high policy, so often classified "top-secret," beyond their ken.

I moved away from Johnson and forced my unsteady sea legs toward the afterdeck of the USS *Denver*. Below, on the helipad itself, another group of evacuees, all Vietnamese, were doing penance, Buddhists and Catholics ranged side by side, mourning loved ones dead and abandoned. A strong breeze riffled the women's *áo dài*s and the red and yellow banner of the lost republic draped over a makeshift altar. I was glad not to be among them, not to have to look into their eyes. The memories were enough.

Memories—already wheeling through the imagination like unsettled ghosts . . . Mr. Han, the translator, screaming over his CIA radio for help . . . Loc, the Nung guard, plucking at my sleeve, begging me not to forget him . . . Mai Ly, phoning just hours before the collapse, threatening to kill herself and her child if I didn't find them a way out . . .

I stared at the *Denver*'s wake, trying vainly to put Mai Ly behind me. She'd phoned too late, I kept telling myself. What could she have expected so late? But there was no consolation in that. The first time she'd called, I'd been chained to my typewriter, hammering out another piece of analysis which I was foolish enough to hope would nudge the ambassador toward the choppers. So I'd told her, "Call back in an hour. I'll be glad to help." But in an hour, I'd been down in the ambassador's office, trying to sell him on the analysis, and she'd left a message, "I would have expected better of you," and then had bundled up the baby boy she'd let me believe was my own and had retreated to that dingy room off Tu Do, and there had made good her promise.

Mother and child: they might have been sleeping when a friend found them hours later except for the blood on the pallet and my misplaced priorities that day. But no more than the ambassador or any of the others I was now so ready to condemn had I troubled to remember that far more than American prestige was at stake those last moments before midnight.

But I remembered now, too late, and the memories plucked at the mind's eye like conscience's own scavengers. Which is why I'd barely slept the past two nights since my own chopper flight out, despite a bone-numbing weariness and a melancholy that already weighed like a sentence of guilt.

As the days passed and the evacuation fleet closed on Subic Bay in the Philippines, the weather cleared, and the Americans on the upper decks took to sprawling in the incandescent May sun like Caribbean vacationers. Below, in the ship's bowels where the Vietnamese were now quarantined, an old man died of heat prostration, a baby was born, and the stench gave appalling measure to the despair and humiliation arrayed on every inch of metal planking.

Sometime midjourney, from Admiral Steele's flagship, came word that my old boss, Tom Polgar, would shortly give a press conference to damp down unhelpful speculation about the way the pullout had been handled. As the reporters among us choppered over for the show, the teletypes in the *Denver*'s signals room beat out preemptive communiqués from Washington, absolving Secretary of State Kissinger of any wrongdoing, quoting

him as saying that the North Vietnamese had been committed to a negotiated political settlement up until the last two days of the war and had
shifted plans so abruptly as to make an orderly evacuation impossible.

I read these dispatches with a rage that was to become chronic.
Kissinger knew as well as the rest of us that our intelligence told a different story, and that it was his own blind stubbornness, not any change in
Hanoi's strategy, that accounted for the delay in the evacuation and thus
the chaos in the end.

When Polgar opened his own dog and pony show, I expected him to set
the record straight. It was his moral duty to do so, for without some acknowledgment of failure, there would never be any incentive in Washington to make amends, no pressure for anyone to mount rescue missions or
attempt diplomatic initiatives to ease the plight of those we'd abandoned.

But to my chagrin, this resilient little man whom I had served so long
merely replayed Kissinger's line, imputing unpredictability to Hanoi and
imperfections to our intelligence to explain his own and others' miscalcu-
lations. And when an opportunity arose for some self-serving scapegoating, he couldn't resist singling out Ambassador Martin himself, claiming
that the old man's inflexibility, his refusal to sacrifice the Thieu regime, had
doomed the prospects for a last-minute political fix.

During this peroration, the accused himself wandered in, munching an
apple. He said nothing in his own defense, but later pulled several reporters
aside and repaid Polgar's slights by suggesting that it was the CIA station
chief himself who had precipitated the breakdown of order and discipline
in the embassy by spiriting his own wife and household belongings out of
Saigon prematurely.

Absurd though this allegation was, State Department officials on board
quickly took up the refrain, and before long brickbats were flying fast and
furious between them and Polgar's apologists. I listened and fumed but said
nothing, confident that back home in official Washington somebody would
insist on getting the facts and the lessons right.

When the task force docked in Subic Bay on May 5, most of my CIA
colleagues were hustled off to the United States for badly needed R&R.
But not I. Believing naively that more intelligence might make a difference,
I volunteered to fly to Bangkok to interrogate some "sensitive sources" who
had just come out of Vietnam.

En route, I stopped off in Hong Kong to replace the wardrobe I'd lost
during the evacuation, and there encountered the *New Yorker* correspondent Robert Shaplen, who had likewise been witness to the fall. He was in
the process of wrapping up a story on it all and asked if I would confirm
some details for him. I consented, since the hulking, bushy-browed Shaplen

had long been viewed as a "friendly" by the Agency and had often been the beneficiary of official secrets-laden briefings by me.

Out at his Repulse Bay apartment, he softened me up with two martinis and some flattery, claiming that my tips to him during the final offensive had kept him from being wholly misled by Polgar and the ambassador. He was so grateful, he said, he wanted to credit me publicly, and despite my demurrals, did so (though with a typographical error) in the May 19, 1975, issue of *The New Yorker.* "Where Martin was more misguided," he wrote, "was in persistently believing that a political settlement was possible, though he had in fact been told for weeks by his military analysts, particularly by Mr. Frank Sneff, a civilian expert well qualified to judge, that the situation was deteriorating very rapidly."

Despite the misspelling, this delicately hedged homage to one who was supposed to be invisible did not endear me to colleagues back home, and though weeks would pass before I'd begin feeling their ire, the start of my long, slow descent into official disrepute can surely be traced to Shaplen's generosity.

As I rose to say good-bye, Shaplen draped an arm around my shoulder and, surprising me again, urged me good-naturedly not to let the story of Saigon's defeat become journalism's preserve alone. There was a book in it for somebody, he said, and given my knowledge of Vietnam and Martin's embassy, what better candidate to write it than I? He'd even supply a preface, he added jocularly.

I looked at him in amazement. A book? Impossible, I told him. Too many reputations at stake. Besides, the Agency always performs its own postmortems, or suffers them, after a foul-up. Witness the Taylor Report after the Bay of Pigs, and the autopsy on Tet '68. There'd be one on this debacle too, no question. A book would be superfluous.

When I reached Bangkok a day later, I'd all but forgotten his suggestion. Would that I could have forgotten the assignment, too. Protestors were raging through the streets in search of fresh pretexts for their resurgent anti-Americanism, and within days of my arrival an American merchant vessel, the *Mayaguez,* was commandeered off the coast of neighboring, newly "liberated" Cambodia by Khmer marauders and the White House had decided to send in the Marines just to show we still had some of our old spunk left. Suddenly, CIA and military colleagues from Vietnam were crowding into Bangkok on their way to staging areas up-country, and for one eerily incongruous moment, American might with flags flying mustered off to war again.

By the time the smoke had cleared, however, this plucky show of force had degenerated into a cruel parody of yesterday's humiliations. Forty-one servicemen had died to save thirty-one crewmen and one tin tub, and the War Powers Act, designed to limit our involvement in such improvisatory hostilities, had been made a mockery again, the president having deployed the troops without fully alerting Congress as required by the law.

To the north of us, meanwhile, another sequel to recent tragedy was being played out around the now irrelevant Laotian capital of Vientiane. Pathet Lao forces had already invested the city, and the few remaining U.S. embassy staffers there were now hunkered down in barricaded compounds awaiting their own inevitable evacuation. Outside the city, beyond any succor, the hapless Meo tribesmen who had once made up the CIA's thirty-thousand-man secret army were already threading their way south toward Thai sanctuaries to escape Communist reprisals. Only a third would make it.

To some of my CIA brethren in Bangkok, the paucity of white faces among the past weeks' casualties seemed to offer consolation. But I knew, as many of them still did not, that the *Mayaguez* losses weren't the only ones to be accounted for. In addition to a CIA officer and several consular officials who had been captured up-country in Vietnam weeks before, two U.S. Marines had been killed in the final bombardment of Saigon, their bodies shamefully abandoned at the airfield, and another CIA veteran, an Agency retiree who'd returned to Saigon belatedly to help evacuate Vietnamese friends, had missed the last chopper out. Now, reports had it, Hanoi's secret police had him under hostile interrogation and were forcing him to finger those he had meant to save.

Given all this and the lingering trauma of my own departure from Saigon, the last thing I needed was to be dragged back through the charnel house. But in the course of the Bangkok assignment, my interview schedule was rapidly expanded to include the debriefing of more and more late arrivals from the war zone—journalists, stragglers, boat people—and with each new source's revelations, I was forced to relive the horrors of the evacuation as few other CIA officers had.

One of my interlocutors, an American journalist who'd just come out of Vietnam on a Red Cross flight, told me of a former Radio Saigon announcer who had been tortured and mutilated, her tongue cut out by her North Vietnamese "liberators," and then allowed to drown in her own blood. Another source recounted summary executions of defectors, CIA collaborators, and cadre of the once feared Phoenix counterterror program. And still another recalled how Communist troops had sought out a CIA billet in Saigon and systematically slaughtered the Vietnamese maids and houseboys who had gathered there in anticipation of last-minute deliverance.

These and other outrages I duly reported in hopes that someone along the chain of command might be shamed into taking ameliorative action, diplomatic or otherwise. But by mid-June, my harping upon betrayed commitments had become an unwelcome dissonance. One morning, by urgent telex from CIA headquarters, I was ordered home.

In my last two and a half years in Indochina, I'd had only five days of leave and few Sundays off, and I badly needed to decompress. But my monthlong odyssey back through the Mideast and Europe didn't do it. My traveling companion, an itinerant CIA secretary, promptly grew weary of my angst, the casual romance she'd anticipated descending quickly into a kind of joyless sexuality which I clung to with the desperation of a drowning man.

Nor was there any comfort in the prospect of heading home. The only real home I knew was the Agency, and the disillusionment I'd suffered these past few months was only a foretaste of worse to come. For this was the Season of the Reckoning, the summer of 1975, and scandal and exposé were now swirling about the Agency like predators on a blood scent. The savaging had begun the previous winter when the press, emboldened by Watergate, had homed in on rumors of CIA kill plots and illegal domestic spying, and since then White House and congressional investigators had joined in the carnage.

During the long months of Saigon's demise I'd been too preoccupied to be able to dwell on any of these indelicacies. But now, with unaccustomed leisure on my hands, I had time to contemplate as never before the overwrought headlines, the tales of murderous excess and lawlessness, and the intimations of perjury by one of my idols, former CIA director Richard Helms, who, it was reported, had deliberately lied to Congress about CIA complicity in the overthrow of Chile's Salvador Allende years before.

Initially, I tried to convince myself it was all spiteful gossip, but the more I read en route the more insistent the truth became, for many of the most serious charges had recently been confirmed by a vice presidential panel, the Rockefeller Commission, appointed (ironically) to dispel them: not only had the Agency, together with the FBI, illicitly spied on thousands of Americans at home, many of them Vietnam War protestors; it had also ripped open and read the mail of countless citizens and exposed still others surreptitiously to deadly drug experiments.

Beyond all this, there was the ghastly prospect, now being avidly explored by congressional muckrakers, that the CIA had systematically tried to rub out foreign leaders like Fidel Castro. Three years before, then CIA director Helms had assured all of us by official circular that the Agency never assassinates anybody. Admittedly, I'd seen that rule bent in Vietnam.

But Vietnam had been a special case, a hot war. All rules were bent there. But now it appeared they'd been bent elsewhere too, with no war to provide excuses. And if that were so, then Helms had lied to us, and the Agency might well be the rogue elephant some congressmen thought it to be.

That prospect was more terrifying than anything else. The rogue elephant can't be forgiven its excesses, and God knows I wanted to be forgiven, to be able to wrap myself in presidential rationales. But if the leash had snapped and the beast was on the rampage, then there were no rationales, no forgiveness. And perhaps no end to it either. The CIA's current director, William Colby, had recently admitted publicly that neither Nixon nor Ford had ever been told of the "family jewels," a ticklist of the Agency's most egregious transgressions compiled by the director's own staff two years before. Two presidents—*not told!* If not, then what else had gone unreported? Maybe much more, and that could mean that the beast had not merely kicked the traces, but blinded the master as well.

No, I couldn't believe it. I wouldn't. Congress was the culprit, not the CIA. Weren't these investigations ostensibly being conducted "behind closed doors"? And yet, just look at the leaks. Could anyone be trusted who permitted such leaks? I took refuge in the most convenient and craven answer.

There was no refuge, though, from my other torments, the demons out of memory that hounded me home. For time and distance only invigorated them, their images, even their pained cries of reproach soon invading my consciousness and conscience and finally my dreams, thus banishing sleep, so that by the time I touched down stateside, I was not only bitter and confused but exhausted, nearing nervous collapse. And still, hard as I tried, I could not rid myself of Mai Ly or Han or Loc, the Nung guard. . . .

Or Le. No, least of all, her. She'd been "U.N. quality," that one, the best interpreter I'd ever taken with me into Saigon's dungeons, her femininity itself an asset in the interrogations, for who could resist unburdening himself to her? The irony was that she'd been more the revolutionary than most of the prisoners we'd grilled. She'd detested the Americans as interlopers and had embraced us only as the lesser of two evils. I'd once tried to fix her loyalties by offering to help her set up a pig farm so she'd have some life outside the interrogation center. She'd politely rebuffed me and gone her own way. By the time the enemy was at the gates this past April, I'd lost track of her, and only later, in Bangkok, had I discovered that those responsible for getting her out had botched it. So she was back there still, with the inmates she'd interrogated. Only they were the jailkeeps now and she the inmate, and God knows how bad off, for they wouldn't forget the role she'd played.

Forgive me.

And Tan—what of Tan? There was no forgetting him either, even though I'd tried and was now exhausted trying, and wished to the pit of my soul he'd never crossed over after the Viet Cong medics had let his wife die in childbirth. They'd been short of medicine as usual, and he'd watched her die in agony; and then, broken and defeated, he had walked out of the jungle and into our arms and had let slip every secret he knew. I'd slapped a defector's label on him and one night had taken him out on the town to an American hangout to try to build rapport. We'd sat at a corner table watching fat, sweating round-eyes wrestle Vietnamese girls around the dance floor, and after a while he'd turned to me, his face ashen, and murmured, "We're going to lose. I've made the wrong choice." A chill had knifed through me, and I'd wanted to send him off into the night, back to his own. But it was too late. He was in. We had him, a certified defector. He could never go back.

Unless we abandoned him—which we did, along with nearly every other defector we'd exploited and turned into a pariah.

Tan must be dead now. An easy death, I hope.

Forgive me.

CHAPTER 2

Reentry

MY FIRST WEEKEND BACK, I spent in New York, remaking old acquaintances and talking of lost ones as if confession might ease the pain.

For almost everyone with whom I shared my punishment called memory, Vietnam was a relic best forgotten, an ancient piece of hubris that had receded from moral relevance in the three years since the last American boys had come home. Only one former drinking companion whose phone number I could remember professed to see things differently; only Linley Stafford seemed to care that Vietnamese had kept on killing one another with our help till just a few weeks before.

I'd first met the garrulous, pipe-smoking Stafford in the mid-1960s, before my stint in graduate school and recruitment by the CIA, and in the decade since, he'd grown rotund and bored as a publicity flack for a national teacher's guild and desperate for an occasional vicarious thrill to take the pall off.

The tales I told him our first night out provided thrills enough to quicken the dead, and by the time I'd launched into the fatal omissions of Saigon's final weeks, he was sweating and hustling his fourth martini and muttering about what a splendid book this would all make if I could only cast off my misplaced loyalties. To buttress the hard sell, he conjured the example of a rogue ex-agent named Philip Agee who'd bailed out of the CIA in 1968 and since made a bundle by blowing its secrets. This born-again Marxist had recently stormed bestseller lists in Europe with a highly publicized CIA memoir in which he fingered countless former colleagues by name, and an American edition was due out shortly. Stafford felt the public's appetite for such exposés, whetted by Watergate, would make Agee a millionaire, and he urged me to take my cue from him.

I reacted as if slapped. *Agee's a turncoat!* I sputtered—a man whose intemperate name-dropping had blown the lid off CIA operations in Central America, the last person in the world who could ever serve as a model for me.

Tossing some money on the table, I bade Stafford good night and retreated to my hotel room to brood over what I chose to view loftily as his moral dissolution. The following morning, rocky from lack of sleep, I hauled myself aboard an Eastern Air Lines shuttle and headed south into the benumbing swelter of midsummer Washington.

— —

The city seemed as far from home as anyplace I'd known in the past five years. The interchangeable bureaucrats who made up its irreplaceable elite were busy stuffing yesterday's secrets into burn bags and packing out for August vacations. The only savagery that tweaked their sensibilities was the ersatz bloodletting of the movie megahit *Jaws,* and out along embassy row the many stretch limousines that normally swaggered through the thoroughfares during high season were fast giving place to bicyclists and ice-cream vendors. Only the omnipresent nattering of the cicadas, so familiar to any displaced denizen of Saigon, struck anything like a sentimental chord with me.

The morning of my arrival, on the way in from the airport, my taxi idled for a moment near the Washington Monument, where antiwar demonstrators had pranced and ranted in early 1972, between my two Vietnam tours. Oh, how their illogic had galled me, their dumb-rote incantations clashing maddeningly with the facts I'd brought home from the field. How could anyone have believed Vietnam was a homegrown revolution! Hanoi controlled the show. Why hadn't those wilted flower children seen that?

In my certainty of the answers—always supported by the latest and most sophisticated intelligence—I'd withdrawn into the contemptuous mind-set the Agency typically reserves for outsiders, know-nothings without the "facts."

Now, of course, the "facts" stood reduced to a mere parody of wisdom, and I was the know-nothing, and so many of those I'd despised, having traded their scruff for establishment tweeds, were hell-bent on putting all illogic behind them.

Even Watergate, that strange incandescence that had doomed Vietnam's last chances the previous summer by incinerating the only madman ever to intimidate Hanoi, was receding onto the press's back pages. There were no familiar reference points anymore, not even repugnant ones.

— —

Over the next several days, the shock of reentry was eased somewhat by the gentle ministrations of an old CIA colleague, Carla Christiansen, whom I'd gotten to know long ago in Saigon. "A very attractive Agency girl," a CIA security officer once remarked of her in a confidential report on our relationship, and impertinent though these attentions were, the conclusion was dead accurate. Carla was everything her Nordic ancestry implied—strikingly blond, relentlessly patient, with long slanting eyelashes that gave her a perpetual come-hither air. She'd been attached to the Saigon station's reports section when I'd first met her, and we'd quickly become intimate friends, occasionally braving the hazards of rural driving in Vietnam to spend a weekend at a crumbling French hotel on the coast.

Nearly a year and too many other emotions now separated us from those passionate times, for Carla had departed Saigon months before the evacuation. But on the afternoon I showed up on her doorstep in mid-July 1975, she greeted me like a returned prodigal and invited me to stay as long as I wanted, as though nothing had changed between us.

"You were so terribly thin," she recalled of her houseguest, "and moodier than I had ever seen you. You couldn't talk about anything but Vietnam."

And talk I did, long into our first night together and into the next and the next—about abandoned agents and blown operations I hadn't been able to reveal to Stafford, for Carla was "cleared" for secrets he couldn't hear.

Magnanimous as always, she listened sympathetically and tried to relate. But the more I plumbed my obsessive memories, the more grudging I became of them, as though only a fellow eyewitness could be trusted to understand.

— —

On a weekend soon after my arrival, Carla drove me down to the Virginia coast to try to help me wind down. It was a bit of therapy she considered essential to both my professional and emotional well-being, for like many others who labored in the Agency's more cloistered vineyards, she no longer trusted in the equanimity of Mother Church. The ongoing exposés had told her more of the Agency's darker side than she'd ever glimpsed or imagined, and she was particularly troubled by newly revealed evidence of its intolerance toward its own. Just weeks before, the Rockefeller Commission had uncovered a lurid surveillance operation run by CIA Security against a staff file clerk simply because she'd dared to sleep with a Cuban expatriate living next door. Bedrooms had been bugged and trysts photographed, all to satisfy some misbegotten suspicions. Carla was convinced that if the Agency could react so excessively to such a benign offense, a stricken conscience would bring down the roof.

I scoffed and scolded, and by the time we returned to Washington I'd persuaded myself the subversive media had co-opted her common sense.

Wrong, of course, and one morning a short while later, as Carla was bustling around her kitchen and bracing for a long day at Langley, she handed me an article from *Harper's* magazine that cinched her case.

As she leaned to kiss me good-bye, she asked if I'd known the author, an ex-analyst named Sam Adams who'd destroyed his career and himself by pressing Langley on a point of conscience. I nodded and waved her off and spent the rest of the morning poring over the article. Oh, I'd known Sam all right. The two of us had worked together in my early Agency days, and what he'd written here merely chronicled the ill-fated crusade he'd waged ever since.

The precipitating event had been a single jarring revelation: in late 1967, Sam had uncovered what he thought was proof that colleagues at the CIA and Pentagon were deliberately deflating their estimates of enemy troop strength in Vietnam to convey a sense of progress where there wasn't any. He'd raged and protested, but to no avail. And then, surprise! Months later, in the great Tet offensive, legions of uncounted enemy had virtually overrun South Vietnam, inflicting heavy casualties on American and allied forces.

Afterward, Sam had demanded an accounting, even prosecution of the "liars" up top, only to be ignored, then pilloried, and finally forced to quit the Agency.

As I thumbed through his article, my mind reeled back to Sam's last year in purgatory, to remembered images of a rumpled misanthrope trudging the corridors, vainly knocking on doors to get someone's attention. Initially, vengeful higher-ups had cut him out of the paper flow, then out of his assigned job, and finally they'd directed the rest of us not to talk to him at all.

I *had* talked to him—I was between Saigon tours in 1972 and no favorite of the bureaucracy's either, having predicted a breakthrough in the Paris peace talks when nobody else had dared second-guess Kissinger's secret diplomacy—and Sam had become my friend.

"Never let 'em make you lie," he'd warned me. "Do that, and we're no better than the Mafia."

That night, I talked to Carla about the article and told her I read it as a challenge to conscience. She saw it as something different. In her view, Sam's story wasn't about the virtue of getting the truth out, but about the dangers of trying.

Remember Sam not for what he did, she counseled me, but for what it did to him.

— —

Sometime during my first weeks back, I traveled to North Carolina to be reunited with blood kin. I'd delayed the journey for as long as I could, for the last thing I needed just now, at peril of my own sanity, was to be cast back into the Faulknerian swamp that had spawned me.

But if such an upbringing teaches you any one lesson, it is not to shrink from pain.

So I went.

As the firstborn of an appropriately dissipated "old" Southern family, I had been nourished on martyr's milk ever since childhood. On many a Sunday, my sainted grandmother had sat me on her knee and regaled me with tales of heroic sacrifice by our Confederate forebears, men such as Colonel John White Gulley—I can still see his bearded features beaming out from aging tintypes—who'd climbed atop a cannon on Cemetery Ridge, raised his plumed hat on sword's point, and upon absorbing the first inevitable volley of grapeshot had cried, "They've got me, boys, but they can't get us all!"

For a child of the South as I was, there was destiny in this vision, the martyr bestride the cannon, tempting fate. Though I'd joined the Agency long after my grandmother's death, that vision had remained a beacon. I'd not wanted to go to Vietnam, not as a foot soldier, certainly not in the late 1960s when foot soldiers were easy fodder. But John White Gulley would never have retreated into a Canadian sunset. So, when a professor of mine at Columbia had suggested the CIA as an alternative to common soldiering, I'd heard the trumpets, raised my hat on my sword, and in mid-1969, less than a year after signing on, had wound up in Vietnam as a spy.

My last gesture upon departing was as foolhardy as the good colonel's mounting the cannon. My newly divorced parents were embroiled in a bitter custody battle, and out of loyalty to my mother, I agreed to testify against my father. It was a patricidal act that should have made any future patron wary, and the hatred my father bore me persisted up through the evacuation of Saigon itself.

But in that improbable moment, the Agency inadvertently brought us back together by mistakenly informing him just after the final helilift that I was missing in action. Eventually, a follow-up message corrected the error, but until then, my father, this icily remote man, sat weeping in a darkened room. Never had he been known to weep about anything, and when my teenage brother told me about this episode, I was moved.

So back I went to the homestead and extended an olive branch, and tried, once the emotions subsided, to explain what I'd witnessed these last months and what I thought I should do about it.

My father listened patiently, as befitted one who'd spent much of his adult life as a state superior court judge, and after I was done he recalled some of the snafus he'd observed as a Marine in World War II, as if familiarity might console. In our awkward groping for common ground, I began to sense the uniqueness of my own perspective. Circumstance and the breadth of my security clearances had left me with far more to deny than many of my Saigon colleagues. And like any bystander at a crime scene, I began wondering: Could I avoid bearing witness?

My father gazed at me apprehensively through clouds of pipe smoke as I picked through these thoughts with him. He knew from the custody battle that in the heat of high purpose I was capable of bringing down the house. Mission over loyalty, ideal over common sense—that was the legend now indelibly impressed on my escutcheon. The kid who'd never connected with the older man had grown into a loner with no instinct for compromise.

Gently, my father opined that maybe the Agency had no such instinct either, particularly given the indignities recently suffered. I reacted predictably, with quivering indignation, pointing out that there were lives at stake, lives still to be saved in Vietnam, and lessons to be learned. And I told him, too, of Sam Adams's remembered admonition. In my five and a half years in the war zone I'd almost forgotten what I was being paid for. I'd lied to the press on cue, shaved analyses to my masters' pleasure, and convinced not a few Vietnamese to trust us. That was the worst lie of all, I told him. It had cost Mai Ly and others more than I could bear imagining. The least I could do was to try to start earning my pay honestly by bringing the truth home. It might not change things. But it might change me, and that was something.

My father nodded tentatively and acknowledged that yes, it might be all right if I tried to prompt a stocktaking, provided there was no vengefulness in it, though, knowing me, he probably thought there would be.

— —

The morning I strode across the CIA foyer for the first time in two and a half years, there was a blood scent on the wind. Otis Pike's House Intelligence Committee was girding for its first public foray into Agency mysteries. Frank Church's counterpart panel in the Senate was reeling from the secret testimony of a Mafia gunsel who'd helped organize CIA kill plots against Fidel Castro. And a *New York Times* reporter was believed to be completing a cautiously admiring review of Philip Agee's names-blowing exposé.

Not a good day for a homecoming.

I paused in the vestibule to contemplate the words of John 8:32 chiseled in the west wall: "And ye shall know the truth, and the truth shall make you free." It was always the last thing you saw as you headed off into the world to do the Agency's bidding, and often the last thing you remembered once you got there.

The security guards at the turnstile frowned at my temporary lapel badge and waved me through grudgingly. As I paused to savor the moment and bless my luck for having survived five years of war, I couldn't help feeling a bit awed by the place. The unremitting purity of the main corridors, the geometric simplicity of the planes of steel and glass stretching away into opposing transepts, gave no clue to the seething conspiracies being hatched two or three stories above. The building itself was a lie, its proportions and population so well concealed that the engineering staff had never been able to find the proper balance between heat and air-conditioning. Still, for all I knew of the frailties of its denizens, and tattered though my emotions were, I nonetheless relished the idea of *belonging*.

An escort officer from Ted Shackley's East Asia division appeared at the front steps and ushered me toward a back elevator. Once alighting on a restricted upper floor, we glided wordlessly past rows of innocuous pastel-colored doors—pastel, blank, pitiless—into the inner sanctum itself.

The master of the domain, Theodore George Shackley, was of a piece with the decor, a chillingly nondescript flaxen-haired technocrat with the blandness of an insurance salesman and the ruthlessness of a born conspirator, all worn comfortably behind a burgeoning paunch and flesh-rimmed glasses.

The "blond ghost," we'd called him in Saigon, where he'd been my first station chief in 1969, and like some wily apparition he'd spent much of his career dodging or dispensing blame for countless collapsed operations and policies. Berlin, Miami, Vientiane, Saigon—everywhere he'd played spymaster, congressional investigators were now finding something to question or condemn: the anti-Castro plotting, the secret CIA war in Laos, the Phoenix counterterror program in Vietnam.

Against this backdrop the last thing Shackley needed was the carping of a malcontent like me.

When I walked into the division enclave, most of the cubicles were deserted, for with typical efficiency the blond ghost had already purged the collective memory. Anyone from Saigon who might have forcefully borne witness had long ago been shunted off to some plush new posting where there would be little incentive to remember or complain. Even my old station chief, Tom Polgar, had thus been disposed of and was now occupying a corner desk in the Latin America division, quietly awaiting reassignment to Mexico.

Since the Bangkok assignment had delayed my return, no one had thought to arrange for me to disappear so felicitously. No new job awaited me, not even a desk or a chair, and certainly no solicitude. On the contrary, since I was still attached to the analytical side of the house despite all my years of clandestine service in Vietnam, Shackley felt no obligation to give me so much as the time of day.

Neither did his minions. None even bothered to ask about the reports I'd filed from Bangkok, and at the end of my first hour of internal exile I might have slipped away unnoticed but for a challenge from Shackley's secretary. Intercepting me at the door, she brusquely thrust a document into my hand and ordered me to read and sign it. Beneath a cover sheet bearing the portentous legend "Classified When Filled In" were attached several pages titled "Vietnam Evacuation Questionnaire."

At first glimpse, these words provoked a tingle of excitement, for here, it seemed, was an invitation to the very stocktaking I yearned for. But a perusal of the opening paragraphs quickly disabused me. While acknowledging that not all of our key Vietnamese agents and contacts had been rescued, the document ascribed the breakdown in the evacuation's "phased flow" to "heavy local enemy action," and ruled out any attempt "to seek scapegoats or to assign blame or discredit any individuals." The reader was then invited to summarize, in blank spaces provided, any instances of abandonment or betrayal that might have "internal flap potential," the capacity to embarrass the Agency. There was space at the end for a signature certifying the accuracy of all of the above.

By the time I'd finished reading, my rage had become volcanic. Anyone who'd been in Saigon at the end knew the evacuation had never approached anything resembling a "phased flow," and not *just* because of "local enemy action."

Dropping the document in a shredder, I stormed out and forever after resisted attempts by Shackley's subalterns to induce me to sign. Too often I'd been made a party to lies in Saigon. I wasn't about to put my signature to another.

That evening as I lay in bed with Carla and recounted the day's events, she evinced no surprise. No one wanted to spring the lock on any more Pandora's boxes, she remonstrated. Forget Vietnam and move on.

But I couldn't. Shackley wasn't trying merely to bury the past but to relieve us of its burden. And if he succeeded, woe betide any Vietnamese who helped us.

Out of sight—and mind.

— —

Within days of my return to Langley, I began prowling the corridors like Sam Adams's ghost, searching for one bleeding heart who would help me get the facts on record.

"Mr. Snepp was concerned that there had not been adequate planning for the evacuation," recalled the director's special assistant, George Carver, "and that the evacuation itself had not been particularly handled well administratively."

"Mr. Snepp would have, and *did,* talk about his concerns that no postmortem or after-action report was being prepared," remembered Carver's deputy, Bob Layton.

"I think he wanted to write his view of how things had collapsed in Vietnam," noted another old colleague of mine.

In a matter of days, I dipped into every major division of the Agency that had had any responsibility for Vietnam, and to my astonishment discovered that truth had preceded me.

"There were a good many people from Saigon who were upset about the way the evacuation had been carried out," confirmed Paul Walsh, assistant deputy director for intelligence.

"Many of Snepp's contacts within the Agency and elsewhere in the government share his view that the evacuation in general and Martin's performance in particular were disastrous," acknowledged Carver's deputy, Layton.

And yet, widespread though this wisdom was, nobody wanted to act on it. And everybody had an alibi. "I felt that there were also a lot of current demands on our time," Carver later explained, "and raking and reraking the coals of the Vietnam War was not necessarily the way that the limited amount of time should be spent."

At one point, in exasperation, I considered kicking over the traces and taking my concerns straight to Director William Colby himself. He'd been a friend of my father's during their student days at Columbia Law School in the early 1940s, and though I'd never even met the man, he certainly would have known my name. But Carver ultimately dissuaded me by promising to broker an introduction himself if I couldn't obtain satisfaction within "proper" channels.

It was a token of my good-soldier mentality that I took him at his word.

Since my only real home over the past five years had been the Saigon station, there was an inevitable temptation, as the frustrations mounted, to turn that way again, back to friends and colleagues and yes, even to Tom Polgar himself. Carla was adamant that I confide in him. However badly he'd disappointed me, he'd once been patron and protector, she argued, and so deserved my candor.

"Mr. Snepp came to me and first of all offered his services in connection with whatever work I was doing as an aftermath of the events in Vietnam," Polgar recalled. "He told me he would like to write such a postmortem."

The afternoon I tracked him to his cubbyhole in the Latin America division, he was agonizing over a possible congressional inquiry and casting about for defenses. I suggested we attempt something substantial, a full-fledged analysis to focus official attention on our obligation to Vietnamese left behind. He pondered that, then shook his head sadly and insisted he had no power to initiate such a study. What he could do, however, was help put me out of my own misery. There was a choice slot open in Mexico City, his own next posting. He wanted to nominate me for it and have me accompany him there.

I should have objected, should have told him no thanks, not after what I'd witnessed the last weeks of the war. But sycophancy dies hard. So I bit my tongue and mumbled thanks and finally slunk away with my resolve newly hostage to second thoughts.

Critics would later fault me for a flawed and fickle conscience. They were only half justified. There was a part of me, a part I had not been obliged to address till now, that remained truly attached to Polgar and utterly beholden. Everything I'd finally become in Vietnam—interrogator of choice, senior analyst, the embassy's principal briefer—I owed to him or through him to the ambassador. And if he'd stumbled at the end, reading too much into our intelligence and too little into Saigon's weaknesses, hadn't I abetted him by not objecting forcefully enough? What right did I have to criticize him now?

How strange I hadn't anticipated this turn. For weeks, I'd been carrying an assassin's stiletto in my sleeve, all the while pretending that it wasn't for him, that truth-telling at Langley could be a victimless crime. I should have known better.

But now what? Was Mexico the inevitable compromise?

Carla thought so, and saw Polgar's offer as a finger beckoning, an unmistakable sign that my future lay not in resurrecting the past but in making peace with it. One night she dragged out some yellowing news clippings she'd been saving and began shoving them at me insistently. Here was President Ford himself ruling out any official investigation into Martin's performance. Here, Kissinger counseling earnestly against public recriminations about the war. All the high priests of our failed Vietnam policies had thrown up revetments and dug in. So who was I to defy them? A young man barely thirty-two years of age with no claim on credibility. How could I ever presume to call any of them on their mistakes?

Over the next several days, the seemingly seamless logic of forgiveness, however, gave way to a new affront: a dizzying escalation of the cover-up Shackley had initiated with his questionnaire. First, I learned that he'd since approached a friendly journalist and offered to open select CIA files to him if he'd pen a "favorable" book about the fall of Saigon. A pack of lies in lieu of a true postmortem.

Then, a few days later, a former aide to Graham Martin pulled me aside at a cocktail party and confided that a similar effort was being mounted on the ambassador's behalf. Two journalists, Bernard and Marvin Kalb of CBS News, he said, were planning a book of their own on Vietnam, and several of the ambassador's supporters had decided to assist them with some discreetly leaked "confidences." The objective was not to rewrite history, he insisted, but merely to ensure that certain "facts" were accurately conveyed. The Kalbs were known to be partisans of Kissinger, having once written an admiring biography of him, and there was always the danger, I was told, that they'd pander to him again, this time at Martin's expense, unless somebody took pains to keep them honest.

It was this task that my interlocutor and his cohorts had taken on themselves, and to make sure "we're all on the same wavelength," he continued, he wanted to double-check a few facts with me. It *was* the cutback in congressional aid that had sunk Saigon? (This, more a commandment than a question.) And hadn't the CIA failed to alert the ambassador adequately to Hanoi's final plans? And then of course there was that scandalous business of Polgar's household belongings. Like the ambassador himself, this apologist was adamant that their premature evacuation was the domino that had set the others toppling.

I stood listening to the man and wondering at the precise definition of justifiable homicide.

— —

At any other point in my CIA career, the righteous indignation that now seized me would have dissolved quickly in the chill waters of cynicism and self-interest. But this time, as luck would have it, my bluff was called. In early August, the Foreign Service Institute, a refresher school for midcareer State Department and CIA officers, invited me to take part in an upcoming seminar on the loss of Vietnam. Nothing elaborate. Nothing for the record. Just a discreet review of the facts.

Feeling a fiery finger prodding me between the shoulder blades, rashly I said yes.

The decision immediately cost me dearly. Fearing that I was tempting my own destruction, and reluctant to be witness to it, Carla asked me to move out and find accommodations elsewhere. Already too consumed to be mindful of her feelings or my own welfare, I hauled myself off the following morning and took a lease on a modest bachelor pad in an Arlington high-rise.

It was here, amid photographs of Vietnam and battle flags of cheap muslin, that I would burrow in to prepare for my first true act of rebellion.

Till now I'd been the perfect ventriloquist's dummy, the man who "always defers to his superiors" and "is careful never to overstep proper bounds," as Polgar had once written of me. But over the next week as I wrestled with the seminar paper, I couldn't even begin to glimpse the proper bounds, and the stress of having to be honest with myself for the first time in so long reduced me to a basket case.

So obvious was my dissolution that it quickly attracted the concerned attention of various colleagues, including Bill Johnson, the Agency veteran I'd last seen on shipboard. Indeed, one morning he drew me aside in the CIA cafeteria to ask if I was well. Since we'd always been friendly, I felt no qualms about leveling with him—about the seminar and my distress at discovering that no one seemed to give a damn about the Vietnamese we'd left behind. Maybe the only way to get the story out, I remarked bitterly, was to get it to a publisher, as Shackley and Martin were trying to do.

Johnson raised an eyebrow and asked if I, too, were considering this course, because if so—he never missed a beat—perhaps he could be of help to me. There was something about the way he tendered the offer, the exaggerated solicitude perhaps, that set off alarms.

"Look," I told him, "my only interest is getting the seminar paper finished, which is proving hard enough, and if I were planning a book, which I'm not, I'd probably turn to"—and here I tossed off a publisher's name Stafford had mentioned, just to close the subject. Johnson nodded gravely and bade me good morning.

Once out of eyeshot, he pulled out a memo pad and, using his own initials to refer to himself, jotted a few words: "Frank Snepp, VN colleague,

breakfasted with W.R.J. Talking about a book with Harcourt Brace . . .
Asked advice. Got little."

— —

On the afternoon of August 13, a heavily pinstriped crowd gathered in a
classroom at the Foreign Service Institute to witness my unburdening. Ad-
libbing beyond my prepared text, I did what I'd thought I couldn't: pinned
blame where it belonged, on friends, colleagues, idols—on Kissinger,
whose "peace agreement" in 1973 had left 140,000 North Vietnamese on
Saigon's doorstep and no hope of political compromise; on Martin and
Polgar, who'd indulged our allies' corruption and shortchanged it in their
accounts to Washington; on former Saigon president Nguyen Van Thieu,
so easily beguiled by American aid promises that he'd never felt compelled
to clean house or trim his defenses to reflect dwindling resources; and on
Congress, which had never demanded much more from Martin than rosy
prognoses.

As for the evacuation, I remarked grimly that only a third of the Vietnamese who'd worked for the Americans at the war's end had escaped,
most of them on their own, with no help from the embassy.

"We left behind on the tarmac or outside the embassy walls four to five
hundred members of the Saigon special police force whom we'd trained—
they were in imminent jeopardy; about twelve hundred members of
Saigon's central intelligence organization—we'd trained them, too; and
thirty thousand cadre of our Phoenix Counterterror program."

I also spoke of security breaches, the loss of CIA documents in the highlands, the ambassador's failure to destroy his own files, the abandonment
of intelligence reports on loan to the South Vietnamese military and police.
Any one of these archives, I warned, could help the Communists identify
those we'd abandoned.

My audience listened in stunned silence. Seldom had these midcareerists
from the State Department and the CIA heard a fellow insider speak so
candidly and intemperately about anything so sensitive. And though the
session had been billed "informal" and strictly "off the record," no sooner
had the room been cleared than news of my heresies was crackling through
the executive suites at Langley.

— —

The following weekend, nerves frayed, I flew to New Orleans to try to min-
ister to a woman named Tu Ha, one of ten Vietnamese refugees whom I'd
helped spirit out of Saigon on cargo aircraft during the final weeks of the

war. She'd abandoned her family in that moment of chaos and was as guilt-ridden as I, and since arriving in New Orleans had succumbed to a crippling new miasma, for as a devout Buddhist she was terrified of placing her life in the hands of the Catholic relief workers who were now her only hope.

And yet, Tu Ha, how lucky you are, I thought as I buckled my seat belt and tried not to imagine her despair. You're here at least. Safe.

Unlike so many others. Unlike Mai Ly.

Midflight and into my third cocktail, I kept trying to reshuffle the script to improve the ending. Two years before the collapse, Mai Ly and I had resumed a liaison that had winked off and on ever since we'd met during my first year in Vietnam. She'd never been the prettiest hostess in the dive off Nguyen Hue Boulevard, where she'd slung "Saigon teas" and talked up the round-eyes. But there'd been a regalness about her—at nearly six feet she could hardly help it—that had made her eternally fascinating.

Then suddenly she'd disappeared. In the spring of 1973, zip, gone. Her friends giggled and said she'd gotten pregnant again—her firstborn had been killed in an American air strike—and had headed home to the delta to deliver.

Nearly two years passed before I heard from her again, before that winter's night in 1974 when she showed up at my door with a year-old baby boy in her arms and a sly smile on her lips. As always, she was coy. First she claimed the child was her brother's; then, her own by an American friend; and then, shockingly, the American friend became me.

I still have a picture of the three of us from that time, that brief five-day reunion that would commit me forever. Mai Ly is standing at the head of her dinner table gazing serenely at the camera like the lady of the manor, her purple *áo dài* skin-tight, as I lift the baby awkwardly with both hands as if fearful of breaking it.

Almost immediately after that picture was taken, she and the child disappeared again, not to resurface until the day before the evacuation and her futile phone call to me, too late to be smuggled out with Tu Ha or any other Vietnamese I'd known, too late for any help against my blind, dumb fixations that day. If she ever confided the baby's name to me, it had slipped away in the soul-wrenching pain I'd suffered afterward, for try as I might, I couldn't remember it.

My God, were they truly dead? The Vietnamese cop who'd climbed over the wall of the embassy the last day to deliver the news had been nearly incoherent with fear. Had he gotten it right? Or was my guilt now simply holding truth in abeyance?

When I reached New Orleans I felt a suffocating desolation, and the situation there only worsened it. Tu Ha, I discovered, had lost the will to fend for herself, and the more I tried to do for her, the more dependent she became, refusing even to board a bus or dial a phone without my help. Within a day, I'd come to realize what she couldn't admit herself. The best I could do for her and the rest of my refugee friends was to withdraw and give up trying to assuage my guilt through them. Otherwise they might never learn to survive on their own in this Lazarus's existence. Perhaps neither would I.

CHAPTER 3

First Temptations

FROM NEW ORLEANS, I booked a red-eye to New York, hoping to buy time to cool down.

No such luck. Stafford, who'd agreed to put me up, remained abrasively committed to my "going public," all the more for having watched with larcenous fascination these past two weeks as Philip Agee's book had sold impressively and even scored with critics.

"Just look at these notices," Stafford exclaimed as he settled himself across from me at a midtown restaurant and dumped an armload of news clippings on the table. "They're saying he's done a public service."

That was putting it too generously. The reviews were carefully hedged. But clearly the nation's literary mavens had a better opinion of Agee than did the CIA.

In the midst of his second course, Stafford presented me with something he hoped would whet my appetite, a dog-eared copy of *The CIA and the Cult of Intelligence* by ex–CIA officer Victor Marchetti and State Department veteran John Marks. I knew of the book—everybody in the CIA did—and like most of my colleagues considered it an abomination on a par with Agee's. Three years before, at the Agency's behest, Nixon's Justice Department had won a court order forcing Marchetti to turn over the still unpublished manuscript for censorship. I'd applauded this victory over infidelity and relished the author's discomfort when the CIA, with the judge's blessing, had sliced great divots out of the text. The edition Stafford had brought with him was riddled with blank spaces, mute testament to battles lost to CIA censors.

"Marks was in Vietnam, you know," Stafford observed teasingly as he thumbed to a prefatory note in which Marchetti's coauthor had condemned the war and prayed the book might help prevent another.

If Stafford was looking to shame me, he was doing a fair job.

Later, he took me back to his office and introduced me to his secretary, Bernadette "Bernie" Longford, whose assistance would be mine for the asking, he said, if I should choose to write a book of my own.

For the first time I felt tempted. Bernie's every attribute, from the aquiline nose to the high cheekbones to the wonderfully sculpted body, seemed lifted from classical statuary, and except for the British accent and the mocha-brown of her skin she might have been the doomed heroine of *Zorba the Greek*.

She was, in fact, an Antiguan of decidedly mixed parentage who'd followed her mother off the island in the late 1960s and had since dabbled in local dance and theater while earning her keep as a girl Friday par excellence. Yet, despite her success in fitting in nicely, her polyglot ancestry had left her keenly aware of what it was like *not* to belong, and like few other "civilians" I'd met since my return, she seemed genuinely sympathetic toward the Vietnamese now swarming across our shores. "Maybe we owe them an explanation," she remarked to me that afternoon. If Stafford had coached her on the line, she was too good an actress to show it.

The next day, a Saturday, Stafford departed on vacation and left his West Side apartment in Bernie's hands. After dinner, she invited me over, danced with me in his cramped living room till well after midnight, and then let me stay. My Southern kin would have been scandalized. NEGRESS BEDS WHITE YOUTH!—you could easily picture the headline. But it was a measure of how changed I was, a measure of Vietnam, that the only thing I found different about Bernie was her generosity.

"Maybe you owe *yourself* an explanation," she said to me sometime before daybreak as I stood at the window gazing at the lost world just behind my eye. "Yourself above all."

On the flight back to Washington, I found myself doodling scenes on a cocktail napkin, marching Martin and Polgar on- and offstage in search of an "explanation." By the time the plane had landed, the scribblings occupied several scraps of paper, and the burden weighing on me seemed infinitely lighter. It was my first taste of the curative powers of exorcism.

— —

Though writing a book remained as far from my thoughts as ever, one thing Stafford had said stuck: if the Agency was to be nudged into cleaning up its act, the impetus would have to come from elsewhere. Right now, the only source for that was Congress, and though I was no more impressed with Otis Pike and his ilk than most of my colleagues, it didn't take any lapse of virtue to be tempted by the idea of dropping some discreet inspiration in the right congressional in-box. With this in mind, I hauled out my seminar paper and began tinkering with it, looking for ways to turn it into bait for the distracted.

By late August a glimmering of promise beckoned from Capitol Hill itself. News reports had it that Pike's investigators were preparing to dig into four intelligence crises, including the Tet offensive of 1968, and that gadfly ex-agent Sam Adams, my old friend, was to be a witness. There was no hint that Saigon's final days might likewise be surveyed, but the very fact that Adams had managed to put Tet front and center bolstered my spirits. If only I could find a sympathetic ear, then maybe, just maybe . . .

But alas, hope died aborning. The morning Pike launched his investigation, CIA officials showed up to decry his decision to make public what they claimed to be highly classified information about one of the crises under examination, and President Ford promptly issued an executive order barring any bureaucrat, high or low, from sharing anything with the panel until it had shored up its security.

As an *ex*–CIA employee, Adams was unconstrained by this injunction. But for all intents and purposes, Congress was now off limits for the rest of us.

— —

Six weeks had passed since my return to CIA headquarters, and despite Shackley's best efforts to put Vietnam survivors out of sight and out of temptation's way, I still was without employment. Normally, the Agency's fastidious bureaucrats have no tolerance for such loose ends. So when personnel finally realized my status, a concerted effort was made to process the job application Polgar had filed on my behalf.

On September 12, it was stamped and delivered. The covering memo informed me that preparatory to heading off to join Polgar's staff in Mexico, I was to report to a clandestine CIA language school to begin a crash course in Spanish.

— —

Five years of war had not equipped me for the tedium of the classroom, and from the moment I showed up to collect my texts and practice tapes I

thought I might go mad. Under any other circumstances, the very monot-
ony of the daily drill might have provided blessed respite. But now, with the
mind idling, the imagination played bully, and day after day, seated in the
language lab with earphones clamped on and the instructor's voice droning
dully, I kept harkening to dead voices, to the bleats and whistles of the radios in the CIA operations room on the final day, the static-laced pleas for
help crackling in over the channels. *I'm Mr. Han, the translator. . . .*

"Soundmares" I called them, and the more I tried to shut them out the
more intrusive they became, tracking relentlessly across the numbing repe-
titions of the language drill like snippets of a movie soundtrack gone hay-
wire.

In the process, day after day, the composition book into which I was to
commit my memory work took on a life of its own, the margins blossom-
ing with quotes and impressions I couldn't put away. One night, sleepless
as usual, I transposed these petals into the text of my seminar paper, and
every night thereafter repeated this ritual so that the draft soon came to re-
semble a shadow of the after-action report no one dared call for.

Had I been less preoccupied or less desperate, I might have understood
that my industry was misspent and my timing abominable. Once Otis Pike
decided to defy the president and persist in his investigation of the Tet offensive, Vietnam ceased to be a forgotten issue in official Washington and
became a forbidden one.

Two days before Sam Adams was to testify, the president announced he
would defy Pike's subpoenas for classified background documents, and
Pike replied that he'd have them or take the president to court. By the time
Adams walked into the hearing room on the morning of September 19,
CIA headqua   was rife with rumor that he would tweak the White
House and the Agency by making an issue of the fall of Saigon itself.

He did not disappoint. After rattling off his familiar charges of blunder
and cover-up circa 1968, Adams announced portentously that those responsible had survived to be deluded again during the last moments of the
war.

The panic was instantaneous. Colby quickly summoned his top advisers
and directed them to review his final Vietnam briefings for the White
House, pluck out the exceptional insights, and fashion them into a document with which he could fend off critics. George Carver's two depu*:-.,
Bill Christison and Bob Layton, were assigned to handle the drudgework.
No one from the Saigon station was alerted, much less invited to contribute. The perspective was to be exclusively that of the man on high.

Knowing nothing of any of this, I was spared the frustration of being
ignored. But Sam Adams's example did inspire, and I continued hacking

away at my seminar paper, adding and refining detail with a view to turning it into grist for a true postmortem. Finally satisfied, I was foolish enough to try to shop my handiwork around headquarters. Most of those who read it reacted as if I'd handed them a skunk's carcass. None offered to pass it up the line to Colby's office, and only Bill Johnson, my friend from Saigon, seemed remotely sympathetic. After thumbing through the draft, he complimented me on its balanced tone and promised to circulate it among colleagues.

But he was concerned about me personally, he added, peering at me over his half-rims. He thought I could use some good old-fashioned camaraderie to lift me out of my doldrums, and luckily he had a prescription. He and his wife, Pat, had taken to holding an open house every Wednesday night for fellow mourners from Saigon. Nothing elaborate, just a few old hands getting together to share solace and memories. If I wanted to take part, I'd be welcome. No need to reserve a place in advance. The door was always open.

I told him maybe, and meant it. During our years together in Vietnam, I'd grown genuinely fond of the Johnsons. Bill had headed an operational unit that had often relied on me for briefings. Pat had worked arm in arm with me in the station's analytical section, and though her patrician's disdain for our enemies had sometimes put us at loggerheads, I'd come to respect her intelligence as I hoped she had mine.

The three of us also shared agonizing memories of the evacuation itself. In the weeks leading up to it, Bill had performed heroically, smuggling many Vietnamese friends and agents out of the country, but Pat had suffered nervous exhaustion and was shipped off to Bangkok to recover. Stranded there during the final pullout, she'd been forced to watch helplessly as her own Vietnamese friends were abandoned. Though once impervious to any criticism of her beloved CIA, she now had as much reason as I to demand an accounting of what had gone wrong.

"Promised to join the Wednesday gr[ou]p," Bill noted in his diary after checking with me again to make sure I'd attend. True to my word, I arrived on his doorstep the following Wednesday night to partake of the free booze and commiseration.

What was actually served up, however, wasn't what I'd expected. Pat spent the evening flitting about like a grande dame, trying to make light of everyone's misery, while Bill sat back eyeing the assemblage suspiciously, as if searching for some sign of insurrection. The prime topic of conversation, moreover, was not our final torments in Vietnam but our current ones on Capitol Hill. Through one round of cocktails after another, haggard Cold

Warriors and eager young pretenders lambasted Congress and the press for daring to question the integrity of the Agency's own. That very afternoon, the CIA's legendary ex–counterintelligence chief, James Jesus Angleton, had been mercilessly cross-examined by the Church committee, and several of my fellow celebrants were convinced that a sinister cabal, perhaps foreign-financed or -inspired, had set him up.

As the evening wore on, resentments came to focus on Director William Colby himself, whose attempts to stonewall Congress, many believed, had been too little, too late. "He should have lied more!" snorted one inebriated true believer. "That's what plausible denial is all about."

Later, driving home, I mulled over what I'd heard and my own discomfort at it. If Colby had been wrong in paying lip service to the truth, what was the point of intelligence work anyway? And if Angleton was a martyr to integrity, then what meaning did integrity have? According to his testimony that afternoon, he and his staff had for years routinely opened and pilfered the mail of countless Americans in search of subversives among them—and had secretly kept on doing so even after being ordered to stop by President Nixon himself. Asked to explain his insubordination, Angleton had conceded that he had "no satisfactory answer."

No satisfactory answer?

A tingling played across the back of my neck, and I found myself glancing apprehensively in the rearview mirror. For the Angletons of the world, my current discontents might well make me a candidate for the sort of mischief for which they had "no satisfactory answer."

— —

If the Johnsons' guests and fellow travelers feared the onset of Armageddon, however, they were grossly mistaken. Over the next few days, Otis Pike caved in to pressure and agreed to let the Agency censor all intelligence documents handed to his committee and all finished reports which the committee might generate based on such documents. Though I'd never trusted Congress or its ability to keep secrets, this double muzzle gave the Agency near total control over the watchdogs. Under these circumstances, the chances of Otis Pike doing justice to any intelligence issue seemed nil.

"I know some bigwigs in publishing," Stafford remarked after listening to me rail on about this. "Let me put out some feelers."

I said I'd think about it.

What if he took some of my letters from Vietnam, diary entries and whatnot, and showed them around, just to prove to his contacts that I could write? Any problems with that?

Again, I'd think about it.

He asked if he could make some calls to see if there was any interest in a book about the fall of Vietnam.

I told him yes, as long as he kept my identity secret.

Tentative though this decision was, it left me debilitated. My weight dropped, smudges blossomed beneath eyes and cheekbones, and Agency friends began *insisting* on buying me lunch, as if eating well might be a cure for my deeper impoverishment.

One witness to my unraveling was less concerned than titillated by it, however. Daphne Miller, a young CIA mapmaker and would-be artist, spied me one morning across the language lab, judged my angst to be intriguingly Byronic, and arranged to be introduced. Not long afterward, she invited me home to meet her father, a ranking official of the CIA's Foreign Broadcast Information Service.

She encouraged me to be candid with him, which I was, believing he might be helpful. But so rigid were his institutional loyalties that he couldn't begin to credit my tales of disgrace and betrayal, let alone the need for anything so exotic as a genuine investigation. The most I deserved for my carping, he told me, was a reminder of where my bread was buttered, and one night at a dinner party he introduced me to someone he hoped could deliver the lesson. A man of massive frame and imperial pretensions, "senior" intelligence analyst Hank Knoche reportedly was on his way to becoming the CIA's next deputy director and surely was one to be reckoned with. He greeted me stiffly, indulged me impatiently for a few moments, then slapped me down. "Naysayers don't belong in the Agency," he snapped. "You really ought to consider resigning."

He might as well have recommended self-immolation. Never had I even *dreamed* of quitting. The very thought was so alien to my well-conditioned sense of dependency as to make me tremulous with fear.

Afterward, I phoned Stafford to tell him not to expect writing samples from me any time soon. I wasn't ready to make the leap, not at the price Knoche had quoted.

And yet, conscience wouldn't be stilled. A few nights later, the CIA's resident group of Army reservists invited me to a showing of newly acquired newsreel footage shot at the Saigon embassy just before and after the Communist takeover. It was a kaleidoscope of fractured nightmares . . . an agent flinging himself suicidally against the bolted gates . . . batons smashing fingers locked around the grillwork . . . a Vietnamese mother being hoisted over the parapet by well-meaning Marine guards oblivious that her child has just been swept away by the mobs below.

I staggered out, shocked and newly determined. However intimidating

Knoche's counsel, there *had* to be a middle way. Rumor had it that Ambassador Martin was about to be hauled in by the Pike committee to testify. Maybe he could be persuaded to speak out about the problems left over from the evacuation.

I placed a call to Foggy Bottom and discovered that Martin was indeed back in the saddle and girding for a fight.

Somebody had told me of the illness, the pneumonia and pleurisy that had ravaged him on shipboard. But nothing could have prepared me for the specter I found in a top-floor cubicle at the State Department the morning Martin granted me an audience. The face, desiccated as parchment, recalled the horrific visages preserved in the wrappings of Egyptian tombs, and the body merely caricatured the dashing figure he'd cut only months before in Saigon. His hands snapped open and shut spasmodically as he gestured me to a chair before a battered desk that not so subtly emblemized his fall from grace.

For all the mortal frailness, though, the mind was still a lethal weapon. The first few minutes, Martin treated me to scatological anecdotes about Polgar as if to gauge my loyalties, and then, finding me unresponsive, canted off into an apologia for his own role in the evacuation, which predictably found fault with everyone else's. If only Congress had voted more aid, if only the Agency had yielded better intelligence, if only . . .

After a moment I interrupted. The intelligence hadn't been all that faulty, I reminded him. One of our sources, a man I'd been dealing with, had called the final offensive just as it happened, and but for Polgar's decision to downgrade the agent's report and others like it, we might have acquitted ourselves better.

Martin cocked his head, claimed never to have seen the report in question, and then abruptly sailed off on another tangent, belaboring Kissinger for trying to suborn history through the brothers Kalb and their prospective book on the evacuation.

Here he paused, and after an eternity of labored breathing acknowledged that he was gathering documentation himself to pass on to the two journalists and would be much obliged if I'd contribute something too, just to keep Kissinger in his place. That report Polgar had ignored, the one from the insightful agent—perhaps I could discuss *that* with the Kalbs, plus Polgar's "irresponsibility."

Wearily, I told him I had a better idea, and then replayed my quest of the past two months, explaining how I'd attempted to prod Langley into a postmortem, but so far to no avail, and how it had occurred to me that I might have to do the job myself in an article or even a book if no one took interest.

Martin perked up. "A book?" he purred, letting his voice trail away like bait on a line. And instantly I knew he was angling. "Do you have a publisher?" he asked, and then offered to help me find one if I didn't.

"The only help I want is Langley's," I told him, and abruptly brought the interview to a close.

On my way out of the building, I buttonholed a State Department friend and asked about the Kalb leaks. He confirmed worse than I'd imagined. Not only had Martin passed deep secrets to the two journalists; so had Kissinger, he said. Even more cynically, the Pentagon had launched its own flank-covering operation by hiring every expatriate Vietnamese general of any consequence to help write a highly classified, tightly controlled study of the war's final days. All had been sworn to secrecy and paid handsomely, and all were made to understand that their handiwork would remain forever the property of the U.S. military. "It's a hush job, pure and simple," my friend assured me.

As I emerged onto K Street, I could feel my pulse racing. Unless I acted quickly, the whole sordid story of Saigon's collapse would almost certainly become forfeit to those who meant to bury it and the Vietnamese we'd forsaken.

— —

"He wanted me to look at the material as a friend. It wasn't in publishable form. It needed a rewrite."

One early October morning—as Stafford later admitted to federal attorneys—I traveled to New York and handed over my promised writing samples to him, mainly letters and diary entries.

Despite my outrage over the Kalb leaks, taking the step hadn't been easy.

"Frank was very pro-Agency," Stafford recalled, "and wanted to do nothing to damage his reputation there."

To help me over my qualms, he offered to prepare the book proposal himself so I'd be spared any immediate soul-searching. If I liked what he pulled together, then maybe we could consider a pitch to one of his publishing friends. If not—end of story, no harm done.

By the time I headed back to Washington, I'd agreed to the plan. More surprisingly, I felt comfortable with it, as if by keeping my hands clear of the drudgery I could escape responsibility for whatever might follow.

Stafford, however, wasn't about to let things play out so casually, not with big money at stake. Sweating at his typewriter for several days, he hammered my memorabilia into impressively readable shape. Then, without breathing a word to me, he slipped a copy to Jim Silberman, vice president of the publishing giant Random House.

Silberman liked what he saw, and handed the proposal along to senior editor Bob Loomis.

A slight, blondish, obsessively dapper man in his early fifties, Loomis seemed the very epitome of the establishment editor—quiet, considerate, a friend of gentility in all its guises. The regimental mustache and small cigars he favored and the immaculate tweed jackets that clung to him like a second skin gave him the comforting look of an Ivy League professor from a well-off family, or even one of those gentleman spies out of the 1950s who wouldn't have been caught dead in anything but Harrods' finest.

And yet the diffidence he cultivated so artfully was mere camouflage for a bomb thrower's daring. It was Loomis who'd edited the first groundbreaking exposé of the CIA, Thomas Ross and David Wise's *The Invisible Government,* and Loomis again who'd shepherded Seymour Hersh through his historic account of the 1968 My Lai massacre in Vietnam.

To Stafford, this infinitely discreet agitator seemed my perfect ally, and if the two of them had had their way, he would have been an *immediate* ally as well, for both were convinced that if Random House didn't strike a deal with me fast the CIA would step in to block it.

Stafford, ever an agitator himself, agreed to try to hasten things along.

— —

While my literary future was thus being shaped by unseen hands, Graham Martin's own political past came back to haunt. The Pike committee conducted a series of closed-door sessions with him from mid-October onward, and though the focus was on his performance during a previous tour in Rome in the early 1970s, intimations of his chronic high-handedness prompted some members to call for an expanded investigation reaching all the way to Saigon itself.

I had no inkling of this, of course—the committee's work was now shrouded in secrecy—but William Colby saw the portents and responded accordingly. On October 24 he asked his inspector general to find out if intelligence reporting in Martin's Saigon embassy had been skewed "to present a favorable picture" and, if so, the extent to which this "represented a conscious policy rather than an unconscious development."

Colby had his own reason for wanting to clear up the issue: to avoid being caught out by Congress. But it was the first and only time the Agency would even come close to probing the war's final traumas, and if Colby had survived in office, he might ultimately have felt secure enough to do the truth justice.

But sadly, it wasn't to happen.

Weeks before, Otis Pike had first gotten wind of the dirty little secret that would prove Colby's undoing. He and his investigators had discovered that thousands of Kurdish tribesmen on the Agency's payroll had been cut loose after a cease-fire in the Iran-Iraq border war the previous spring, and had been abandoned to the mercy of marauding Iraqi forces, who'd promptly massacred untold numbers. Amidst the bloodletting, the Kurdish leadership had begged for help—from the Agency, Kissinger, and the president himself—but had been ignored.

When Pike learned of this outrage, the White House implored him not to go public. But on Sunday afternoon, November 1, Daniel Schorr of CBS News blew the lid off by reporting the story in ghastly detail.

As the story spilled into the evening newscasts, Kissinger absorbed the first withering barrage of criticism, but within hours, blame had been shifted, and by the following day word was swirling through Washington that both Colby and Defense Secretary James Schlesinger would be fired.

Twenty-four hours later the administration made a show of even-handedness by announcing that Kissinger would pay a price too, by forfeiting his secondary role as the president's national security adviser. But humiliating as this "demotion" may have been for him, its practical (and doubtless intended) effect was to put him out of harm's way, for once shorn of the White House job he no longer had to answer any congressional subpoenas directed to him in that capacity.

Similarly, though Colby's fall from grace was less ambiguous, there was a bit of calculation to it. Indeed, four days after removing him, the White House disclosed that he would be staying on until his designated successor, U.S. envoy to China George Bush, could get home for confirmation. Thus in a stroke the director of the CIA was reduced to lame-duck status that would make it impossible for him to police the Agency effectively or speak for it authoritatively to Congress. If reformers had been cheered by Colby's denigration, their elation was premature.

— —

The morning of Colby's ouster, I skipped language class and stayed home, nursing a deepening case of despondency. First the Vietnamese—now the Kurds. Where in God's name was our morality?

"Where's *yours*?" Stafford snapped as we bruited all this long-distance. "You still want to protect these bastards?"

I confessed I wasn't sure, and told him to expect a visit from me the following weekend. "We can talk about 'laying' the 'wallpaper' then," I said, "wallpaper" being our previously agreed code for the writing sample he'd pulled together, and "laying" my cryptic way of suggesting an approach to a publisher.

I still didn't realize he'd taken that step for me.

It may be difficult for an outsider to understand how a seasoned spook could have been so easily manipulated by someone so transparent as Stafford. Ironically, part of the answer lies in the very psychology of the spy business. Trust always comes hard and is grudgingly bestowed. But because of the rigors of the tempering process a bond, once forged, is well-nigh unbreakable. (Why else my unswerving attachment to the agents and collaborators we'd abandoned?)

Moreover, even as Stafford worked his wiles, a sudden distraction turned my attention elsewhere. In early November, the CIA's inspector general sent me a note inviting me to an interview about the quality of the analysis and reporting in the Saigon embassy. Unaware that the exercise was simply part of an effort by Colby to hedge against a possible congressional inquiry, I quickly convinced myself that the heavens had opened.

Sadly, that illusion died fast. When I showed up for the interview on the afternoon of November 7, it wasn't the inspector general who greeted me but one his water boys, a former intelligence analyst of muddled mind and demeanor named Norman Jones. Moreover, as Jones quickly made clear, he'd come here not to ferret out the truth but simply to decontaminate it so as to make it fit for congressional consumption. "I might have said something to the effect," he later recalled, "that . . . because Congress is most earnest in its investigative capacity . . . we have to make sure our own house is in order."

Someone less obsessed than I might have walked out then and there. But as the impulse stirred, I reminded myself of all the other missed opportunities and decided: not yet.

"My interview with Frank Snepp," Jones noted in his subsequent report, "began to come to the heart of the issue. But the Byzantine complexities are such that this memo will only attempt to provide a confidential setting for Snepp's point of view—not a balanced, objective statement for the official record. Frank Snepp aimed his gun, pulled the trigger, and the barrel smoked. The indictment was made—but the target, I am convinced, is not Polgar but the complicated piece of history known as Saigon in its final hours."

With this overheated preamble, Jones set the tone for all that was to follow, a jumble of snide one-liners and comic-strip images too fantastic to be believed. Ambassador Martin emerged "a gray figure . . . an ideological colleague of Polgar but by no means his master," while Polgar himself became "a warm, sensitive idealistic individual who could come to Snepp's office to cry tears of frustration when plans went awry."

Jones was honest enough to record some of my criticism of Polgar's reporting practices, including what I described as his unwillingness to recognize the Saigon army's morale problems and his penchant for burying unwanted intelligence in the garbage that flowed back to Washington in our lowest-priority, least-read ("ops") channels. But in each instance, Jones managed to insert a jokey aside to take the edge off. Polgar's practice of editing offending "nuances" out of intelligence documents was breezily dismissed as "Polgarization." His use of the Agency's sewer pipes to sink objectionable reports out of sight became "a clever way of circumventing the ambassador's own censorious sieve." And on the most critical issue of all, Jones insisted that "Polgar never suppressed outright anything Snepp wanted to say," even though in another part of his narrative he carelessly let slip that Polgar had canceled my final briefings for the ambassador and sidelined several of my more alarmist reports.

"Taken literally," Jones concluded, "Snepp's description of Polgar's biases and shortcomings are serious indeed. But the important question is how literally should they be taken." He then provided his own answer by dismissing "the very unusual relationship between the two men" as "a classic father-son relationship, with strongly emotional elements of both love and hate, respect and disgust," as if all this made me untrustworthy. He also warned that I exhibited "an unwillingness to accept a sort of shade of gray," a quality which he said I shared with CIA renegades Sam Adams and Victor Marchetti.

None of this did Jones confide to me, but his antagonism was apparent from the pinched expression he wore throughout. Even so, as the interview wound up, I couldn't resist broaching the issue he'd studiously avoided: the evacuation itself. Pleading for an inquiry, I offered to help set one in motion if need be.

"Too difficult," he snapped, abruptly cutting me off. "Beyond our mandate." With that, he terminated the interview.

Though the Saigon station had numbered in the hundreds, only eight other witnesses were summoned, and Jones managed to bend and twist their testimony as easily as he had mine. Later in a written report, he claimed to have found "no evidence whatsoever that there was a policy, conscious or unconscious, to suppress any information that might have cast a less favorable light on the Vietnam situation." He did acknowledge that another interviewee and I had spoken of "an 'atmosphere,' an unwritten code not to report on certain subjects." But, he added nimbly, neither complainer had "any proof that this 'atmosphere' was based on a conscious effort on the part of station management to suppress information." Turning my own testimony upside down, he concluded: "Indeed, of the two officers, the one most closely associated with Mr. Polgar emphatically denied that he strove to prevent certain information from being disseminated."

Thus, just as Colby might have wanted, our final intelligence failures of the war were reduced to the salutary status of an "unconscious development."

CHAPTER 4

Leaks, Lies, and Loomis

WHEN BERNIE pulled me aside in New York the following weekend and told me Stafford had braced Random House on his own, I could barely work up a temper. After my session with Norm Jones, any further injury seemed redundant.

Stafford, sensing my disillusionment, touched only gently on the hard choice it implied. "Maybe you won't have to quit," he ventured. "Maybe you can stay on and write in your spare time."

In theory he should have been right. As I'd discovered from my experience as a press briefer in Vietnam, the Agency had never been reluctant to let friendly voices tell tales in print. Indeed, the Pike committee was even now looking into how the CIA had underwritten a slew of propagandistic volumes over the years, including the bestselling *The Penkovskiy Papers,* a ghostwritten, largely fictional "memoir" of a "mole" inside the Soviet Union.

Still, the operative concept was "friendly," and even a benign insider's commentary on Agency affairs might not win approval in the current climate of recrimination.

— —

As I pondered and agonized, the recriminations intensified. By mid-November, Senator Frank Church was preparing to release his preliminary findings on CIA-sponsored assassinations, and nervous nellies all over

Washington were howling down the winds to try to intimidate him into silence.

On November 19, Colby called a press conference to warn that lives of CIA agents would be jeopardized if the report were released uncensored. Church ignored him and two days later unveiled a detailed summary.

It was enough to shame even a true believer. By Church's account, four foreign leaders had died in Agency-inspired violence over the past two decades, many more killings had been attempted, and nowhere was there a scrap of convincing evidence that the White House had sanctioned any of it. Moreover, in perhaps the sickest of revelations, it turned out that several of the "agents" whose safety Colby had feared for were Mafia hitmen who'd been enlisted in CIA kill plots against Cuban leader Fidel Castro.

Editorialists across the country reacted with outrage. I felt betrayed and terrified; betrayed by the fictions the Agency had spun to keep those of us in the trenches from suspecting the worst—and terrified at the thought that nothing had *ever* been beyond the pale.

The Agency, meanwhile, moved aggressively to repair the damage. Suddenly, lame-duck William Colby was available to any and every journalist who seemed likely to give the Agency "good press," and not merely on matters related to CIA "wet operations."

Even Vietnam came in for varnishing, and according to subsequently released CIA security memos, Colby himself met with CBS's Bernard and Marvin Kalb to share secrets on the very subject he would not submit to official postmortem—the fall of Saigon. He also arranged to have George Carver's deputy, Bill Christison, brief them further.

Christison took up the challenge and ran with it. Not only did he talk at length with one of the Kalb brothers; he even handed over a copy of the top-secret digest of Colby's final White House briefs that he and his colleague, Bob Layton, had just completed.

A gregarious and self-inflated man, Christison had long suffered from a bad case of braggadocio, and in the wake of the Kalb briefing he couldn't resist boasting to colleagues about it, about how he and the director had given the two journalists the run of the house.

Shortly before Thanksgiving, at a cocktail party, he made the mistake of boasting to me.

I kept my cool through the rest of the evening, since there were "civilians" present who weren't cleared for a top-secret shouting match. But the following morning I roared into Christison's office to have it out with him and Layton.

In the course of the angry give-and-take, neither of them let on that a secret document had changed hands, and Layton tried to convince me that nothing sensitive had been compromised. But I wasn't buying. If the briefings had been so benign, I cried, why not give me access to everything the Kalbs had seen so I could write a book too!

Layton cringed. Christison bolted for the door. Moments later, George Carver sent word that he wanted to see me at once.

Hallway gossips had long insisted that the diminutive Carver kept his chair padded with pillows so he'd always be gazing upon the world from regal heights. Once ushered into his presence that morning, I remained standing, the defiant courtier, so I could look him straight in the eye as I delivered my ultimatum. Either the Agency performs an autopsy on Saigon's collapse, I told him, or I proceed with one of my own—inside or even *outside* the Agency if necessary! The Kalb leaks had destroyed whatever rationale there was for silence.

Carver shrank ever deeper into his pillows with each new challenge and finally—reluctantly—promised to get me in to see Colby himself.

Over the next two days, I called his office repeatedly to see if the interview had been arranged. Each time, Carver contrived to be unavailable.

After the umpteenth brush-off, I phoned Stafford in New York and asked him to set up an immediate meeting with his "friends."

— —

The San Marino on Manhattan's East Side is a posh but noisy eatery, particularly at lunchtime, the perpetual clatter of dishes providing a perfect mask for confidential tête-à-têtes. Maybe that's why Bob Loomis and Jim Silberman of Random House chose it as the venue for our inaugural get-together two days later.

Seated to my right, Loomis did most of the talking. But it was Stafford who remembered most of what was said. "The discussion was exploratory," he would later tell government investigators, "because Snepp still intended to write inside the Agency. . . . There was no discussion of a contract or anything, simply exploratory stuff."

Exploratory or not, the banter turned quickly to my writing sample. Loomis inquired if I'd consider expanding it into a manuscript. I vacillated, saying that yes, I'd consider it, if the Agency consented. Across the table Stafford groaned. Loomis seemed exasperated too and invited me to get back to him if and when I could respond more definitively.

Meanwhile, he continued, he wanted to make sure we understood each other. In the event that I did elect to do a book, he'd insist that it be secret-free.

This was no casual injunction. Having edited other CIA exposés,

Loomis knew that the publication of certain secrets, cryptographic or photographic intelligence, or atomic energy data is strictly forbidden, and he wanted nothing to do with that. Neither did I, I assured him. The last thing I meant to do was compound the injury we'd inflicted on our Vietnamese allies.

Loomis nodded gratefully, relieved that he could count on my discretion. It never occurred to him, he said later, that he might have read me wrong, since he'd dealt with enough potential whistle-blowers to have a feel for them. Nor did he have any doubts about my capacity for keeping secrets. He'd learned from Stafford that I'd been a press briefer and assumed that anyone with that kind of background must be practiced at censoring out what the public shouldn't hear.

Later, over coffee, he brought up another precondition. Just as he'd expect me to protect the Agency's interests, he said, he'd demand similar consideration for Random House. Which meant no one was to know he was dealing with me. It wasn't cynicism that prompted this requirement, he continued. Experience had taught him that any publisher who dabbled in material critical of the CIA, secret or not, was courting big trouble.

I agreed immediately. Stafford had already given me a blow-by-blow of the difficulties Random House had faced in bringing out Ross and Wise's *The Invisible Government* in 1964. The CIA had stolen galleys, threatened Loomis with espionage charges, and had finally offered to buy up all editions of the book. Random House had responded by promising to keep it in circulation regardless, thus prompting Langley to commission a spate of unfavorable reviews from such perennial hatchetmen as CIA alumnus William F. Buckley.

In spite of all this, the book had sold well and inflicted not a whit of damage on the nation's security. Still, warning had been served. Next time, the Agency wouldn't be thwarted.

Next time had come soon enough: the Marchetti case of 1972. This time the CIA had prevailed, persuading a federal judge to force Marchetti to turn over his manuscript for censoring. Later, his publisher, Knopf, a Random House subsidiary, had challenged the censors' deletions in court. No use: a federal appeals panel had ultimately sustained 168 of them, leaving Knopf with a mangled manuscript and $150,000 in legal fees.

This was why Loomis was so determined to keep a low profile. I couldn't say I blamed him.

Despite the tentativeness of our discussion, Stafford sailed out of the San Marino on a cloud of high expectation. Fully convinced that I would finally opt to write, he offered to act as my agent and secret intermediary, so there would never be any thread or footprint linking me directly to Random House. Of course, he added, he'd require a modest service fee: say, ten percent of my advance and profits. But that was scarcely exorbitant compensation for the risks *he'd* be running—or against the sizable advance he was sure I'd command.

He then asked me to name my price. I conceded that my needs, should I take time off to write full-time, would doubtless approximate my current salary of twenty-five thousand dollars a year.

"Twenty-five thousand!" he exclaimed incredulously. "With your story, you could get four times that amount." On this jubilant note he ushered Bernie and me off to a nearby saloon for celebratory cocktails.

Later, as we savored our drinks and prospects, Stafford returned to Loomis's insistence on anonymity. It wasn't simply paranoia that inspired it, he asserted, but a very real concern that if the publisher's name got out, the Agency's second-story artists would soon be dropping in. That's what had happened with Marchetti, after all. Somebody working for the Agency had stolen his book proposal out of a publishing house in New York, and it was this same purloined document that the CIA had later used to obtain a judge's restraining order, obliging the renegade author to surrender his manuscript to the censors.

"So you see, Bob's fears aren't exaggerated," Stafford concluded emphatically.

I agreed and said I knew enough of the Agency's bad habits to be quite certain that it was capable of far worse than a little second-story job.

Stafford froze. "You don't think they'd kill us?" he asked in a frightened voice. In light of recent revelations, I wasn't nearly as confident of my reflex skepticism as I might once have been.

— —

Once back at Langley the following day, I immediately contacted Polgar and told him I was bailing out of the Mexico assignment to be free to write a book about all we'd been through. He took the news equably, perhaps realizing, as I did not, that I had about as much chance of winning CIA support for such a book as of prompting an inquest into the evacuation.

As word of my intent spread, lamentations echoed through the corridors. Nobody could later recall if I'd ever been seen as a security threat, but that wasn't the point, of course. "The Agency had been deluged with publicity, much of it unwanted," George Carver remembered, "and anyone who was thought to be pounding a typewriter was regarded as a source of additional distress, of which we already had more than enough."

The only Agency acquaintance who immediately endorsed my plans was the admiring cartographer Daphne Miller. She saw in them a chance to realize her own artistic promise and generously offered to prepare whatever maps and drawings I might need for my book. Her enthusiasm was seductive, encouraging me to tell her more than I should have, including the one thing I'd assured Loomis I would keep confidential, the name of my prospective publisher. Oh, what a mistake! When Daphne mentioned to her father that I might be a fledgling author, he responded hysterically that Philip Agee wrote books too, and that I could be another such traitor in the making. By Thanksgiving, her ardor had cooled. So had our friendship, leaving Random House's identity in the hands of a young woman who now owed me no loyalty at all.

— —

"Mr. Snepp felt that he had come to some kind of turning point, decision point, some moment in his career when he wanted to take stock of himself," recalled senior CIA analyst William Parmenter.

On December 1, only days after Daphne had bid me farewell, I sailed into Parmenter's office and asked him to give me official sanction for the book I wanted to write. Parmenter was chief of a small analytical unit that had inherited responsibility for me after the scuttling of my Mexico assignment. So the overture to him was not only appropriate but necessary.

As I explained what I wanted to do and why, Parmenter listened politely like a man who could empathize. But by the time I'd finished outlining my themes, his normal conviviality had vanished. "My impression," he later reported, "was that what Frank wanted to write was essentially critical of American policy in Vietnam, and more specifically, as I recall it, of Secretary Kissinger's policies and Ambassador Martin's implementation of them. And what I told him was that I doubted very much that the Agency would approve of such an article or book."

But *why?* I demanded incredulously. My security record was flawless. No one could expect me to blow secrets.

Parmenter smiled bleakly and flicked the air with his hand as if dismissing an irrelevancy. Security was only one of the grounds on which the Agency could keep an employee from speaking out on matters of official interest, he explained. The other was *propriety*—the appropriateness of any active-duty CIA agent engaging his superiors in public debate about how they'd performed their duties. On this ground alone, he felt my proposed book would never pass official muster.

I protested, reminding him of the CIA's willingness to peddle its own truth to the press. But he stood fast. To write and be true to my scruples, I'd have to resign. Otherwise: no book. My employee's status and the demands of "propriety" forbade it.

That night, I called my father and told him I felt trapped. He suggested wryly that given my propensity for backing myself into corners, this might be my natural state.

Two days later, a mote of the story I was so eager to tell wafted through Otis Pike's hearing room. An Army colonel named Henry Shockley, once of the defense attaché's office in Saigon, advised the committee that Martin's embassy had been a cesspool of corrupted intelligence. "The deadly combination of 'can do' and 'let's not feed a hostile press,' " he declared, "led well-meaning and patriotic officials to suppress even routine reports that indicated the operational readiness, the morale, or the general capability of the armed forces was not what it should be."

His testimony was delivered in secret, as a footnote to Pike's investigation of Graham Martin's career. Not a whisper of it reached me, and no one on the committee bothered to ask for more.

But Martin himself got wind of it and quickly concluded the entire intelligence community was conspiring against him. On this suspicion, he called me. He'd heard that Colby had ordered up backgrounders for Bernard and Marvin Kalb, he ranted, and had shown them transcripts of his own final White House briefs on Vietnam. What did I know about that?

I knew nothing and told him so. But that night, I lay awake agonizing. Any verbatim snippets of Colby's White House briefs could contain secrets enough to compromise countless abandoned agents.

The next morning, I descended on Layton and Christison to demand an explanation. Both urged me to take my concerns to Colby himself.

I called Carver to see if Colby would grant me an audience at long last. As usual, Carver ducked my call.

That tore it. I stormed out of headquarters, found a corner pay phone, and dialed up Stafford in New York. I told him the deal with Random House was on.

The following Thursday, December 11, Stafford met with Loomis for lunch to discuss a possible contract. To his dismay, the advance Loomis proposed fell short of expectations. True spy stories, he explained, never sold well, and since Vietnam itself seemed a dead issue, he couldn't afford to gamble. Even so, Stafford did manage to lever him up from an initial offer of eleven thousand dollars to one twice that amount—half up front, the rest upon delivery of an acceptable manuscript.

Stafford was anxious to tie up all loose ends, but Loomis said that given the sensitivity of this project, he'd have to check first with Random House president Robert Bernstein. Another round of litigation like the Marchetti suit could make me a costly investment, and since Random House's parent company, RCA, thrived on government contracts, legal fees might not be the only hidden cost of collaborating with me. Thus, the need for Bernstein's involvement.

In an industry not known for daring, Robert Bernstein was the odd man out. A lanky, perennially well-tailored marketing whiz with rusty-blond hair and improbable freckles, he was notorious for championing free-speech causes even at risk to himself and the company. Given this dubious propensity, nobody who knew him could imagine that he'd pass on a book like mine. But neither would he be likely to bestow his blessing blindly. As one whose very livelihood depended on strict enforcement of the First Amendment to the U.S. Constitution, Bernstein had a fixation with the law. Years before, he'd rallied to Marchetti in his own battle with the CIA's censors precisely because Bernstein had convinced himself that they had overstepped the law. More recently, he'd refused even to *bid* for the publication rights to Philip Agee's *Inside the Company: CIA Diary* in the belief that the book's revelatory glossary of CIA names was illegal.

That he should condition approval of my book on the advice of Random's soft-spoken lawyer in residence, Gerald Hollingsworth, was thus wholly in character.

Hollingsworth himself had learned the legal risks of taking on the CIA in print the hard way, for he'd played a critical role in the Marchetti litigation. And though he knew of my promise to include no secrets in my book, he shared Loomis's view that no disenchanted spook was ever likely to slip into print easily. So after weighing the pros and cons of "the Snepp project," he gave his approval with Loomis's own caveat: Random House's identity must be kept secret.

Bernstein duly concurred.

With company policy now locked down, Loomis began fashioning an editorial strategy to fit it. Never before had any mainstream American publisher produced a book in near-total secrecy. So considerable improvising would be required. On December 17, he advised Stafford by letter that he was "investigating various methods by which we might bring [the book] out" without tipping off the CIA.

Ironically, at the very moment Loomis put the book deal in motion, Colby made a final effort to close the book on Vietnam. His aides had already done the preliminary work, drawing up lists of those from the Saigon station who seemingly deserved to be cited for their efforts during the final days of the war, and now the recommendations lay before him for review and approval.

Shortly before Christmas, Colby began poring over them, scratching off names, adding new ones, and scrawling his signature across reams of foolscap to be scissored and framed into exaggerated tributes to individual bravery and foresight.

Months later, scores of bureaucrats would try to distance themselves from his decision to include me among the honorees. Ted Shackley couldn't remember approving any commendation for my Medal of Merit, and William Parmenter huffed defensively, "I sign documents like that by the bale." For all their indignation, though, their signatures bore witness to the fact that they'd been none too reluctant in the winter of 1975 to try to flatter a malcontent into silence.

The day before the awards ceremony, I told Stafford I'd decided to stay away. He was incredulous. "You want people to believe your story?" he groused. "Then accept the damn award!"

The following afternoon, two hundred or more CIA officers filed solemnly into the Agency's secure bubble-top auditorium where Colby had so often railed against Pike and other troublemakers. As I walked past the security guards in the underground accessway, I wondered if I *could* play this out in conscience. No question that Stafford was right in urging me to think strategically, and no question, either, that any act of protest would embarrass the few genuine heroes among us. But wouldn't Colby simply use this gathering to sanctify a lie?

As I hesitated at the entrance, a friend from Vietnam named John Stockwell shouldered his way over. Looking every inch like a down-and-out country-and-western singer with drooping mustache and tumbling forelock, he confessed to suffering reservations too. He'd even gone to the top to see if he could bow out. "I called Colby's office," he remarked, "and asked what I could do to refuse the medal, and was told that Colby had given an order that no one could refuse medals."

No one could refuse?

I nodded, remembering Parmenter's injunction to propriety, his insistence that as long as you took the king's shekel, you owed decorum in return. That was the answer, wasn't it? Conscience had no place here, only obedience. Turning away, I entered the spectator's gallery and found a seat not far from Bill Johnson, who smiled in greeting. Behind me, Stockwell paused, then ambled in, though clearly with no relish. "I went there," he remembered, "thinking there could be an equal number of court-martials instead of medals being handed out—except that the Agency has no provision for court-martials."

If Stockwell shared my disillusionment, he had double my incentive.

The previous summer, after returning from Vietnam, he'd been anointed chief of the Agency's task force for Angola and had since watched in horror as the war there had degenerated into a great-power bloodletting by proxy, Cuban troops battling CIA-funded mercenaries and South African irregulars who were stand-ins for the Angolan factions we favored. To Stockwell, it all seemed a heartbreaking replay of Vietnam in different costume, right down to the impossible promises of American aid and Colby's public disingenuousness about the viability of our allies. This time, though, Congress hadn't tumbled, and even now several senators were writing legislation that would end CIA operations in Angola forever.

As Stockwell settled down to listen to Colby's paeans to our "successes" in Vietnam, his tolerance for such hypocrisy was thus at exceptionally low ebb.

The man in the pulpit himself, prim and stiff-backed as a New England deacon, devoted his sermon that afternoon to belaboring the devil rather than the transgressors before him. At no point did Colby, whom I'd never seen before, mention any of our final intelligence failures or our delay in preparing for the evacuation. Except for Hanoi's eleventh-hour reliance on conventional forces, he said, the antiguerrilla strategy he had helped devise in the early sixties, when *he* was Saigon station chief, would have carried the day. No question.

By the time I stepped up to receive my Medal of Merit, I felt as disoriented as I had on shipboard in the South China Sea. But only after glancing at the accompanying citation did I realize how far I'd stepped through the looking glass. It was a ringing tribute, in Polgar's own words, to all the reports I'd written that he'd ignored. "The importance of Mr. Snepp's work during the final days and indeed hours of the American presence in Vietnam could hardly be overestimated," he'd asserted. "His total unflappability, his ability to organize the necessary material along with his own thoughts during periods of the most intense pressure, his courage under fire, and above all, the perspicacity of his analyses were such that it is my opinion that they deserve and indeed demand special recognition. . . . In summary, during the most critical final days of the American presence in Vietnam, Mr. Snepp turned in a kind of performance which I have never seen equaled nor even approximated during my long years with U.S. intelligence."

I stared at the words in disbelief. The most that could ever be said about my performance at war's end was that it had been irrelevant.

As I walked off the stage with flashbulbs popping and applause rolling up around me, I felt tears on my cheeks and an ineffable sadness, for I knew that if I was to do any justice to the truth, the generosity Polgar had shown me could not be reciprocated. There could be no gratuitous commendations, no white lies to spare the emotions. And inevitably, he would wind up feeling betrayed.

If there is any place in the Agency where betrayal is a permanent fixation, it is the office of Security, official warden of employee loyalty. That same afternoon, as the awards ceremony unfolded, senior Security officer Leo Dunn sat at his desk, flipping through personnel files and informant reports, trying to unravel a case of disloyalty that was beginning to pique his interest.

Bullet-headed Leo Dunn—"Skip" to his friends—had spent most of his career in Security and had acquitted himself well. During Watergate, Director Helms and then CIA comptroller Colby had called on him to help eradicate all traces of the CIA's complicity with Nixon's White House Plumbers, including its role in supplying wigs and technical paraphernalia to the chief Plumber, ex–CIA agent E. Howard Hunt. The cover-up had failed; the wigs and the skeleton keys had been found out. But Dunn had prospered anyway, rising from the debris of the scandal to become one of Security's leading lights, responsible for, among other things, rooting out in-house dissidents.

Three weeks before, a troubling blip had appeared on his radar screen. As he later noted by memo, "a confidential source in the State Department" had disclosed that "a young Agency employee allegedly had written a very controversial manuscript about the Agency and . . . was now writing another article that would be even more critical." The tipster hadn't been able to identify the author, except to say that he was a "former boyfriend" of "the daughter of Mr. Thomas Miller." It had taken Dunn many hours of staffwork to put a name to the lady in question. In the process, he'd turned up some information about poor Daphne Miller even I didn't know.

During a recent, purely routine CIA polygraph test, Daphne apparently had been forced to admit that she'd smoked marijuana from time to time. Since such an indulgence is strictly forbidden in Langley's puritanical clime, she'd been put on probation and given six months to clean herself up.

Dunn had uncovered this blemish on her record quite fortuitously. But now, as he pored through paperwork, trying to identify the putative new "CIA author," he suddenly realized that Daphne's lapse might be a godsend, that it might be used to force her into fingering her "former boyfriend." By the end of the afternoon, he'd written a memo to his superiors urging that she be brought in for questioning.

If the memo proved anything, it was how ignorant of the left hand the

Agency's right hand might be. One phone call to George Carver or any number of knowledgeable supergrades would have enabled Dunn to identify me without having to rough up Daphne Miller.

Still, nobody could ever have accused him of not getting his priorities straight. Having discovered that a disenchanted employee was about to tattle in print, he'd rightly taken it on himself to ferret out the scoundrel. He'd even mobilized two of Security's largest subcomponents, numbering scores of agents, to help in the dragnet.

Whether this may have required skimping on manpower elsewhere remains unclear. But history tells us that on the very day Dunn completed his memo about Daphne Miller, an unforgivable lapse in CIA *physical* security, likewise the responsibility of his office, led to the murder of a ranking Agency spymaster abroad.

The story was all over the headlines the following morning. Richard Welch, the CIA station chief in Athens, had been returning home from a Christmas party when masked assailants had cornered him and gunned him down on his doorstep.

Normally, the residential address of any CIA station chief is cloaked in secrecy. But Welch's had recently become cocktail gossip in Athens and, shockingly, CIA Security had failed to take remedial action in time. Thus, when the luckless spy chief returned home that fateful night, he'd had no shred of anonymity to shield him.

Tragic as his death was, however, it was not entirely in vain. Indeed, proving once again its capacity for turning adversity to advantage, the Agency was soon able to parlay the murder into a propaganda coup. The circumstance that made this possible was the intemperance of its enemies. A few weeks before, an anti-CIA magazine in Washington, *Counterspy,* to which Philip Agee was a regular contributor, had identified Welch as station chief in Peru. Though this garbled disclosure had in no way abetted the abomination in Athens, CIA officials figured the public wouldn't know the difference and that with the right kind of spin they just might make Agee the fall-guy for the murder.

In no time they had the spigots cranked open and the toxic leaks flowing. In the process they also began hinting to the media that congressional investigators had contributed to the bloodletting by making CIA-baiting seem acceptable.

It was a cheap shot, but effective. Over the next several days, as photos of Welch's flag-draped casket dominated front pages across the country, the public bought into the Agency's complicity theories and the steam went out of the Church and Pike investigations.

Peering out over the ramparts of his own paranoia, Stafford assessed the situation and concluded that my writing plans were doomed as long as I was an agent-in-good-standing. If the CIA could treat Otis Pike as an accessory to murder, what hope was there for any criticism from within?

Sometime after Christmas, he sent me a draft of the Random House contract and urged me to resign—and sign.

CHAPTER 5

Sudden, Bitter Good-bye

A S THE WORST YEAR of my life entered its final hours, the Senate voted to suspend all financial support for our only outstanding secret war, the CIA's guerrilla operations in Angola. Many in Congress and the press were moved to find footnotes and meaningful parallels to Vietnam. Some recalled that we'd stumbled into *that* conflict by stealth and presidential subterfuge, and saw the Angola vote as a repudiation of such end runs around the Constitution. Others argued that the administration's reliance on secrecy and covert action, so much on display in the Angolan bush, was the coming thing, an attempt to compensate for the defeatism and paralysis left over from Vietnam. If the imperial presidency had died on April 29, 1975, they said, Angola was its Mount of Olives, and there was a resurrection of sorts in the offing.

The irony implicit in that was not lost on me. The ghost of "my war" was reviving a passion for clandestinity that would make writing about the CIA in Vietnam about as easy as growing sunflowers at midnight.

— —

During the New Year's break, Bernie, Stafford's secretary and my new-found lover, visited me in Arlington and accompanied me on the inevitable social rounds. Listening enrapt as I reminisced with other Vietnam hands, she quickly concluded that a book was my only way of neutralizing the past and urged me to sign the contract Stafford had sent me.

Having still heard nothing from Carver or Colby, I weighed her advice and, on January 6, hauled out the contract and put my signature to it. Before mailing it back to Stafford, however, I attached a note instructing him *not* to pass it along to Loomis until I gave the word. Even at this late date I couldn't muster the courage to abandon my career.

As usual, Stafford ignored me. Fearing that any further delay might scuttle the deal with Random House, he promptly delivered the contract, picked up the first slice of my advance—an eleven-thousand-dollar check made out directly to him as my agent—and slipped it into an account under his own name.

When later asked by federal investigators why he hadn't alerted me, he replied: "There was just no point." He considered my resignation a foregone conclusion and figured he could fill me in when the time came. It never occurred to him that the CIA might take umbrage at my being hired out to a publisher while I was still on the public dole.

— —

At Langley, meanwhile, Skip Dunn was beginning to pick up the scent. The morning after the New Year's holiday, he dispatched an emissary to the CIA's "confidential source" at the State Department to forage for more on Daphne Miller's "former boyfriend." The source offered a crucial name— Frank.

A few hours later, Dunn hauled Daphne herself in for interrogation. Reminding her slyly that her career was at peril because of her "marijuana problem," he led her to believe she could repair the damage by answering a few questions about "Frank."

"Miss Miller," Dunn recorded in his notes, "immediately identified her former boyfriend as being Frank Snepp, because she assumed I already had his name."

She then rambled on about me for over an hour, parceling out confidences we'd shared and embellishing them when memory failed. Under her imaginative brush, I was transformed into an indefatigable writing machine, already cranking out dangerous tomes and nudging deadlines I hadn't even begun to glimpse.

"The Subject reportedly is attempting to complete the book by March," Dunn noted, "and he has said that 'the book will blow the Agency wide open.'"

"Miss Miller speculated," he continued, "that Subject has written the book because he is quite bitter; and he probably feels some guilt because of his involvement in the Vietnam 'travesty.' She stressed that the Subject is an extremely intelligent individual who likes the James Bond–type adventure. He is said to be very calculating, and thus Miss Miller speculated that he might enjoy writing the book under the noses of security."

Admitting "a rather sudden break-off" of her brief association with me, Daphne told Dunn that she was puzzled that I'd confided in her at all. "She did indicate," Dunn observed, "that Subject advised her to keep the information in confidence and . . . she was disposed [to do so] . . . until the death of Richard Welch. She has since discussed this again with her father, and there was agreement that the book could do damage to individuals who remain in Vietnam."

So there it was, Daphne's rationale. "The execution of Athens station chief Richard Welch," she later remarked, "spurred me to volunteer . . . what information I had about Snepp's book. If, as I then believed, he would violate national security by naming names, I hoped it could be prevented."

For all of her patriotic fervor, however, Daphne resented Dunn's rough way with her and immediately scheduled a remedial hearing with the CIA's associate general counsel, John "Jack" Greaney. "Having been totally unnerved," she recalled, "yet still anxious to assist the Agency, I informed Mr. Greaney that I would be willing to discuss any aspect of the Snepp case with him"—provided that Dunn be cut out.

The CIA general counsel's office had always been an oxymoron in the CIA's closed moral spaces. Staffed by a half dozen earnest young lawyers and older keepers, its main purpose was to keep the CIA free of the law. To this extent, Greaney was a perfect fit. In one of his more recent coups, he'd managed to dissuade the Justice Department from prosecuting a Thai drug trafficker who happened to be a CIA asset by refusing to turn over crucial background documents on him.

When Daphne arrived at Greaney's office the morning of January 7, the middle-grade house advocate knew nothing about me. But after hearing her out, he quickly conferred with Dunn, then contacted Paul Walsh, assistant deputy director for analysis, and asked him to pull me in for questioning. Walsh suggested that he and my former superior, William Parmenter, handle the interview together so there would be no confusion about "who struck John." His secretary then called me at home, where I was convalescing from flu, to summon me to the shakedown.

Promptly at ten A.M. the following morning, I walked into Walsh's office and found him with Parmenter at his elbow. Both apologized for rousting me from my sickbed. But, said Walsh, "a problem had arisen which required immediate action." A secret source had revealed that I'd written a book about Vietnam. True or false?

False, I replied in bewilderment. The only manuscript I'd written was the controversial talking paper I'd delivered months before to the Foreign Service Institute. Surely they'd heard about it.

They said they hadn't.

Well, then, surely they knew I was *considering* writing a book. I'd made no secret of that. Just ask Parmenter.

Both let that pass. To be truthful, Walsh continued smoothly, their concern was not whether I had written a book or was planning one, but only to remind me of my "obligation to submit any such manuscripts for security review."

Confused, I turned to Parmenter and reminded him that he'd already vetoed my proposed book for "propriety" reasons. Walsh glanced approvingly at his colleague and confirmed that sure enough, the Agency could keep an active employee from publishing anything "detrimental."

Should the employee persist, he added, "he would have a difficult decision."

I told him wearily that if I persisted, I would resign.

As both men later testified, they both came away convinced I now understood my "obligations." Wrong. The only thing I understood was that as an employee I was handcuffed. But what if I resigned? Would the same strictures apply? Parmenter later acknowledged that this was never discussed with me.

When John Greaney learned what had taken place, he felt uneasy. Not enough had been pried loose. No one had demanded to see what I actually had on paper. He considered going to court immediately to seek a judicial restraining order—a gag—to keep me from jumping into print without official approval. But he knew there was a discrepancy he'd have to clear up beforehand. Daphne had insisted a manuscript existed; I'd denied it. On this issue the case could founder.

He called Dunn and suggested that they put Daphne back in the hot seat.

— —

The summons left Daphne thoroughly miffed. Bad enough to have her testimony challenged; worse to have to confront Dunn again.

On the day of the interview itself, she brought her father along for protection. His presence steadied her, so much so that she quickly cast all caution to the winds and began responding so expansively to questions that Greaney could barely scribble notes fast enough.

On the most crucial question of all, she was unambiguous, insisting that there *was* a manuscript, "at least two inches thick," spanning 250 pages and permanently consigned to a "cocktail table" in my apartment. Not only had she handled it, she said; she'd even "reviewed" parts of it. But—noted Dunn, who was also keeping record—"she had no recollection as to the overall contents or the title." Even so, she was confident, he added, that it posed a threat, largely on the strength of "Subject's" repeated assertions that "the book would blow the Agency apart."

As to whether it would blow actual secrets, Daphne couldn't be sure. She did expect me to use pseudonyms to protect the identities of CIA agents under cover ("Pseudo, minor characters," ran Greaney's shorthand), but she doubted that anonymity would be accorded major players like Polgar. Greaney asked what my rationale for this might be, and recorded her response with chilling succinctness: "True names . . . Tom Polgar . . . Pay the price along with the rest."

Asked about my immediate plans, Daphne recalled that I'd once mentioned resigning as a way of freeing myself to write. According to Dunn, she interpreted this to mean that "Subject did not intend to have the publication reviewed by appropriate components of the Agency." At this point, Daphne's father interrupted to say that he, too, had this "impression." In fact, observed Dunn, "the father felt that the Subject never had any intention of going to Mexico City" with Polgar.

Dunn puzzled over this and asked why, then, I hadn't resigned months before. Daphne had a mischievous explanation. "It was her feeling," recalled the security man, "that the Subject intended to remain in the Agency as long as possible, so that he might use Agency facilities and the Agency library to do research while working on a manuscript."

Greaney now leaned back and eyed Daphne Miller curiously. Despite the recurrence of speculative buzzwords—"feeling . . . inference . . . impression"—her testimony had seemed reasonably credible so far. None of the acrimony he might have expected from an ex-girlfriend had shown through.

Still, even if she was telling the truth, would any court gag "the Subject" on the basis of her statements alone? In the Marchetti case, the Agency had been able to present the judge with a copy of a book outline lifted from one of the author's publishing contacts. Such a coup might be necessary here. So, the next logical question for Miss Miller was: Who'd bought the rights to the "Subject's" book? Who was the publisher?

In this, as in everything else, Daphne was wonderfully forthcoming, albeit excessively optimistic about my earning power. As Dunn recollected in his notes, she "pointed out on a number of occasions that the Subject was to receive a $100,000 advance, and he was dealing with Random House in New York."

The ease with which she volunteered this information caught Greaney off guard. This, after all, was the ultimate betrayal, for it would enable the Agency to snare the manuscript itself. For a moment, he reacted mechanically, merely shorthanding her words without keying on the implications: "Random House . . . Publisher . . . $100,000 advance." Only after he lifted his pen did the full significance sink in and the first twinge of doubt assail him. A *$100,000 advance*—for a book by a *total unknown*! It didn't make sense. And if Miss Miller had this detail wrong, what else? Maybe she was wrong about Random House, too.

Greaney would later be hard-pressed to explain his incredulity. "She didn't sound at all sure that this was a publishing house," he exclaimed testily.

If she was unsure, however, Greaney shouldn't have been. He'd been part of the CIA team that had litigated against Random House and its subsidiary, Knopf, in the Marchetti case. They were Marchetti's publishers!

So why did he discount her testimony on this crucial point? Was it that he couldn't bring himself to trust a pot smoker? Or was she simply too glib for his tastes? Whatever the reason, the fact remains that John Greaney refused to believe that Random House was in cahoots with me.

So did Dunn. Although the company's name appears in his own record of the interview, there is no evidence that he or anyone else ever attempted to follow up this priceless lead. Instead, the Security office and the general counsel's staff simply pigeonholed and forgot the one piece of intelligence that might have enabled them to stop my book cold.

At the end of the interview, Daphne inquired whether it would be in the national interest for her to spurn me if I tried to contact her again. Dunn and Greaney declined to play Miss Lonelyhearts, but did ask her to let them know if the relationship revived. "It was at this point," observed Dunn, "that Mr. Miller, speaking as a father, took a rather strong position that he would not want his daughter to have any further discussions or contact with the Subject."

— —

For Greaney, one issue *had* been resolved. He now believed unequivocally, based on Daphne's testimony, that a manuscript, or something like a manuscript, or something that could be presented to a judge as a manuscript, did exist.

But still, he wasn't confident that he could obtain a gag order against me in court. The problem was my intentions, or more precisely, the uncertainty surrounding them. Would I submit to clearance or not? Daphne had assumed the worst. But again, her testimony might not be enough to sway a judge.

So Greaney decided to go back to the culprit himself. He and Dunn would take another swipe at me.

The moment I walked into Dunn's office on the afternoon of January 22, I realized I was facing a classic interrogation, with Greaney playing good cop to Dunn's bad one. It was just the sort of grilling I'd often conducted in Vietnam. So I knew how to roll with the punches.

During the two-hour ordeal, I acknowledged I had in my possession 150 pages of letters, diary notes, and unclassified briefing papers—but was emphatic that I'd produced no manuscript.

Dunn scoffed and, in his notes, expressed certainty that I'd already completed a book that was "quite anti-Kissinger and anti–State Department" and "quite critical of Mr. Thomas Polgar."

Equally skeptical, Greaney demanded I turn over whatever I'd written, be it manuscript, diary notes, whatever.

"The Subject quite strongly and repeatedly emphasized that he would not," recorded Dunn, "for fear that we would censor the material."

Greaney countered by insisting that I sign an affidavit pledging to surrender the manuscript at some future date.

Dunn noted that I was "very firm" in refusing.

At this point, Greaney, exasperated, challenged me to demonstrate my truthfulness by submitting to a lie-detector test. From my own experience as an interrogator, I knew it would take him only a few cleverly phrased questions to turn my 150 pages of memorabilia into something he could label a "manuscript" and use to persuade a judge to restrain me.

"The Subject," reported Dunn, "stated that he would concede to no such interview. He mentioned that he was familiar with the way the polygraph can be utilized and he had no intention of being pulled into semantics on a definition of a manuscript."

As the interrogation wound up, I threw out a challenge of my own, suggesting that Security might better spend its time investigating the CIA's leaks to the Kalbs. Neither Dunn nor Greaney batted an eye.

Assistant Deputy Director Paul Walsh was hovering at Dunn's door when I stumbled out, and noted that I seemed "rather perturbed." Small wonder. Though I'd survived the skirmish, I'd certainly lost the war. Any CIA officer who refuses a polygraph might as well resign on the spot.

A few floors above, I found William Parmenter hunched over his desk, writing furiously against the traditional five o'clock deadline for analyses destined for the White House. When he saw me, though, he shoved the work aside and bade me be seated. As I began pouring out my story, he jotted a note to himself—"Frank Snepp, resigning."

"In the course of our conversation," he later wrote, "it developed that he felt the Agency's attitude, illustrated by Mr. Greaney's request that he sign a second secrecy agreement and take a polygraph test, was or would be basically obstructive of his desire to publish. . . . He contrasted this with the cooperation he asserted the Kalb brothers were receiving from Agency officials; he felt this smacked of news management."

Parmenter indulged my plaints with apparent sympathy but made no attempt to persuade me to stay on. "I told Mr. Snepp," he remembered, "that for his protection and the Agency's, we would handle his resignation by the book."

The only question was—when.

Tomorrow morning, I replied, wanting to be done with this as quickly as possible. He extended a hand to seal the bargain. "The conversation was not acrimonious," he remarked afterward. "We parted, from appearances, more in sorrow than in irritation."

Across the Potomac, only a few minutes from where I lived in those days, stands the Lincoln Memorial, a tribute in majestic symmetry to the man who turned loyalty to the Republic into a martyr's vision. Shortly after nightfall, I made my way there, a kind of pilgrimage.

As I wandered among the crystalline porticos, surveying the inscriptions, a chill settled over me, for I realized that in breaking with the Agency this way, I would forever set myself apart from so many who shared my memories and my values.

Pausing under the Great Emancipator's lifeless gaze, I reminded myself why I'd come this far and vowed to go no further—to get the truth out, but to keep the secrets, no matter how tempting the prospect of easy vindication or how crushing the isolation.

Often, in the succeeding months when the isolation deepened or the ego swelled, I would return to that spot to remind myself of the vow. But I would never feel at ease. As a Southern conservative nurtured on thirty-two years of middle-class mores, I had none of the skepticism that might have comforted a practiced dissident. The textbook precepts of honor and loyalty were the only ones I knew.

Next morning, groggy from lack of sleep, I dragged myself out to Langley to begin my "outprocessing." All along the exit route, I received instant attention, as though the natives were impatient to be rid of my contaminating presence.

As my first order of business, I typed a curt note of resignation, but accidentally misdated it "23 January 1975." On that date, one year before, Saigon still had over three months to live.

While I made my way along a well-marked paper trail toward the turnstiles, Dunn, Greaney, Walsh, Parmenter, and Security Chief Robert Gambino debated what to do about me. According to contemporaneous memos, all agreed that I was prepared to expose secrets and would refuse to sign the CIA's "Termination Secrecy Agreement." Dunn suggested a body search at the exit to see if I'd pocketed any classified documents. But Gambino worried that this might prejudice their hand if they were ever obliged to take me to court.

Halfway through the morning, Parmenter summoned me to his office to assure me I wouldn't be "surveilled or otherwise harassed gratuitously." He also emphasized that the only obligation I now faced was to "abide by the terms of the secrecy agreement." He did not elaborate. As he later acknowledged under oath, he was already convinced that my book would be so chock-full of secrets that it would be a candidate for censorship on that ground alone.

From Parmenter's office, I moved on to a cubbyhole occupied by a fulsome, red-faced Security officer named "Meehan," who was to read me my final rights.

Blinking rapidly, he reached into his desk and produced photostatted excerpts of the espionage statutes. I read them over and discovered that I was forbidden, at risk of jail time, to steal national defense documents or hand them over to a foreign power for the purpose of hurting the United States. "Any problem?" asked Meehan. "None," I replied.

Next, this aging leprechaun presented me with a two-page document titled "Termination Secrecy Agreement." It required the signatory to seek Agency approval before publishing "classified information or any information concerning intelligence or the CIA that has not been made public by the CIA." Since I had no intention of publishing anything that might further imperil abandoned Vietnamese, I saw nothing here to object to either.

To be doubly certain, however, I asked if the agreement covered all my obligations. Meehan said it did, and assured me that the termination pact was identical to the agreement I'd signed on joining the Agency in September 1968. I nodded and scrawled my signature.

No wonder Greaney had wanted me to sign an affidavit pledging him my manuscript under any circumstances. Without it he had no legal power to stop me from publishing a book that exposed no confidences.

Before waving me out, Meehan stripped me of my ID lapel badge and gave me an anonymous "Visitor" one to see me through the rest of the day. He then sat down and typed out a "contact" report for Dunn, noting that "Mr. Snepp had displayed no animosity." Dunn immediately relayed the message to his own high command. "The Subject," he wrote, "was somewhat quiet and subdued."

With my odyssey now well past the point of no return, George Carver finally roused himself on my behalf. Late that afternoon, he told Walsh of my request to see Colby, and suggested that it might now be safely granted. Since Colby was only days away from his own retirement, he'd be in no position, by the time we met, to press for the official inquiry I'd so long demanded.

— —

The remainder of the afternoon, with the temporary visitor's badge banging my chest like a leper's bell, I stayed clear of the main corridors in hopes of avoiding old friends and painful farewells. But one old friend, Bill Johnson, spotted me at the elevators and descended. Clapping me on the shoulder, he assured me I was doing the right thing and reminded me that I had a standing invitation to his Wednesday-night soirees. "Please stay in touch," he remarked earnestly. I told him I would and was touched by his kindness. At least I wouldn't be a pariah to everyone at Langley.

As I hurried away, Bill paused a moment, then pulled out his notebook and jotted my words verbatim.

Later, toward the end of the day, I visited the Latin America division to say good-bye to another friend, Tom Polgar. Unbeknownst to me, he'd been agonizing for hours over a piece of bad news that he believed to be related to my departure. Ambassador Martin, it seemed, had just persuaded a House subcommittee to hear his side of the evacuation story, and Polgar was fearful that I was resigning in order to help Martin prepare. Though in fact I knew nothing about his planned testimony, rumors of our impending "collaboration" were already circulating through the Security office, and as Dunn noted by memo, he and his colleagues spent part of the afternoon fielding queries from Agency officials concerned that I might create "a public controversy" at the hearing.

Anxious and irritable, Polgar asked point-blank what I knew about Martin's testimony. I said I knew only that Martin was out to burnish his record in any way possible and that he'd been leaking freely to the Kalbs to ensure favorable treatment in their book. "For whatever [it's] worth," Polgar later advised associates, "Snepp claimed that the Kalb book, which he said was being written with full access to info[rmation] in possession of

Secretary Kissinger and Ambassador Martin, would be strongly anti-CIA."

By the time Polgar relayed his impressions up the chain of command, I'd reached the end of my long day's journey. Before surrendering my visitor's badge to the guard in the downstairs foyer, I paused to read again the inscription on the south wall: "Ye shall know the truth and the truth shall make you free." For the first time, it occurred to me that herein lay the Agency's most valuable bequest to me, the key to my own deliverance from Vietnam.

PART II

MIGHTIER THAN THE SWORD

CHAPTER 6

Martin's Artful Dodge

A FEW HOURS after leaving CIA headquarters, I called Stafford and endured his hosannas. "You're on your way, m'boy!" he shouted. "Fortune beckons."

I wasn't so sure. My purest sensation was confusion, and any satisfaction I might have felt at having finally made the leap was quickly dampened by news that seemed to trivialize my daring. Indeed, when William Colby announced the following Sunday that he was planning to write a memoir of his own, I began to wonder what all the fuss had been about anyway.

His declaration was virtually his last word as director. The Senate confirmed George Bush as his successor twenty-four hours later, and in a backhanded gesture to the departing regime, the House voted to cut all funding for CIA adventures in Angola, as the Senate had weeks before.

The vote, which owed so much to our failures in Vietnam, couldn't have been more exquisitely timed. That very afternoon, Graham Martin showed up on Capitol Hill to deliver his own apologia for Saigon's end.

— —

From start to finish, it was a dazzlingly self-serving performance, as indeed it had to be, for though the audience was a House subcommittee on foreign affairs with no direct sway over Martin's next appointment, he needed to establish here, before God and country, that he was still worthy.

I got to the hearing room early to be assured a good seat, only to discover that the two front pews had already been cordoned off at the witness's request. Knowing that even a congressman can be distracted by a comely leg or fluttering eyelash, Martin had reserved these ringside seats for several gorgeous female friends.

Shortly before his own regal entrance, *they* paraded in, setting the congressmen twittering and the TV crews along the wall gawking in admiration. Whether their presence served to soften the subsequent interrogation, I can't say. But clearly, Martin was taking no chances.

Looking every inch the ambassador, white hair neatly trimmed and glistening under the lights, he took his place at the witness table shortly after two o'clock. Representative Lee Hamilton, chairman of the subcommittee, called the session to order, his flat Indiana drawl booming through the conference room. "Mr. Ambassador, we welcome you back," he said, adjusting the microphone. "Perhaps you would like to make a few brief remarks on the events of last spring before we start with questions from members."

For the next two hours, Martin proved himself a master of the artful dodge. While blaming congressional parsimony for Saigon's collapse, he didn't exactly blame Congress itself. Arab sheiks with their inflated oil prices had ravaged the small pittance of aid allotted Saigon, he said, and though Congress had cut its final appropriation far below what had been anticipated, the fault lay not with stingy legislators, but with a sinister anti-Saigon think tank here in Washington, the left-leaning Indochina Resource Center, which had lobbied effectively against additional aid.

At no point did he hold the South Vietnamese themselves responsible for their defeat. Nguyen Van Thieu had been "a very good leader" until U.S. aid cutbacks had destroyed the morale of his army. And if there had been corruption in his regime, Martin considered it beneath comment, for he offered none.

As for the evacuation, he declared it "a hell of a good job," and juggling figures to prove his point, claimed credit for the rescue of sixty thousand Vietnamese, though in fact, over half of these had been smuggled out on U.S. cargo planes by embassy officers acting in defiance of his orders. Asked why the evacuation hadn't proceeded more rapidly, he cited first his fear of panic, and second, creaking U.S. immigration policies which, he said, had limited the number of high-risk Vietnamese he could ship to the United States. What he didn't say was that he'd repeatedly ignored requests from Washington for realistic evacuation estimates that would have enabled immigration officials to adjust quotas accordingly.

Nor did he even hint at the real reason for his foot-dragging, his inability to admit defeat. While claiming to have realized four weeks before the end that Thieu couldn't survive, he argued that there had been a chance for some kind of last-minute "fix," the creation of an "interim regime" headed by a neutralist.

Several congressmen wagged their heads at this. Hadn't there been intelligence reports to the contrary? one asked. Martin stiffened. "We did have information from a long-range penetration of the so-called COSVN, the central Communist unit in South Vietnam," he conceded, "which indicated that, regardless of all the other byplay, the North Vietnamese were now determined to press a strict military solution.

"Now I hesitate to say this," he continued, "but that report was not given that much credibility by the CIA station chief. It was not sent back by the CIA station chief in normal reporting channels. It was not until he was pressed by the officer who was in direct contact with this particular penetration"—Martin swung around and gestured toward me—"that this man was allowed to send it back through operational channels."

Representative Hamilton demanded: "Who is that man?"

"Mr. Frank Snepp," replied Martin, "the person who was in direct contact with the penetration."

My stomach wrenched violently. Martin had just committed an astonishing security breach; the very existence of the COSVN source was secret. And if I was now asked to comment, I would have to refuse.

Hamilton stared down his nose at me. A long moment passed. Finally he turned back to the ambassador himself.

"That mid-April assessment concerning the North Vietnamese decision to push for total victory," he continued, "did I understand that you saw that?"

"Yes," replied Martin.

"You did not accept it as accurate?"

"I put considerably more credibility on it than the station chief did, as a matter of fact."

Suddenly Martin checked himself, as if realizing he'd said too much. He had. For if, as he contended, he'd believed the COSVN source, why hadn't he called for an accelerated airlift?

To duck that one, he took a leaf from Kissinger and Polgar and imputed inconsistency to the North Vietnamese themselves, claiming that they'd "changed their signals" at the last moment "and appeared to shift suddenly to a military option. The possibility of a negotiated settlement was ruled out."

It was all I could do to keep from howling. Having just betrayed one of our most sensitive sources, Martin was now attempting to repudiate the source's intelligence!

None of the congressmen seemed troubled by this, however, for none objected, and emboldened, Martin reverted to his favorite pastime, scapegoating, accusing Polgar of rank insubordination and Kissinger of having ultimately been responsible for everything.

"I have never forgotten," he observed slyly, "that in the end, the policy was never mine."

He also reminded his audience pointedly that both the secretary and the president himself had publicly commended his performance. The only reason he was speaking out now, he added, was that certain parties had dared fault him.

Even so—and here he paused for a long sip of water—he wasn't sure if Congress should pursue this inquiry any further. "I would think Vietnam has been divisive enough," he said. In short, with today's testimony, Martin hoped to have the final word.

Based on what followed, he seemed destined to get his wish. Hamilton closed the proceedings without calling for follow-up, and as staff aides began scurrying about, gathering up briefcases and papers, I stood alone and ignored by the dais, wondering if anyone in Washington cared what had happened in those last moments of the war.

If press coverage was any measure, nobody did. Apart from brief honorable mention on local TV news, Martin's testimony dropped into oblivion.

It didn't escape Polgar, however. When a summary of it reached him in Mexico City, he immediately denounced the ambassador's "falsification of history" in a cable to Langley and demanded to be allowed to set the record straight.

He might as well have spit into the wind. George Bush was about to take over as director, and his mandate was clear. "The abuses of the past have been more than adequately described," President Ford declared at Bush's swearing-in.

In a reply cable, Shackley advised Polgar not to expect any satisfaction and insisted that even Martin's ill-considered remarks about the COSVN source were unworthy of protest. "Given temper of the times and other public disclosures of CIA activities," he argued, it was doubtful that "we can make case against Martin for reference to agent in these unspecific terms."

In short: leave well enough alone.

It wasn't to be that easy.

The morning after the hearing, a reporter from National Public Radio called the CIA's press officer, Angus Thuermer, to ask about the "spook" the ambassador had mentioned. Thuermer pretended not to know my name, but immediately alerted Dunn, who in turn alerted Shackley, that

Snepp was already causing trouble. That afternoon, the Agency's senior cadre circulated several all-points bulletins about me.

To all "CIA Duty Officers and Watch Officers": "Frank Snepp . . . has resigned from the Agency rather than agree to submit for review a book he is writing. . . . Anyone talking to him should be mindful of his status."

To all CIA "Group Chiefs": "Frank Snepp of DDI has retired from the Agency. . . . [H]e is writing a book—probably about Indochina—and . . . has choosen [sic] not to submit the book to the Agency for review."

By February 4, as Dunn noted by memo, Shackley was pressing for a campaign of active surveillance against me. Dunn's own immediate boss, Security Chief Robert Gambino, agreed to allow "passive monitoring" by CIA volunteers.

That afternoon, Shackley sent a cable to Mexico to update Polgar. In an effort to ease his nerves, he glossed over the danger I posed and claimed I'd agreed to submit to CIA censorship even though the watch-officer memos told a different story. He also informed Polgar that no one knew who my publisher was.

Replying instantly, Polgar argued I was too crazy to be trusted. The individual he'd observed at headquarters seemed "increasingly irrational . . . heavily involved financially—probably over his means" and "under pressure to make money quickly." For this and other reasons, which Polgar felt might be "best analyzed in psychiatric terms," he advised Shackley that "we may have a real problem on our hands, even though Snepp repeatedly has stated that he is not going to be another Agee or Marchetti." Urging that my testimony to Norm Jones be reexamined, he believed it to be the "key to Snepp's thought processes" and a harbinger of worse to come. "Probably, as memory grows dimmer and he comes under increasing financial pressure," said Polgar, "his exaggerations will increase, particularly as he realizes that earning potential may be great when emphasis is on alleged incompetence of his superiors."

Taking these warnings to heart, Shackley ordered all his immediate subordinates to shut me out: nobody was to answer any requests for information from me or even return my phone calls. I was effectively reduced to nonperson status. The Kremlin couldn't have done it any better.

There was, however, one crack in the stonewall. Just before leaving Langley for good, William Colby had sent a note to Paul Walsh advising him to arrange the interview I'd long asked for.

"Pl[ea]se get in touch with him," he told Walsh, "and say that I would be glad to chat with him either officially or personally (as a Columbia friend of his father's). His option."

The afternoon of the interview, as I climbed the icy front steps of

Colby's modest home in suburban Washington, I remembered an anecdote my father had told me about their student days together at Columbia Law School, where they'd been close friends—so close, in fact, that Colby might have been my godfather had not World War II intervened. As my father remembered it, he and Colby had been out swilling beer at a student hangout—it was the winter of 1940—and *pfft,* Colby had disappeared, just like that. Days later, unshaven and bedraggled, he'd shown up for class and confessed he'd been holed up at Princeton, his old college alma mater. Having climbed aboard a train in an alcoholic daze, he'd wound up there as if by instinct, blindly homing in on the institution he knew and loved. "That's the way Colby was," my father mused every time he told the story. "Once he signed on somewhere, he could never break away. He was always ready to defend the stockade."

As the front door swung open and I found myself staring into Colby's zippered smile, the one he'd so often worn for offending congressmen, I knew at once that this was no remove from the stockade, but a mere extension, and that I'd find no comfort here.

He motioned me to a chair, inquired politely about my parents, offered a good Catholic grimace when I mentioned "divorced," and then mumbled something about the two of us being in the same boat now, since he too was "retired" and contemplating a memoir. But he was no egalitarian about this. "Pitchers should leak from the top, not from the bottom," he counseled primly.

When I asked why he'd allowed secrets to be leaked to the Kalbs, he became a veritable iceman, disclaiming any knowledge of this at all.

Substantively, he echoed the platitudes he'd dispensed at the awards ceremony and only once allowed any emotion to creep into his nasal monotone. In defending the Phoenix counterterror program, which he'd helped devise in Vietnam, he waxed positively indignant. "They were *Communists,* those people, just no damn good," he said of Phoenix's numberless victims.

— —

A few days later, at the start of the Vietnamese Tet New Year, I traveled to New York to wrap up what I thought was a still incomplete publishing deal. Over a lavish lunch at Ho Ho's midtown restaurant, Stafford lubricated me with wine and flattery and then casually let drop that he'd already wrapped it up himself. Not only had he turned my draft book contract over to Loomis, he'd banked the eleven-thousand-dollar down payment on my advance.

My expression must have frightened him, for he hastily shoved a promissory note into my hand and assured me that he'd done nothing rash, that his every action had been in my interest.

"But how could you *presume!*" I gasped.

At this, he grew indignant, as if I had no right to question his intentions, and immediately called for the check. It would be many months before I realized he'd glossed over the most critical detail of all, neglecting to mention that he'd finalized my Random House contract *before* my resignation from the Agency.

— —

For anyone who'd done time in Vietnam, the very word "Tet" conjured clashing images of strife and celebration, of jittering papier-mâché dragons, exploding firecrackers and the flash of incoming artillery.

My last Tet, I'd been in Saigon, up late into the early hours of the morning writing an "analysis" designed to convince congressional fact finders that Thieu's regime was a Thousand-Year Reich. This Tet New Year's Eve I spent with the ravaged survivors of that lie, in a school auditorium in Arlington, amid the trappings of a pageant that now belonged only to the past.

Arlington's Vietnamese community was then the second largest in the country. So the spectacle that night was standing room only. As I stood back in the throngs, watching exquisite Vietnamese girls turn and genuflect through traditional dances, I found myself weeping openly, the delicate cymbals and muffled drums beating out echoes of a part of my life I'd lost forever.

Later, in the foyer, moving among plywood stalls redolent of fish sauce and bedecked with memorabilia from the old country, I felt a hand on my shoulder and turned to find my Agency friend, John Stockwell, gazing at me quizzically, as if surprised to discover I was still among the living. "You've done the right thing, quitting like you did," he said after a long pause. "But don't kid yourself. They'll crucify you and no one will care."

CHAPTER 7

Muzzled

A N OLD CIA friend of mine used to liken the Agency to a stained-glass window too scuffed and weathered to be repaired. "You'll never get it to shed much light," he'd muse sadly. "All you can do is polish up a frame or two."

It never occurred to me, as I began writing, that I could do any more than polish up a frame or two. I was still too much the Southern conservative to be able to think in bolder terms.

I wasn't alone. Until recently, nobody had done much polishing. A half dozen congressional panels claimed to be overseeing the CIA, but classified briefings had become routine only in the past year and a half, and the juiciest stuff continued to be reserved for a few "trustworthy" committee members.

When the White House appointed the Rockefeller Commission in early 1975 to look into CIA murder plotting, Congress created two special committees of its own to pursue parallel inquiries. Senator Frank Church's group forged ahead gamely, but the House panel kept stumbling. Its first chairman was attacked for being too close to the CIA; its second, Otis Pike, was denounced as security-lax, and by the time he fired back, the CIA and its supporters were lobbying hard to persuade the public that nobody in Congress could be trusted with the nation's secrets.

The Welch killing and the propaganda surrounding it strengthened this impression, and on the eve of Bush's swearing in as CIA director, the entire House of Representatives voted to keep Pike's final report secret.

The decision was a bell tolling. From now on, the equation governing any new gesture toward increased accountability would be: one part reform and two parts increased secrecy.

If the trend seemed clear and inexorable, however, the disillusioned did not go quietly. On February 11, Bernie called breathlessly from New York to tell me *The Village Voice* had just published massive excerpts of the suppressed Pike report that had been leaked by parties unknown.

An infuriated President Ford mustered out the FBI to track down the culprits, and even the media cried foul. When TV journalist Daniel Schorr confirmed that it was he who'd fenced the leaked report and sold it to the *Voice*, CBS News suspended him, and ultimately fired him, after watching him stagger through a lengthy House ethics investigation.

— —

In the midst of all this, Stafford panicked. "Who wants to go to jail for one damn book!" he wailed, and overnight his instinctive hauteur gave way to fried nerves and ever heavier drinking. He bought an extra dead bolt for his already barricaded West Side pad and became so obsessed with phone security that he was soon fielding calls like a veteran spy, using code words reflexively for whatever might betray us: "wallpaper" for the manuscript, "Janice" for Loomis, and "Virgil Black" for me.

Being more inured than he to living dangerously, I was better able to hide my fear. But it was there nonetheless, deep and metastasizing. The changing political climate, the co-opting of the press, the persecution of Daniel Schorr made me feel increasingly uneasy, and always I was haunted by the prospect that the Agency might shut me down before I could get enough on paper to liberate me from the memories. And I knew that if that happened, I might go mad.

So I took care to preserve my running room, applying every shred of tradecraft I knew to keep the Agency guessing. Code words, dead-drops, surreptitious hand-offs became my daily choreography, and whenever I'd venture forth beyond the bolted doors of my Arlington apartment, I'd keep to less traveled thoroughfares, avoiding the lights, hugging the alleys, pausing briefly before the odd storefront window to search the reflections for presentiments of a tail.

So exacting were these rituals that I soon fell prey to a chronic, paralyzing exhaustion that robbed me of every emotion but fanaticism. Inevitably, the first casualties were my friends. Laura Palmer, a journalist pal from Saigon, received little more than a cold shoulder for the many long nights she played confessor to me, and Bernie might as well have been a seaman's wife for all the thanks I gave her as she slaved away on my behalf, transcribing the cassette tapes I sent her, nudging my jumbled ramblings into the first semblance of a manuscript.

And when, in early spring, my Agency confidante, Carla Christiansen, called to patch things up and offered help, I fastened on to her with the same singular intensity, extorting so many favors—from fact checking to proofreading to occasional if passionate sex—that her Agency chums soon came to suspect her loyalties. In time, she and Bernie were sharing everything I had to offer but my heart. That I reserved for my only true mistress, the book that was to cleanse me.

Oh, but there *was* a price to be paid, for the many cruelties I inflicted were duly borne back on me by the treachery of lesser friends. Throughout the spring, countless Agency "buddies" showed up at my door to encourage and sympathize and to offer an inside tip or two, but almost invariably, as subsequently released CIA memos reveal, they scurried back to Langley to spill everything they'd learned. By early summer, Dunn and his associates in CIA Security had parlayed these little gratuities into a promising intelligence file on me.

— —

For all the petty betrayals, however, one set of acquaintances, Pat and Bill Johnson, remained steadfast and considerate. Every Wednesday night they'd throw open their doors and let me commingle, unjudged and unchallenged, with their closest Agency friends. So seductive were their attentions, and so great my need for acceptance in the world they represented, that I soon came to rely on them as a surrogate family. And once my manuscript took on some semblance of what it was supposed to be, I began passing large swatches of it to Bill to annotate and critique.

Always encouraging, he repaid my trust in kind, scouring CIA files and smuggling out helpful documents for me to use in my research.

Among these purloined pearls was one that would prove critically important, a commentary on the North Vietnamese victory by Hanoi's field commander, General Van Tien Dung. Intercepted from Radio Hanoi and rendered by CIA translators, it virtually confirmed my worst fears: Not only had lives been abandoned in our rush to the choppers; so had reams of highly damaging intelligence reports. At Saigon's military and police headquarters, Dung wrote, his legions had discovered "top-secret files and documents of the puppet commanders" and "a modern enemy computer containing the records of each officer and enlisted man of the puppet armed forces of more than a million."

How the victors meant to use this find was telegraphed in another intercept that Bill turned over to me, a warning from Radio Hanoi that all American "lackeys" with "blood debts" to repay would soon be hauled before "secret people's tribunals." Anyone who knew Vietnamese history could guess the implications. In the mid-1950s, such tribunals had been used to cleanse the Communist north of an estimated fifty thousand "bourgeois elements."

— —

Given its import, Dung's memoir was bound to attract attention outside intelligence circles, and it soon did. Don Oberdorfer of *The Washington Post* learned of it, sought out a copy, and immediately glimpsed the potential for an explosive news story.

Fortuitously, as he began his research, another account of the Communist victory that had been recently published abroad showed up in translation in American bookstalls. Written by an Italian journalist who'd stayed on in Saigon after the takeover, the book expanded on Dung's disclosures, revealing that North Vietnamese forces had captured not only computerized troop lists in their move on Saigon but "all the dossiers that had been compiled over the years by the secret police in collaboration with the American CIA."

For Oberdorfer, this was priceless gilding, exactly what he needed to turn the Dung memoir into front-page news. But he knew that such a story all but required an insider's perspective.

So he turned to me.

It wasn't a cold call. Having once worked as a reporter in my own hometown, he knew and respected my father and figured that some of the integrity might have rubbed off. He asked if I would comment on Dung's disclosures.

When Loomis found out, he wasn't pleased. Anything but silence, he remarked anxiously, could be taken as provocation.

But silence *was* the provocation, I shot back. Official silence had given Hanoi a free hand to set up those tribunals. Maybe what was needed was a little hue and cry.

I told Oberdorfer I would help.

His "Saigon Secrets Seized" appeared as the *Post*'s lead story on Memorial Day. Describing me as a former CIA strategy analyst hard at work on a Vietnam memoir, he quoted me confirming many of Dung's allegations and decrying the "wishful thinking" that had kept Martin and Polgar from ordering up the evacuation in time or ensuring the destruction of intelligence documents we'd spread around Saigon. Some of these files, I said, "may reveal to the Communist authorities a great deal about U.S. intelli-

gence operations and permit them to identify well-placed U.S. agents behind Communist lines as well as anyone who helped us."

As other newspapers picked up the story, the aftershocks rolled through
official Washington. President Ford demanded an accounting of all compromised files. Shackley whipped up a brief that blamed careless Vietnamese authorities for what had been lost, and Polgar grabbed a plane
home from Mexico to deal with me personally. Upon arrival, he phoned to
invite me to a "friendly" lunch at a motel diner.

Friendly it wasn't. For over two hours he chided and bullied, accused me
of flirting with treason, and warned of the "insurmountable" competition
I was facing from the Kalbs. Later, in a note to Shackley, he harped again
on my sanity or lack of it. "I think Snepp is basically honest, very capable
but emotionally somewhat unstable and under great strain," he wrote. "He
is not doing well financially, and he feels himself driven into a corner. When
the pressures on him become great enough he will lash out against whatever he can."

The warning registered. A week later, Bush's newly appointed deputy,
Hank Knoche, summoned me to Langley for an "informal" chat.

— —

I hadn't seen Knoche since that night at Daphne Miller's so long ago, when
he'd warned that Agency naysayers had no choice but to resign, but as he
peered at me across his brilliantly varnished desk the afternoon of June 25,
he made a show of being attentive.

"Snepp believes," he later remarked by memo, "that we not only left a
good many loyal Vietnamese behind, but that the compromise of classified
documents dooms many of them to death unless the [State] Department is
willing to try to warn the North Vietnamese against such extreme mea-
sures."

In the course of our conversation, he invited me to elaborate on another
of my concerns, the leaking of Agency secrets to the Kalb brothers. Afterward, he made no effort to pursue the matter, perhaps for fear of discovering more than he could sweep under the rug, but he wasn't so indifferent to
me. Summoning Bob Layton a few days later, he directed him to begin dog-
ging and documenting my every move so the Agency would never be
caught off guard again.

— —

Since I knew nothing of Layton's new assignment, I wrote off the meeting
with Knoche as a waste of time. But I did come away with one impression
firmly fixed: the Dung memoir was *gold.* More than anything I'd done on

my own, it had focused attention where it mattered. Could it be that the general actually had the power to accomplish my objective for me—to shame official Washington into remembering?

The more I pondered, the more I thought so. *The bastard could do it for me.* With this in mind, I dipped into my paltry savings and booked a flight to Paris. I told Stafford I was going to approach Vietnamese Communist officials there to see if I could open a dialogue with Dung himself!

Stafford nearly fainted dead away.

Five days before my departure, Layton called and asked to see me. Fearing that my trip had been discovered, I told him I had no time to spare, that I was going abroad to interview Nguyen Van Thieu, who was then living in London. It wasn't a lie, since I did hope to meet with Saigon's fallen leader, but it wasn't the full truth either. I asked Layton to keep my plans quiet lest Thieu be frightened off. "Snepp requested that the fact he planned to interview Thieu not be spread about," Layton told Knoche, "but it seems to me you should be aware of this."

By the time I arrived in Paris, I was so sure I'd been found out I didn't even try to elude potential tailgaters as I made my way to the cold gray building on the Rue de Verrier that served as the Vietnamese Communist embassy.

Outside, looking up at the chancery's great wooden door, I could almost feel the prickle of surveillance along my spine.

The moment I stepped across the threshold into a high-ceilinged foyer, the door slammed shut behind me, a bolt shot into place, and I found myself gazing into the gaunt face of a Vietnamese gentleman who introduced himself as "Mr. Thong, the press officer." I was petrified.

Having already decided that honesty was the safest policy, I told him who I was and handed him a copy of the Oberdorfer article by way of proof. Without a word, he turned and ushered me into a marble-encrusted sitting room with a brightly polished floor-to-ceiling mirror. Squinting into it, I wondered how many cameras peered back, and whether the lights of the chandelier had been deliberately angled to illumine the couch where Mr. Thong bade me be seated. The faint whirr of a wall fan seemed just loud enough to mask the whisper of an unspooling tape.

Mr. Thong slipped into a chair opposite me and leaned forward as if encouraging me to speak up. I did, sliding into a little spiel I'd memorized in French. Reminding him of the American Civil War and the subsequent reconciliation, I suggested that the same might be accomplished between our two countries through dialogue and understanding. To this end, I said, I was writing a book and hoped to travel to Hanoi to interview a knowledgeable Vietnamese official, preferably General Dung, about the war and its aftermath, *particularly* the aftermath, since that's what most concerned me.

I then produced a photo of a North Vietnamese prisoner I'd interrogated in Saigon, a top-ranking intelligence officer who'd reportedly been killed by his Vietnamese jailers just before the Communist takeover. I'd once promised the man that if he didn't survive the war, I'd inform his family. I related this to Thong as he studied the picture. "You can tell his wife and children he spoke of them often," I added. Thong glanced up, his eyes betraying nothing, and returned the picture. He denied, as I'd expected, that he knew the prisoner, but assured me that he'd convey my interview request to the "proper authorities."

As I stood to leave, I expressed hope that those same authorities would be as considerate of their captives as I'd tried to be of this one. The corner of Thong's mouth twitched ever so slightly, though I couldn't tell if he was suppressing a sneer or a smile.

During the remainder of the trip, I called him daily to ask for news. Invariably, over innumerable mysterious clicks on the line, he replied, *"Pas encore."* Meantime, Thieu sent word from London that he couldn't receive me. Kissinger's State Department had threatened to bar him from visiting relatives in the United States if he spoke publicly about anything.

No sooner had I returned from Paris than the agency locked on to me again, Layton phoning immediately to demand an audience, and not for social reasons, he emphasized.

The moment we sat down together, he informed me crisply that he'd been assigned to keep book on me. "I wanted Snepp to be aware," he later advised Knoche, "that if there was information that he did not want known within the Agency, he'd best leave it unsaid."

Trying to be as forthcoming as possible, I told him of the trip and my session at the Vietnamese embassy, and offered to show him the latest draft of my manuscript "informally," outside official channels, so he could assure himself it exposed no secrets. He shrugged and said that wouldn't be necessary, since he assumed I'd be "playing by the rules." He didn't elaborate, and I didn't press him. The last thing I needed was to be confronted with a newly contrived set of CIA regulations designed to handcuff me.

The conversation ended amicably enough, but once back at Langley, Layton brooded—not about my proposed trip to Hanoi, which he considered "less than a sure thing," he informed Knoche, or about my discretion, which he felt could be relied upon.

What did trouble him, though, was the likelihood of my giving the Agency a massive black eye. In the current political climate, that would be as troublesome as the betrayal of secrets, and Layton knew that *he* would be held accountable if he hadn't served fair warning. So rather than give me the benefit, he hit the panic button and leaned on it. In two separate memos—one for Knoche, the other for George Bush himself—he turned me into a potential bomb thrower, a "loner" driven by "opportunism . . . often willing to bend the rules . . . not a team player . . . not a person to be fully trusted.

"Although this is purely a personal opinion," he told Bush, "I believe that Mr. Snepp has great potential for causing trouble for the Agency." In his memo to Knoche, he expressed doubt that anything could be done to "defuse" me, but urged "a relatively low-key approach to Snepp" since "an open confrontation would serve his purpose and probably increase the publicity surrounding him."

His alarms resonated through the CIA's Security offices. "Subject continues to refuse to provide a manuscript," Skip Dunn told his staff on September 16. "I would appreciate it if you would continue to review and monitor the case from a CI standpoint."

"CI" stood for "counterintelligence"—which meant I was to be treated as a hostile foreign spy.

— —

Since Layton shared none of his impressions with me, I couldn't be sure that he was poisoning the well. But I assumed the worst anyway and acted accordingly. From a friend in CIA logistics, I obtained a .38 automatic, just in case some overzealous patriot came in over my balcony, and I began secreting copies of my manuscript all over town. One agency friend stashed parts of it in a safe at CIA headquarters on the assumption that the pit bulls would never go snuffling around their own sandbox.

None of my confederates bore the new pressures equally, and Linley Stafford actually began cracking under the strain. By late summer, he'd persuaded himself that I was a kamikaze pilot in free fall and that I'd take him down with me if he didn't bail out fast. What finally tipped him over was Layton's arrival on the scene. With a CIA baby-sitter now assigned to me full-time, Stafford decided it was indeed time to make his exit.

But he was not about to go empty-handed, not after everything he'd done for me. Convinced that he'd practically invented Frank Snepp, he was determined to be recompensed, and in early autumn began shifting large sums out of the account he'd set up for my book advance and using them to pay off personal debts.

Needless to say, he did not bother to inform me. But one morning, while going through her normal secretarial duties, Bernie found evidence of the drainage and sounded the alarm.

When I composed myself sufficiently to confront my old friend, he hemmed and hawed, denied, then confirmed what he'd done, and ultimately tried to absolve himself by denouncing the Paris trip and the Oberdorfer article as ill-considered provocations. Indignantly, he then wrote me an IOU for the missing funds and declared our business and personal relationship dissolved.

For days I couldn't write, and I might well have succumbed to terminal paralysis but for Bernie. It wasn't simply that Stafford had betrayed my trust; that was bad enough. But worse, he could do so again, ad infinitum, for he was privy to everything the CIA needed to know about me and could rat me out at will.

Bernie, however, refused to let me surrender to such alarm. Never mind that I'd lost my go-between, she told me. She'd gladly assume the role herself and handle it even better than Stafford, since she was an actress after all. And if he even attempted to raise a finger against me, she'd take care of that too, for she'd reviewed his accounts and knew how he'd stiffed the IRS over the years, and could muscle him as he'd never been muscled before.

Cause a problem? He wouldn't dare.

Her ferocity surprised and awed me, and finally shamed me out of my self-pity, causing me to acknowledge for the first time that I had in Bernie far more than an ally and helpmate. Oh, I'd sensed it before, just as I'd sensed Carla's deepening love for me, but now that I was vulnerable and newly desperate, I could no longer afford my usual detachment. So in late September, I began spending more and more time with Bernie, and she in turn made good on her offer, taking up where Stafford had left off, becoming my secret emissary to Random House, mediating all contacts, shouldering all risks. And though Stafford was too terrified of both of us to oust her from her secretary's job, her first commitment now was to me.

— —

The instant Bernie slipped into Stafford's role, I alerted Loomis and altered our own dance steps accordingly. Bernie was to be our sole cutout, I told him. Whenever a face-to-face was required, she'd call his office and direct him to a random pay phone to pick up precise instructions. Street-corner rendezvous were out from now on due to the threat of surveillance. All our meetings would be confined to a handful of vest-pocket parks in midtown Manhattan, and depending on the time of day and where the shadows were longest, Bernie would make the choice for us, always reserving the decision to the last minute to minimize the risk of our being discovered.

Loomis needed only one briefing to get the hang of it all and soon slid into our new minuet with the aplomb of a true professional. Before long, we were conferring regularly and discreetly in the postage-stamp parks Bernie selected for us.

It was in one such cloister that I slipped him my first completed chapter a few weeks later. With nary a fumble, he palmed it behind an unfurled section of *The New York Times* as Bernie, hovering nearby, kept watch for inquisitive passersby.

By the time my third chapter was wrapped up, we had the routine down pat.

— —

As my writing picked up so did my research needs, and I began filing carefully honed Freedom of Information requests with the Agency in hopes of prying loose something useful. I should have known better. Each time, Ted Shackley responded with a flat-out veto or dragged his feet until his staff could eviscerate what I'd asked for. Indeed he felt only one set of documents could safely be released to me: copies of the watch-officer memos issued at the time of my resignation. Since they made me out to be to a thoroughly bad actor, unwilling "to agree to submit for review" the book I was writing, he figured their airing might chasten me.

Even without Shackley's hostility, however, the Agency could scarely have been expected to be generous anyway, for by the fall of 1976 it was awash in new sewage spills that made any whiff of accountability seem noxious. Former director Richard Helms was facing indictment on perjury charges growing out of his congressional testimony about Chile. The everraucous liberal left was trying to implicate the CIA in the murder of a Chilean leftist who'd recently been car bombed on a Washington street. And Shackley himself was wallowing in a deepening scandal involving an old friend and former colleague, an ex-agent named Edwin Wilson. A few weeks before, an informant had advised Langley that Wilson was busily selling lethal hardware to Libyan terrorists and that two active-duty CIA employees, who were likewise close to Shackley, were lending unofficial assistance. The inspector general's office had immediately leapt to Shackley's defense, cranking out a report that found him innocent of any complicity, and Deputy Director Knoche had moved to head off adverse publicity by allowing Wilson's two in-house collaborators to keep their jobs and their anonymity. But anyone with an ounce of savvy could see that the cover-up wouldn't hold for long.

On top of all this the Agency was now facing a new round of recriminations from one of its own, for a former operative named Joseph Burkholder Smith had just slipped an unapproved memoir, *Portrait of a Cold Warrior,* onto the fall book lists.

Astonishingly, nobody had seen it coming. In fact, "Little Joe" Smith had labored so unobtrusively in the long shadows cast by Agee and Snepp that he'd managed to complete his confessional of twenty years in mufti without arousing a prickle of suspicion. Only at the last minute, as advance copies plopped onto reviewers' desks in New York and Washington, did the trip flares go off—and all hell break loose.

Within hours, Dunn's security staff pounced on the book and "discovered" low-grade secrets sprinkled throughout. Shackley bristled at a plethora of unflattering references to himself, and the CIA's new general counsel, a man named Anthony Lapham, acted promptly to have the book suppressed.

To admiring friends and colleagues, Lapham seemed more than equal to the challenge. Scion of a respected San Francisco family and brother of *Harper's* editor-in-chief, he'd earned his diplomas from Yale and Georgetown Law School, and his battle spurs as an assistant U.S. attorney in protest-ridden Washington of the mid-1960s. During Watergate, as a private attorney, he'd bargained for and won immunity for White House Plumber David Young by offering to turn over to authorities a document Young had stolen from official files that implicated others in the scandal.

On the strength of this accomplishment, Lapham had gained cachet among conservatives and a ticket to Washington's fast track, and the CIA job had come along just in time. But he knew he would have to score fast if he was to prosper. The Smith case gave him the opportunity.

— —

Tampering with free speech is always a dicey proposition in this country, but Lapham felt he had a fighting chance. The Marchetti ruling of 1972 had empowered federal judges to gag any signatory of a CIA secrecy agreement and to seize the author's manuscript, if it could be shown that secrets might otherwise be compromised. Smith *had* signed a secrecy pact, and advance copies of *Portrait* contained enough arguably "secret" material to warrant such a restraining order.

To buy time to build a case, Lapham flew to New York to ask Smith's publisher, Putnam, to delay distribution of the book. Three years before, the CIA had persuaded another publisher, Harper & Row, to let the censors screen an explosive book about CIA drug connections before publication. In that instance, the author had been a private citizen with no CIA ties. This time the Agency's case was much stronger, since Smith had been an employee in good standing.

Lapham made his pitch and connected: Putnam agreed to pull *Portrait* from distribution. But the victory was a Pyrrhic one. Too many copies had already reached private hands, too many to be retrieved. The scheme had to be abandoned.

As a fallback, Lapham and Justice Department officials considered suing Smith for breaching his secrecy agreement to teach him and other potential tattlers a lesson. But ultimately, that plan was scuttled too. As Lapham later explained, his concern was that a lawsuit might give the book the very thing he wanted to deny it, visibility. "I felt it would have had the effect of stimulating sales and readership and distribution," he said, "[and] would be counterproductive."

If fear of hype saved Joe Smith, however, it didn't save me. Days before, with Smith's book on the verge of release, CIA management had alerted all employees to finger anyone else believed to be working on an unauthorized memoir. Suddenly scores of patriots came forward with new tips and guesswork about me.

The groundswell quickly convinced Lapham's deputy, John Greaney, that he was about to have another Joe Smith on his hands. So on October 8, he sent me an ultimatum, a four-line letter demanding that I turn over my manuscript at once in accordance with the secrecy agreement I'd signed on joining the Agency in 1968, my entry convenant. Enclosed was a copy of the document.

As I read through it, a coldness rose in the pit of my stomach. One paragraph obliged me to seek CIA approval before publishing *anything* about "intelligence matters generally," classified or not. Another declared it to be "established Agency policy" to keep any sort of CIA memoir out of print. If that were true, my book was already a dead letter.

The Agency would later claim I'd known about these strictures all along, that I'd been well aware I couldn't publish anything without clearance. But the opposite is true. I hadn't seen this document since my first day on the job and hadn't even been reminded of it at the time of my resignation eight years later. Instead, the debriefing officer had assured me that the much more limited termination agreement, which I signed that day, was identical to the original one. Clearly, he'd misled me. The entry document imposed obligations I wouldn't have conceived in my worst nightmares.

How could I ever have put my signature to such a thing?

As I thought back, trying to tease out an explanation, barely recollected impressions began to coalesce into a hazy vision of youthful gullibility, of a callow twenty-five-year-old dazzled by his first day at Langley, and by the heroic aura of the induction officer who'd come across as a real-life James Bond. It was this dashing figure who'd put me and the other starstruck inductees through our inaugural paces and had finally handed us the entry agreement to read and sign.

In recalling that moment, I experienced a twinge of misgiving, for I remembered my unease even then: the young man raising his hand timidly, asking James Bond how, given the way this document was worded, you could even write a postcard home. His answer came floating up out of the depths like a bubble freed from decay: "No, Sonny, this doesn't mean you can't send a letter to Mommy."

Down through the years, the discomfort I'd felt had given way to a sense of latitude defined by the five subsequent secrecy agreements I'd signed, all of them, including my last one, imposing but one limited obligation: to seek official approval only before publishing secrets.

Frantically, I scoured Greaney's document for an escape hatch, some clause that would return me to that looser standard. Deep within, I found what I thought might pass—a guarantee that the inspector general stood ever ready to hear any employee complaints. Had the Agency ever given me such a hearing on the evacuation? *No.* And if not, could this document be enforced? I comforted myself with what seemed to be the only possible answer.

I flew to New York to talk all this out with Bernie. She asked me to tell her honestly what I thought my obligations were.

To protect secrets and no more, I replied. The Agency had had an opportunity to commit me to something broader upon my resignation, but had blown it and was now trying to change the rules in the fourth quarter.

She listened and agreed this wasn't fair. But she wasn't sure what I could possibly do now to save myself. "You can't say anything that will cause them to doubt you," she observed pensively. "But you can't lie to them either. How will you do that?"

"Very carefully," I told her. "Very, very carefully."

CHAPTER 8

Betrayed

WHENEVER BOB LOOMIS was feeling particularly chipper, he allowed himself three Jack Daniel's at lunch. By late November 1976, the Tennessee sour mash was flowing freely and frequently, for he'd read the secrecy agreement Greaney had sent me and concluded I was right about it. Having failed to hear me out about the evacuation, the Agency had violated its part of the bargain, thus rendering the compact null and void.

Bolstering his optimism was the people's verdict on Gerald Ford, who'd just lost out in his reelection bid to a peanut farmer from Georgia. It was Ford's CIA, after all, that had given me such grief over the past year, and any change in command had to be a change for the better, particularly since his replacement seemed refreshingly enlightened about my former employer. "If the CIA ever makes a mistake," President-elect Jimmy Carter advised reporters, "I'll tell you and the American people this is what happened, these are the people who violated the law, this is the punishment I recommend." With such a champion of openness at the helm, need we fear gag rules or excessive secrecy any longer?

Like Loomis, I felt entitled to that extra celebratory cocktail.

Nor was I the only repentant spy who took heart from the election. Former colleague John Stockwell dropped by my apartment soon afterward to tell me he was now so confident of intelligence reform that he'd decided to pen a cautionary tale of his own—about the CIA's recent intervention in

Angola. Having seen much of the worst firsthand as chief of the CIA's Angola task force, he needed only to find a publisher. Could I help him?

I felt a slight tug of apprehension. If the CIA was looking to plant an informant next to me, what better candidate than this soft-spoken Texan with the Vietnam experience and remorse to match my own?

Bernie was even more suspicious, believing that Stockwell's charm concealed a rampant case of opportunism. And in fact, as he would have been the first to admit himself, he'd never been immune to self-interest. He'd joined the Agency convinced that good works would earn him a place in heaven, and over the past fifteen years had labored hard and kept an accounting. Up until Angola he'd felt duly recompensed, but in recent months, as choice assignments had slipped away to less talented rivals, resentment had replaced thanksgiving.

Stockwell had too much messianic rage in him, however, to be dismissed simply as a frustrated Sammy Glick. "Appalling, sloppy" were his favorite thunderbolts for the Angola operation itself, and "soft, corrupt" the wonderfully categorical epithets he reserved for those who'd run it. Nor did he limit himself to a single sermon. Vietnam, too, had spawned sinners worth his loathing, and what galled him most was that so many had come home to rewards he considered undeserved. But no more! he told me. The two of us would right the scales, no question.

"Be careful," Bernie counseled. "It's not justice he wants, but simply a piece of your action." But I was too weary of my own solitude to risk putting him off with hard questions. Misery loves company, and in Stockwell I found enough to equal my own. So I suspended judgment, wrote his hyperbole off to nerves, and finally, after introducing him to Loomis around Christmas, stood watching like a proud matchmaker as the two struck a contract.

It would take Stockwell several more months to resign, during which time he'd quietly review CIA files for information to gild his book. I didn't feel comfortable with that. It seemed too calculating, too deliberately mischievous. And yet who was I to judge? Many suspected me of far worse chicanery, and were quite ready to say so.

Indeed, by early winter a rumor was swirling through CIA headquarters that I'd publish my exposé and embarrass the Agency just in time for Carter's inauguration, and on December 12 a "personal source" advised Security Chief Robert Gambino that one "Mr. Snepe" had recently been overheard discussing a possible trip to Hanoi. This was merely a belated echo of very old news, but Greaney chose to interpret it as a new threat aborning, and panicked. Believing that I was about to skip the jurisdiction of American courts, he hastily phoned a friend at the Justice Department,

Assistant Attorney General Irwin Goldblum, to see if a restraining order couldn't be obtained against me at once.

Goldblum told him no; more was needed on the Hanoi trip, the sensitivity of the manuscript, and the author's intentions. Greaney relayed this to Hank Knoche, and Knoche reverted to habit. He dispatched Bob Layton to try to pin me down.

The interview took place three days before Christmas. "Snepp offered nothing concerning the Hanoi trip," Layton reported afterward, "and I chose not to raise the matter on my own."

Nor could he persuade me to name my publisher or surrender even pieces of the manuscript for clearance. The most he got from me was a threat: Should I be faced with a restraining order, I told him, the manuscript would be turned over to the Senate Intelligence Committee so its revelations couldn't be squelched.

"Although the conversation with Snepp was pleasant and low-key," Layton advised Knoche, "I sense that he realizes that a crunch point with the Agency may be fast approaching. This is the first time in my conversations with him that he was so direct concerning what he might do should the Agency try to impede his book."

That was all Knoche needed to hear. He directed the general counsel's staff to do whatever was necessary to get me hauled into court.

Four days after Christmas, Greaney began pulling together the necessary paperwork, much of it eyewitness testimony as to my unwillingness to submit to censorship. Normally, in national security cases, federal courts will impose a restraining order only if the government can show that an author's work threatens irreparable harm or contains verifiable secrets. But as Greaney explained to Security's Skip Dunn, he was hoping to achieve the same result simply by identifying "the classified information which it was assumed Mr. Snepp had access to."

Greaney and his boss, Tony Lapham, spent several days compiling an inventory, then presented it to Knoche. Lapham warned that despite this plethora of material, a judge might still refuse to act if he felt there was a chance that I'd submit to censorship voluntarily. However, "even if an injunction were not issued," Lapham added, "this legal action would certainly have a desirable psychological effect on Mr. Snepp."

Knoche liked that—the idea of terrorizing me into silence—and directed Lapham to prepare a memo for the Justice Department urging immediate action.

Greaney drafted the document and allowed himself considerable poetic license in the process. While acknowledging my concern over "alleged" leaks to the Kalb brothers, he neglected to mention that they'd actually occurred. And while admitting that I had sought an after-action report on the evacuation, he insisted falsely that Colby had looked into my complaints and found them *unjustified.* "The conclusions of this investigation," he asserted, "appear to have been responsible for a feeling of disillusionment on the part of Snepp."

Having thus reduced me to a rebel without a cause, he went on to cast me as a rebel beyond redemption. "It is certain," he declared, "that Snepp has finished at least some portions or chapters of his manuscript. He has refused to submit the completed portions . . . and there is every reason to believe he may persist in his refusal."

George Bush, only days away from leaving the director's office, reviewed the memo and sent it off to the Justice Department without comment.

— —

It was bitter cold and snowing gently when I arrived at Pat and Bill Johnson's the following Wednesday night with a batch of manuscript pages in hand and the anxiety of an expectant father. I'd just finished redrafting a critical chapter in which they figured prominently and was anxious to plumb their reaction.

The crowd on hand for this evening's soirée was larger and more raucous than usual, for Bill had just announced his retirement from the Agency and Pat was on her way out too. Many old friends had shown up simply to bid farewell. Only after midnight did the last of them depart and my host and hostess find a moment to look over what I'd brought them. To my chagrin, they liked none of it. Pat objected to the way I'd portrayed her and Polgar, though I'd adhered to descriptions she'd given me herself. Bill denounced the chapter as too "negative" and urged me to seek the CIA's help in redrafting it so it would come out more "positively."

When I finally left, I was desolate. Didn't they realize I was writing history, not propaganda?

— —

If I got little help from the Johnsons, however, the law treated me considerably better. Within days of receiving the Agency's petition for a lawsuit against me, outgoing Attorney General Edward Levi decided there was not now grounds for one. CIA officials would later claim that I'd dodged the bullet by offering "false assurances" that I'd voluntarily submit my manuscript. But Lapham, for one, knew this wasn't so. "There were no assurances that were satisfactory that existed in January 1977," he later conceded under oath.

In fact, the real stumbling block for Langley was its own spent credit at the Justice Department. Two spy cases had just broken into the open, one involving two young defense contractors known popularly as "the Falcon and the Snowman," and the CIA had infuriated Levi's prosecutors by refusing to let Agency secrets be used in open court.

Even more significant, Levi had come to suspect that there was something about renegade ex-agents that brought out the worst in the Agency itself. He'd discovered, for instance, that in its zeal to stop Philip Agee over the years, the CIA had badgered his ex-wife and children, tracked him across Europe, even slipped him a bugged typewriter, the better to surveil him. Levi and his staff were now conducting an investigation to determine if Agee's civil rights had been violated, and until the findings were in, they could see little percentage in picking up another hot potato.

— —

The reprieve they granted me might have become a lasting one if President-elect Carter had followed through on his plans for CIA reform. Midway through the transition period, he made a first significant step in this direction by nominating a bona fide liberal, Theodore Sorensen, to become Director of Central Intelligence. Sorensen, a onetime adviser to President Kennedy, had sat out the Korean War as a conscientious objector and was on record as favoring less official secrecy and less reliance on "covert action." His politics and temperament would certainly have made him wary of the Agency's ongoing vendetta against me.

But sadly, Sorensen did not survive the confirmation process, and the fallout would leave me more vulnerable than ever.

What did him in was the very thing that had commended him to Carter: his liberalism. Agency supporters and hard-liners couldn't imagine having a former conscientious objector as director, and from the moment Sorensen's nomination was announced, they worked assiduously to derail it. The weapon they finally used to finish him off was a bundle of court documents known as the Pentagon Papers case. Back in 1971, two employees of the RAND Corporation, Daniel Ellsberg and Anthony Russo, had landed themselves in a legal acid bath by committing one of the great security breaches in American history. Disenchanted with the Vietnam War, they'd attempted to register protest by leaking a highly classified and immensely candid history of the conflict prepared by the Pentagon itself.

As the documents began showing up in *The New York Times* and other newspapers, Nixon officials went to court to obtain an injunction against publication. They also elected to prosecute the two leakers for espionage. The first case collapsed when the Supreme Court held that the government had failed to show sufficient justification for such "prior restraint" of the press. A year later, a judge threw out the second case after discovering that Nixon's Plumbers, a group of ex–CIA agents hired to plug leaks, had burglarized the office of Ellsberg's psychiatrist.

Before that stunning denouement, liberals across the country had rallied to the defendants, and Sorensen had filed an affidavit on their behalf. In it, he'd admitted that as adviser to President Kennedy he'd slipped secrets to the press and later, after Dallas, had hauled off boxloads of classified documents to use in preparing his memoir of those years. It was this ancient document that now came back to haunt him.

As his confirmation hearings got under way, his critics hauled out the affidavit and used it to savage his credibility as a potential guardian of the nation's secrets. President-elect Carter tried to defend him by claiming that such indiscretions were a way of life among luminaries of both parties, but Sorensen read the portents and on January 17 pulled his nomination.

At Langley, the rejoicing was instantaneous. Not only had a reformer been routed and the Agency delivered from the hand of moderation; for the moment the old guard stood unchallenged.

The most immediate beneficiary was Hank Knoche, who was invited to stay on as "acting director" until a suitable nominee could be found. The most immediate casualty, apart from Sorensen himself, was me. With Knoche in the saddle and the old guard ascendant, the Agency could be counted on to pursue the proposed lawsuit against me with a vengeance.

— —

Knoche in fact wasted little time in picking up where he'd left off. No sooner had the dust settled from the Sorensen episode than he importuned Greaney to draw up a new legal brief against me. Greaney immediately began casting about for fresh sources of incriminating information. Polgar suggested two names.

Pat and Bill Johnson.

Until that moment, Greaney had been only vaguely aware of the Johnsons and their relation with me. But as he began digging, he realized he'd struck pay dirt. According to official files, the Johnsons had recently tattled on me not only to Polgar but also to Bob Layton. Even more astonishing, as early as the summer of 1975, right after my return to CIA headquarters, Bill had begun slipping diary notes and other observations about me to old pals in the CIA's counterintelligence office. So ample had been his reporting that CI was now a virtual storehouse of privileged insights into my publishing plans, my manuscript, and my hopes and fears. Except for the traditional reluctance of its principals to share confidences outside their own circle, Greaney might have learned of and recruited the Johnsons long ago.

Still, better late than never, he decided. And no matter that they were on the verge of retiring and that the CIA was legally barred from spying at home. If Pat and Bill were willing to help, he'd find a way to justify it.

I hadn't a clue to their treachery, of course, but ironically, if I had, I could have understood it. The Johnsons were not so much false friends as perfect exemplars of a mentality I knew all too well, a mentality that read evil into dissent and the devil into nonconformity. Anyone not a member of their club was automatically assumed to be against it. For all my disenchantment, I'd desperately wanted to remain a member in good standing, and their feigned kindnesses and generosity had over the past twelve months convinced me I still was. Only in the moral isolation imposed by the CIA can the mere *illusion* of love and trust seduce so easily.

On Monday morning, February 28, Bill arrived at headquarters to brief Greaney for the first time on what he knew about me. Holding nothing back, he confirmed that a manuscript existed and that he and Pat had read parts of it and expected me to have it finished by late March or early April. He also offered to provide an affidavit attesting to all this.

A few days later, he returned with Pat in tow to hand over three cassette tapes on which I'd recorded a marathon interview with them in their home months before, as part of my early research. Bill had recently asked to borrow the cassettes, and I'd willingly handed them over. At various points in the taped conversation, he and Pat could be heard discussing highly classified topics with me.

Though Greaney didn't ask for *proactive* assistance, Bill provided that, too. A day or so later, he buttonholed an acquaintance of mine, Philip McCombs of *The Washington Post,* and told him that everything I knew about Vietnam was "government property" and that I'd be guilty of "theft" if he didn't help shut me down.

"McCombs took this thoughtfully," Bill advised Greaney, "and I rather hope it will get back to Snepp."

It didn't. McCombs refused to be manipulated. But no matter. Bill had another card to play. That night he called me to insist that I be on hand for the next Wednesday's soirée.

From the moment I showed up, he came on like Pater Familias, addressing me fondly as "son" and "dear boy" even as he and Pat pumped me for information. By the time they'd sent me off into the night, they'd gotten what they thought would be more than enough to satisfy Greaney.

Much of the following day, Bill sat hunched over his typewriter, hammering out a nine-page memo, the purpose of which he spelled out up top. "Possibly some of this information," he wrote, "can be used in drafting affidavits for use by the general counsel in court action against Snepp."

The document was a curious amalgam of diatribe and error that read in places like the carping of a jealous literary rival. Glossing over the fact that he'd perused hundreds of manuscript pages, Bill maintained that he and Pat had seen only two chapters and had been impressed with neither. The last of these, he said, "thunders away at the war and embassy" from such an "Olympian perspective" that one had "to wonder whether any publisher would want to put it out"—"especially if a nobody is making comments of a lofty nature without having established the dramatic context of his utterances."

For all his soaring contempt, however, Bill was quite ready to acknowledge that the chapter had real potential for causing trouble. Its contents were "basically denigrating" to Martin and Polgar, he told Greaney, and included "factually inaccurate" information that "we would like to see suppressed." He also tried to hang a security rap on me by suggesting I was another Philip Agee in the making. "Our discussions with Snepp and our perusal of one chapter of his book," he remarked coyly, "indicate that his method is to use personalities and names throughout his material."

On the most crucial question of all—"Will Snepp clear the book?"—Bill wanted to believe the worst so he could give Greaney the dirt he needed. But here he was faced with a quandary. Since, as the tapes revealed, he and Pat had shared classified secrets with me, he couldn't now tag me a scofflaw without raising questions about why they'd carelessly indulged me. So rather than risk such embarrassment, he simply fibbed, insisting that I'd repeatedly assured him I would clear my manuscript. He also asserted more accurately that he'd recently urged me to seek "a sympathetic reading" from a qualified CIA official "so that what came out would be favorable to the Agency, accurate in its history, and saleable as a published product.

"Snepp's reaction to these suggestions," he recalled, "was that he doubted much sympathy would be forthcoming."

— —

When Greaney read Bill's memo, the enthusiasm went out of him like air from a punctured balloon. If, as Bill maintained, I would willingly submit to censorship, what was the need for legal action? Gloomily, Greaney advised colleagues that his best gambit had just gone bust.

The fledgling Snepp case might have gone bust too if he'd had no other sources to draw on. But fortuitously, Ted Shackley had been working overtime, and on March 10 he was able to advise Greaney by memo that my manuscript was nine hundred pages long, "just about finished," contracted out to "a prominent New York publisher, and highly critical of Kissinger, Martin and Polgar." In a covering note, he named his primary sources, Keyes Beech of the *Chicago Daily News* and Bud Merick of *U.S. News and World Report* magazine, both longtime friends of his.

Greaney eagerly perused these gleanings and urged Shackley to dig for more. Shackley promised to do even better. He'd contrive to question me directly.

The opportunity presented itself two days later at a cocktail party thrown by Merick and several of his friends. Shackley had persuaded them to include me in the guest list.

I didn't realize I'd been set up until I found myself backed against the hors d'oeuvres table by Shackley himself. Fixing me with a merciless eye, he demanded to know if I meant to submit to censorship, and insisted that I answer a simple "yes" or "no." I dabbed idly at the cheese dip, responded that I'd meet my obligations as I saw fit, and slid away. "If one had to make an educated guess," Shackley later informed Greaney curtly, "one could only conclude that the odds did not favor Mr. Snepp sending a copy of his book to the CIA."

For Greaney this was, perversely, very good news. It gave him what he needed to demolish the Johnsons' false optimism and to spur the Justice Department to action. Determined to prevail this time, he urged Tony Lapham to approach Carter's new nominee for CIA director, a naval officer named Stansfield Turner, and plead the cause.

— —

It wasn't a seemly thing, an old man being pushed out the door, but even as Greaney began preparing for another run at me, the Saigon evacuation took its final casualty. In early March, former ambassador Graham Martin was forced out of the State Department and into retirement.

For all of my problems with him, I felt uneasy about the way he'd been treated. For two years he'd been allowed to languish in bureaucratic limbo, two years without rehabilitation or meaningful assignment.

A lesser man would have been broken, would have tucked tail and disappeared. But Graham Martin was not the disappearing kind. Humiliated? Oh yes, he'd been humiliated all right. But the lust for revenge he carried away with him overwhelmed all other emotion and kept him focused and animated. Nor had he allowed himself to be cast into the wilderness with an empty quiver. On the contrary, in his final weeks of public service, he'd smuggled out of the State Department any and every document he might need to lend authenticity to his version of history, mountains of classified files which he intended to use to indict the man whose support, he felt, had been too little, too late: Henry Kissinger.

"I was looking over them the other day," he told Shackley's friend Keyes Beech. "They make mighty interesting reading."

Beech quoted the remark in a news story marking Martin's retirement, but no one noticed or cared.

— —

Meanwhile, as the Ides of March came and went, my own world turned increasingly hostile and forbidding. *Very* distant acquaintances from Langley began showing up at odd hours to offer solicitude and to note my rituals, and on many a night hang-up calls, interspersed with menacing ones, anonymously whispered threats of mayhem and retaliation, persisted well into the predawn hours. Shortly after Shackley's encounter with me, somebody broke into Bernie's New York pad and took *nothing,* and soon afterward a State Department friend with whom I'd been sharing confidences exposed his true colors by signing up for a government seminar that I knew to be reserved for CIA officers alone.

Ever fearful that a "crunch" *was* coming, I stayed constantly on the move, spending alternate weekends with Bernie in New York and Carla in Arlington, Bernie always ready with a jug of wine and Antiguan hospitality as she prepared to take down in shorthand my amendments to her latest transcriptions, and Carla laboring just as selflessly, checking and rechecking facts and jotting outlines for manuscript to come.

There were no diversions for any of us, and no joy either.

Throughout it all, Loomis continued to operate like a wily spymaster, betraying nothing, concealing all. After a year, only Random House lawyer Gerald Hollingsworth and company president Bob Bernstein even knew I existed, and though Loomis was diligent in reading and annotating each new increment of manuscript, he made sure none of it was ever in plain sight, the growing accumulation of pages remaining dispersed among countless anonymous storage boxes in his office.

Nor did he commit to file or memo the title he'd recently chosen for my book. Fittingly it echoed what many of Kissinger's critics had said of the Vietnam cease-fire agreement he'd concluded in 1973—that it promised no honorable peace, but merely a "decent interval" before the inevitable Communist takeover.

Loomis liked the irony. So *Decent Interval* it was.

Had the Johnsons known of the choice, "decent interval" would doubtless have found its way into the CIA's expanding files on me. But weeks before, Pat had tendered an offering of her own, urging me to call my book

Waste of Shame after a Shakespearean sonnet about unrequited love. She felt the phrase elegantly summed up Vietnam's implications for us all, and persuaded herself and John Greaney that I'd adopted it as my title. Accordingly, no one at Langley ever bothered to look for a book under any other name. The distraction may have bought me time.

CHAPTER 9

Showdown

W HEN ADMIRAL STANSFIELD TURNER was sworn in as CIA director on March 9, President Carter showed up at the ceremony to decry the "revelations of past mistakes" that had so damaged the Agency in recent years. This didn't quite sound like the man who only a few months earlier had campaigned against the cynicism and duplicity of "Vietnam, Watergate, and the CIA."

What had happened?

For one thing, the Sorensen episode, the humiliation of the Kennedy-esque liberal whom Carter had wanted as his CIA director. That embarrassment, as one deputy later explained, had left Carter grimly determined "to hit the pacifism [issue] in the neck," to show everybody he could be as hard-nosed about national security as any Republican. With the arrest of the Falcon and the Snowman, moreover, the new boy on the block had been instantly sensitized to the wages of lax security—a lesson amply buttressed during his first days in office by a spate of disastrous leaks. One of them, picked up by *The Washington Post,* revealed that for twenty years the CIA had been dolloping out secret annual gratuities to Jordan's King Hussein. By malign coincidence, newly installed Secretary of State Cyrus Vance had just arrived in Amman to meet with the diminutive monarch. When the story hit the stands, the discussions hit the rocks.

Carter himself hit the roof. Immediately, his new CIA director, speaking for him, called on Congress to enact tough criminal or civil sanctions to punish leakers.

For those who were gunning for me, all this sounded like an answered prayer.

— —

To judge from his résumé, Stansfield Turner ought to have been on the *other* side of the secrecy debate. A Rhodes scholar and former commandant of the Naval War College, he came draped in the aura of a thinking man's warrior, a descendant of the likes of George Marshall or Maxwell Taylor, men devoted to the Platonic ideal of freewheeling intellectual combat.

But there was something in Turner that had skewed the balance, turning the scholar into a dogmatic, and the dogmatic into an apostle of dogged rote and lockstep loyalty. Some blamed religious fervor, pure and simple. A devout Christian Scientist who took only hot water and lemon for breakfast and never a drop of alcohol, Turner had a fastidiousness about him, and a moral certitude, that did not suffer contradiction easily.

Nor did he come encumbered with any need for delicacy or false deference. He owed his appointment to a personal relationship with the president dating back to their days together at Annapolis, and his ability to call on that friendship reinforced his already formidable self-confidence.

Once he stepped across the threshold at Langley, moreover, the suspicions of the always self-protective old guard provoked similar feelings in him, and the arrogance he'd worn so dashingly on the captain's bridge quickly gave way to a peevish paranoia that tended to view any hesitation or bleat of criticism as a personal betrayal.

The first to feel the heat was Deputy Director Hank Knoche. During Turner's confirmation hearings, Knoche had declined to lobby for him for fear of embroiling himself and the CIA in partisan politics, and sensible though this decision was, Turner never forgave him for it. "My reaction," recalled the admiral, "was that if Hank could not shift his loyalty to a new superior, something that is quite normal in the military as seniors come and go, he was going to have an uphill battle to hold his job as my deputy. Loyalty has always meant a lot to me in the selection of associates."

Loyalty, in fact, was both an ideal and a fixation of Turner's. Asked at the hearings if he would ever alert Congress to any policy differences he might have with the president, he confessed he would not. "I believe that if every member of the executive branch who disagreed with the president went to the press or to Congress independently," he said, "we would have anarchy."

To Turner's chronically suspicious eye, the Agency itself seemed on the verge of anarchy the day he took over. CIA operatives were at "risk of giving in to the temptation to cut corners," he observed, and the upstart clandestine service appeared determined to rewrite any order it didn't like. "Unless I could rely on someone to check," he later noted in his memoirs, "I could not be sure that my directives were being transmitted faithfully to the espionage branch."

Such insubordination outraged his military sensibilities and quickened the autocrat in him. After only the briefest hesitation, he ordered wider use of polygraph tests to root out troublemakers, and upon discovering that a senior operative was romancing a female agent and lying to superiors about it, he fired the man as an object lesson to other potential miscreants.

From the outset he also paid court to the Agency's own obsession. "One of my first and most urgent concerns was to put the CIA's much criticized past behind us," he noted. "I doubted the CIA could survive another round of damaging criticism and publicity such as that of 1975–1976."

Military experience had taught him that official secrecy was an effective way of buttoning lips, and from the moment he arrived at Langley he was zealously protective of the Agency's vast security interests. As the Falcon and the Snowman case progressed, he stood firmly against allowing the Justice Department to introduce classified CIA documents into open evidence, and on the morning of March 10, he listened attentively as General Counsel Tony Lapham outlined an antileak initiative that seemed equally well advised, the proposed lawsuit against me. Though the case had been on hold for over a year, Lapham felt it might now have a new lease on life and so informed Turner. An old Georgia crony of Carter's, a conservative named Griffin Bell, had just been appointed attorney general.

— —

A down-home Southern judge with a drawl and rigidity to match my father's, Bell had no tolerance for anyone who offended his sometimes selective sense of the law. For precisely this reason, he would defy Turner and insist on allowing CIA secrets to be used in the Falcon and the Snowman case. By the same token, he could be expected to have little sympathy for a scofflaw like me.

Accordingly, in late March, with Turner's blessing, Lapham wrote Bell a letter urging a lawsuit against me on grounds that were familiar but compelling. "We still had nothing," Lapham recalled, "that could fairly be regarded as a reliable assurance that we would have the book for review."

Within days the Justice Department sent back a response: the CIA could have its lawsuit—*if* I was given a last chance to commit myself to clearance, and refused.

— —

Pathetically, as the blade descended, I remained convinced I was unassailable, at least from a legal standpoint. Not only had I broken no law, exposed no secrets, and shown no propensity for doing so; whatever mischief I was suspected of would surely be seen to pale alongside the greed and opportunism of Carter's *natural* enemies. According to news reports, both Ford and Nixon were in the process of negotiating sumptuous book deals based on the promised revelation of insider secrets, and Kissinger, using the same bait, had just sold his prospective memoirs to Little, Brown and Co. for two million dollars, and his consultant skills to NBC for one and a half million.

Bernie clipped an article about all this and sent it to me with a note attached: "So who's trying to get rich off secrets?" The moral implicit in the message boosted my spirits, for I couldn't imagine that that great American ideal, Equity, wouldn't favor me as easily as Henry Kissinger.

— —

With so many insiders now taking up pen for profit, my friend John Stockwell ought to have felt as justified as I. But he didn't. Indeed, one morning in late March I found him leaning nervously on my doorbell, obviously discomfited with the choice he'd made.

After we'd settled ourselves on my open-air balcony, away from any potential eavesdroppers, he tried to explain why. He still wasn't convinced, he said, that there was any real hope of life beyond Langley, that he wouldn't simply drop away into oblivion once he did drop out. Given that uncertainty, he'd decided not to go quietly. Instead, he'd announce his resignation as ostentatiously as possible, through an open letter in the press, a missive to Admiral Turner himself warning of the corruption and inefficiency around him. Not only would this bring much needed attention to "responsible critics" like ourselves; it would bell the old guard before they could seduce the new director.

Would I help him?

When Bernie learned what Stockwell was after, she begged me to beg off. "He's just looking for publicity to bid up his price," she argued. But I wasn't so sure. After another month or two, Turner might indeed be so in thrall of the old guard that he wouldn't even acknowledge "responsible critics." Maybe this *was* the moment to strike.

I contacted Don Oberdorfer, the *Washington Post* reporter whose "Saigon Secrets Seized" had earned me infamy the previous summer, and through him arranged for Stockwell's letter to be published as an op-ed piece.

Meanwhile, the author himself finally did what he'd been delaying: he quit the Agency. On his way out, he refused to sign the termination secrecy agreement on the ground that he'd been recruited under false pretenses, and thus unfairly sworn to secrecy, since no one had ever told him the Agency routinely broke the law.

Stockwell's letter dominated the front page of *The Washington Post*'s editorial section on April 10, Easter Sunday. A blistering indictment of the CIA's old-timers, it damned the incompetence that had given us disaster in Angola and Vietnam and warned that those responsible would only benefit from a muzzling of the CIA's critics. If new antileak penalties were enacted, declared Stockwell, "cynical men such as those who gravitate to the top of the CIA could then, by classifying a document or two, protect and cover up illegal activities with relative impunity."

Official reaction to this cri de coeur was exactly as might have been expected. In seething interoffice memos, CIA division chiefs and senior supervisors impugned Stockwell's motives and sanity and demanded that Turner rally round the flag. Sensing a rare opportunity to curry favor among them, Turner obliged. In an Agency-wide bulletin, he castigated Stockwell for taking his complaints public, and in a private phone call, bit his head off.

Stockwell was not one to suffer such abuse gladly. A proud, combative man who'd grown up among missionaries in Africa, he quickly applied the easy moral dichotomies he'd learned from them to rationalize his fury. With the certainty and force of religious conversion, he came to see his tormenters as worse than wrong, as devils incarnate, and the Agency itself as some dark temple worthy only of damnation. Agee and Marchetti, devout Catholics both, had experienced a similar inversion of faith, and the prism Stockwell now held up to the world admitted as few shadings as theirs.

He had come to his epiphany, however, not quite so spontaneously as they. As I would discover only later, Marchetti's coauthor, John Marks, had been the tempter, befriending and coddling Stockwell in recent weeks and offering to help bargain him into a better deal at Random House, and luminaries from a liberal Washington think tank had played chorus to his discontents. Once Turner confirmed his worst suspicions by throwing in with the sinners, an evangelist was born.

Predictably, Stockwell did not see fit to announce his new friends or philosophy to me. But he didn't have to. His fervor betrayed him. When Loomis pleaded with him to stop baiting the Agency, Stockwell replied indignantly that he'd *only just begun*—that to be true to his mission he might have to include secrets in his book.

I was both appalled and outraged. But much as I might have wished to dissociate myself from my quixotic friend, it would have been disingenuous even to try. The best I could do, I decided, was to try to help bank the fires by making his critics understand that he was no voice in the wilderness, that others stood ready to second him. Then, just maybe, they'd back off, pay heed, and give him reason to believe he needn't pull out the stops to win respect and attention.

I immediately called the Johnsons and asked them to pass word to the Agency "not to push Stockwell." I implored Layton to try to determine if Stockwell and I were under FBI surveillance, as I'd heard rumored, and I warned my old office chief William Parmenter that it would be imprudent to write off Stockwell's concern about institutional corruption since I too knew of cases in point. To make the threat palpable I mentioned a CIA operative who'd embezzled operational funds in Vietnam and been allowed to walk, and I also noted that Shackley, while serving as Saigon station chief in the late 1960s, had paid himself a secret subsidy to support a second household in Hong Kong. Why had neither case been investigated or referred to the Justice Department?

Parmenter gulped and promised to try to find out.

— —

Given my own lack of credibility, none of this would have been enough to cow any of Stockwell's enemies. But by blessed coincidence, *The Washington Post* did what I couldn't. On April 12, Watergate reporter Bob Woodward published the first of several stories about a scandal that had been long simmering at Langley. By the time he came out with his third installment, he had the details down pat. For months, he reported, the Agency had known that Shackley's old friend Edwin Wilson and two active-duty CIA operatives had been playing quartermaster to Libyan bomb throwers.

When Turner read the story, he was aghast, and all the more after learning that Hank Knoche had long been aware of Wilson's two CIA collaborators but had declined to fire them. Shackley's role was equally troubling to him. "I had no evidence of wrongdoing on Shackley's part," Turner later remarked, "yet I could not understand how he could associate with someone like Wilson. I expected a higher sense of integrity in a man who held a position as sensitive as his."

From the moment the scandal broke, Shackley's days were numbered; so were Knoche's, and John Stockwell, ostentatious decrier of fraud and deception, stood vindicated.

— —

The fairy dust did not rub off on me, however. By mid-April, CIA lobbyists had asked for and received assurances from the Senate Intelligence Committee that it would support legal action against me, and Turner had decided to proceed lest the flouting of discipline à la Stockwell and Snepp become epidemic. Two weeks later, Lapham, Knoche, and other senior Agency officials met with him to review the bidding.

According to the running minutes, Lapham reminded all present that "there has been a problem with seeing that [Snepp] abides with his secrecy agreement and submits anything he intends to publish for review. He has not said he won't, but he has not said he will." He also pointed out that the Justice Department was willing to file suit if I persisted in my ambivalence. After some discussion, Turner urged Lapham to write me a letter demanding a clarification of my plans and "citing our intent to go to court" if I refused.

Across the Potomac at the Justice Department, two young staff attorneys from the Civil Division had already been assigned to prepare a case against me.

The flashier of the two was a lacquered young blond named Sally Whitaker, but the true cunning belonged to her partner, Brook Hedge, a laconic workaholic given to down-at-the-heels Guccis, a severe pageboy, and a good-soldier view of her job.

"I'm not paid to have opinions," she would later tell a reporter who wondered at her determination to trash me. As she saw it, her only responsibility was to get the job done, whatever it might be. And right now, trashing me was it.

On the morning of May 5, she and Whitaker trooped out to Langley to confer with Layton for the first time. He had nothing encouraging to tell them, and to their consternation seemed vaguely contrite that he'd never been much more than an "empty conduit to me," as he put it.

By coincidence, I happened to call Layton just after his meeting with the attorneys. I was trolling, trying to tease out a response to my latest Freedom of Information requests, and for once Layton talked to me straight. "Look," he said wearily, "if you've got anything constructive to discuss, you'd better take it up with Turner himself. Otherwise there's gonna be legal action." He then clicked off without saying more.

As I put down the receiver, I was trembling. Legal action? An overture to Turner? It took me several days to muster the courage.

Meantime, Hedge and Whitaker worked feverishly to complete their preliminary briefs. By May 10 they were so far along that Knoche felt obliged to advise Turner to stand clear. "As you know, we are in the preliminary stages of taking [Snepp] to court as we did Marchetti," he reminded the admiral by memo. "Tony Lapham is preparing a final request to Snepp that he submit his book. . . . I recommend that you not get personally involved."

It was not to be. Two days later, I drew Turner into the vortex myself by calling him to request the interview Layton had suggested. The admiral's secretary quickly cleared his calendar for the following Tuesday afternoon.

Over the next five days, according to contemporaneous records, Turner's assistants coached him on every aspect of my case except one: the fact that in the course of my CIA career I'd signed six totally different secrecy agreements. They never showed him a copy of any of them. They neglected to point out that five of them, including my last one, required clearance of only confidential writings and that only the entry agreement extended further. Instead, they let him believe that I was bound by a single "unambiguous" contract obliging me to submit everything—and that I'd cynically refused to comply. "I believe you should remind Mr. Snepp," Lapham advised him by memo, "that we have not yet received satisfactory assurances as to his intention to abide by his secrecy agreement, and that he can expect us to pursue this matter further."

Because of other pressing business, Lapham would not be able to attend the interview with me. But given what was at stake, he decided to have his deputy, John Morrison, sit in for him. Morrison, a perennially dour-faced veteran of the Agency's legal wars, knew my secrecy agreements by heart and was well aware, as he would later testify, that my final one did not encompass unclassified writings and that a broader commitment would be needed if the Agency was to see my manuscript regardless.

Though I had no inkling of the trap being laid for me, I knew that I would have to do some fast footwork if I was to elicit any sympathy from Turner during our face-off. So I drew up a memo for him in which I tried to explain why I'd resorted to writing a book and why I now found it necessary to play my cards so close to the chest. "In attempting to cordon itself off from any criticism at all," I wrote, "the Agency has made it nearly impossible for former employees like myself to deal candidly and responsibly with it on any issue."

— —

When I was ushered into Turner's top-floor suite the afternoon of May 17, I had this document in hand. But after gesturing for me to drop it on his desk, he lifted his eyes to focus on me.

A handsome, fleshy-faced man with the commanding presence of a soap-opera patriarch, he gracefully invited me to tell him "all about" my grievances. Since my most immediate concern was whether the FBI had me under surveillance, I asked him to clarify. He smiled indulgently and said he didn't think so—then, after a pause, added breezily that he couldn't, however, speak for the rest of the security community.

My pulse spiked. *Wrong* answer. The Director of Central Intelligence most certainly could speak for everybody else.

But before I could press him, a side door swung open and in strode Morrison and one of Turner's Navy aides-de-camp. As they pulled up chairs across from me, I realized instantly: ambush!

Trying to compose myself, I slid into an apologia for Stockwell, describing him as a "sincere and religious individual" convinced of the righteousness of his cause. Morrison blinked through thick-paned glasses and jotted a note to himself. "Parenthetically," he wrote, "Snepp's description of Stockwell possibly could be applied to Snepp."

Impatiently tapping a finger, Turner invited me to come back to my own situation. I did, *warily,* groping my way forward as through a minefield, telling him first of my concerns about the evacuation, then of my outrage at having been unable to prompt an after-action report even as the Agency had leaked protectively to the Kalb brothers.

At the very mention of the Kalbs, Turner flushed. "I won't be a party to giving out any classified material!" he sputtered—then paused, and injected contritely: "But no journalist gets preferential treatment on my watch, either."

After some back-of-the-hand consultations with Morrison, he promised to see if the top-secret documents the Kalbs had received could be "sanitized" and released to me. The irony didn't seem to register on him: I'd been cleared for secrets, the Kalbs had not.

With this irritant now disposed of, Turner turned to my book. "A lot of people around here are pretty emotional about it," he remarked with a hint of reproach.

Picking up on cue, Morrison launched a barrage of questions, demanding the identity of my publisher, the specifics of my contract, my "pub date." I told him bluntly that I would say nothing about my publisher for fear of exposing him to reprisals, and that my pub date was still some months off, since it had taken a lot longer than expected to wrestle my seven hundred pages of scrawl into a coherent manuscript.

Rousing himself again, Turner asked when the Agency would get a look at these seven hundred pages. Not before they were safely deposited in others' hands, I responded. He frowned and inquired if I intended to abide by my "secrecy agreement."

Yes, I replied, adding that I had no intention of publishing secrets. Morrison realized I hadn't said enough and insisted peremptorily that my "contractual duties" required more—the submission of everything I might want to publish, secret-free or not.

Your interpretation, I shot back.

Whereupon Morrison dropped his air of forbearance and warned that he and his colleagues were awfully upset over Joseph Smith's uncleared memoir and would brook nothing of the sort from me. "Are you threatening me with legal action?" I asked. Turner adopted an angelic expression and swore that there was *no* consideration of that at all.

As I got up to leave, I placed on his desk another document I'd written, a list of modest proposals for improving the Agency, including the suggestion that all new recruits be fully appraised of their legal obligations, whatever they were, before being asked to sign away any of their legal rights.

Turner picked it up and handed it to Morrison. "Somebody look at this," he muttered. He then grasped my hand briefly and waved me out.

As Turner would later testify, he came away convinced that he'd finally brought me to heel and disposed of the "Snepp problem" forever.

CHAPTER 10

First Reprisal

OVER THE NEXT WEEK, whenever anyone asked about the "Snepp interview," Morrison played cheerleader, lauding the director for his "exercise in patience" while ridiculing my chances of getting anything published.

Still, for all his gloating, Morrison knew the meeting had been bollixed, that neither he nor Turner had remembered to ask me for the one thing the Justice Department had demanded: a new written commitment.

To compensate, he hastily drew up a letter to me that was the epistolary equivalent of a steel trap. He was "pleased," he said, that I'd agreed to submit to censorship—which of course I hadn't—but knew I understood the Agency's "need" to have me "acknowledge" this in writing. Prompt compliance, he concluded, "will make it unnecessary to take any further action at this time."

Scarcely had the letter dropped through the mail chute before I was on a plane to New York to hash it out with Loomis and Random House attorney Gerald Hollingsworth. Both felt Morrison had blown it, that by pressing for an "acknowledgment" of what he said he already had, he was effectively admitting that he had nothing at all.

I wrote a letter back to him pointing this out and explaining that his request "[could] only lead me to believe that the original document" I'd signed on joining the Agency "and my signature on it were not adequate."

The letter landed in Morrison's in-box like an incoming rocket, exploding what remained of his equanimity.

"Snepp's response," he advised Turner, "leads me to believe that he either misses the point of my letter or is trying to be coy or evasive."

Turner was shaken, too. "Let us keep our fingers crossed," he moaned, "and hope that he can't pull those seven hundred pages into a manuscript and get it published."

Morrison, however, wasn't quite so ready to fold. "My inclination right now," he told the admiral, "is to respond to Snepp with a low-key note explaining that we merely wanted to be certain we had not misunderstood his intention to abide by his secrecy agreement, and that we now understand from his letter that he does."

It was another cutesy ploy, an attempt to rewrite the script to the Agency's advantage. If I replied to him in the affirmative, agreeing that he'd read my letter right, he'd have the commitment he sought. If I balked and said no, he had no such commitment from me, I'd be giving him convincing justification for legal action.

He discussed his scheme with David Anderson, chief of litigation for the Justice Department's Civil Division. Anderson, backed by Hedge and Whitaker, gave his blessing.

— —

Turner was not so enthusiastic. This whole sordid affair was taking on a complexity he didn't think it deserved. Was there something about the censorship system that had eluded him? A flaw, a little glitch that could come back to bite him in court?

To find out, he did some digging and quickly confirmed the worst: there was no "system" at all. From time immemorial, the vetting of manuscripts had been handled on an ad hoc basis by the office of security without any clear guidelines to light the way. No one could even say for sure how many manuscripts had been cleared over the years or what secrets approved for publication. A plan drawn up the previous spring for a formal prepublication review board still languished in Knoche's bottom drawer.

Turner knew there was no time for major repair work. A suit against me was imminent. The best he could do was throw up some window dressing so the Agency wouldn't appear foolish in court. Hastily, he activated the prepublication review board ("PRB") and put his own chief public-relations officer in charge.

Officially, the PRB became operational Thursday morning, June 23. Only then, with the window dressing in place, was Morrison permitted to send me the "low-key note" he'd proposed two weeks before.

Like the earlier letter he'd sent me, it was a snare wrapped in camouflage. Claiming to be writing to me to "correct any misimpression," he insisted that *the* "secrecy agreement" (as if there were only one) was a "valid contract" requiring me to clear all my writings. "In view of your assurances that you will do so," he concluded, "we consider that the matter has been resolved."

I instantly realized what he he was trying to do: sell me a bill of goods. If I didn't object, I'd be stuck with it, like an unsolicited main selection from the Book-of-the-Month Club.

Initially, my impulse was to object and risk the consequences. But the more I pondered, the more I thought not. No one could conclude from the record that I accepted the Agency's view of my obligations, and any further fencing might expose me to hazards I couldn't begin to calculate. So I decided to stay silent.

I couldn't have known that this would effectively stop Hedge and Whitaker in their tracks, but it did. Since Morrison's letter would have all the world believe that I'd given him the commitment he wanted, and since I'd said nothing to the contrary, the two prosecutors suddenly had no cause for legal action against me.

— —

If Turner had had his way, he probably would have washed his hands of me at this point. Yet, never one to be seen a piker, he remembered the promise he'd made at our meeting and meant to keep it. In late June, his office called to tell me I would soon receive the fifty-six pages of classified insights that Colby had released to the Kalbs two years before.

I was both shocked and gratified at the consideration, particularly since there had been so little of it before. But after the package arrived and I looked through it, only the shock remained. Contained within was enough top-secret material to imperil countless agents and collaborators abandoned in Vietnam. For the first time, I understood how completely Colby had betrayed his trust in disclosing these secrets to the Kalbs—and how hypocritical the censorship rules were. If Colby could leak so profligately and irresponsibly, how could anyone dare try to silence me?

— —

My indignation deepened when, in early July, Carla gave me a copy of a chilling commentary on CIA censorship recently published in the CIA's unclassified in-house newsletter. Written by a former general counsel, it recounted boastfully how the CIA had cynically *over*censored Victor

Marchetti's manuscript after seizing it through court injunction in 1972. Far from suppressing real secrets, the author recalled, the censors had cut out even "soft" items, marginally classifiable information, so the Agency would have plenty to bargain with if Marchetti ever challenged any of their deletions in court.

I was sickened, both by the article and by the incredible smugness of the author. If this was what "prepublication review" amounted to—a game of one-upmanship—only a masochist would want any part of it.

— —

Authoritative volumes about great historical events normally come festooned with candid portraits of the principal players, centerfold pictures of both heroes and villains. David Kennerly, once President Ford's personal photographer and a friend from my Vietnam days, had recently agreed to let me use some of his prized shots of Ford, Kissinger, and Martin, and I'd managed to isolate from my own photo collection a hazy image of Polgar partying it up at a diplomatic reception in Saigon.

But Loomis felt we needed something more dramatic and urged me to cast about for other sources. Somewhat hesitantly, I told him I had one. My alcoholic mother, whom I hadn't seen or heard from recently, had trained as an artist, and though her hands shook and her eyes were failing thanks to the booze she absorbed so copiously, she just might be able to execute a few drawings if given time.

Loomis said it was worth a try.

When I called my mother to let her know, she broke down and wept. It had been a long time since anyone had offered her such an opportunity to showcase her considerable talent.

The first picture she conceived took her only a few days, and when she sent it to me I felt like weeping myself. It was a pen-and-pencil rendering of a horribly mutilated Vietnamese, a gash of crimson spilling from his wounds and congealing into the contours of South Vietnam. I knew it was too brutal for *Decent Interval,* but didn't have the heart to tell her. Instead, I delicately suggested that what I really needed was a group portrait of Polgar, Martin, and Nguyen Van Thieu. She sensed the rejection and polished off a bottle of vodka, but after a day or so of drying out, managed to stagger back to her drawing table. Painstakingly, she produced images that both surprised and inspired, and struck Loomis as perfect. Not in a long while had I seen my mother so happy.

During one of my trips home that summer, I paid a call on the other half of my family tragedy. After the usual awkward salutations, my father expressed concern for my welfare and offered to try to mobilize his old school chum William Colby on my behalf. I told him not to bother. Colby wouldn't like what I was writing.

My father considered this and asked warily if I was about to break the law. I said the Agency seemed to be inventing law as it went along and that I'd rely on justice to protect me. The old Southern judge wasn't impressed. The law and justice seldom coincide, he warned me. Better make law my surety.

I told him it was probably too late for that.

— —

Because of the sheer bulk of my manuscript, Loomis entrusted its final pruning to someone inured to such ponderous tomes, Bertha "Bert" Krantz, James Michener's personal copy editor. A diminutive gray-haired generalissimo whose penchant for blue-penciling would have put any CIA censor to shame, she approached her task with a vigor that left even Bernie breathless. If anything dimmed her star it was only an irrepressible garrulousness. Invariably, whenever Bert would ring up Bernie to discuss editorial matters, she'd drop into a stage whisper as if that might foil any eavesdropper and then blurt out references to "Frank" and "*Decent Interval*" in blithe disregard for the code words she'd been urged to use instead. The Agency's failure to pick up on these cues convinced me falsely that Big Brother was napping.

Except for Bert and two or three others, Loomis's myriad colleagues and subalterns were allowed to remain blissfully ignorant of the subversive tome taking shape in their midst. Though this made perfect sense from a security standpoint, the effect was to ratchet up the pressures on me. Whatever editorial burdens Bert couldn't handle herself, I had to shoulder or shuck off on others still brave enough to acknowledge me. Three State Department officials agreed to comb the manuscript for errors, provided that I keep their identities secret, and Carla, working furtively by a neighborhood pool on weekends, clipped and pasted maps and proofread my countless rewrites until she could decipher my marginalia even better than I.

The stress of bringing out the book this way inevitably took a heavy toll all around. By late July, Bernie and Carla were both stumbling tired, and I was worse, a zombie, too weary to write with any facility and too besieged by demons to keep from writing. One night, while dozing fitfully at Carla's side, I was seized with such graphic visions of rampaging Viet Cong that I leapt up and inadvertently popped my hostess on the jaw.

Nobody who behaves so inhospitably is likely to keep old friends or win new ones, and the isolation I brought upon myself blossomed around me like a toxic cloud. Though Carla forgave my excesses and Bernie indulged them, others simply drifted away, and those who didn't I began cold-shouldering anyway, out of the misbegotten belief that only a CIA informant would be so masochistic as to try to remain my friend. I stopped accepting invitations or returning phone calls, and though the Johnsons had urged me to contact them in Colorado if ever I pined for a friendly voice, I tore their number out of my address book and tossed it away, the better to resist the temptation.

On many an evening after a long day at my writing table, I'd drag myself off to a Georgetown pub, to Clyde's or some other haven for the habitually young, and sit there alone, amid the press of bodies, trying to connect with the world beyond my obsessions. But the harder I tried, the more distant I felt, and the more contemptuous and jealous, too—contemptuous of all these idling souls who had nothing more to worry about than the latest baseball scores, and jealous of their very freedom to squander time at all. And invariably, after listening in on them for an hour or two, I'd haul myself off, more morose than ever, more chillingly sober, and all the more aware that Vietnam had left me an outcast.

— —

Meanwhile, at Langley, the "Snepp problem" was fast giving way to other crises far more urgent. In June, the Soviets unmasked a key CIA penetration agent in Moscow, thus obliterating American spy operations there. By late July, the Justice Department was seriously debating whether to prosecute Richard Helms for perjured congressional testimony, and his many supporters were beginning to leak stories to discredit the man they held responsible for his plight, Helms's onetime friend and colleague, William Colby.

It was Colby, after all, who'd first called Helms out, alerting the Justice Department in late 1974 that the ex-director had lied to Congress the year before about CIA involvement in the overthrow of Chilean president Salvador Allende. Colby had fingered Helms to spare the Agency. But the old guard had never forgiven him, and by late summer anonymous leakers were accusing Colby of everything from incompetence to treason.

Even in the best of times such backbiting would have served the CIA poorly, but coming as it did on the heels of the spy bust in Moscow, it caused an unwelcome stir on Capitol Hill. The House of Representatives had just created a permanent intelligence panel to match the one set up a year before in the Senate, and many CIA loyalists worried that the new watchdog might start poking into the Helms-Colby imbroglio simply to justify its existence.

For Turner, the prospect of any such heightened scrutiny was discomfiting indeed, for by the end of the summer he had a lot to answer for himself. The loss of the Moscow agent had triggered rancorous debate among insiders about his competence as spymaster, and though he could scarcely be faulted for wanting to clean up the Agency as Stockwell had suggested, he'd recently launched a housecleaning from hell. Suspicious of the old guard, he'd brought in outside efficiency experts to help plan it. They knew nothing of espionage and lacked both subtlety and finesse, and as they began muscling their way through the bureaucracy, taking names and demanding answers, the atmosphere turned sulfuric.

Deputy Director Knoche tried to sound warning. After two years of intense proctological examination, he told Turner, the clandestine service couldn't take any more. But Turner ignored him, and before the summer was out Knoche resigned.

On August 7, Turner met with his remaining top lieutenants to discuss the shake-up and try to make it seem reasonable. Since the end of the Vietnam War, the clandestine service had been underemployed and overstaffed, he argued, and needed to pare down. This explanation didn't sway Shackley, who was now associate deputy director for operations, or anybody else who was likely to feel the axe. As resentments swelled, so did the inevitable vindictive leaks, prompting Turner to worry anew about a possible breakdown of discipline in the ranks.

In my weariness, I didn't glimpse the omens or see how any of this might redound against me. If anyone deserved to be sanctioned for imprudent disclosures, I reasoned, it was Helms and his unruly confederates.

For once, as William Colby would later confide to me, he and I were in agreement. The continuing indiscretions of the Helms camp not only set a terrible example, he felt, but were damaging to him, and he wasn't about to sit mum and unprotesting. So as the summer waned and the leaks intensified, he began pressing hard to complete the memoir that was to be his answer to Helms and his ilk. By late August, with the help of a collaborator, he'd produced a respectable manuscript.

Since Colby had been a moving force behind the Marchetti lawsuit, he felt obliged to do some obeisance to the CIA's censors. But he also knew that they might hold up his manuscript indefinitely, leaving him at the mercy of Helms's sniping. So rather than let them have the first look, he slipped the manuscript to his editors at Simon and Schuster. Only on September 8, two weeks later, did he trouble to surrender a copy to Turner's newly constituted prepublication review board.

Agency officials knew as well as Colby that this violated the very rules they were seeking to enforce against me. CIA lawyer John Morrison had declared in one of his letters to me: "you may not submit an outline, manuscript or any other material or information you propose to publish to a publisher, agent, or any other unauthorized person prior to a review by the Agency." Colby had already overstepped this line. But did anyone raise a hue and cry?

Not quite. Not even close. Instead, the CIA agreed to let him leave the manuscript with his editors even as the censors looked through it, provided he ensure that any changes they demanded be cranked in before publication.

— —

If consistency had been any part of the CIA's playbook, a comparable dispensation should have been offered to me. But too many had too much invested in stopping me. So the Agency said nothing.

Still, I wasn't forgotten. In late August, when a routine polygraph exam fortuitously put my friend Carla on the chopping block, CIA Security spied an opportunity—and grabbed it.

Carla and I should have seen it coming. Polygraph tests are humiliations to be endured periodically as part of routine CIA security evaluations, and we ought to have realized that her next one might be turned against me. The Agency had tried everything else—surveillance, blackmail, entrapment. So why not the manipulation of a friend?

Even so, we were blindsided, the ordeal awaiting Carla in the testing lab that terrible morning catching us wholly off guard.

Around midday, she called in tears to tell me what had happened. For several excruciating hours she had been strapped to the machine and grilled mercilessly about me. She fielded all questions gamely except one, but unfortunately it was a crucial one: Had she ever given classified information to unauthorized persons? Each time she answered negatively, she sent the needles spiking. She knew it was a bogus reading; she had never given me anything classified since my departing the Agency; her nerves were playing her false. She tried to make her inquisitor understand. But the most he would cede to her was a second chance, an opportunity to be "boxed" again the next day, on pain of losing her job, should she stumble again.

I scooped up my manuscript, hid it away, then raced over to her apartment to help arm her for the rematch. Reassuring her that she'd never made any unauthorized disclosures to me, I urged her to make certain the questioner posed the issue to her in precisely these terms.

The following morning, she did as I suggested—and came through clean. Still, the inquisitor kept on badgering her, pressing her to inform on me. She resisted, and time and again turned his questions back on him, demanding to know why the Agency should be so interested in me when it didn't give a damn about the Vietnamese. "Your treatment of Frank is criminal!" she thundered.

"Are you emotionally involved with Mr. Snepp?" the inquisitor asked snidely.

"Yes!" she snapped back.

"Isn't that a conflict of interest?" he continued.

"No, because nothing he's doing is in conflict with Agency interests!"

On that note the interview ended, and Carla walked away convinced that even if she hadn't saved herself, at least she'd saved me.

— —

That was always Carla's way of course—save Frank and damn the personal cost—even though she knew I had Bernie in New York and a claim on her affections, too. It was a curious conspiracy the three of us had forged, recognized but never declared, struck from shared passions, yet so compartmentalized that each of us could sustain our illusions.

In all the months these two women had supported me, I'd never told either of them the worst of my secrets, the full truth about Mai Ly and the child. Keeping that hidden had enabled me to go on pretending to be the white knight. But it had also kept me at such a distance from them both that all intimacy remained superficial.

Still, I'd seen too much of betrayal to be a mere thief in the night. If I couldn't give either of them the love they deserved, at least I could spare them further pain.

So I stepped up the pace, working furiously to bring our ordeal to a close, eating little, skipping sleep, and spending less and less time with either of them. Miraculously, by the end of August I was launched on my final chapter, a summing up that would explain, among other things, why I'd ignored the censors.

I made no attempt at a reasoned defense, only an honest one: "In my view, if the Agency could officially leak to the press to whitewash its role in Vietnam, it had forfeited the right to censor me in the name of national security."

Strangely, after dictating this final line and mailing the cassette off to Bernie in New York, I felt no elation, no relief, only a terrible emptiness, as if the shambles of a life I'd salvaged from Vietnam had abruptly lost even a semblance of meaning.

Bernie stayed up all night transcribing the tape, and agonizing, as she later told a reporter, over "the weariness and horror" she detected in my voice. The following morning, crushingly exhausted herself, she delivered the last chapter to Loomis and picked up a check for eleven thousand dollars, the final installment of my book advance.

It had taken me just under twenty months to reach this point in my long journey out of Vietnam.

— —

The arrival of the final chapter ratcheted Random House into full alert. With the manuscript now easily recognizable for what it was, Loomis knew that any breach in his own security could subject both book and publisher to instant legal retaliation. So he set out to narrow the risk. His normal six-month production schedule he slashed in half. Galleys were dispensed with. The first and only imprint of *Decent Interval* would be the final page proofs themselves.

He also arranged to have the manuscript fed into the production system with no title page or author's credits, so that none of the myriad technicians soon to be mobilized to process it would know how sensitive it was.

Since the dust jacket of any book instantly telegraphs its contents, Loomis took special precautions in preparing mine. Rather than farm the job out to an independent contractor as was normal, he had the dummy pasted up in-house and wrote the flap copy himself. His typed draft was incorporated into the jacket design through a photo-offset process that eliminated the need for countless prying eyes.

Even after corrected page proofs were delivered to the printer, he insisted on keeping my name off the cover and title page. Up until the last minute, "Virgil Black" would remain the ostensible author of this nameless entry in Random House's fall book list.

One problem did tax his imagination, though: publicity. For obvious reasons, no advance copies of *Decent Interval* could be hawked to book clubs or professional reviewers, and all the usual marketing venues were likewise closed to us. If the book wasn't to die on the shelves, an alternative had to be found. Loomis decided our only choice was to slip a copy to a single trustworthy journalist—and pray.

His own favorite journalist was Seymour Hersh of *The New York Times,* whose account of the My Lai massacre he'd edited years before and who'd made a career out of exposing CIA illegalities. Loomis considered Hersh a close friend and promised me we could rely on him.

I wasn't so sure. Having never met the man, I was wary of entrusting my fate to a stranger. Moreover, I knew that Hersh had once spiked an exposé in deference to William Colby, a story about a top-secret CIA operation to salvage a sunken Soviet submarine. Colby had persuaded him that publishing it would endanger national security.

Loomis assured me that his friend had lapsed only this once, and for legitimate patriotic reasons. But to me, one lapse seemed one too many.

Indeed, apart from Don Oberdorfer of *The Washington Post,* I knew of only one journalist I felt I could trust: Mike Wallace of CBS News's *60 Minutes.* Years before, during summer breaks from college, I'd worked as his researcher and had become a friend, even at times a very pale substitute for a son he'd lost to an accident. Though I hadn't seen Wallace since joining the CIA, I was confident he wouldn't betray me.

On impulse, I contacted him to see if he might be interested in doing a television piece about my book, and in mid-September I began slipping him page proofs. I also asked Oberdorfer to read the manuscript for accuracy. No promises were made or understandings reached with either journalist. All I could do was dangle the bait and hope for a strike.

Until that happened I saw no profit in challenging Loomis on Hersh's suitability. I simply let the matter lie.

— —

The discipline Loomis had imposed on the editorial process carried us smoothly into the final stages of publication. Though an expanding number of Random House employees quickly became aware of *Decent Interval,* the discretion they exercised would have done any spook proud.

Had John Stockwell been less ambitious, he might have realized that the trail Loomis was blazing would serve him well, that the lessons learned from my experience could be applied toward the safe and efficient publication of his own book.

But the notoriety Stockwell had earned in recent months had blinkered him. The article I'd helped him publish in *The Washington Post* had bloated his self-confidence, and the interest Congress had taken in his allegations had encouraged him to believe that he deserved far more from Random House than had been proffered—more money, a bigger publicity budget, greater deference. His new friends on the left had cheered him on, and one of them, John Marks, acting as his agent, had approached Loomis during the summer and demanded a new and more lucrative contract for his client.

Loomis gave the overture short shrift. The manuscript pages Stockwell had produced so far were unimpressive, and Loomis was doubtful that Angola would sell half as well as Vietnam. He told Stockwell to play by the agreed rules or take his game elsewhere.

From a strictly business standpoint, this was a reasonable position. But for the ego-driven Stockwell, it was an invitation to high noon. By the time I'd begun correcting my page proofs, he was in a rage. He approached Sy

Hersh for advice; he vented his frustrations to passersby; he began preparing a film documentary to hype his own story. At the very moment I was most vulnerable, with the presses rolling and *Decent Interval* on the verge of release, John Stockwell kicked up a ruckus that threatened to set off alarms all over Langley.

Blessedly, his fury peaked quickly. Unwilling to endure Loomis any longer, he abruptly broke off all contact and stormed off to look for another publisher—without even offering to return any of the advance he'd received so far.

Bernie proclaimed "Good riddance!" But Loomis and I weren't so sanguine. Once free of Random House, Stockwell had no incentive to do us any favors. Though I couldn't imagine him fingering me to Langley—he *hated* Langley—I was determined to limit the risk. If he tried to learn anything more about *Decent Interval,* I'd freeze him out.

As it turned out, he did try. One night in September he called me at Bernie's to inquire about my pub date. I let him believe it was months away.

— —

Stockwell's defection, jarring as it was, cinched one decision for me. Much as Loomis might admire Seymour Hersh, I wasn't about to gamble on anyone about whom I knew even less than Stockwell. If Mike Wallace wanted my story exclusively, he would have it.

In early October, as Wallace finished reading the page proofs, I asked what he thought. He clapped me on the shoulder and declared *Decent Interval* a "perfect" *60 Minutes* piece.

Soon afterward, he invited Loomis to his East Side townhouse to nail down "arrangements." Loomis had only one stipulation. While delighted to have *60 Minutes* on board, he would insist on keeping Seymour Hersh in play. If Hersh wanted to break a print exclusive in *The New York Times* after the broadcast, he would be free to do so.

Reluctantly, Wallace agreed.

— —

The day of the *60 Minutes* interview itself, a steady drizzle converted Manhattan into a Léger-like tableau of bleak grays and browns with occasional disquieting flashes of red. My own condition was a thin film of bluster stretched over a bad case of nerves.

Early that afternoon, Wallace's silkily gracious producer, Barry Lando, treated me to a tranquilizing lunch reinforced by two Bloody Marys. He then marched me over to the Essex House on Central Park South where a suite had been rented out under a false name, CBS's own studios having been deemed too insecure to accommodate my special need for anonymity.

Moments after we arrived, Wallace glided in, jittery as a cat. After a curt lecture to the floor crew—"anybody who talks, walks"—he began tinkering with the lights and camera angles. Only after Lando handed me a snifter of cognac did Wallace's eyes shift to me. "Nervous, Frankie?" he inquired after my first long draught.

"What for?" I replied gamely. "I've got to know this stuff better than you."

The eyebrows lifted. "We'll see."

The filming lasted all afternoon, three cameras rolling at once—one focused on Wallace, two on me—so there would be no need for retakes or reverse shots of the interviewer or his subject. Questions and answers, and the two talking heads, could be interspliced at Lando's whim.

—— ——

Having now committed my story to both celluloid and print, I couldn't have escaped a reckoning if I'd wanted to. But the conditions under which I was to play out my little drama would soon change for the worse, for, as luck would have it, Turner chose this moment to put his long-proposed housecleaning into effect. Nothing about it would be pain-free.

On the very afternoon I unburdened myself to Wallace, Turner met with his senior advisers to discuss final details. In selecting which heads to lop, his imported efficiency experts had opted for flowchart logic over seasoning and experience, and in timing out the executions, they'd rejected a leisurely drawdown in favor of a sudden, massive bloodletting. The date they'd chosen was ghoulishly apropos: October 31, Halloween.

Never one to be overly sensitive, Turner proved a perfect hobgoblin on the witching day itself. Nowhere in the hundreds of pink slips he had circulated was there even a whiff of thanks for a job well done. No salve was offered for wounded feelings, no executive bulletin to ease the pain of the condemned, and over the next several days, as their howls of protest echoed through the media, he added insult to injury by mocking them. "You really heard them crying, haven't you?" he snorted to *Newsweek*.

His callousness obliterated what remained of institutional discipline, and he and his critics quickly came to agree on one thing: prompt and decisive countermeasures would be needed to keep the Agency from slipping into terminal chaos.

Except for my own chaos, I might have taken note and been sobered. Turner's incompetence had precipitated a crisis that would make my book a provocation he couldn't ignore.

—— ——

If that fact escaped me, however, another one profoundly affected the way I would view the odds and my obligations.

On the very day Turner launched the Halloween massacre, a man who'd once occupied his chair, ex–CIA director Richard Helms, marched into a federal court in Washington, D.C., to face a long overdue comeuppance for that disingenuous testimony he'd given Congress four years before about Chile. Since lying under oath is a criminal offense, a felony, it should have been an open-and-shut case.

But after a few uneasy moments in court and a lecture from the judge, the great Richard Helms beat the rap. Far from being hustled off to jail, he received a mere two-thousand-dollar fine, a suspended two-year sentence, and a sweetheart deal that enabled him to plead no contest to a misdemeanor charge that held him liable simply for testifying "incompletely."

Weeks before, federal prosecutors had agreed to bargain for one reason: Helms had convinced them that his CIA secrecy agreement had entitled him to keep the truth from Congress—had *justified* lying!

At the Halloween hearing itself, he repeated this alibi. "I'd sworn my oath to protect certain secrets," he proclaimed from the witness stand.

After the actual sentencing four days later, Helms walked out of the courtroom and declared through his lawyer that he would wear his conviction like a badge of honor. Four hundred retired CIA officers anted up to pay his fine, leaving him financially unencumbered and free to embark on a new career as a business consultant to the Shah of Iran. It was a job to which he could bring the most unique asset imaginable: knowledge gained from three decades of exposure to the CIA's most vital secrets.

Meanwhile, just hours after the sentencing, Griffin Bell tried to convince the public that the defendant deserved every favor he got. "You can rob a bank and get promoted," the attorney general snapped to reporters. "It doesn't set so well with me to say that we haven't done enough to somebody who is a first offender."

I didn't quite agree. Helms had lied and made his secrecy agreement an excuse. If there was any inference to be drawn, it was that such agreements didn't have a shred of legal—or moral—authority.

One of the federal attorneys who'd prosecuted Helms seemed to share this view. As he later admitted to the press, not once had he or his colleagues bothered to ask for, much less read, the secrecy agreement that had saved the ex-director's hide.

CHAPTER 11

Unveiling

BY LATE OCTOBER, Random House salesmen were quietly urging "jobbers," the independent middlemen who move books to retail outlets around the country, to stock up on a hot new item to be released within weeks. None of the sales reps knew title, content, or author. The most they could say was that prerelease secrecy was mandatory and that orders had to be made on good faith alone.

Normally, books aren't marketed this way. Since jobbers have limited time and resources and are liable for what they order, they naturally want to know as much as possible about the latest offerings. This time they were being asked to gamble.

To tweak their interest, Random House circulated a discreet flyer promising "tremendous publicity" upon the mystery book's release. How the hype was to be accomplished was not explained, though an ever-widening circle of Random House employees knew that Mike Wallace was to debut the book, with Seymour Hersh offering a follow-up in *The New York Times.*

Because of his friendship with Hersh, Loomis took it upon himself to keep him supplied with page proofs and background for his story. I was grateful to be spared. Hersh still worried me, not for any specific new reason, but because I now had enough time on my hands to indulge any ugly fantasy. To make things worse, the letdown I'd suffered on finishing the book had left me morose and distracted, incapable of focusing on much of anything, and I found myself wandering blearily through my days like a drunk coming off a binge.

If anything seemed worthy of attention, it was the latest grim news out of Vietnam, Hanoi having recently offered to release the remains of twenty-one American servicemen and one civilian missing since the war. The gesture was meant to win sympathy and warm liberal hearts, but it had quite a different effect on me. Among the fragments of flesh and bone to be turned over was the shattered body of a retired CIA officer who'd returned to Saigon just before the end to help Vietnamese comrades, only to be abandoned himself. Captured and tortured mercilessly, Tucker Gougleman had succumbed months later in a prison outside Hanoi. I'd known him well during my first Vietnam tour, and his loss and belated resurrection in a body bag only underscored what our last-minute negligence had cost.

Adding to this overload of emotion were reports of larger calamities, famine, and ethnic persecution throughout the "new" Vietnam and an expanding bloodbath in neighboring Cambodia. The flow of human detritus out of both countries was fast reaching flood tide, swamping refugee camps from the Philippines to Japan, and though President Carter had vowed to lift immigration restrictions to help ease the pressure, the American electorate was already grumbling that one more wave of little yellow people could sink an already listing economy.

I didn't sleep easily through any of this, and my crushing sense of helplessness flayed an incipient ulcer into a bleeding one. By late October, I was facing a doctor's ultimatum: ease up or crash.

Under this imperative, I hauled myself off to a squalid tourist resort to try to wind down. But the place I chose had a decrepitude eerily evocative of Saigon. By the afternoon of the third day, I was straining over the whap-whap-whap of the long-stemmed ceiling fan on the hotel veranda for intimations of gunfire and trying not to imagine that a distant figure floating in and out of the rising heat along the boardwalk might be Mai Ly.

On the morning of the following day, Bernie called to say that Loomis had failed to clarify some obscure point about his dealings with Hersh, and suddenly I convinced myself with the certainty of the truly unhinged that I was about to be betrayed, that Hersh would surface my book prematurely. That evening, I packed up and flew home to deal with a crisis that existed only in the synapses of my addled brain.

— —

By the time I resurfaced on November 5, the first of the inaugural fifteen thousand copies of *Decent Interval* were winding their way unbidden to bookstores around the country and Bernie had telegraphed my wholly un-founded misgivings to Wallace's producer, Barry Lando.

Over dinner at Washington's Trader Vic's, Lando warned me that if Hersh did jump the gun, *60 Minutes* would drop my story. He demanded to be reassured.

Next morning, I flew to New York to confer with Loomis. If Hersh did step out of line, I told him, he'd lose his exclusive. Don Oberdorfer of *The Washington Post* already had a copy of the book in hand and could turn a story just as fast.

Loomis went pale. No other print reporter was even supposed to know of *Decent Interval,* he insisted. If *The Washington Post* had a copy, we were honor-bound to alert Hersh.

I shrugged and said I'd do so myself.

— —

The restaurant Torremolinos is an intimate watering hole on Manhattan's East Side around the corner from Random House, and Loomis was already on his second Jack Daniel's when I showed up shortly before cocktail hour. The tension was thick enough to cut, and I quickly ordered a stiff drink for myself. Just as it arrived, so did Hersh, trenchcoat flailing about him. "Great book!" he shouted at the top of his voice. "So great it will never sell."

He plopped down across from us and yanked out a notebook. He wanted a few quotes for his story, he told me. Would I mind? For a moment he sat gazing at me expectantly, pen poised over the page. I drew a breath and shook my head. No quotes, I told him. In fact, the situation had changed. I'd decided to let *The Washington Post* in on my secret.

Hersh's eyes narrowed behind his thick glasses, and for a second I thought he'd spring across the table. "If I don't get this goddamn exclusive," he roared, "the *Times* doesn't touch this story! I mean, this is hard-ball!"

Loomis dropped back about a thousand yards. "Frank, be reasonable," he gasped. "Think what a *Times* story could mean." But I wasn't thinking any longer, let alone reasonably. "*No,*" I barked back. He'd get no exclusive.

Face flushed, Hersh leapt up and pinioned Loomis with a murderous eye. "We'll talk about this later," he snapped.

"Oh no," I injected. "The decision's mine, and *final.*"

"Then there's no more to talk about!"

With that, Hersh rocketed out of the restaurant.

Loomis inhaled the rest of his bourbon and begged me to reconsider. I told him, "No chance."

Even now, it's difficult to imagine how I could have been so foolish. Hersh had betrayed no one and violated no understanding. I was the double-crosser, not he. And once I stiffed him, he had no obligation to protect me any longer. In a wink, I'd created the one thing I least needed right now: an unguided missile.

The following Monday, flush with paranoia, I raced back to Washington and informed Oberdorfer that *Decent Interval* would soon be fair game. With Carla's help, I then duplicated several copies of page proofs and asked her to be ready to distribute them to other select journalists if Hersh should go to press early. At least he wouldn't have a lock on the story.

In New York, meanwhile, Hersh's editors consulted an ombudsman and prepared a preemptive strike of their own. On Tuesday morning, they advised Loomis that all deals were off: my book would see the light of day a bit earlier than planned. That afternoon, Random House's publicity department hastily drafted a new flyer announcing that *The New York Times* would be breaking an "exclusive" on a nonfiction opus titled *Decent Interval* in its *Friday* edition—two days before my *60 Minutes* interview.

On Thursday morning, ignorant of all this, I flew back to New York and arranged to meet Loomis outside the headquarters of Doubleday Publishing on Third Avenue. I'd chosen the spot carefully. On the chance that CIA tailgaters were following me in an effort to identify my publisher, I figured it wouldn't hurt to wave Doubleday under their noses. The distraction might buy us a few extra moments to get the last copies of *Decent Interval* into circulation.

But alas, there were no longer any extra moments, as Loomis himself seemed to realize when he showed up coatless against the chill. Scuffing the ice-encrusted pavement with the toe of his shoe, he confessed to being "fairly certain" that Hersh was about to break his story, possibly as early as the following morning.

I was too stunned even to reply. Loomis scowled at me, then turned and stalked off.

A short while later, I returned to Torremolinos for a long-scheduled appointment with Random House's publicity director. Having recovered enough to be truly apoplectic, I told the good woman that if Hersh did go to press the next day, I'd tape a postscript for *60 Minutes* accusing him of torpedoing me for the sake of a meaningless scoop. She slugged back her drink and fled. Soon the maître d' summoned me to the phone. It was Loomis. "Hersh *is* breaking the story tomorrow. No question," he sighed over the line.

Moments later, I was pushing through the revolving doors at Random House's headquarters on East Fiftieth Street with Bernie clattering after me on spiked heels. It was the first time I'd ever set foot inside this august citadel of American letters.

In a cluttered office on the eleventh floor, I found Loomis frantically trying to reach Mike Wallace by phone. As I flung myself in a chair, he turned to me ashen-faced and handed me the receiver. Fearfully, I gave Wallace the bad news straight up: his story had been hijacked.

"You've lied to me!" he shrieked with such vehemence that I was sure he could be heard without benefit of amplification all the way to Langley. The line then went dead with a thunderous click.

Bernie put a consoling hand on my shoulder. "Don't worry, Mike's not your only hope."

Summoning up my last reserves, I phoned Oberdorfer's boss at *The Washington Post,* Larry Stern, and told him that if he didn't want to be caught up short by Hersh, he'd better be ready to headline *Decent Interval* at dawn's early light. I then called Carla and asked her to distribute the page proofs she had in hand to other journalists.

No sooner had she rung off than a *Newsweek* reporter punched through the switchboard. He'd seen the latest publicity flyer and wanted an interview. I hesitated, reluctant to tempt Wallace's ire any further. But Loomis warned that we couldn't be picky now, particularly if *60 Minutes* was on hold.

That evening, he and I met with the journalist at Bernie's apartment and gave him highlights of my story. By the time we were done, I was so drained I would gladly have shriveled up and blown away, if I could have managed it. But it was already too late. Shortly after Loomis and the newsman departed into the night, I got a call from John Stockwell. He'd just come from a glittery soirée across town where the talk of the cognoscenti had been—*Decent Interval.*

"Why didn't you warn me?" he asked tightly.

I made some excuse and hung up, my nerves thrumming like high-tension wires. If *Decent Interval* was already an open secret around this city, the wolves might be only moments from the door.

In fact, they were closer than I imagined. Later that night, Loomis received word from a Random House warehouse that some suspicious gentlemen had come around asking about me just after the last copies of *Decent Interval* had been shipped out. It had been a very near miss.

Near or not, however, it saved me, and the following morning I clawed my way out of a fitful sleep to find myself the talk of the eastern seaboard.

Both *The New York Times* and *The Washington Post* gave *Decent Interval* front-page billing, and *The Washington Star* followed suit that afternoon. Not only had Hersh been denied his scoop; he'd been matched by his fiercest rivals.

But if he was resentful, his story didn't reflect it. Planted just below the fold on page 1, it ran an eye-popping five thousand words and occupied more space than had been reserved for any national security story in any single issue of *The New York Times* since the publication of the Pentagon Papers. If the CIA had ever been inclined to ignore me, it couldn't now.

— —

All the initial coverage, including Hersh's, keyed on a theme buried in the postscript of *Decent Interval*. "It is not too much to say," I'd written, "that in terms of squandered lives, blown secrets, and the betrayal of agents, friends, and collaborators, our handling of the evacuation was an institutional disgrace." It was a scathing verdict. But the press loved it.

My other key themes—Martin's duplicity, the corruption of intelligence—received extensive treatment too, though only Hersh troubled to explore the political and legal implications of what I'd done. "Because of its central accusation and dozens of other disclosures, the Snepp book poses an immediate problem for the CIA," he wrote, noting that Turner's housecleaning had unleashed resentments that could be transformed by my example into "more books and more disclosures."

Drawing on tips from Random House, he made much of our surreptitious publishing tactics and pointed out that they'd been designed to ward off the kind of restraining order imposed on Victor Marchetti. He also suggested that my publishers hadn't always been comfortable with me. "The concern at Random House," he wrote, "was complicated by the fact that high-level CIA officials, including Admiral Stansfield Turner, had permitted Mr. Snepp to interview present Agency employees as part of his research. He did so on the basis of Mr. Snepp's assurance that he would submit his manuscript to the Agency for clearance before publication."

When I saw that, I didn't know whether to laugh or to cry. After all the trouble I'd had in leveraging *anything* out of the Agency, how exquisitely ironic to be accused of welching on a sweetheart deal with Turner!

Bernie realized immediately how dangerous these distortions were, and begged me to ask Mike Wallace for help. With no one else to turn to, I dragged myself down to the CBS broadcast center early Friday afternoon to plead for forgiveness.

Blessedly, it wasn't a hard sell. Wallace's cigar-chomping executive producer, Don Hewitt, had just spotted wire copy about a possible injunction against me and scented a story within a story. After only a brief hesitation, he offered to restore my interview to the Sunday lineup *provided* I talked to no one else between now and then. Not realizing what I was giving away, I agreed.

With this stricture in place, Wallace immediately began dialing up magazine editors around town to try to shop highlights of our interview for the next week's editions—only to discover that *Newsweek* already had "highlights" aplenty. Enraged, he put in a call to Random House president Robert Bernstein. "That *Loomis*," howled television's coolest interrogator, "is the worst bum I've ever met!"

Reaction to my book among Washington's elite was hardly any more temperate. Kissinger denounced my allegations as "nonsense." Former ambassador Martin, speaking from Italy where he professed to be "picking some olives," thundered indignantly that the evacuation had *too* been a success, and William Colby assured Hersh that 130,000 Vietnamese and all the Americans who'd wanted to get out, *had.*

As for Polgar, he had only one comment when Hersh tracked him down. Although he'd always held me "in the highest regard," he said, "what he's giving is the private's view of the war."

The CIA was far less charitable. Midmorning on Friday, as the wire services began beading out pearls from Hersh's story, the chief of the prepublication review board, Herbert Hetu, released a press statement, "Answers to Inquiries," that transformed me into a virtual Benedict Arnold. Alleging that I'd explicitly promised Turner my manuscript, he claimed that the admiral had given me "unclassified information" in return, as if I'd duped him into being generous. Afterward, "the director had no word from Mr. Snepp until he read descriptions of the book in today's newspaper."

As for my substantive allegations, Hetu declared that the CIA's inspector general had "thoroughly investigated" them all and sent an "authoritative" report to Congress.

Another of Turner's aides told Hersh, "Mr. Snepp promised orally, without qualification, that he would provide us with a copy of the book.

"It's one thing to go ahead and take your chances," he added, "but it's another thing to deliberately mislead."

So serious was this allegation that Hersh felt obliged to check it out with Random House. Unfortunately nobody there checked with me. "Random House officials," reported Hersh, "acknowledged that Mr. Snepp had deliberately misled Admiral Turner at their meeting in May."

As the potshotting intensified, I was sorely tempted to fire back. But up through Saturday night, Wallace kept me cooped up and incognito at CBS headquarters, thus enabling the CIA to go on peddling its version of the truth without correction or challenge.

— —

Sunday dragged by in slow motion, and by the time seven o'clock rolled around and Bernie and I had settled ourselves in front of her pinched-screen Motorola to watch *60 Minutes,* I was feeling like a panic victim on high-grade speed. The first tick-tick-tick of the televised stopwatch heralding another hour of exposé and confession nearly launched me through the ceiling.

"Tonight, an exclusive interview with a former CIA intelligence analyst of North Vietnamese strategy," Wallace announced, as my image flickered briefly on the screen. "He charges that the U.S. government covered up the mishandling of the American evacuation of Vietnam."

To the CIA's chagrin, this edition of *60 Minutes* would attract more viewers than any other installment to date, since the lead-in segment was given over to something truly spectacular, a play-by-play via satellite of Anwar Sadat's historic arrival in Jerusalem. Nobody who tuned in for it, however, could have been in any doubt that another spectacle was in the offing, for coming out of the first commercial, Wallace teasingly reminded viewers that they'd soon be hearing "from the former CIA agent who has broken his secrecy oath to talk about America's last days in Vietnam."

Displayed in a blowup over his shoulder was a mock intelligence file with SECRET emblazoned across it. With that single image, viewers were encouraged to believe I was about to commit a massive security breach right on national television.

Twenty minutes into the hour, after the Sadat piece and another commercial break, Wallace returned to set the stage for the longest interview *60 Minutes* had ever broadcast—"one man's report of America's last unhappy days in South Vietnam.

"You've been reading stories about it the last two days in your newspapers," he told his viewers. "But no one has yet heard from the ex–CIA man responsible for this charge of cover-up." He then introduced me: "senior intelligence analyst . . . awarded the CIA's Medal of Merit . . . two tours in Vietnam." But lest anyone mistake what was coming for a recycling of old news, he promised fresh insight into my decision to defy the CIA's secrecy agreement. "Frank Snepp," he noted coyly, "will tell us why he now sees fit to break that oath."

With that, the screen ignited with images lifted from the *CBS Evening News* broadcast of April 29, 1975. Dan Rather, substituting for anchor

Walter Cronkite that day, set the scene as the camera tightened on a colored map of Vietnam, a configuration as familiar to most Americans in those days as the skylines of their own hometowns.

Rather: "South Vietnam is now under Communist control. Early today, beginning with a jeepload of ragtag Viet Cong soldiers, then truck after truck of heavily armed North Vietnamese regular troops, the Communists entered Saigon in force."

Now—a quick cut to correspondent Ed Bradley, caught up in the chaos of the city's final hours. As the camera's eye flicked through a montage of panicked mobs and crashing helicopters, Bradley spoke breathlessly of "desperate scenes," of Americans trying vainly to push Vietnamese wives and children onto buses, of Marine guards beating back throngs at the embassy walls.

Finally, Wallace's pouched features reappeared. He ticked off my basic charges—the "institutional disgrace," the abandonment of "hundreds, perhaps thousands" of Vietnamese who had worked for the U.S. embassy. Then to me, as I'd appeared in our filmed interview weeks before: "You describe all this leaving behind of people who had worked with us or for us—Vietnamese—a 'callous act of betrayal on the part of the CIA,' " prompted Wallace.

"In some cases betrayal was involved," I replied. "We saved the people in the white skin. We left behind the Vietnamese." I went on to accuse the CIA of a "host of sins," including failure to ensure destruction of documents that could help identify abandoned allies and sensitive sources and methods. Enough had been compromised, I said, to enable an experienced Soviet counterintelligence operative to develop a picture of how the United States operates in a crisis. "And this is strategic intelligence any way you put it."

Wallace wanted to know which American officials were responsible. I named them: Colby, who'd failed to perceive the need for intensified evacuation planning in time; Polgar, with his overreliance on duplicitous diplomatic contacts in Saigon and his desperate yearning for a face-saving way out; Kissinger, misled by skewed intelligence into believing additional aid could offset South Vietnamese corruption—and deceived by the Soviets into thinking that a last-minute fix had a chance; and finally, the ambassador himself.

"Martin was a Cold Warrior in the old stripe," I explained. "He could not conceive of being beaten by Communists. He had lost a son in Vietnam. His life was fraught with all sorts of tragedy. And he was determined to make this last stand."

As for his misbegotten hope for negotiations, I continued, it had defied intelligence from our best agent, who'd told me three weeks before the end: "there was no chance for a negotiated settlement."

Wallace wondered if the CIA had ever managed to plant spies in Thieu's cabinet. "Not only spies," I told him, "we had the cabinet bugged so the South Vietnamese could hardly cough without our picking up the data."

And what of the North Vietnamese—had they planted such agents too?

I acknowledged they had, and pointed out that the CIA had even had an inkling of who they were, but had never moved against them for fear of embarrassing itself, since each suspect had once been close to the Agency. So the spy, or spies, had remained in place.

Who'd used their spies better, our side or theirs? asked Wallace.

Theirs, I told him. "They believed their intelligence. We didn't believe ours."

Worse still, I continued, our reporting had often been trimmed to fit policy considerations, to de-emphasize corruption in Saigon and security problems in the countryside so as to keep the South Vietnamese looking worthy of continued aid. Not that the ambassador had ever lied about any of this, I stressed. "He was merely stretching the facts to fit the case."

Shifting focus, Wallace remarked that Martin had repeatedly justified delaying the evacuation by claiming that any premature rush to the helicopters would have sown panic. I replied that this had been a red herring—that on occasion, he'd actually courted panic by spreading horror stories in the press about an impending Communist bloodbath, so as to win congressional sympathy for the South Vietnamese.

Wallace: "To what degree was the press 'had' by the United States in Vietnam?"

I collapsed my answer into several names: Keyes Beech of the *Chicago Daily News,* George McArthur of the *Los Angeles Times,* Robert Shaplen of *The New Yorker,* Bud Merick of *U.S. News and World Report.* "All these reporters," I explained incautiously, "were 'favored' journalists during my two tours in Saigon. We would leak to them on a selected basis, draw them into our trust, into our confidence, and then we could shape their reporting through further leaks, because they trusted us."

Recalling a case in point from my book, Wallace noted that "in the final days, the U.S. embassy continued to leak stories, pushing the chances for a negotiated settlement. . . ."

"And one particular reporter who bit all this hook, line, and sinker," I picked up, "was Malcolm Browne of *The New York Times.* He and Polgar became very close during Saigon's final days, to the point that we were using Browne on April 28 to pass messages to the Communist delegation at Tan Son Nhut."

Wallace: "Do you know of any American journalists paid by the CIA?"

"I know of foreign journalists paid by the CIA whose stories appear in *The New York Times* and various other newspapers."

"Who?"

"I cannot identify them because, as I have pointed out in the book, I am against dealing with sources and methods explicitly."

Harkening to other revelations, Wallace led me through a summary of how Kissinger had negotiated the Paris peace agreement without keeping Thieu informed, how he'd even contemplated kidnapping the North Vietnamese leadership, and how the U.S. embassy had often blinked at the peccadillos, including drug trafficking, of South Vietnamese officials deemed too important to offend. He then wondered if there'd been any corruption in the CIA itself, and I told him of the sticky-fingered CIA officer whose embezzling of operational funds had proved so costly, depriving us of assets in Vietnam's western highlands where the final Communist blitzkrieg had begun. Wallace raised an eyebrow and inquired about the officer's fate. "He was called into Saigon, sent home, and then released from the CIA," I told him. "But he was not prosecuted."

From there the interview veered toward things personal, with Wallace probing my reasons for going public—the Agency's refusal to sanction an after-action report, my anger over official leaks aimed at obscuring the failures of the evacuation. "What you're talking about is a calculated cover-up," he volunteered.

"Not merely a cover-up, but a whitewash," I told him.

Wallace then returned to the most ticklish issue, my secrecy obligations. "You signed an oath that you would not go public," he declared, brandishing a copy of my original secrecy agreement that I'd given him. I acknowledged having signed it, but explained why I no longer felt bound by it. "If you read on in that," I told him, "there is a clause there which specifies that an officer can go and register his complaints with appropriate authorities within the Agency. I tried to do this. I wanted *not* to go public. I wanted to do my after-action report on the inside, and was rebuffed at every turn. I feel I have met my obligation."

Wallace interposed: "The CIA knows you've been writing this book?"

"That's correct."

"Do you really think the CIA does not know how far this has gone and that you're talking to us?"

"I think if they did, Mike, I would have been enjoined. I think they would have gotten a gag order to silence me." Pausing, I then extended

Turner a courtesy, giving him the benefit, never dreaming how much I'd been shadowed and hoodwinked over the past eighteen months. "I think it should be brought out," I continued. "If the Agency were operating in its bad old ways, monitoring telephones, surveilling people illegally, I wouldn't have gotten this far."

Wallace smiled slyly. "You're an arrogant young man, aren't you?"

"That's the only way you can survive in the CIA, Mike—by being positive, arrogant, and hoping you know where you're going."

— —

As a tag to the interview, Wallace told his audience that he'd recently contacted many of the principals I'd criticized and had found them generally contemptuous of both me and my charges. Many, he said, agreed "with Henry Kissinger, who called Snepp 'a man of the second level in Saigon,' ten thousand miles away from Washington, who couldn't possibly have had any full understanding and knowledge of what decisions were made and how they were reached." And all "deny blame for the thousands of Vietnamese left behind in jeopardy."

That being said, he continued, a number of them "tended to point the finger of blame at each other." Martin had repeated his claim that Washington had waited too long in granting him authority to evacuate large numbers of Vietnamese. "But various others criticized Martin's performance," said Wallace. "One calls him too strong-willed. Another said he was physically sick toward the end. Another called him batty."

Wallace did not identify the source of that last slur. In fact, as he later told me, it was Kissinger himself.

Wrapping up his summation, Wallace quoted William Colby as denying "categorically leaking any secret material." Though he knew that CBS's own Kalb brothers had been beneficiaries of Colby's leaks, he chose not to confirm this. Indeed, the only point he finally conceded to me had to do with the *Times* reporter I'd mentioned. "Malcolm Browne of *The New York Times* acknowledges that he carried information from one side to the other in the final days," observed Wallace. "He says he was probably 'had' to some degree, by both sides in the chaos at the end.

"And finally, what about Frank Snepp?"

Wallace hesitated a beat, then added a zinger: "CIA director Stansfield Turner says he has spoken with the Justice Department, looking to the possibility of prosecution for Snepp's breaking his oath of secrecy."

The moment Wallace signed off, the phone on Bernie's night table jangled. It was Loomis. "The interview was fantastic!" he exclaimed.

Over the next several hours, applause wafted in from other quarters. A

New York Post columnist urged readers to "give thanks for a nation that still produces such stubborn young men." The *New York Times* pundit Tom Wicker mocked the anonymous CIA official who, in lambasting me two days before, had snorted: "It's one thing to take your chances, it's another thing to deliberately mislead." Retorted Wicker: "Let him tell that to Richard Helms and the Senate committee Mr. Helms deliberately misled."

Murray Kempton, in a CBS radio commentary, expressed amazement that the CIA should be trying to suppress "what we had the best reasons to suspect: as our presence in Vietnam disgraced us, so did our departure."

Still, there were discordances too. Elliot Fremont-Smith of *The Village Voice* was put off by my television presence: "a teenage Nureyev with a whiny singsong voice" whose "cockiness didn't help credibility." Other less flattering epithets were dumped on me by the journalists I'd described as CIA-friendly. Bud Merick, Keyes Beech, and George McArthur all denied having been manipulated. *The New Yorker*'s Robert Shaplen dismissed my "whole performance" as "shocking and deplorable . . . an ego trip.

"I at no time accepted at face value what the Agency, Snepp included, told me about anything," he snapped.

For all of the carping, though, none of my journalist-critics disputed my main message, that the evacuation had been a disaster. Said Beech: "No American who was in Vietnam could help but view the whole thing with extreme distaste. I felt soiled." Malcolm Browne, whose wife was Vietnamese, waxed mournful: "To me it was a desperate trauma. I too left many people behind, including members of my family. . . . It's a hateful memory. It's like resurrecting a funeral at which everybody was killing each other."

The press's ambivalence carried over to the public. Some who'd witnessed my *60 Minutes* performance weighed in with accolades. Others echoed an anonymous Bible thumper who, in a note to Wallace, likened me to a "Judas" who'd betrayed his master for "thirty pieces of silver."

Controversy being the staff of commerce, however, such hostility scarcely hurt sales. By Monday morning, November 21, orders for *Decent Interval* were pouring in at such a clip that Loomis ordered up a second printing.

The uptick in demand may not have been entirely spontaneous. As with Ross and Wise's *The Invisible Government* in 1964, the CIA initially tried to buy the book off the shelves. By Monday afternoon, operatives had purchased six hundred copies in the Washington area alone.

A reporter who was following the story quipped, "Thus are bestsellers made." It was a prescient remark. A week later, *Decent Interval* sprang onto *Time* magazine's bestseller list and several others.

— —

"Oh Lord, I reckon he's made everybody mad now." The morning after my *60 Minutes* appearance, my mother told the press that my nickname was "Trey" and that I'd always been trouble.

"If I just sat down and started worrying, I could worry about Trey all the time," she confessed as she brandished a cocktail tumbler at bemused reporters. "He's never backed down from a fight. His writing the book and taking the stand he has doesn't surprise me a bit."

"All of us are really outspoken," conceded my younger sister Fran in an outspoken interview of her own. "I guess Mike Wallace called it arrogance."

My father acknowledged to *The Charlotte Observer* that he hadn't yet bought a copy of *Decent Interval*. "I haven't been able to find fifteen dollars yet," he joked in his usual heavy-handed way.

But he added soberly, "I knew he was working on the book and I knew how he felt about the CIA. When he came back from Vietnam, he said they had pulled the rug out from under the people there who had helped them, and it was being covered up by the high brass."

"The book has become a moral issue with him," Fran confirmed. "He's worked on it night and day. He feels he has a personal commitment to these people who didn't get out. He said they were as far as the eye could see."

My mother expressed surprise at some things I'd said to Mike Wallace, particularly my criticism of William Colby.

"The funny damn thing is that Bill Colby was nearly Trey's godfather," she remarked jauntily. "When he was in law school, I thought he was fun. I suppose I would still like him."

"He and I were very close friends," my father acknowledged. "I haven't seen Colby in a long, long time."

The reporters wondered if I'd ever been careless with CIA secrets.

My father said no; even my ruminations about the evacuation had been circumspect.

"Trey was a very good agent," Fran snapped. "He never talked about the CIA or his work."

My mother recalled that I'd been so closemouthed with her that she'd never even understood why I'd joined the Agency. "He told me for my own protection he wouldn't tell me much about it. I learned to be a CIA mother a long time ago."

She sucked at her drink and added wanly, "He's a very strong patriot. This decision he made must have been a very dreadful one for him, because he believed in what he was doing over there."

— —

As my family tried to cover for me, the CIA moved beyond casual sniping to a considered campaign of retaliation. Up until Christmas, the Security staff provided daily screenings of the *60 Minutes* broadcast in the CIA's bubble-top auditorium in hopes of inflaming the faithful and coaxing some of them into volunteering dirt on me. Skip Dunn, meanwhile, launched a preliminary "damage assessment" to see if he could find enough secrets in my book to hang me. According to subsequently released CIA files, he came up cold.

Still, he and his Security staff knew they'd have to give Turner *something* or risk his ire. So in two separate memos, they conjured a case for deceit, claiming that I'd managed to sneak my book past them only by promising falsely that I'd submit it for clearance. "He consistently lied to Agency officials all through 1976–1977," they contended, adding that my minder, Bob Layton, had received nine such bogus promises himself.

Layton would later deny this under oath, and even the Security boys themselves let slip a contradiction, acknowledging in one of their memos that both Dunn and Greaney had concluded after meeting with "Subject" in late 1975 "that he would not submit the manuscript."

So why hadn't anybody taken steps to stop me?

To stave off that question, Dunn and his colleagues devoted considerable space in their memos to hyping my alleged virtues ("a recognized expert . . . brilliant . . . hard working") *and* my vices ("not a team player . . . not above bending the rules") so they could never be accused of having been outwitted by a nincompoop. By the time they were done, I'd been transformed into the perfect spy, so adept at subterfuge and dissembling that nobody could wonder why I'd slipped through their fingers. "Some of the very qualities which made him a strong performer for the Agency," they concluded, "can now be viewed as indicative of the problems Subject has caused."

Turner may not have recognized the irony implicit in this. But no matter. He now had what he needed to dignify his yearning for revenge: testimony from the Agency's own impeccable sources that I was a conniving cheat.

CHAPTER 12

Self-Inflicted Wounds

T HE EASE with which a director of Central Intelligence can sling mud and make it stick might have chastened some incumbents.

But not Turner.

Scarcely had his security people hung their Judas label on me before he was out shopping it to the public.

In an all-stations advisory beamed to CIA operatives around the world, he urged that I be portrayed to the international media as an insider turned thief who'd extorted privileged information through false promises. In an effort to shape opinion at home, he wrote an op-ed piece for *The Washington Post* that made "Answers to Inquiries" look like a valentine. Laying a major guilt trip on me, he insisted disingenuously that I'd given him an oral and written promise to surrender my manuscript and had never challenged the Agency's view of the rules, even though my letter to Morrison the previous summer had done just that. He also maintained that the Agency had never attempted to monitor my activities, as if the Johnsons, Daphne Miller, and Bob Layton had never existed.

Nor would he credit Security's ultimately benign assessment of what I'd written. While deriding "this case" as "not worthy of this much discussion," he judged my unsanctioned rush into print to be as potentially damaging as Daniel Ellsberg's leaking of the Pentagon Papers in 1971. "The logical extension of the Ellsberg-Snepp syndrome is that any of our 210 million citizens is entitled to decide what should and should not be classified information," he thundered, even though I'd scrupulously kept my text secret-free.

Incensed, Random House president Bob Bernstein dashed off a rebuttal, accusing Turner of trying to smear through innuendo and of ignoring such perennial leakers as Nixon and Kissinger, whose self-serving indiscretions, he declared, had made a mockery of official secrecy.

His analysis was deadly accurate. But when he submitted it to *The Washington Post* as an answer to Turner, the editors rejected it as a bid for free publicity.

Fearing that media indifference might expose me to something a bit more lethal than a poisonous op-ed piece—yes, I *was* thinking this way—I quickly issued a rejoinder of my own, advising the Associated Press that I'd never promised Turner *anything* concerning submission of my manuscript. A CIA spokesman responded evasively that the "promise" had been "oral not written." No one at the AP bothered to get back to me for clarification.

— —

As might have been expected, the ferocity of Turner's attacks emboldened his confederates to go after my own. Being within easy range, Carla took the first hits. Within days of the publication of *Decent Interval,* the chief of the CIA's clandestine division wrote a memo to Security questioning the propriety of her helping me. Security Chief Robert Gambino then sent a report to the inspector general pointing out that she'd admitted under polygraph examination the previous summer that she'd "proofread portions of Mr. Snepp's book" and "performed some research on his behalf in the CIA library." While conceding there was no proof she'd provided me classified information, he wondered pointedly if she might have made improper use of the library's staff or facilities. Immediately, the inspector general sent his own gumshoes rummaging through library files to find out. After an investigation surpassing anything ever done on the Vietnam evacuation, the inspector general reported back with a hint of exasperation, "She apparently conducted her library research for Mr. Snepp without assistance."

Though Carla herself was unaware of the specifics of this inquiry, she could feel the rising heat and knew there would be no quick end to it. Within days she decided to spare herself further grief by taking a one-year unpaid sabbatical from the Agency. Generous as always, she urged me not to blame myself and assured me that time and distance would surely make things better. But I knew, if she did not, that the chances of that were zero. I'd compromised her future as completely as I had my own, and in my obsession to redeem my own conscience, I'd exploited her love as heedlessly as I'd exploited Bernie's and abandoned Mai Ly those last terrible moments of the war.

Whatever was to happen to me, I began to believe I deserved.

— —

Meanwhile, the casualty list continued to grow. CIA Security opened investigations into the character and loyalties of other acquaintances, and the inspector general and his staff dusted off their files on Stockwell and perused the fine print for some clue to his relationship with me.

Though Stockwell wouldn't have been pleased with their conclusion—he was deemed a mere bit player in my excesses—he had more than enough to worry about already. With the Agency now in high dudgeon over alumni memoirs, he was finding it difficult to snag a publisher to replace Random House. Even worse, from his standpoint, my whirlwind dance through the media had upstaged him as the Agency's most visible critic.

It is one of the ironies of our complicated relationship, however, that Stockwell's bruised ego ultimately worked to my advantage, for in his determination not to be eclipsed, he began bragging to reporter Seymour Hersh that he'd had experiences equal to my own, that he, too, had "pressed for an early evacuation" and had later had his protests quashed back home. Self-serving though these remarks were, they convinced Hersh that my own story was believable, and soon he was cranking out article after article to support it.

In due course, his sympathetic coverage won me an improbable new constituency that I could never have attracted on my own. Despite my refusal to renounce the war or the Agency—how could I renounce what had been so much a part of my life?—many of Hersh's left-leaning admirers quickly concluded that anyone so high on his A-list couldn't be all bad, and began rallying round.

Among the most enthusiastic was Gloria Emerson, an icon of the political left, and normally an implacable foe of people like me. I'd first met the defiantly eccentric Ms. Emerson at a Saigon cocktail party in the early 1970s, when she'd been a correspondent for *The New York Times*. The virtual conscience of the local American press corps, she'd helped inflame antiwar sentiment back home with impassioned stories about the cruelty of combat and the perfidy of the American commitment and was about as popular with the embassy as a Viet Cong sapper squad. That first encounter, I'd cold-shouldered her, as was expected of those of my station, and she'd reciprocated, knowing me to be a "spook," like one of her apparently unlamented ex-suitors. Later, whenever I'd spotted her bustling around Saigon, I'd dutifully informed on her to my superiors.

But now, with such offenses fading into memory and her own perennial enemies baying for my blood, Gloria found little in me she couldn't rationalize or forgive.

The two of us, in fact, had long been far closer geographically than she realized, for the apartment she rented on New York's Upper West Side happened to be just down the block from Bernie's. Often in recent months, I'd seen Gloria sailing along the sidewalk, chin out, hair flying—but I'd never spoken, for I had my prejudices too.

But one morning, shortly after Hersh published one of his more helpful articles, I took a deep breath, scuttled up to her door, and knocked. "I'm the fellow who wrote the book," I said as she tore off the locks and peered out.

"Snepp looked like a man on the run, as if on the Upper West Side he might be seized," she later wrote. "Perhaps like any man who has changed sides in one way or another he needed to explain why, to be with someone who knew the dead language of the war. . . ."

Gloria and I would never see eye to eye politically. She was, if anything, more paranoid than I, always fearful that thugs in jackboots would come battering down our doors. Still, she seemed to understand my personal odyssey better than anyone, for she too had been to the manor born, and had turned her back on it. A descendant of the crankily conservative Ralph Waldo Emerson, Gloria knew instinctively what it cost to betray one's past.

Fascinated to find a fellow traveler in me, she asked if she could do a profile for *New York* magazine. The portrait she rendered several weeks later caught facets of my character I was too myopic or cowardly even to admit to myself.

"What Snepp wants to do," she told her readers, "is avenge the abandoned Vietnamese, to feel somehow he has earned their forgiveness."

As an operative's ex-lover, she could understand my abiding loyalty to the CIA and its own, even if she deplored it, and she could appreciate too, without condescension, my chronic mistrust. "Sometimes, walking in the neighborhood," she wrote, "Snepp stops dead until people close behind him have passed. He is calmer in New York, where paranoia is as common as a cough, than in Washington."

Nor was she deceived by the mask I wore any more than a practiced spy might have been. "Snepp has trained himself not to show he is a sentimental man," she remarked. "You have to hear him speak of some of the Vietnamese he knew to understand the fury and the sorrow he felt. When he does, some of the self-assurance, the silkiness of the CIA man, lifts to show a different Snepp, not the glib man on *60 Minutes*."

For all that she found sympathetic, though, Gloria the activist could never abide my choirboy faith in reform. "The most startling thing about Snepp—a complicated, combative, stubborn man—is his naïveté," she wrote, noting incredulously that I'd actually *expected* some act of repentance by the Agency once the truth came out.

She was also struck by how uncomfortable I was in the unaccustomed role of whistle-blower and speculated that I was half yearning to be punished for it by way of atoning.

In this, she may have been right. Martyrdom comes as naturally to a Southerner as a long morning's walk up Cemetery Ridge. Gloria was less confident than I, however, that the government would deny me such a purifying moment. "Snepp is still without a lawyer," she observed at the close of her article. "I asked why. His reply was defiant, the answer of a man still convinced that if the truth is told then the guilty will repent and reform. 'I don't have a lawyer because I haven't broken any laws,' he said."

— —

It is a token of how topsy-turvy my world had become, and how politically chaotic, that even as Gloria embraced me, so did her polar opposite, William F. Buckley. Immediately following publication of *Decent Interval,* he wrote a column extolling its virtues—"weighed against the scales of the Old Testament, the justification for this book is in its contents"—and time and again invited me to appear on his *Firing Line* TV show, even pairing me at one point with Nixon apologist Roy Cohn, whom he expected to despise me. Surprisingly, Cohn didn't. Both he and Buckley felt the fall of Vietnam could have been averted if their hero, Richard Nixon, hadn't been hounded from office, and to the extent that my book put Vietnam back in the headlines, they saw it as a chastening answer to the Woodward and Bernstein crowd.

To a certain extent, Buckley may also have been shamed into championing me. As an ex–CIA agent himself, he was under the same clearance obligations as I and yet had never been punished for ignoring them. He would later try to rationalize his privileged treatment by arguing that his many spy novels were merely "imagined," while my writings "arguably reveal CIA habits." But after some honest reflection, he was willing to allow that "abstractly" he might be the beneficiary of a double standard that spared the Agency's "friends."

— —

To Admiral Turner himself, the very breadth of the pro-Snepp lobby, stretching as it did from left to right, suggested the existence of a sinister cabal carefully designed and orchestrated to embarrass him and the

Agency. In one public statement, he even accused *60 Minutes* and *The New York Times* of being complicit in it.

He couldn't have been more mistaken, of course. Sy Hersh and Mike Wallace had practically trampled each other in an effort to score an exclusive, and the morning after the *60 Minutes* piece, the coverage I received had simply assumed a life of its own. NBC's *Today* show and ABC's *Good Morning America* had featured me in back-to-back appearances, and within hours, requests for interviews were pouring in from TV stations around the country.

In response to this demand, Random House hastily laid on a book tour for me in mid-December that would send me whizzing across the country over the next two weeks. It would turn out to be just long enough for one dazed, utterly exhausted ex-agent to do himself, if not the CIA, irreparable harm.

— —

The average, bleary-eyed, early-morning TV host who greeted me along the way hadn't read my book and couldn't have cared less about the tragedy it chronicled. What he or she wanted was a juicy secret or two to jolt viewers out of their precaffeine stupor. Finding me invariably tight-lipped on that score, "Bob" or "Jane" would then typically fall back on the "sexiest" part of my personal story: the "breaching" of my secrecy agreement.

"How could you betray your oath and your country this way?" I was asked repeatedly. Time and again, I pointed out that *Decent Interval* betrayed no legitimate obligation or national interest, only official hypocrisy. Since no one could accept that so little might provoke such a furor, I was usually repaid with a skeptical sneer.

Nor could I ever quite get across why an ex-spook might be morally exercised by anything the CIA did. "Why join such a corrupt organization?" huffed one barely pubescent anchorwoman, who clearly considered me culpable for having signed on in the first place. I reminded her that the Agency had once been bathed in glory, that the Church and Pike revelations had come well after my recruitment, and that secrecy often kept even the best-intentioned operatives from glimpsing the rot around them.

Honest though these protestations were, they dropped like stones into glimmering shallows.

"It seems to me," oozed one typical talk-show caller, "that Mr. Snepp's desire for making this story known rather coincides with his own personal enrichment."

Patiently, I explained then, and many times afterward, that profit had never been my motive, that I could have earned twice my book advance if

I'd stayed at Langley and collected my CIA salary these past twenty-one months. Such accountant's logic, however, didn't begin to persuade the countless millions who assumed that writing was as simple as falling off a log.

It didn't go down well, either, that I'd sidestepped the ordained guardians of the public weal. "Didn't it occur to you," scoffed one skeptic, "to go to the people we elect either to make public or keep secret different pieces of national security information?"

I explained then and many times that Congress had always been off limits, that in the fall of 1975 both the president and the CIA director had disallowed *any* contact with congressional investigators, and that under the CIA's interpretation of the rules, any unapproved disclosure to *anybody*, senator, congressman, or book editor, could land you in court.

Each time I ticked off this litany, you could almost hear listeners snoring off.

If any topic could be trusted to inspire boredom, though, it was our failure to do enough for abandoned Vietnamese. Whenever I threatened to stumble too far down this rocky path, there'd be a fast cut to a commercial break, followed by a segue into sports or weather, during which I'd be hustled off stage, always trailing the aura of a man near collapse. Which I was.

— —

During these weeks on the road, echoes of the Agency's Mighty Wurlitzer followed me everywhere. A syndicated editorial distributed by Hearst newspapers mechanically recycled Turner's claim that I'd hoodwinked him, and *The Arizona Republic* declared confidently: "There's no question but that Snepp broke" a pledge "never to divulge any classified information."

Nor did sympathy always play well, either. Writing in *The New Times Magazine*, Kevin Buckley and Jon Larsen, two old reporter friends from Saigon, remembered me fondly as "everybody's favorite CIA source" in "ever-present dark glasses and silk blue sport shirt open to the breastbone . . . never without his .45 and CIA bleeper, which he always concealed in a briefcase."

A *Washington Post* reporter, Tom Zito, not realizing this to be satire, promptly recast it in darker hues. "Snepp comes on like a nasty spook," he wrote in the *Post*'s "Style" section. "He wears a black-leather overcoat, tough-guy boots, and a Clint Eastwood face, and carries a slim little black attaché case and a bulging brown jiffy bag. Back in Saigon, acquaintances say, he used to push bar girls aside with his attaché case and carry a .45 in a brown paper bag. Now he will only say that his pain pills are in his case.

"Snepp tells a lot of stories with that I've-been-there-so-you-better-believe-it look," Zito advised his readers teasingly—and then proceeded to recount one with zealous embellishment. "I was in a bar in Saigon with a friend," he had me say, "and two Viet Cong guys came in and started shooting, and I flipped a whore over my shoulder and ran up into one of the rooms upstairs. They hit her in the leg, and there was blood streaming out of her, and she said to me, 'Your friend is still out there.' So I went out, and the two of us grabbed the rifles from the two guys and we just beat them to death."

My first reaction to such doctored snapshots was simple bemusement. I'd never owned a silk shirt or "tough-guy boots," never bullied bar girls or anyone else, and never, ever gloried in the violence of war. I couldn't imagine anyone taking such nonsense seriously.

But Bernie wasn't so sanguine. "I don't recognize the person coming across in these articles," she moaned to Gloria Emerson, who had her misgivings, too. Journalists like Zito had sat out the war and were feeling guilty about it, Gloria told me. So be careful about rubbing their noses in testosterone.

I considered her advice and tried to follow it in future interviews, muting the war stories or avoiding them altogether, no matter how often I was asked about them, and once, in a flush of indignation uncharacteristic of me, I even contacted my *New Times* pals, Kevin Buckley and Jon Larsen, to protest their satirical portrait of me.

Buckley offered to buy me a friendly dinner and reserved a table for us at a trendy Manhattan café called Elaine's.

The night of our friendly reckoning, an arctic wind was whipping snow flurries through Manhattan like volcanic ash, and in deference to the weather, I'd draped myself in the black leather trenchcoat that had so offended Zito.

Bad choice. On arriving at Elaine's, I inadvertently snagged part of this cast-iron vestment in the cab door, and before I could disentangle, the driver pulled off, dragging me over ice-pebbled asphalt for several feet. By the time I'd freed myself and stumbled into the bar, I looked like agent 007 himself after Goldfinger's worst depredations. A ripple of applause went up, and praises were tendered all around for my "imaginative" entrance, so in keeping with *the* persona.

— —

The bruising I suffered that night was nothing, however, compared to the injuries I inflicted on myself as my publicity tour drew to a close. Oh, I tried to avoid imprudent candor, as Gloria had counseled. But in striving to put a patina of reason on what had essentially been an emotional act, I often wound up sounding (unforgivably) like a lawyer—and an ill-informed one at that, since the Agency had yet to give me a copy of any secrecy agreement but my first one. Thus, when asked as I always was whether I'd breached a contract with the CIA, I was usually reduced to arguing tortuously that while yes, I might be seen to have broken my original agreement by not submitting to clearance, the Agency had broken it too, by not allowing me to air my grievances as it was required to do.

This mind-bender not only trivialized my actions but defied compression into a ten-second sound bite, so that all too often I seemed to be admitting guilt, as when I conceded on the *Tomorrow* show: "I did violate my secrecy agreement in the sense of not turning my manuscript into the Agency for clearance."

I also wounded myself grievously by attempting to deal charitably, like the genteel Southerner I was, with Turner's claim that I'd promised him my manuscript. On far too many occasions, I resisted the temptation to call the good admiral a liar and simply allowed that if he was indeed so convinced that he'd have my manuscript, then apparently I'd misled him or he'd misled himself. In soft-pedaling his dishonesty, I strengthened the impression that I was guilty of the same or worse.

On top of all this, exhaustion often led me into disastrously garbled exchanges, as when *Today* show host Tom Brokaw declared imperiously, "When you met with Stansfield Turner, you deliberately misled him about your plans to publish this book." Having missed the word "deliberately," I responded, "That's right."

No interview was so devastating, however, as one I staggered through in Los Angeles at the end of my book tour. Invoking my original secrecy agreement, TV newsman Jess Marlow asked if I'd broken it by *blowing secrets*. Practically somnambulent, I answered, "I surely have"—then realizing my error, I tried to backtrack: "as a matter of fact, I published the book without any Agency clearance whatsoever because I felt the Agency had to learn from its mistakes."

Scenting blood, Marlow continued: "You made an additional agreement in promising Director Turner last May that you'd submit the manuscript of your book to him." This time I lapsed into near-incoherence. "Yes, I did," I started, then corrected confusedly: "I did *not* because I had to outflank Admiral Turner. He was moving in on me. In fact, he ordered FBI surveillance, so I turned the Agency's tactics against them and really fooled them into believing I was doing nothing at all."

Nonsense. I knew, and had said many times before, that I hadn't "fooled" the Agency, "blown" secrets, or pledged Turner anything except that I wouldn't betray classified information. But now, reeling under the stress of five and a half years of war plus twenty months of nonstop writing, I stumbled—badly.

Luckily, Los Angeles was the end of the line. But the many bomblets I'd left scattered in my wake were quickly gathered up by CIA officials and preserved for future use in court.

— —

If my own intemperance set me up for the fall, however, it was Congress that snatched away the safety net.

The morning after my *60 Minutes* interview, the Senate Intelligence Committee began badgering Langley for information about me, and I began badgering the committee's staff director for an opportunity to testify. For days, he stalled. In the meantime, Turner gained a critical march. He advised House and Senate overseers in two secret sessions that I'd "exposed" classified information to the "risk of disclosure" and had tricked him into calling off legal action by lying about my intentions. "I feel I have been 'had' by Mr. Snepp," he told the Senate group. "I put my confidence and trust in his word, and he violated it as well as his oath."

On December 6, in the wake of these briefings, *The Washington Star* reported that neither watchdog group intended to investigate the evacuation, since it was now viewed as an "administrative" problem rather than an "intelligence" one. If there was to be any inquiry at all, it would be limited to my allegations of CIA misconduct.

Two days later, in a speech at Yale, Turner attempted to trivialize those allegations. "I haven't read Snepp's book," he told his student audience, "but it's about a piece of history that I'm not finding terribly relevant, and Mr. Snepp is not qualified to tell it."

Given such advance notices, it's small wonder that when I finally did get in to see staffers of the Senate panel on December 12, I was accorded a leper's welcome.

For the next two days I struggled to recoup, assuring them I was not out to expose the Agency's secrets and that I'd misled Turner only by omission, by refusing to respond to trickily worded letters his lawyers had sent me *after* I'd declined to sign an affidavit that would have pledged him my manuscript.

Some of the listeners nodded sympathetically. But most seemed convinced that I should have done Turner the favor of giving him the rope to hang me. Few expressed any concern about the evacuation. And when I happened to mention that Graham Martin had slipped into retirement with hordes of classified documents in his possession, all I got back was a collective yawn.

Finally, on December 14, came the actual shoot-out, a closed session with the full Senate committee itself.

I realized I was doomed the moment I saw who was to preside. Substituting for committee chair Daniel Inouye, who as a Hawaiian of Asian descent might have been sensitive to the issues I'd raised, was a man of excruciating neutrality, Adlai Stevenson III.

Alone at the witness table, I led with the only defense I knew, explaining that I'd written my book as a substitute for the after-action report the CIA didn't want, to force the Agency to acknowledge our debt to the abandoned.

As for my alleged transgressions, I denied having knowingly or deliberately broken any law, but pledged to stay put and submit to the judgment of the courts if it came to that. In any event, I concluded, "I do not really care what happens to me now. I have done what I thought was right, and as honorably as I could, given the circumstances and the moral ambiguity of the espionage business."

My presentation drew not a flutter of applause, and afterward, for nearly two hours, I was subjected to a torrent of personal abuse that utterly obscured the issues I'd brought to public attention. One distinguished conservative impugned my patriotism. Another, Senator John Morgan of North Carolina, found me "dishonorable" for breaking my "oath." And several of his colleagues, forgetting that this committee hadn't even existed in 1975, were indignant that I hadn't come to them first, before going to Random House.

Browbeaten and bloodied, I finally demanded in exasperation whether anyone there had even read my book.

Dead silence greeted me. Dead, dead silence.

Within a week, *The Washington Post* reported that "there was little inclination on the part of the senators to pursue a full investigation" of *anything* I'd said, even though "the questioning of Snepp by the committee was often sharp." Explaining this reticence, an anonymous source told *The Washington Post:* "We don't want to fight the Vietnam war all over again." Besides, the source added, there wasn't much in *Decent Interval* "that could be construed to violate the CIA's sources and methods," as if that somehow disqualified it for serious consideration.

— —

If you're born and bred in the chivalric tradition of the mythic South, you do not take easily to being called a traitor. Though I realized the senators had been too well coached by the Agency to be able to come to their own conclusions, my shock, pain, and rage were not assuaged. Something died in me at that hearing, perhaps the "naïveté" Gloria Emerson had perceived, and healthy though this humbling may have been, it made me realize for the first time that I might never be able to help anyone we'd betrayed.

Immediately after the hearing, I booked myself a flight home, believing there might be some solace in the unquestioning acceptance I could expect from my father and the brother and sister still living in North Carolina. And maybe I'd see my mother, too. Sure, my mother. We could share a few drinks and talk about the virtues of soldiering on alone.

But as soon as I landed, all hope of succor fled. A TV reporter sought me out and asked me to comment on the way Congress had treated me. In a splenetic rush, I found myself remembering how North Carolina's own Senator Morgan had questioned my loyalty, and without thinking, I looked into the camera and said, "You know, that Morgan—he called me a traitor and he hadn't even read what I'd written. What kind of man is that? Maybe a know-nothing who doesn't read at all."

It was a juvenile remark, and when I arrived at my father's home, I found him livid. In case I didn't know, he snapped, Morgan had the power to nominate candidates for the federal bench and had offered to support my father for such a posting. But now that I had opened my big mouth, now that I'd put my own ego ahead of everything else, what incentive could Morgan have to see the nomination through?

That night, I flew back to Washington with emotional lacerations that would never heal. Nor would the hurt I'd done my father. Within weeks, Morgan indeed turned his back on him, leaving him to languish forever at a stall point in his judicial career.

When a reporter later asked me how my father was coping with the knowledge that his son was in trouble with the CIA, I replied, "I don't know. I now do him the favor of staying out of North Carolina."

— —

Once Congress abdicated its responsibility to investigate my charges, Turner faced no obstacle to exacting vengeance. But to make doubly sure he could proceed with impunity, he appointed an Agency task force to scour the terrain for land mines.

Needless to say, the group was never supposed to be fair or objective. The chairman's slot went to a Polgar supporter; two other members came from Turner's public relations staff; and a fourth was drawn from the liaison unit that had been attempting to discredit me on Capitol Hill. Representing the analytical division was Bill Christison, the bureaucrat who'd helped Colby slip secrets to the Kalbs nearly two years before.

Among the topics slated for inquiry, there was no mention of the evacuation. But up top was Turner's own pet concern. He wanted to determine once and for all if I'd tried to air my complaints about the evacuation with the CIA's inspector general. If that could be disproven, *Decent Interval* would be shorn of all moral justification.

Among the first witnesses summoned was Norm Jones, the investigator who'd interviewed me for the inspector general's office back in 1975. As it turned out, hard as he tried, he couldn't be certain that I *hadn't* asked for a postmortem on the evacuation. Disappointed, the task force turned to a half dozen others who could be trusted to be more helpful, including Polgar himself.

Fearing a fix, I sent a letter to the Agency offering to testify. No one even bothered to reply.

In the end, the panel gave Turner exactly what he wanted. While acknowledging that I'd met with Jones, it concluded that, since he had set up the interview himself, I was "in error" in claiming that I'd brought my concerns to the inspector general. Based on this nitpick, I was judged to be a liar.

— —

By the time the task force completed its work, Agency security experts had again scoured *Decent Interval* for secrets and again had found it benign. In early February, Turner confirmed this publicly. "Even Snepp was circumspect in writing his book, as far as I can see," he told *Newsweek,* thus contradicting the dire warnings he'd peddled earlier in his *Washington Post* op-ed article. He also admitted that *none* of the criticism leveled by anyone at the Agency in recent months had scared off any foreign intelligence sources. "I have zero evidence," he said, "that it has resulted in a degradation in the quality or quantity of information we get from them."

Turner's inability to hang a security breach on me made the findings of the task force all the more important. For if he couldn't portray me as indiscreet, he would need some other rationale for a lawsuit. By bolstering the impression that I'd cheated my way into print, the task force strengthened his hand with Justice Department officials who would finally decide whether the game was worth the candle.

PART III

TRIALS

CHAPTER 13

Suit and Subterfuge

S HORTLY BEFORE NOON on February 14, the *Washington Post* reporter Larry Stern placed a frantic call to me from his office off the city
room. "Have you heard?" he croaked between smoker's coughs. "Bell says
they're going to sue!"

The news had just been phoned in by a reporter covering an American
Bar Association conference in New Orleans. A few minutes earlier, Attorney General Griffin Bell had casually let drop that the government would
seek a gag order against me *and* a fine for alleged, unspecified injury inflicted by *Decent Interval.* The suit would be civil, not criminal, based on a
contractual interpretation of my original secrecy agreement. Since Bell
hadn't mentioned any compromised secrets, Stern inferred that something
"imaginative" was in the works, maybe the first legal test ever of the CIA's
presumed right to clear *anything* an ex-employee might commit to public
screed.

As I hung up, I felt dizzy. I hadn't expected Turner to be able to pull it
off, or at least not this way. Oh sure, I'd had my nightmares: trumped-up
claims that I'd divulged secrets in *Decent Interval.* But I'd always been confident that if the government sued me for a security breach, as it had Victor Marchetti, I could answer easily by demonstrating that the secrets in
question had been compromised already. I'd been the Agency's principal
press briefer in Vietnam. I knew as well as anyone what had been kept se-

cret and what hadn't. But to be prosecuted for publishing *anything*—that blew me away.

— —

The Director of Central Intelligence cannot, unilaterally, sue anybody on the Agency's behalf. All he can do is plead for the attorney general to act for him. That's what Turner had done. According to the Agency's own records, he'd twice, in recent weeks, fired off "strongly worded" letters to Bell demanding that I be punished for my unapproved revelations. His main concern, as he put it to the Senate Intelligence Committee, was "the long-term effect such disclosures can have on our national intelligence efforts.

"Agents simply will not be recruited to an intelligence source that appears to be an information sieve," he argued.

Anybody who'd read Turner's recent *Newsweek* interview might have been surprised at these alarms. Hadn't he pooh-poohed the impact of any recent anti-CIA disclosures? What had changed his mind?

Short answer: panic. Only two months had passed since that orgy of pink slips known as the Halloween massacre, and the Agency was now thoroughly "demoralized," as Hank Knoche conceded publicly. Anyone who came marching into this mess trumpeting defiance and thumbing his nose at authority was about as welcome as a freak spark in a gunpowder factory.

For Turner, moreover, the tensions between us had become intensely personal. Not only did he feel "had by Mr. Snepp"; on an existential level he'd somehow come to identify me with the youthful upstarts who'd outraged his entire conservative generation. "My blood boils at the obvious callousness and selfishness of such persons," he told the Senate Intelligence Committee one morning, after likening me to Dan Ellsberg. "Rather than being the patriotic heroes as some are wont to believe, these individuals are self-serving charlatans in quest of fame or fortune."

Though many of Turner's senior deputies shared these sentiments, not all of them saw me as the ideal stand-in for a ritual hanging. One associate general counsel argued that if Turner wanted a test case, he could surely find someone who better fit the bill, someone who'd betrayed secrets. Even my old enemy, Ted Shackley, seemed ambivalent. By late winter, he'd been ousted from the clandestine service and reassigned to a do-nothing interagency job as a belated consequence of the Halloween massacre, and he had no incentive to support the hated Turner in *anything.*

Still, whatever objections he or anyone else may have offered were quickly lost to the pure, practical logic of revenge. Polgar and others were already muttering about suing me for libel, and Turner realized that if that happened, the whole ugly story of the CIA's final days in Vietnam might be replayed in open court with all of the aggrieved spewing secrets from the witness stand. Better to let the Justice Department fashion a reckoning more compatible with the Agency's interests.

CIA general counsel Tony Lapham cast the decisive vote. He did not realize, as he would later testify, that my offense was the norm, not the exception at Langley, and that many other unauthorized CIA memoirists had been allowed to slip into print with impunity. As he saw it, I'd committed a singularly impertinent act worthy of the most singular punishment. "Snepp took his secrecy agreement and said, 'Here, stick it in your ear'!" he snarled when asked on one occasion why he wanted me skinned alive.

— —

No one would ever have accused Griffin Bell of harboring such a bloodlust or of being a toady of Lapham or Turner. But in making up his mind to sue me, he drew much of his inspiration from them. For one thing, he bought entirely into the admiral's demon image of me, describing me contemptuously, in his memoirs years later, as a "phony" and as a "critic of the government who simply broke a contract and then tried to wrap himself in the flag of the Constitution." Even more excessively, he accepted Turner's contention that the dikes of official secrecy would soon burst if an example weren't made of me. "Several hundred other agents recently had been discharged in a purge of the CIA's clandestine service," he wrote. "If Snepp were allowed to flout the secrecy provisions, other ex-agents were likely to follow his lead, and agency secrets could be compromised."

Beyond all this, Bell had a controversial espionage case in the works that virtually dictated his prosecuting me. The previous summer, the FBI had discovered that a Vietnamese expatriate named David Truong had been passing U.S. secrets to the postwar regime in Hanoi with the help of an accomplice, Donald Humphrey, who worked for the U.S. Information Agency. Humphrey had been drawn into the caper because his Vietnamese wife had been abandoned in the evacuation, and he'd hoped to buy her out by peddling secrets to Hanoi.

Both men had been under surveillance for months. But to cinch the case against them Bell needed to have a CIA double agent, a Vietnamese woman, testify against them in open court.

Turner and his colleagues balked, believing rightly that the agent, once identified, would be useless. But Bell managed to sweeten the pill by offering them what they wanted almost as much as the agent's anonymity—me.

No, there was never any formal agreement sealing the deal. But there didn't have to be. By dragging me into court as Turner wanted, Bell could demonstrate in the most dramatic way possible that the law needn't always inconvenience the CIA.

The message got through. Immediately after the suit against me was announced, the CIA agreed to let its double agent testify against Truong and Humphrey.

— —

"We never gave the Snepp thing much thought," a deputy of Bell's once told reporters. "We just knew we had to sue."

In fact it wasn't *ever* that simple. Initially, Turner demanded a scorched-earth strategy, the confiscation of all copies of *Decent Interval* and the prosecution of both Random House and *60 Minutes* for their role in bringing my unapproved story to the public. Justice officials said no, for fear of offending the media and First Amendment purists. But even after the proposed suit was narrowed to focus on me alone, the chief of the Civil Division, Barbara Babcock, dug in her heels. As an avowed liberal who'd come to the Justice Department from Stanford Law School, she warned of a massive backlash from the press.

"I virtually had to order the Justice Department's Civil Division to file the suit," Bell later recalled. "I told them that the suit concerned breach of contract and had nothing to do with the First Amendment or censorship. If Snepp did not want to work for an employer who required him to obtain clearance for what he wrote about his employment, he didn't have to take the job. There's no longer involuntarily servitude in this country."

In the bowels of the Civil Division, the two staff attorneys assigned to litigate my case were decidedly more enthusiastic about it than Babcock. Sally Whitaker and Brook Hedge had been bird-dogging me since the previous summer, and having been outmaneuvered at that time, they were delighted to have another shot. In addition, both saw the case as the chance of a lifetime. Everybody was watching: the president, the attorney general, Congress. Careers would be made, and it was time—oh yes, it *was* time. For too long, women had labored in the shadows of their male colleagues in the Justice Department's hidebound bureaucracy. A sure win against Snepp could help change that.

— —

Though many aspects of the prospective case would daunt and harry the two government attorneys in the weeks ahead, one built-in problem posed an immediate challenge to them. Ever since Colby's unchastened indiscretion the previous summer—his slipping his unapproved memoir to Simon and Schuster without sanction—an air of discrimination had hung over the government's expanding brief against me. Why forgiveness for one sinner and not the other? Why had Colby been allowed to get away with what I was to be pilloried for? The CIA and Justice Department had tried to finesse the issue by keeping Colby's transgression secret. But in mid-December, as Hedge and Whitaker began mulling over ways to finish me off, the specter of selective justice came back to haunt with a vengeance.

Improbably, the force behind the reckoning was none other than former ambassador Graham Martin.

Though months would pass before I'd learn the story myself, the trouble apparently began with my *60 Minutes* interview. When Martin learned of it he was apoplectic, and immediately resolved not to suffer in silence. A week before Christmas, he packed out of the country house in Italy where he'd been vacationing and flew home to answer me.

Touching down in Washington, he went immediately to his daughter's apartment to pick up a footlocker he'd stashed there. Inside: the treasure trove of top-secret documents he'd stolen from the State Department—and which he now intended to use in selective leaks against me. "I thought the historians might be able to do a better job of telling the story than has been done so far," he would later explain.

On the morning of December 22, he packed the footlocker in the back of his daughter's car and drove south to his family home in Winston-Salem, North Carolina. Arriving late that evening, and too weary to unpack, he left the footlocker in the car, and, inadvertently, the key in the ignition. Sometime before dawn, a gang of young car thieves made off with the whole shebang.

Two weeks later, shortly after New Year's, two high school girls happened on a curious stack of papers just off Summit Road in suburban Winston-Salem. Splashed across each page was the label "Top Secret" or "Secret," and tucked in amongst the documents was an envelope with Martin's name and address. The mother of one girl alerted Deputy Sheriff Ed Gaylor, who in turn summoned the FBI.

Within hours, federal agents were swarming all over Graham Martin. Under questioning, he conceded the documents had been stolen from him, but swore there were no more. A few days later, a high school student guided FBI agents to an abandoned shack where the rest of Martin's booty had been dumped, hundreds of super-secret papers tracing the history of the Vietnam War from 1963 to the pullout.

Months before, on retiring from the State Department, Martin had signed a secrecy "oath" pledging to surrender or dispose of responsibly all classified material in his possession, on pain of ten years in prison and a ten-thousand-dollar fine. Clearly, he'd violated that promise and deserved punishment. But suddenly, the Justice Department officials who were so anxious to hang me found themselves paralyzed. "The man has lung cancer," one of them rationalized months later. "Nobody wants to give him any more grief." An FBI agent offered a more cynical view: "Martin is part of a network that has run U.S. foreign policy for thirty years. If they go after him, he can turn up a lot of skeletons."

Ultimately, such considerations saved Martin, prompting the government not to prosecute. But that didn't end the Justice Department's own quandary, for how could it make the public understand that one transgressor deserved such dispensation while the other did not? Rather than test the public's tolerance for such inequity, those who were determined to pursue the case against me decided simply to bury the one against Martin. By mid-February, a protective smokescreen had been laid down from Washington to Winston-Salem. As Deputy Sheriff Gaylor confessed much later, "The FBI guy I talked to asked me not to put anything about the secret documents in my report and to keep quiet about it." Even the car thieves, once arrested, were enlisted in the cover-up. Recalled one FBI investigator: "When Washington found out about the papers, they went crazy. They promised those kids immunity if they turned them all in and didn't say anything to the press."

As for Martin himself, he was allowed quietly to "volunteer" his documents to the LBJ Library in Texas and thus to escape exposure. The fix was laid in just a day before Griffin Bell announced I was to be sued.

— —

If the government thus preserved the seeming "impartiality" of its case against me, Hedge and Whitaker did pay a price. From now on, no matter how tempting it might be for them to up the ante and accuse me of leaking secrets, they couldn't do it. For under the rules of legal procedure, any such expansion of the charges would immediately give me pretext to ask questions and probe in directions that could lead me straight to Martin's footlocker and Colby's clearance dodge. Not about to risk that, Hedge and Whitaker had to keep the secrets issue in cold storage.

And yet, without it, did they have a case? Would any judge agree to gag and impoverish me for publishing *non*secrets?

In late January, they began noodling with a CIA lawyer named Ernest Mayerfeld. According to one insider, they labored "for three weeks to get Snepp" and finally hit on two formulas—one to reduce me to penury, the other to silence.

— —

Penury: In medieval England, under common law, if a serf was caught stealing from the manor house and making money from a fence, all his "ill-gotten gains" were automatically forfeit to his master as compensation for a "breach of trust." Today, this precedent is preserved in a body of American law that makes it illegal for an employee of one company to sell its trade secrets to another. Anyone who commits such a transgression can be stripped of his "ill-gotten gains" without a jury trial or even proof of injury to anyone. All the wronged employer has to do is convince a judge that the miscreant broke a "fiduciary" duty, an implicit contract of loyalty.

Proceeding from the assumption that my book profits amounted to ill-gotten gains, Hedge and Whitaker followed this thread back to relevant case law and found that it fit their needs perfectly. Without having to prove injury or endure a jury trial, they could reduce the serf to penniless contrition.

Attractive though this option was, however, there was a hitch. Nowhere was it established in American law that you could be held liable for a breach of trust simply for disclosing nonconfidential information about your employer. Without raising the secrecy issue, could Hedge and Whitaker hope to dun me?

Ultimately, they decided to gamble. In the Complaint they drew up, they charged me with violating a trust simply by virtue of having published without clearance. For added insurance, they also claimed that I'd broken a contract, my original secrecy agreement, and demanded not merely my "ill-gotten gains" but compensatory damages and "such other relief as this court may deem just and proper." To help the court along, they portrayed me as the sort of deceitful bastard who deserved a huge punitive fine for his mischief. "Defendant Snepp repeatedly expressed his intention to abide by the terms of the agreement," they declared. "The Agency relied on these representations to its detriment and to the defendant's unjust enrichment."

— —

Muzzle: For Hedge and Whitaker, the relevent precedents were not very promising. In 1971, the United States Supreme Court had refused to bar the press from publishing the top-secret Pentagon Papers—had refused to impose a "muzzle"—because the government hadn't been able to demonstrate a sufficient threat to the national security. A year later, in the Marchetti case, a federal judge had agreed to gag the defendant only because the CIA could prove that he'd already violated his CIA secrecy agreement by leaking secrets.

If I hadn't imperiled the nation or leaked secrets, how could any of this be made to work against me?

It was Turner who gave Hedge and Whitaker their cue. He'd been grumbling for weeks that my refusal to submit to censorship, and my public gloating about it, had created the *appearance* of a breakdown in security that could discourage friendly foreign intelligence agencies from cooperating with us. It was a muzzy charge and contrary to his recent *Newsweek* interview. But Hedge and Whitaker figured it could be made to sound convincing to any judge who knew nothing about the intelligence business. So they cribbed it and included it in their Complaint against me.

"The United States," they intoned, "has been damaged inter alia by the undermining of trust and confidence in the Agency, thereby hampering the ability of the Agency and the director of Central Intelligence to perform their statutory duties."

To punish this grievous sin, they demanded that I be gagged and forced to submit to CIA censorship for life.

Not since the McCarthyite fifties had the government offered so little to justify such an assault on a citizen's right to free speech. Nowhere in the Complaint was there any hint of a security breach, concrete damage, or impending peril. The government was seeking to silence me and break me financially for having published unclassified criticism of a federal agency.

CHAPTER 14

Enter the Defense

WHEN I TOLD BERNIE of the impending lawsuit, visions of a summary lynching came swarming out of some dark place in her imagination. That afternoon, she caught a flight to Washington and proceeded to hover like a guardian angel. Meanwhile, I began casting about for what I needed even more than her solicitude just now: a lawyer.

Weeks before, at the prodding of a very agitated Gloria Emerson, I'd contacted the *New York Times* columnist Anthony Lewis to inquire about candidates. He'd urged me to consider a "big gun," like Edward Bennett Williams or Mitchell Rogovin, on the chance that a monster lawsuit might be lying in wait. I'd procrastinated, believing the monster to be ephemeral and the protection to be prohibitively expensive. Only about four thousand dollars remained out of my advance, and though I was to receive my first royalties within the next six to eight months, nobody could predict what they'd be. Since a lawyer's meter runs continuously, I figured I'd better wait.

It was Random House's Bob Bernstein who finally jolted me into a proper panic. Only days before Bell's announcement, he arranged for me to meet Alan Dershowitz, the flamboyant constitutional scholar from Harvard.

Even at this early stage in his career, the bespectacled Brillo-haired Dershowitz enjoyed wide renown as an advocate of the controversial, having defended the likes of *Deep Throat*'s Harry Reems (against obscenity charges) and errant heiress Patricia Hearst. Bernstein hoped he'd be impressed with me. He wasn't.

"I was surprised at Frank Snepp's appearance," he recalled. "He looked like a model for a CIA recruitment poster: quietly handsome in a West Point sort of way, polite almost to a fault (he even called *me* 'sir'), fiercely loyal to his country, and discreetly careful not to reveal too much. . . . Indeed his book, *Decent Interval,* was like its author in several ways: graceful; low-keyed; brimming with information; cautious in its revelations—and on the whole, a bit boring."

Despite the lack of personal empathy, Dershowitz was fascinated by the looming case against me, and for nearly an hour he stormed around Bernstein's office, pelting us with inspiration. What I needed, he concluded, was a combination of big guns and straight shooters: a Williams or Rogovin backed by First Amendment purists from the American Civil Liberties Union.

Back in Washington later that day, I ran all this by journalist Larry Stern. He grunted approvingly and offered a name: Mark Lynch, a young ACLU attorney. Again I hesitated. To the Southern conservative I still was, the ACLU glowed pure pink, a bunch of lefty goody-goodies who'd skewer the nation on a bent flagpole. Besides, hadn't they lost the Marchetti case?

"You need help fast!" shrieked Bernie when I broached my reservations. "Okay," I murmured, fearing her ire even more than the CIA's. But maybe Williams and Rogovin weren't ideal big guns. Both had been a little too cozy with the Agency for my tastes, Williams as Richard Helms's attorney in the recent perjury proceedings, Rogovin as counsel to Colby during the Church-Pike investigations. Could either be trusted to defend me?

Having been too long in the CIA to know how or where to find a good lawyer, I decided the best choice was the obvious one. That night I called Dershowitz. Generously, he agreed to serve as my "personal" counsel, without pay, provided the ACLU handled the drudge work. I groaned but figured the fates had spoken. A few minutes later, I dialed up Mark Lynch.

As it turned out, the ACLU was fairly itching to represent me. Its legal staff was still smarting from the bruising it had suffered in *Marchetti,* and saw my case as an opportunity to even scores.

Brusque on the phone, Lynch could not commit to me definitively. That decision was up to his national directors. But he was optimistic. I then told him about Dershowitz and detected a hesitation. Mark did not seem to relish the idea of having to share the initiative with anyone. Even so, he agreed to accompany me to Boston to confer with the potential competition.

The urgency of shoring up my legal defenses was underscored the following morning when Bell announced the suit against me. Next day, the Complaint was filed in the Alexandria federal court, and twenty-four hours later, a sheriff's deputy showed up on my doorstep to serve me with it. He couldn't have been more terrifying if he'd had swastikas on his epaulets. For once, Bernie, who was in residence, couldn't utter a word.

A few hours later, still badly shaken myself, I appeared on a local TV show to share first impressions with Marchetti's coauthor, John Marks. A former Foreign Service officer with the scrambled locks and mien of a sandlot evangelist, Marks railed against the double standard that invariably punished critics of the CIA for "blowing secrets" while allowing more favored leakers to walk free.

Listening, I experienced the sudden panic of a man who's blundered into the wrong cocktail party. Not only had I blown *no* secrets (a point I delicately emphasized); to my insufferably self-righteous eye, Marks seemed a poor claimant to the moral high ground. In the Marchetti case, I recalled (but did not say), he'd tried to dodge the bullet by arguing that as a State Department alumnus, he could not be held to his coauthor's CIA contract. He'd then promised to leak no more, only to do just that. Hauled back into court, he'd "taken the Fifth" to avoid being cited for contempt. Was this anyone with whom to make common cause? Later, walking out of the studio, I realized with blinding clarity that I'd turned my back on the only fraternity where I'd ever truly felt at home.

— —

On the morning of the trip to Boston, I found Mark Lynch lounging near the Eastern Air Lines counter at Washington National, his gangly frame and rumpled suit only half-hidden by a waist-length down jacket. The eyeglasses, broken and taped with adhesive, listed precariously on a sharp, uncompromising nose, and the sandy hair shot helter-skelter as if teased with electric shock. Surveying him across the lobby, I suffered a spasm of despair. My God, is *this* my defender?

During the flight, our conversation faltered, as it often would when we were alone together, for I would never find it easy to banter with Mark. Indeed, from the instant we first spoke, there seemed to be an odd rivalry between us, not because I could match him intellectually—far from it—but because we had so much in common, from volatile tempers to unyielding views on Vietnam to youthful self-righteousness. Ours was truly a match made by a mischievous god.

A "Yalie" with a meticulously cultivated blue-collar air, Mark had once considered going into the ministry, his model being fellow Yale alumnus William Sloan Coffin, who'd given up a budding CIA career to become a social evangelist. But for all the allure of a life in the pulpit, Mark had quickly veered off in a different direction. Like many of the rest of us, he'd been taken with Jack Kennedy's vision of a world under America's moral sway, and in 1966 had hied himself off to Vietnam, not as a Special Forces officer as he'd originally intended, but as a field hand for a private relief group. He'd learned Vietnamese, "worked with the people," and had soon realized, by his own account, that the war was being lost.

In 1970, my second year in Vietnam, he'd headed home to help activists like Coffin agitate against people like me. But now, as a seasoned eyewitness, he'd communed poorly with those whose indignation came secondhand, and soon he was back in Vietnam as a stringer for *Newsweek*. Quickly dispirited, he'd returned home again in 1972, to Georgetown Law School, and a year later had been corralled by consumer advocate Ralph Nader to help nudge amendments to the Freedom of Information Act through Congress. It was Mark's first major brush with First Amendment law. The magic would never wear off.

Through Nader he met John Shattuck of the American Civil Liberties Union and Morton Halperin, a former Pentagon official who now headed the liberal Center for National Security Studies. The two of them, mightily impressed with Mark's legal skills, soon invited him to join their "Project on National Security," a scrupulously respectable anti-CIA lobby.

For his initial assignment, Mark was enlisted in a grand crusade: to help Halperin pursue an ambitious lawsuit against the ultimate "warmonger," Henry Kissinger. Years before, as a member of Kissinger's White House staff, Halperin had so spited his boss—finally resigning in protest over the invasion of Cambodia—that he'd wound up being surveilled illicitly, with a tap on his phone. The lawsuit was his way of repaying the insult.

As our plane landed in Boston, I still felt uneasy about my new advocate. In my heart, I knew that Mark was not the sort I would ever have associated with during my CIA days, except perhaps to gather intelligence on his friends in the antiwar movement.

— —

Alan Dershowitz's cubbyhole of an office at Harvard Law School was draped with publicity posters for off-color movies and dance-hall revues he'd defended against Boston's censors. When Mark and I walked in, the champion was poring over briefs and humming like a high-voltage transformer. Seated across from him was a gnomish, moon-faced man who I was surprised to learn was none other than Halperin. Like Dershowitz, he saw the case against me as a dangerous new bid to expand official secrecy and had agreed to help me.

As Mark and these two good Samaritans began kibitzing, I realized how far out of their league I was. Terms like "discovery" (the pretrial hunt for evidence) and "interrogatory" (a written query to be answered under oath) zinged past me without sparking a tic of recognition. Equally baffling was one of the charges against me: "breach of fiduciary obligation." Mark helpfully explained what it meant ("like cheating on your wife"), and marveled at the government's audacity in introducing it. If merely working for the government made me a fiduciary—and merely writing without permission made me a sinner—then anyone who worked for the government and wrote unsanctioned would be a sinner too. In Mark's view, the Justice Department had opened the door to censorship throughout the government.

Yet, however ominous this seemed, he felt it might help us politically by causing the press and public to take notice. The Marchetti case had all but been ignored outside the intelligence community because of its seeming irrelevance to anyone but former spooks. By nailing me to the cross of "fiduciary trust," the government had given *Snepp* far broader implications, and far greater "fright potential."

More immediately significant, he and my other counsels agreed, was the government's failure so far to allege that I'd published secrets. Knowing nothing of Martin's footlocker or Colby's easy way with the censors, we couldn't figure why the prosecutors had handicapped themselves this way. But whatever their reasons, they'd indeed made their own job harder. For one thing, there was no precedent for arguing that a fiduciary's obligation extended to protecting *non*secrets.

Nor did my "contractual" obligations seem to stretch that far either. In the Marchetti case, the appeals court had declared: "the First Amendment limits the extent to which the United States, contractually or otherwise, may impose secrecy requirements upon its employees. It precludes such restraints with respect to information which is unclassified or officially disclosed."

If that caveat were applied as written, said Mark, the government didn't have a contractual leg to stand on—unless it accused me of publishing secrets.

By the time the meeting broke up, I was feeling pluckier. My three new associates seemed determined not to repeat the mistakes of Marchetti's attorneys, who'd subordinated contract law to an idealist's view of the First Amendment. Instead of hanging our hats on high principle, we'd concentrate on spotting loopholes in contract law and build our defenses from there.

— —

That night, I sat by my phone debating whether to call my father. How often as a child had I fidgeted and pouted as he'd droned on at the dinner table about some turgid legal principle that had caught his fancy. And how

I'd hated those forced father-son outings in which he'd dragged me into his courtroom to sit through some incomprehensible trial he was presiding over. Was it any wonder that I'd chosen to make a career in an agency that held the law in utter contempt?

But now here I was, in desperate need of his expertise and unable to reach out to him because I'd embarrassed him with his senatorial patron. Would he have glimpsed some flaw in the government's case that had eluded Mark and the rest? Would he be as cautiously optimistic?

No boring pedant now, dear old Dad. I would have willingly endured your tyranny for your wisdom.

But I was still too ashamed of what I'd done to you to make the call.

— —

Having spent the last eighteen months hunched over a writer's pad, I'd developed the habit of thinking on paper. So, to be sure that I understood what Lynch and the rest had told me, I played their thoughts back in a quirky memo that ultimately wound up as an op-ed piece in *The New York Times.*

Decrying the CIA's secrecy agreement as "the most elastic thing since rubber bands," I noted that Richard Helms had stretched it to cover a lie to Congress and that Turner was now trying to turn it into a gag for dissent.

When I handed the piece over to the *Times,* Mark drew a deep breath and held it. Though I'd written carefully to avoid even a whiff of classified information, I hadn't sought CIA clearance either. How would the government react?

Bernie thought she knew, and threw up her hands in despair. Why was I tempting them so?

To test the waters, I told her, to see if there was consistency to the rules Hedge and Whitaker were seeking to enforce against me. Consistency would make me liable for the op-ed piece. But if the government failed to react, then why was I being censured for *Decent Interval?*

"You enjoy this, don't you?" she replied tartly.

I shrugged, knowing she was right. Living on the edge has a way of becoming addictive.

This time it paid off. Days passed and the government did nothing.

— —

Sometime in early March, as the gravity of the lawsuit sank in, Bob Bernstein sent a note to his superiors at RCA, Random House's parent company, warning that they might be in for some backdoor reprisals—that the government might try to punish them for Random House's association with me by withdrawing federal contracts vital to RCA's profitability. The board of directors gulped but offered no objection.

In the meantime, Bernstein made clear to me that he would stand by me regardless, whatever RCA did, out of principle and personal sympathy. Soon afterward, he threw money behind the assurance by buying a huge ad on *The New York Times*'s op-ed page to protest the government's case against me. "That this lawsuit has been brought," he wrote in the copy, "diminishes the democratic ideal and in fact diminishes us all as Americans."

His indignation caught on, prompting sympathetic editorials across the country. *The New Republic* thought it "politically stupid" for the administration to try to punish disclosures that embarrassed only its Republican predecessors. *The Boston Globe* saw my book as "the sort of risk we take in an open society." *The Tennesseean* remonstrated: "To spies and traitors, the oath is meaningless. . . . So the oath becomes a device used by government officials to cloak the failures of their agencies."

At his confirmation hearing, newly nominated Deputy Attorney General Benjamin Civiletti predicted defeat for the government unless it could prove that I'd done the country irreparable harm.

— —

As Griffin Bell would later acknowledge, he'd kept the White House in the dark about the "Snepp suit," not mentioning it to anyone there until the day before his announcement in New Orleans. But once he did his hard sell, the president himself fell quickly into line, and in a press conference on March 2 explained why. "I don't look on Frank Snepp as one of the greatest whistle-blowers of all time," Carter groused to reporters. "He signed a contract, later confirmed this agreement with the CIA that before his book was published it would be examined."

Admitting that he hadn't read *Decent Interval,* he nonetheless doubted that it "revealed anything that would lead to an improvement in our security apparatus or protection of American civil rights.

"If everyone who came into the CIA felt free to resign because of a dispute and then write a book revealing our nation's utmost secrets," he concluded, "it would be very devastating to our nation's ability to protect ourselves."

When his comments hit the headlines, the fragile confidence I'd carried away from Boston evaporated. Here was the president himself suggesting that I'd compromised "*utmost secrets*"!

— —

A week later, Mark filed our first legal brief at the Alexandria courthouse. While conceding that I'd published without clearance, he argued that the First Amendment barred the CIA from requiring approval of a benign book like mine. He also maintained that the CIA had violated its own obligations under my original secrecy agreement, and thus rendered it unenforceable, by refusing to hear me out about the evacuation.

He didn't mention the secrecy pact I'd signed on leaving the Agency, since we still had no copy of it. But a few days later, Hedge and Whitaker finally handed one over in response to our initial discovery requests.

Mark read the document and whooped for joy. Just as I'd remembered, its clearance requirements were limited to "classified information, or any information concerning intelligence or CIA that has not been made public by CIA." Unless Hedge and Whitaker accused me of publishing Agency confidences, they couldn't claim that I'd violated my *final* set of obligations.

— —

It was still too early, of course, to run up a victory flag. Though Turner had described me as "circumspect" in his *Newsweek* interview, there was the president's own suggestion that I'd revealed "utmost secrets." Which view was to prevail?

To find out, Mark drew up ninety-two interrogatories for the CIA to answer in writing. Syndicated columnist Mary McGrory obtained a copy of the questions and wrote a wry article about them, remarking that some "are of a nature to make CIA director Stansfield Turner's blood run cold."

"The last thing in the world that the CIA needs right now is civil liberties lawyers tracking through its demoralized corridors, asking the decimated ranks how they feel."

Officials at the Justice Department agreed. Within days, Hedge and Whitaker petitioned the court in Alexandria to rule on my case immediately, without letting me dig any further into CIA business.

In their Motion for Summary Judgment, they declared that I'd conceded guilt by admitting to having published without clearance, and asked the court to gag me forthwith and impose an "appropriate" financial penalty, the determination of which, they said, would require only "a limited amount of discovery." To reach this abbreviated calculus of justice, they brushed aside any distinction between Marchetti and me—never mind that he'd leaked secrets, and I hadn't—and insisted that even absent an agreement, the unwritten common law of trusts would imply an across-the-board clearance obligation "to protect classified information."

When Mark spotted this passage, he popped the cap on one of his beloved Budweiser long-necks and took a long draught to douse his fury.

If *even absent an agreement* the government could require clearance of all job-related information, then Hedge and Whitaker were indeed peddling an argument that could lead to the censoring of anyone in government.

Anthony Lewis of *The New York Times* was equally chagrined. "If the Justice Department wants all former government employees to have to clear their manuscripts before publication, why doesn't it ask Congress to pass a law?" he demanded in a commentary on the case.

"The answer, of course, is that such a proposal would have no chance. It would arouse cries of alarm about an Official Secrets Act. But raise the idea in litigation, and no one may notice until it's too late."

Rattled by this broadside, Attorney General Bell responded publicly that there were only two ways for the government to protect secrets—by prosecuting leakers under the espionage laws, as in *Truong-Humphrey,* or by bringing civil suits against them for breach of contract, as in *Marchetti* and now *Snepp.* "But you can't prosecute if it's much of a secret," he added, "because you have to make the secret public in court. The contract may be the most important device we can have, if we can have one."

CHAPTER 15

Roarin' Oren

BY MID-MARCH, a corner of Loomis's desk was piled high with letters threatening libel action against me. None of the aggrieved, mostly ex-embassy types, ever followed through. But the incessant cawing did have the effect, no doubt intended, of spooking the faint of heart. *Book Digest,* already quavering before the prospect of *United States v Snepp,* dropped plans for serializing *Decent Interval,* and the producers of NBC's *Today* show ruled out any further interviews with me lest, as they explained it, they risk prejudicing the *government's* chances of a fair trial.

Against this backdrop, a scathing review published in *Inquiry* magazine wounded me more than it should have. Denouncing *Decent Interval* as a softball critique of the Agency, the reviewer flayed me for not penning an indictment worthy of his own spleen. The byline on the story was Victor Marchetti's.

On an abnormally frigid night in mid-March I drove out to his home in Langley, Virginia, hard by CIA headquarters, to have it out with him. Several inches of snow and a bunch of rambunctious dogs so slowed my progress up his darkened driveway that I was practically homicidal when I slammed a fist into his doorbell. After a long pause, the door swung open, and instantly my hostility drained away: the potbellied munchkin with the double chin and Buddy Holly glasses who greeted me was so unrelentingly pathetic that I found myself mumbling apologies for even disturbing his evening.

I'd read somewhere that Marchetti considered himself a "functional alcoholic" but, given the marinated persona he presented that evening, "functional" didn't begin to describe the debris.

He staggered theatrically as he introduced his wife, and couldn't stop winking as he assured me she considered me "a real hero," though for *what*, he didn't say. He then slipped out of his trousers and hung them on a breakfront, the better to avert creases and an unnecessary laundry bill, he told me. "You gotta save where you can," he added, noting that his battles with the government had left him with nothing but his house and a prayer.

Downstairs, in his basement study, he struggled briefly with a pair of dusty barbells as if to prove that a critic of the CIA needn't be a wimp, and bragged soddenly about having "stuck it out" in this community with its notoriously high concentration of CIA families. I asked why he'd stayed and subjected his own family to such uncongenial neighbors. He puffed himself up and sputtered: "I wouldn't give the bastards the satisfaction of running me out!"

He said his sons had reached a détente of sorts with the local "CIA brats" by always being able to match them taunt for taunt—"Your old man's a traitor!" "No, *yours* is a dirty killer!" But the traitor himself, I could see, had reached a détente with no one, least of all himself. Though he offered a perfunctory defense of fellow Catholic Philip Agee, who he said had acted out of conviction, tears soon began rolling down his cheeks and he stopped abruptly and stammered: "Goddamn, I wish *I* had never done it. I shoulda kept my own mouth shut. Never taken on the CIA."

Shocked, I asked him why, then, he'd been so quick to condemn me for not pulling out all the stops. He looked at me from a million miles out and whispered: "Because I knew if I attacked you, you'd come. I was lonely. So lonely."

At dinner, he confessed to me, as his wife choked back tears of her own, that he was still "in love" with the Agency. "I even have dreams about it at night," he murmured, adding blearily that he had not set out to be a rabble-rouser. On the contrary, *this* son of a Pennsylvania coal miner had once seen the CIA as an escalator out of his squalid past, the Agency's rigid discipline and pretensions to holy purpose comporting neatly with the evangelism that had nearly propelled him into the priesthood.

But once he'd attained the heights, as an assistant to the deputy director with all the concomitant access to privileged wisdom, he'd seen too much, too much of the meddling, mendacity, and hypocrisy that were the CIA's daily fare. In 1969, my own first year in Vietnam, he'd stepped off the escalator and resigned.

But he'd done so quietly. "I was unable to speak out publicly," he sighed over the lip of his wineglass. "I was still imbued with the mystique of the Agency. I therefore sought to express my thoughts—more accurately, my feelings—in fictional form."

The novel he wrote, *The Rope Dancer,* celebrates a CIA official who spies for the Russians after suffering epiphanies similar to Marchetti's own. Never cleared by the Agency, it prompted no formal retaliation. But its informal reception by CIA loyalists turned the author overnight into Satan incarnate, a role for which he was unprepared emotionally or theologically, and he retaliated in the surest way he knew how, first by dribbling out lurid secrets designed to confer demonhood on the Agency itself, and then by circulating a scathing nonfiction work in outline that would ultimately become *The CIA and the Cult of Intelligence.*

"Everybody at Langley went bonkers," Marchetti explained, chin sinking toward his dinner plate. "People were so paranoid, so frightened."

And no wonder. Ellsberg had just dropped the Pentagon Papers on the press's doorstep, and the bulldogs of CIA Security were getting their first whiff of Philip Agee's intentions as the ex-agent flitted from Europe to Cuba and back again researching his own prospective exposé.

To head Marchetti off, CIA director Richard Helms ordered him surveilled and his mail traced, and finally prevailed on the Nixon White House to take him to court, a favor in exchange for which Nixon later tried to extract CIA cooperation in the Watergate cover-up. "I was the price to be paid," Marchetti hiccuped blithely.

Colby devised the legal strategy, and the Justice Department implemented it. CIA witnesses filed sealed affidavits with the federal court in Alexandria accusing Marchetti of having violated his secrecy agreement by leaking myriad secrets, and one day in April 1972, the unsuspecting defendant woke up to find himself facing a gag order, obliging him to surrender his manuscript to the CIA for clearance.

"He was so depressed," his wife put in. "He had to get John Marks to help him finish the book."

Once it was finished and submitted for censorship, the sharks feasted. "Yeah, they *over*censored it," I injected helpfully.

"Overcensored!" he shrieked. "They bloody tore it to shreds!"

He grasped a shaking finger and began ticking off examples. Deleted was a reference to the fact that Helms had mispronounced the name of the Malagasy Republic at a White House meeting. Deleted was one of Kissinger's more contemptuous remarks about Chile under the left-wing Allende regime—"We can't let a country go Communist just because of the irresponsibility of its people." Deleted was any passage that made the "holy men" at Langley, as Marchetti described them, look fallible.

Eventually he and his publisher, Knopf, bargained the CIA down to 168 deletions and then went to court to try to get those overturned. By then, the trial judge had become so impatient with the CIA that he restored all but twenty-seven. But a less sympathetic appeals court reversed that decision, leaving the book perforated like Swiss cheese.

"After I lost, I stayed in bed a week," said Marchetti. "I didn't shave or bathe or even turn on a light."

"I was working in a doctor's office at the time," injected his wife. "Many of our patients began staying away because they thought Vic was a traitor."

I sat frozen, staring at my host and hostess, wondering if such misery might be contagious.

Marchetti topped his wineglass shakily and tried to rationalize his rage. "You're picked for the Agency because of certain personality traits," he muttered. "And they're gonna give you big problems. You're buffeted between guilt and the feeling that what you've done is worthwhile. The Agency always wins in court. The loser in the end is going to be the guy who spoke out. It's a goddamn lonely feeling."

Later, after treating me to a farewell brandy, he shuffled with me out to my car. As I was about to climb in, he embraced me hard. "From now on," he said, "you're gonna be an outlaw, a gunslinger all by yourself. And every time you walk down the street there's gonna be somebody waitin' to take a shot at you."

"It's happening already," I told him.

He nodded, burped, and replied with steely calm: "Just keep your gun well oiled."

— —

One thing you quickly learn about lawsuits is that they generate paper as profligately as any federal bureaucracy. Having opened the sluice gates with his ninety-two interrogatories, Mark was now obliged to meet the government's counterattack in foolscap by pouring on more of the same. During the hectic week leading up to the hearing on the government's summary judgment motion, he churned out rebuttals by the ream, as Dershowitz peered over his shoulder, dropping suggestions like flowers from the queen's carriage.

From my pen flowed an affidavit setting out in layman's terms why I deserved a jury trial. Mark did the same in a legalistic memorandum. Together, our handiwork provided a fairly complete summary of the "points" and "authorities" we'd wield throughout the litigation.

For starters, I tried to nail down the secrets-free status of *Decent Interval* by echoing Turner's remark to *Newsweek* about my being "circumspect." Mark played on it too, using it to rebut the government's claim that I was no different from Marchetti and thus no more immune to a gag order.

He also took hammer and chisel to the government's theory that I was *implicitly* obliged to submit to censorship. Under existing precedent, he argued, any restriction on a bureaucrat's constitutional rights must be based on explicit authorization from Congress or the president.

He then moved on to another constitutional point, letting me pave the way. Noting in my affidavit that the CIA could be pretty arbitrary in enforcing clearance regulations, I recalled that two old spooks, Joseph Burkholder Smith and a legendary operative named Miles Copeland, had published uncleared memoirs of their own and suffered no consequences, even though Copeland had brazenly thumbed his nose at the censors. "I have been associated with intelligence agencies long enough to realize how futile it would be for one such as myself to request official permission to publish even the most antiseptic book," Copeland had written in the preface to his *Without Cloak or Dagger.*

"So I have been my own censor, and if I have included cases and information that have until now been held under tight security wraps, it is because I cannot accept the reasons for their continued secrecy."

These were the defiant words of a man who'd actually taken it on himself to declassify secrets. Yet in the four years since he'd published his memoir—four years, incidentally, which had seen Marchetti censored and Agee harassed—Copeland had never been sued.

Why?

The same question, Mark continued in his own brief, deserved to be asked about all the CIA operatives who routinely leaked to the press. He also pointed out that if one accepted the government's claim that public service alone conferred a fiduciary obligation to submit to censorship, the potential list of scofflaws extended to every statesman-memoirist of the past half century, from Henry Stimson and Dean Acheson to John Kenneth Galbraith and Henry Kissinger. "Under the theory in the case which is now being pressed against the defendant," he wrote, "each of these men violated their fiduciary duties to the United States and unjustly enriched themselves with the proceeds from their publications."

Had we known of Colby's clearance dodge or Martin's footlocker, the selectivity of the government's censorship theory would have needed no further explication.

Speculating on why I'd been singled out, I noted in my affidavit a remark Bob Layton had made months before. He'd told me my book was seen as an *embarrassment.* Was this the CIA's reason for picking on me? If so—and here Mark picked up the thread—"then this violates the defendant's First and Fifth Amendment rights" to free speech and equal protection under the law.

— —

Knowing that judges often like to rule on the narrowest possible grounds, Mark devoted the rest of his brief to simple contract law, emphasizing that I hadn't broken the only contract that bound me, my final one. As for my original agreement, not only did he consider it a dead letter because of the Agency's refusal to hear me out about the evacuation, he also insisted that since the CIA officer who briefed me on the day of my induction had assured me the agreement didn't apply to *all* writings, he had suckered me in under fraudulent pretenses that now excused what I'd done.

Mulling over this argument, I was reminded of another instance of fraud that might work for me. On my first full day at the Agency, the same induction officer had declared that the CIA never engages in assassinations—a claim that was clearly untrue. Hadn't that been an act of misrepresentation?

When I posed this to Mark, he frowned skeptically and asked if I'd ever believed such claptrap. "What about the CIA's notorious Phoenix counterterror program in Vietnam?" he demanded testily, his liberal ruffles showing. Surely I'd known *it* was a covert killing machine.

The war itself was a killing machine, I replied, the Phoenix just one weapon of many. The first time I'd realized assassination was a routine part of the CIA's *peacetime* repertoire was when the Church committee had confirmed it just before my resignation.

Mark pawed and snuffled but ultimately went back to his brief to expand the section on fraud, arguing that the induction officer had tricked me by leading me to believe that the CIA never kills. It was the one argument he put forward that I know he never believed.

— —

By the time Mark completed our answer to the government's summary judgment brief, the Snepp case had become a cottage industry, both defense and prosecution teams having swollen impressively. A half dozen government attorneys, including the CIA's Ernie Mayerfeld, had joined Hedge and Whitaker on the attack, and Mark had picked up two new shotguns of his own: John Cary Sims of Ralph Nader's Public Citizen Litigation Group and Geoffrey Vitt, a private attorney from Alexandria. Both had agreed to pitch in free of charge simply for the glory of it all. Neither knew squat about the Vietnam War except that they'd opposed it. But since I knew squat about the law, maybe we were even.

Having long practiced in the Fourth Circuit, Vitt brought some badly needed parochialism to the table. A sharp, eminently preppy graduate of George Washington Law School, he knew, at age thirty-two, every judge, clerk, and bailiff who might have anything to do with my case. Moreover, behind the oval-rimmed glasses and thin puckish face ticked the mind of a natural-born interrogator capable of reducing even the most reluctant witness to quivering acquiescence.

The other recruit, John Sims, was Machiavelli to Vitt's Borgia. Wonderfully calculating—a former editor of the *Harvard Law Review*—John worked best as a behind-the-scenes strategist, his very brilliance and grasp of detail robbing him of the verbal agility that his two colleagues employed so effectively. Yet, of the three, Sims, this slight, nearsighted genius with a prominent lower lip and wash of unruly black hair, was the easiest to live with. Always patient, he took pains to help me understand the filigreed logic being spun on my behalf, and whenever I seemed incapable of rubbing Mark or Vitt the *right* way, which was often, he invariably stepped in to mediate, perhaps realizing as they did not that my inquisitiveness sprang not simply from arrogance, but from mortal fear.

As the day of the hearing approached, Sims found himself increasingly cast in this peacemaker's role, for I couldn't forgive Mark one omission in his counterbrief: his failure to mention Colby's leak to the Kalb brothers. Since it was this outrage that had helped persuade me to go public, I was incensed that Mark had ignored it, and told him so.

With considerably more tact than I could have commanded, he explained that the case so far was about clearance, not revelation, and that unless and until the government accused me of publishing secrets, it was *pointless* to harp on the secrets leaked by others.

"Better not cloud the picture," Sims agreed delicately. "Better focus on what's central to this case."

And so we did, with the result that many of the issues most critical to me simply dropped from sight, including the botched evacuation itself. Since the government's own briefs shortchanged the topic, so did ours, leaving me to wonder if this suit was really about me at all.

— —

On the other side of the battle line, preparations were running no more smoothly. Griffin Bell had taken Anthony Lewis's recent remonstrances to heart and was now concerned about one key element of the government's

case, the theory of fiduciary duty, which could expose even Bell himself—
a government fiduciary, after all—to the threat of censorship. On the very
eve of the summary judgment hearing, he ordered Hedge and Whitaker to
pull back.

His diktat left them floundering, with little to hold on to but the tangled
strands of contract law. But as luck would have it, in the week before the
hearing, the case was delivered into the hands of a judge whose prejudices
would more than compensate for any deficiencies in their arguments. As
Vitt chillingly observed, this newest player, seventy-five-year-old Judge
Oren R. Lewis, would have made Genghis Khan look like a civil libertarian. Around the Alexandria courthouse he was known unfondly as
"Roarin' Oren."

The assignment could have gone to any of his colleagues, and any one
of them would have been preferable. Mark had hoped to have the case remanded to Judge Albert V. Bryan, Jr. He'd presided over the Marchetti trial
and, despite having initially ruled against the defendant, had later become
skeptical of the CIA's extravagant national security claims. Sadly for us,
however, Bryan was given *Truong-Humphrey,* and Judge Lewis had been
summoned to the battlements to deal with me.

Everybody had stories about him. One local attorney liked to quip that
Lewis merited a Blue Cross finder's fee for having "done more to increase
the incidence of lawyer high blood pressure and ulcers than any other force
of nature." Columnist Mary McGrory surmised that if you were looking
for a summary judgment, "you could probably find no more summary
judge" than this one. "His honor is a white-haired, ruddy-faced man who
looks like a country squire who would rather be out hunting than listening
to the prattle of lawyers," she observed. "He interrupts frequently, joyfully
galloping over the carefully manicured lawns of their arguments."

"When you describe me, you can use the word 'crusty,' " Lewis himself
once told a reporter. "I am combative by nature. I'm either for you or
against you."

A lifelong Republican, Lewis had been nominated to the bench in 1960
on the recommendation of a lawmaker he'd campaigned for. The American Bar Association found him merely "qualified," not "well qualified," for
the appointment. But with Eisenhower in the White House and the Republicans riding high, he got the job anyway.

Over the next fifteen years, as the civil rights struggle spilled into the nation's courtrooms, Lewis dispensed justice erratically. In one case he refused to allow county schools in Virginia to close down rather than be
integrated; in another, he kept an all-black school open rather than shift its

students to segregated white ones nearby. In a third case, he praised a restaurant owner for his courage in ejecting blacks during a lunchroom sit-in, then jailed the man for violating their civil rights.

"He tries to be fair," remarked one defense attorney. "But he's totally unpredictable."

Apart from civil rights, one other social issue of the turbulent 1960s and 1970s had repeatedly brought out the worst in Lewis: Vietnam. Indeed, it was his dubious distinction to have jailed Norman Mailer and the other demonstrators whose march on the Pentagon had inspired Mailer's masterpiece, *The Armies of the Night.*

How Lewis himself felt about the war was not entirely clear. He'd once publicly condemned it as wrong, but he'd invariably ruled against any anti-war activist who'd had the misfortune of winding up in his courtroom. During one such trial, he took it upon himself to cross-examine the defendant through thirteen pages of transcript without letting defense lawyers get a word in edgewise. The appeals court, in reversing the guilty verdict, chided him for these high-handed tactics and said there was "every indication" he'd come to court with his mind made up.

"I never let a deserter try the Vietnam War," Lewis later explained. "They wanted to use the court as a forum to espouse their political philosophy."

If the government was looking for a judge who would be instantly suspicious of my disenchantments, it couldn't have found a better candidate than Oren Lewis.

— —

But it wasn't so much Lewis's political views that chilled me as his social ones, which seemed all too familiar. His ambivalence about civil rights recalled a world I thought I'd put behind me, one where prejudice passed for civility and where none of my friends of color, neither black nor Vietnamese, neither Bernie nor Mai Ly, would have been welcome except at the servants' entrance. My beloved grandmother had steeped me in its paradoxes. As head of the local Humane Society, she'd been known to weep over an abandoned puppy and to spend days trying to place a stray cat, but as a spiritual descendant of Scarlett O'Hara, she'd once struck our black maid for speaking out of turn and had never forgiven me for calling her on it. The biases she'd harbored would never have tolerated my relationship with Bernie, and had my grandmother been in the judge's box, which—given Lewis's own similarly warped perspectives—she might as well have been, she would have ruled against me simply for having slept with the wogs, the burrheads, the little yellow people.

In consideration of this, I came to the most damning decision I would make in the course of the lawsuit. Bernie would have to stay away—not for her sake, but mine, to save me from the prejudice she might inspire in Oren Lewis.

I did not explain this to her, of course. I was too craven for that. When I flew to New York the weekend before the hearing to ask her not to come, I made exhaustion my excuse and begged her to understand that I was too strung out to be able to endure any distraction.

So trusting was this woman that she never doubted or questioned. As always, Bernadette Longford, who had sacrificed so much for me, who had spent eighteen nerve-racking months transcribing and typing my manuscript, watching my back, deflecting the risks, and running interference, agreed to do what was best for me. Her only concern was that I should have to confront the dragons alone without the moral support she thought I deserved.

At the end of the weekend, she delivered me back to the airport, kissed me tenderly, and asked me to keep her up to date by phone "when it's convenient."

— —

The day of the summary judgment hearing, March 31, not a cloud blemished the sky over Alexandria, and the ninety-eight-year-old courthouse was bathed in a summerlike radiance. Inside, I found reporters everywhere, some hovering outside the chamber where the latest skirmishing in *Truong-Humphrey* was taking place, others jockeying for choice seats in the hearing room assigned to me. As I slipped in, Mary McGrory shot me a curious glance, and Sy Hersh rushed over and gleefully snatched some notes I'd been jotting to myself, which he never returned. Mark's endearing British wife, Gail, and his ever-suffering secretary, Sally Householder, already occupied a front pew and were watching attentively as lawyers for another defendant wound up their arguments under Lewis's imperious eye.

My own lawyers were nowhere to be seen, and would sorely test my nerves by delaying their arrival till what seemed like the last possible moment. Finally, Mark burst in, hair flying, with Vitt and Sims in ragged pursuit, and slammed to a screeching halt upon realizing that the court was already in session. "Don't worry—somebody *else's* case," Vitt whispered as he nudged the suddenly shaken Mark toward a seat near me.

For the next several minutes, as we sat awaiting our turn, I studied the peppery little man in black robes and square-framed glasses who would pronounce judgment on me. A dynamo of unfocused energy, Lewis alternately swiveled, gesticulated, bucked, and wriggled as he needled the lawyers at the defendant's table, who were trying gamely to conclude their arguments. One of his wisecracks sent a ripple of nausea through me. Glowering down at one of the more loquacious attorneys, he barked maliciously: "You sound like someone from the ACLU!"

By the time my case was gaveled in, the courtroom was packed and stifling. Alongside Hedge and Whitaker sat Bell's right-hand man, Michael Egan, and Deputy Assistant Attorney General Thomas S. Martin, who was to argue the prosecution's brief this morning. CIA associate general counsel Ernie Mayerfeld slouched in a pew behind them.

My own cheering section seemed positively puny by comparison. Dershowitz hadn't been able to get in from Boston. None of my relatives was present, and no one from Random House. Bernie's absence was excruciating in its conspicuousness.

Before inviting opening arguments, Lewis flashed a fawning smile at the high-level delegation from the Justice Department. Mark glanced at me and rolled his eyes. It wasn't going to be an easy morning.

According to protocol, Martin was first up at the lectern. He was young, lean, and ill at ease in his pinstripes, and judging from his curriculum vitae, unburdened by any firsthand knowledge of Vietnam.

His presentation was predictably dismissive. Describing the action at bar as a simple contract case, he portrayed me as a brash opportunist who'd cynically and surreptitiously broken his secrecy agreement for money and whose sins were so obvious as to merit no further comment, or court time.

At a nod from Lewis, Mark fought back valiantly, insisting that since I'd compromised no secrets, I'd kept faith with my only valid contract, the termination agreement.

Martin objected: "We say the second agreement is not a contract." But before he could complete his thought, Lewis leapt in. "Lawyers have a knack of writing agreements," he remarked airily. "I love single-line agreements."

Blinking at this non sequitur, Mark protested that even if the original agreement was the controlling one, the government itself had voided it by ignoring my grievances. But once again, Lewis broke in, warning that no one here would be allowed "to try the Vietnam War or the deficiencies of the CIA, *if there are any.*"

I bowed my head.

Mark took several deep breaths, turned a page, and tried another tack, arguing that the entry agreement had been fraudulently obtained.

"You'll never get off the ground with that," Lewis shot back.

With most of his cards now trumped, Mark played the only promising one still left: precedent. The Marchetti decision, he asserted, far from sanctioning suits like this one, had left signatories of CIA secrecy agreements free to publish unclassified information. For the first time, Lewis seemed interested. Turning to Martin, he asked if the government would truly allow me to claim that I'd published no secrets.

Martin equivocated, declaring vaguely that the government had made "no contention one way or another." That miffed Lewis. Chiding the young attorney for being too "elusive," he grumbled that the main issues of the case might be rendered moot by the government's unwillingness to point a finger. "If there wasn't much classified material," he muttered, "there isn't much damage."

I held my breath. Would Martin recoup by abruptly pointing to "secrets" in *Decent Interval*? Or would he fall back on the government's theory of fiduciary trust, importuning Lewis to seize all my profits without any proof of damage?

To my astonishment, he did neither, but merely stood down. As he later confided to reporters, he'd been directed by Bell not to raise the trust issue. And he couldn't cry wolf about blown secrets without immediately rendering the case too complex for a summary judgment.

Before gaveling the session to a close, Lewis offered some preliminary impressions. As Mary McGrory recalled, he "inveighed against agents who decide for themselves what to print" and "commiserated with the CIA because it didn't see Snepp's book until publication—'after the horse had been stolen.' " Clearly, he'd read the government's briefs and *believed*.

Even so, he couldn't bring himself to rule against me based on the record so far. So, in the end he declined to render summary judgment, ordered the CIA to answer our interrogatories, and directed Martin and his colleagues to prepare for a jury trial within two months. "You'd better get your machinery ready," he warned them. Then, as if in apology for having given them so little, he added dreamily, "You *are* interesting people."

As I walked out of the court amid a phalanx of reporters, I felt anything but reassured. Besides being just short of senile, Lewis had steamrollered Mark's favorite arguments. And though he'd seemed baffled by the CIA's failure to accuse me of any security breach, his alarms about agents declassifying secrets on their own suggested he had his own views on the subject.

As often happens with a battered client, I chose to blame my lawyers for what hadn't gone right. Mark had been too nervous, too slow on his feet, I convinced myself foolishly. He'd put too much emphasis on my final agreement and not enough on the Agency's bad faith. Why not argue simply that *all* my obligations had been nullified by the Agency's nonresponse to my grievances? Why all this gobbledygook about one agreement superceding the other?

At lunch, Mort Halperin and the ACLU's John Shattuck sensed my anger and begged me not to sound off to the press, lest I give Lewis additional fodder. Mark smiled ruefully and told them they "might as well try to get a brown bear not to shit in the woods." Besides, he added, Lewis seemed already to have made up his mind; he'd probably find some way to rule against me on liability.

Shattuck agreed, but struggled to tease out a silver lining. Maybe we could bargain any damages down to a single dollar. Maybe Frank Snepp wouldn't be impoverished.

That night in a call to Bernie, I vented my frustrations and vowed to get Dershowitz more involved. He'd show Mark a thing or two!

Misdirected though my fury was—Mark was the best ally I ever had—Bernie reacted with alarm. An hour or so later, *her* confidante, Gloria Emerson, exercised as well, called to urge me desperately not to be so hard on my defenders. Better to think strategically, she said. Better to look for a way to extricate myself from Oren Lewis. She had a suggestion: since Random House was in New York, why not file a motion to shift the case to that venue? There were a lot of liberal judges in Manhattan accustomed to dealing with subtle First Amendment issues.

I broached the idea to Sims the next morning. "No way," he said sadly. Random House was not a party to this case. The government had cleverly locked me into Lewis's courtroom by focusing its charges on me alone.

CHAPTER 16

Inquisition

WITHIN A WEEK of my first day in court, a sun-drenched, betel-brown Carla showed up at my door and pretended not to be hurt that I hadn't been in touch these past six months, since her last trip home. Had it been *that* long! I stammered, truly surprised.

She was up from the Virgin Islands for a few days to deal with some personal business. But she'd read in the press in St. Thomas that I was being sued, and had grown fearful for me.

She stayed an hour or so and agreed to attend a speech I was giving somewhere. But she did not offer or invite any greater intimacy. At some point, she did ask about Bernie and how she was holding up, for she seemed to sense that my "New York friend" had usurped whatever sparse terrain I still reserved for emotion. I had to struggle for an answer, not because I had anything to keep from Carla but because my life was now so tightly coiled that I had little sense of anything beyond my own anxieties. I knew I'd talked to Bernie after the hearing, but couldn't remember what about, or why, except that I'd burdened her as usual with my woes.

Carla did not ask why Bernie hadn't flown in for the hearing, but I think she guessed the answer. She had experienced enough of my selfishness herself to know I had a limitless capacity for it.

— —

In the wake of the hearing in Judge Lewis's courtroom, no one at the Justice Department donned any victory laurels. But Hedge, Whitaker, and their colleagues had seen enough of His Honor to know where his sympathies lay. Thus, as we began pushing them over the next few days to answer our interrogatories as he'd directed, they arrogantly began pushing back, brushing aside any they considered inconvenient, out of confidence that he'd never cite them for contempt.

Infuriating as their intransigence was, Mark had read the auguries too, and realized it would be pointless to protest. So on April 5, he simply dumped forty-four of the interrogatories and modified eleven others to suit Hedge and Whitaker. Not only did he agree to give up trying to determine if the CIA had ever surveilled me, he consented to let the two government lawyers withhold anything from the CIA's files on me that they deemed irrelevant to the case.

Predictably, these giveaways bought us nothing. Though Mark had asked for expedited security clearances for him and his cocounsel, Hedge and Whitaker continued to delay, thus making it impossible for me to discuss many things with my lawyers that were vital to my defense. They also continued to stiff-arm our now truncated interrogatories, including all requests for documents relating to my "complaints" about the evacuation, which they dismissed as "clearly irrelevant."

"The defendant once again seeks to litigate the question of the government's performance in the final days of Vietnam," they objected to the court.

This was too much. Mark quickly requested a remedial hearing with Judge Lewis on April 14.

In the week leading up to it, Hedge and Whitaker moved deftly to keep me on the defensive. Pulling together my most infelicitous press quotes, they trimmed and edited them into a compendium of what they called "admissions of guilt," then drew up a motion asking Lewis to force me to swear to their accuracy. Included in this poisonous stew were all my garbled and disjointed references to misleading Turner and dodging the censors.

— —

On the morning of the fourteenth, Sally Whitaker took to the podium for the first time. Lewis seemed delighted to have such pulchritude to fence with and quickly agreed to her request that I certify the "admissions." He also extended her a favor that she liked far less. Although she'd wanted to put some interrogatories to me, Lewis decided this would be too much to my advantage. "He'd get his counsel to tell him what to say," he warbled, gesturing contemptuously at me. "He'd have more time to confer with his lawyer."

A far better course, he declared, would be a deposition, a face-to-face interrogation under oath. To make sure I had no time to polish up my act, he suggested that she make her first pass the following Sunday, just two days away.

Sally tried to force a grateful smile.

"Now you won't be worried about lawyers helping him answer," Lewis reassured her.

As for our own concerns—the interrogatories we wanted answered—he granted us only enough leeway to satisfy his own curiosity. Still puzzled that the CIA could claim injury to itself without charging a security breach, he commanded Sally to answer a few pertinent questions.

Biased as his rulings were, Mark didn't even consider challenging them. With my deposition just around the corner, he knew we'd need every waking moment to prepare.

Since Bernie had stashed most of my personal files in remote hiding places around New York, assembling the necessary paperwork proved a nightmare. Nor did I show much promise as a potential witness on my own behalf. As Mark's cocounsel, Geoff Vitt, quickly discovered during rehearsal interrogations Saturday afternoon, I'd been too well indoctrinated by the CIA to be capable of easy candor. Whenever pressed on a delicate point, I'd feint and parry rather than answer head-on, thus conveying an impression of duplicity and evasion.

Equally troublesome was the sad legacy of Linley Stafford's own duplicity toward me, especially his failure to level about the circumstances in which he'd closed my book deal with Random House. I'd long known, of course, that he'd acted prematurely, turning over my signed contract to Loomis without my permission. But what he'd never let on was that he'd made the handoff *before* my resignation from the CIA. This fact had become clear only recently, after Bernie had discovered a fully executed copy of the contract among Stafford's papers, and though I'd assured Mark and my other lawyers that I'd never seen it before, let alone realized I'd been committed to Random House while still a CIA officer, they clearly didn't believe me.

By late Saturday evening, they were pushing their incredulity in my face to see if I could take it, and before long I was raging at them, trading vitriol for sweet reason. It was not a good omen. If I couldn't keep my cool tomorrow, Hedge and Whitaker would tear me to shreds.

Later, back at my apartment, I sat for a long while riffling through memories of interrogations past in search of some lesson that might insulate me. Gradually a face coalesced through the haze, the gaunt, grim visage of a Vietnam casualty named Nguyen Van Thai.

My toughest challenge, that one, the highest-ranking Viet Cong we'd ever captured, a top official in Hanoi's intelligence service. Even after two years in solitary, two years in a hermetically sealed, snow-white cell, he'd remained so exquisitely self-controlled that he could tell the time of day simply from the changing chemistry of his own body. But in the end, the chemistry had failed him, the rage surging forth one morning to consume and betray him. Reflecting on that moment, I felt an odd affinity for the man in the snow-white room, for I realized that what had breached his defenses was something I knew too well: shame. I'd shamed him that morning with the memory of his father, whom he'd betrayed on his way up the Communist Party ladder, and for once he'd been unable to hide from himself.

There was a moral to be drawn from that, I decided, and I would harken to it in tomorrow's interrogation and many others to come: Never let them shame you with your betrayals. Never let them near the shame that can consume you.

— —

"When did you first consider writing a book?"

"Around Thanksgiving."

"And when did writing *Decent Interval* crystallize?"

"The day I left the Agency."

Room 3618 of the Justice Department, where we convened promptly at ten A.M., had all the charm of a cheap coffin, and the conference table where we sat with subpoenaed documents scattered before us was as battered as any well-worn lie. Sally Whitaker, bleached curls teased into a Shirley Temple coif, tried repeatedly, through nearly six hundred pages of transcripted testimony extending over three days, to confirm the government's ungenerous image of me.

"Did you advise the CIA prior to your resignation that you were writing this book?"

"That I was *contemplating* writing."

Throughout the grilling, Whitaker's colleague, Brook Hedge, and several CIA attorneys including Ernie Mayerfeld, whose hooked nose and greasy gray hair gave him the antic slovenliness of an Al Capp cartoon, whispered cues from the sidelines. Remembering Nguyen Van Thai, I tried to remain composed, always addressing Sally politely as "ma'am" even though she was certainly younger than I.

During that first morning, she attempted to dismantle my motive for writing.

"Well, you tell me, Mr. Snepp, what your grievance was."

"The mishandling of the evacuation, number one. And number two, the Agency's failure to deal with the question."

"I want to know, after you finish telling me about the evacuation, do you have any *others* you are going to tell me about, other *grievances*?"

"Don't you think that is sufficient?"

In expanding on this answer I named names, the unclassified names of nearly a dozen senior Agency officials, from Polgar to Ted Shackley to George Carver and Paul Walsh, who'd found it convenient to ignore my grievances and my plea for an official after-action report.

Tilting her head slightly, Sally gazed at me as if I were a specimen under a slide. "Did you *specifically* mention the Vietnam evacuation in each of these conversations?"

"Yes, I did."

"Did all these people say they couldn't deal with these things?"

"They said: 'No, we can't deal with it. We can't follow this thing through.' "

Endeavoring to show that I'd never pursued my grievances through proper channels, she taunted me with the fact that my one brush with the inspector general's staff had come at *his* initiative.

"So, Mr. Snepp, you never contacted the inspector general with respect to your attempts to write an after-action report?"

"Did I *initiate* the contact? I didn't feel it was necessary once I was called in. Are we quibbling over semantics here?"

The brightly varnished lips tightened into a thin line. "Just *answer* the question! Yes or no."

To flesh out her portrait of the money-hungry young mendicant, she tried relentlessly to get me to admit that I'd kept colleagues ignorant of my burgeoning book plans, and refused to believe that I could have been un-aware of Stafford's premature delivery of my book contract to Random House. "When did you learn *that*?" she asked scornfully.

"Not until the book was published."

She could barely suppress a guffaw.

Nor did she consider my professed lack of business acumen any more credible. Firmly convinced that I was hiding millions under the bed, she pressed me hard on how much I'd earned in royalties, whether I'd had a job on the side, how much in taxes I'd paid on my advance. On two of the three, I could easily oblige: No job; taxes paid in full, albeit a bit late. But with so much of Random House's paperwork still hung up in New York, I couldn't be sure of much else.

Mark did his best to bail me out. "I think the testimony," he put in gen-tly, "amply indicates that Mr. Snepp is not a businessman."

Hoping to lard the record with intimations of grave threat, Sally repeatedly harkened to Turner's image of me as a latter-day Dan Ellsberg out to declassify anything I wanted.

"Do you contend that you have the discretion, when you write a book about your Agency employment, to determine what is and what is not classified?"

"Yes."

Seeing Mark wince, I tried to clarify, pointing out that as a CIA briefer and interrogator in Vietnam, I'd become so adept at spotting secrets that I could censor myself without clearing a script with anybody.

A shadow of exasperation crossed Sally's face. "Is it your contention that the book, *Decent Interval,* contains no classified information?"

"No information that I obtained while I was at the CIA that was classified."

"You felt for that reason you did not need to submit it?" A flick of the lashes.

"Correct. Yes."

Suddenly she slapped a document on the table, a copy of the letter that CIA lawyer John Greaney had sent me nine months after my resignation, demanding submission of my manuscript *regardless.*

"Does *that* reflect your understanding of your obligations!" she cried.

Calmly I replied that it didn't, that the letter had arrived just after the publication of Joseph Smith's CIA memoir, *Portrait of a Cold Warrior,* which the author had made clear was unapproved. The Agency's failure to act against him, I said, had convinced me Greaney was blowing smoke.

Eyeing me coldly, Sally asked if my CIA case officer, Bob Layton, hadn't advised me differently.

"I can't recall."

"You have a *fine* memory!"

Instantly Mark leapt in—"Let's knock off comments like that!"—and for a moment she seemed stunned.

Soothingly, I explained that Layton's preoccupation had been with the emotional distress I was causing his colleagues. "He told me they were concerned about embarrassment, not classified information."

Mayerfeld chuffed in disbelief.

"Would you *listen!*" I injected quickly, fearing he might lunge across the table.

"I *am* listening!" Sally shot back.

Willing myself to stay calm, I told her about my offer to Layton, how I'd volunteered to let him read my manuscript "informally" to reassure him of my discretion, how he'd declined, saying this was "not necessary."

I also pointed out that two other Agency contacts hadn't been so hands-off. My "very good friends," Pat and Bill Johnson, I said, had often given me help with the manuscript.

"And what did Mr. Johnson advise you your obligations were?" Sally inquired without missing a beat.

"He didn't advise me. *I* said, 'Will you look over pieces of the manuscript?' And he did so."

Not about to let on that the Johnsons were anything but very good friends to me, Sally quickly returned to my own "chicanery," bearing in on what she considered the most egregious example, my face-to-face meeting with Turner.

"Did you state that you would submit your book for prepublication review?"

"I felt it had been left ambiguous," I told her. "Mr. Morrison came in and recited a long litany of implications for the secrecy agreement."

"How did he tell you that classified information was going to be protected?"

"He said the Agency has a right to review *classified* information."

Sally shifted her gaze to Mayerfeld, who shrugged disgustedly. Slowly she turned back to me. "Did you *tape* your meeting with the director?"

I shot an amused look at Mark. "Is that privileged information?" I quipped. Mark realized she wasn't kidding.

"No," he said tightly.

I looked back at her and shook my head, "No, I didn't tape it."

Having failed to turn me into the complete scoundrel, Sally tried next to put me at the center of a well-orchestrated conspiracy, suggesting that Random House and I had carefully colluded to breach my clearly defined "obligations."

Soberly, I told her she had it wrong, that, far from working in diabolical harmony, Loomis and I hadn't even been able to agree on publicity tactics!

Refusing to let go, she asked why then, if everything had been so innocent, I'd insisted on publishing surreptitiously.

Fear of interference, I told her. Had Random House's identity been revealed, there might have been court action which could have cost me the publisher's support.

"Why would that have been a problem," she countered, "if you were not going to publish classified information?"

"I was under the impression, because of what happened in the Marchetti case, that we might have to negotiate over pieces of the manuscript that simply *embarrassed* the Agency."

She opened her mouth to challenge that one, but on a cautionary glance from Mayerfeld, thought better of it.

For the balance of the inquisition, Sally played a lawyer's game, trying to trick me into misstating or repudiating my more complex legal defenses.

Scoffing at my claim that I'd been "defrauded" of the truth about CIA assassinations, she challenged me to explain why I hadn't resigned in protest after the first public intimations of such kill plots in early 1975.

I reminded her that I'd been a bit distracted—by the collapse of South Vietnam.

"Did you in fact ever assassinate anyone!"

"No," I answered softly, struggling to remind myself that I'd always been an accessory, a source of deadly intelligence, never the actual trigger.

Her gaze lingered. Finally she roused herself.

"You are alleging that you have been singled out," she continued in obvious reference to my "discriminatory enforcement" defense.

"Seems that way."

"Why do you believe that?"

Because, I told her, other ex-agents who'd published uncleared books had gotten off scot-free.

She gave me a deprecatory smile, knowing that I hadn't said enough. Only by pinning a nasty motive on the government, only by suggesting I was being picked on for a vengeful reason, could I meet the standard of proof required in cases involving discriminatory enforcement of the law.

She pressed me again.

"Do you consider your book basically embarrassing to the CIA? *Yes or no,* Mr. Snepp."

"Ask the CIA."

Mark sighed dispiritedly. I was being too dodgy for my own good. My answer should have been: Yes, I've embarrassed the Agency and that's the only reason I'm here.

— —

By the third day of the deposition, Whitaker was so nerve-fried that she was popping off at anything. At one point, after failing to wrench a desired response from me, she wheeled on Mark furiously: "Counsel, would you *instruct* the witness to answer the questions responsively, or I am going to move for costs in this deposition!"

Mark kept his voice level: "If you don't start asking questions that he can answer, *I* am going to move for costs."

In another fit of pique, she demanded that I immediately hand over the names of all undercover CIA operatives who might testify for me, even though Mark still was not cleared for such secrets.

"Is he going to be able to give a copy of the list to me?" he asked her politely.

She wagged her head. "The names are still classified."

Mark's jaw clenched. "My client is not going to give you any piece of paper which he can't give to me."

"So you are *refusing* to provide those names!" She drew out the words like an accusation.

"Absolutely," snapped Mark. "If you need this information, you can clear me so I can look at it."

The confrontation left her rattled, and for the next several minutes Sally kept opening herself up to sucker punches. Through one awkwardly worded question, she gave me a pretext for blasting the Agency's policy of controlled leaks to the press. Through another, she inadvertently introduced an issue Griffin Bell had wanted her to avoid altogether.

"Do you contend, Mr. Snepp, that you owe no fiduciary duty to the Central Intelligence Agency?" she began.

Mark interjected: "Fiduciary duty to what?"

"Tell me what a fiduciary obligation means?" I chimed in.

She hesitated, trying to get her bearings. "It means to hold something in trust for another," she said finally.

"What is that *something*?" Mark persisted.

She paled, and I almost felt sorry for her. If she answered, "secrets," she could kiss this case good-bye. I'd held all the secrets I knew "in trust"—in confidence—and continued to do so.

"I think we are really quibbling and playing games here," she simpered.

Mark smiled malignly. "Does he have a fiduciary obligation to pick up his tray in the cafeteria?"

Sally gulped, tears welling.

— —

It was nearly twilight, Wednesday, April 19, when I fielded her last question. Immediately afterward, I raced to a hallway phone booth to call Bernie. In replaying the highlights of the seemingly endless inquisition, I didn't gloat. It had been too painful. But I did feel that the government understood for the first time that I was no dollar-grubbing lowlife out to destroy the CIA.

There was one moment I was particularly proud of, I told Bernie. It had come when Sally challenged me to explain why I didn't consider my behavior dishonorable.

"I could have blown sources and methods," was the way I'd answered her. "I could have gone abroad and been publishing anything I want. That is what I consider dishonorable."

Bernie listened and approved and assured me the government couldn't possibly mistake me for Agee or Marchetti any longer. Maybe this was the beginning of the end of the lawsuit.

That was overstating it, of course. But not even my opponents felt I'd suffered any real damage. The CIA's Mayerfeld, who'd sat in on most of the deposition, told me afterward that Sally hadn't landed a punch, though his reasons for thinking so scarcely did me credit. As he saw it, I'd proven myself to be as slippery a customer as any of the professional liars he counted among his colleagues at Langley.

Unfortunately, my own colleagues agreed. Geoff Vitt warned that if I diddled Judge Lewis as I had Sally, I'd wind up in jail for contempt. "Try to be forthcoming," John Sims counseled more soothingly. "You're not a prisoner of the Viet Cong!"

For all the strong opinions pro and con, though, the deposition would ultimately count for little. The "admissions," which Sally and her colleagues had distilled from my public interviews, were far more damaging than any answer she'd elicited from me.

Realizing this, Mark urged me to repudiate the admissions as misstatements made for publicity reasons.

I refused. Rash as some of the quotes were, none had been inspired by publicity considerations, I told him, and all were offset by less garbled, more helpful interviews, including the deposition itself.

Mark picked up the 595-page deposition transcript, weighed it with one hand, and then hefted the 5-page admissions with the other. He didn't have to tell me what he was thinking. To a judge of Lewis's tastes and attention span, only one of these dead mackerels would seem worthy of consumption.

CHAPTER 17

Pat and Bill

W RITTEN INTERROGATORIES are not normally the stuff of bomb-
shells. Lawyers for one side draw up impossibly convoluted questions which lawyers for the other side answer in the most evasive way
possible.

And yet, just two days after my deposition, a set of interrogatories we'd
previously submitted to the government produced a written response that
would define the case from now on.

Question: "Do you contend that *Decent Interval* contains classified information or any information concerning intelligence or CIA that has not
been made public by the CIA?"

Answer: "For the purpose of this litigation, the plaintiff does not so
contend."

It *was* a bona fide bombshell, a much needed confirmation from the government that I wouldn't be accused of any kind of security breach. The
CIA's own lawyers had signed off on the response package, the signature at
bottom being that of Ernie Mayerfeld, the rumpled general counsel's representative who'd sat glaring at me throughout my deposition.

When news of the breakthrough reached ACLU headquarters on Pennsylvania Avenue, the huzzahs would have roused even comatose boozers at
the nearby Hawk 'n' Dove bar. Even if Mayerfeld hadn't quite given me
Good Housekeeping's seal of approval, his response seemed more than suf-

ficient to set me apart from Marchetti and to render me blameless under the only contract we considered binding, my last one.

Over the next two weeks, Mayerfeld disposed of the rest of our interrogatories, though less satisfactorily. In one set of answers, he accused me of lying to eight different Agency officials about my intentions. In another, he claimed that my failure to submit to clearance "demonstrates the potential vulnerability of all information provided on a confidential basis.

"Any foreign government or individual who could provide confidential information to the CIA may be deterred from doing so," he intoned portentously.

If there was any proof for this outrageous allegation, he didn't feel compelled to provide it, and he gave equally short shrift to the few questions Lewis had permitted us about the Agency's discriminatory enforcement of the rules. Instead of addressing each one, he finessed them all by claiming to know of only two ex-employees—Joseph Burkholder Smith and Philip Agee—whose clearance violations had been allowed to go unpunished.

Two problem cases? *Come on.*

— —

"Mr. Bernstein, I presume your counsel has explained to you why you are here today. Your statements will be taken and they can be introduced at the trial later on in the case of Defendant Snepp."

Barely a week after I'd been interrogated, the prosecution summoned Robert Bernstein and Bob Loomis of Random House for back-to-back depositions, and announced that my onetime literary agent, Linley Stafford, would soon follow. Despite having ceded the secrecy issue to me, Sally and her colleagues remained convinced that my "admissions," those garbled press statements, exposed the conspiratorial nature of my offense. Hence: their determination to wring my "coconspirators" dry.

"Did Mr. Loomis make any statement to you that Mr. Snepp had indicated he was not going to submit his book for prepublication review?" Brook Hedge asked the president of Random House.

"At some point we became aware that he was not going to submit his book."

Why the prosecution chose not to put Bernie and Carla under oath I'll never know. Maybe they felt that "girlfriends"—Sally had already noted snidely that my dance card seemed unconscionably full—were too partisan to be useful. In any event, they kept their subpoenas focused solely on my *male* collaborators.

As it turned out, Bernstein and Loomis proved far tougher to handle than the government had imagined, and not merely because they had nothing to hide. Rather than travel to Washington to be interrogated, they exercised their right, as New Yorkers, to be heard on their own turf, in the offices of the Wall Street law firm Cahill, Gordon and Randel, whose senior partner, Floyd Abrams, was Random House's favorite outside counsel.

The setting itself would have awed the Queen Mother. The beautifully appointed conference room, with its wraparound windows, afforded a breathtaking view of the East River, which from eighteen floors up looked deceptively pristine. Even the lavatories, with their faint hint of pricy men's cologne, conveyed a sense of power and damn-their-eyes exclusivity.

No less impressive was Abrams himself, veteran of such landmark First Amendment battles as the Pentagon Papers case and *Knopf v CIA,* the publisher's challenge to the Marchetti deletions. A graceful, balding man with surprisingly spare eyebrows and a little gray over the collar, Abrams dominated the proceedings with his very insouciance, alternately yawning, stretching, and flipping through newspapers and a copy of *Decent Interval* as the opposition rambled on.

Still, he never missed a beat. Once, when Brook Hedge tried to maneuver Bernstein into admitting he'd sought legal advice about my book, Abrams cut her off simply by *warning* that he *might* invoke an attorney-client privilege.

Sally, who also was on hand, seemed equally starstruck. While leaving the questioning to Hedge, she deferred constantly to Abrams and policed her own like a nervous den mother, once even admonishing the CIA's representative, a bulbous young attorney named Chris Winkle, not to expect more than one beer at lunch. "I want you to be awake for this one," she remarked uncharitably.

My own counsel, uncharacteristically resplendent in a stylish suit, appeared duly awed himself. When time came for Mark to pose his own questions after the government's initial round, he began each one in a tremulous voice and then proceeded to spin syntactical pretzels that only a Jesuit could have digested with relish.

The two witnesses themselves, both remote and eminently respectable in their muted pinstripes, played on the deference accorded them and their attorney to keep Hedge off balance, even as she attempted to nudge them to the center of a conspiracy that existed only in her imagination.

"Was there any agreement that counsel would be provided to Mr. Snepp if the government interfered?"

"None at all," Bernstein assured her.

"Did you see it to your advantage that the book had not been submitted for prepublication review?" she inquired of Loomis.

"I would never recommend doing that"—the indignation was palpable—"for *publicity* purposes."

Hedge asked why, then, there'd been *any* need for subterfuge.

Loomis gave her a rueful smile. "I had been involved with other such books," he replied. "Not one with an agent. But we had published a book called *The Invisible Government* years back which was about the CIA. The CIA at that point either stole or bought a set of the galleys somehow. I was threatened on the phone. They tried to stop the book. So we were very wary of that kind of interference."

In his follow-up questioning, Mark pressed for detail, asking Loomis to recall exactly what he'd been told on that occasion by the director of Central Intelligence.

"That we were bad Americans," Loomis replied softly. "That if this manuscript had been given to a foreign national, the authors would have been put in jail immediately, and perhaps we would have been threatened with some other action."

Pursuing this line with Bernstein, Hedge wondered if he'd ever been worried about a preemptive strike against my book. Templing his fingers, he nodded. "I felt that if it got involved with the CIA, its publication could be delayed, whether or not there was a reason."

As the depositions continued and Hedge found herself frustrated time and again, her equanimity wore thin. Finally reverting to her characteristic machismo, she asked Bernstein nastily if he'd ever been advised by his lawyers that his decision to publish *Decent Interval* might expose him to a "tortious interference suit," that is, prosecution for "interference with business relations, interference with a contract."

"I think much later on we discussed that," he responded coolly.

Hedge let the matter drop. But in insinuating it just this way, she'd reminded us all that Random House was not beyond Griffin Bell's brand of justice.

During the lunch break, Abrams treated the defense and its witnesses to a sumptuous meal at one of those tony Wall Street clubs where only the host is given a copy of the menu with the prices listed. Over dessert and coffee, Mark, luxuriating in the ambience, thanked Abrams for his hospitality.

"You're welcome," Loomis popped in, knowing full well that Random House was feeding the meter.

Still, considering what he and Bernstein had avoided at the government's hands—"a tortious interference suit"—the bill probably was a bargain.

— —

Three days before the government was to take on its fourth and final deponent, Linley Stafford, I sat down with Bernie and gave her an ultimatum to pass on to him, since I was afraid that if I confronted him myself I would kill him. I wanted him to understand that if he trifled with me again, I'd let his children know he'd sacrificed friendship to avarice by rushing the contract with Random House and by trying to skim my advance. "Just tell him to tell the truth," I urged her.

She gave me a pained look and begged me not to ask this favor of her. There was this dream she'd been having recently, a dream in which she'd imagined driving a knife into a shadowy unidentifiable figure and feeling no regrets. Was this any frame of mind in which to approach her own boss!

Not once considering that the shadowy figure might be me, I refused to spare her. The following morning, she reluctantly let Stafford know that his self-interest had better coincide with my own.

— —

The heavy bifocals gave his eyes an elusive split-level quality. Blink or not, Stafford betrayed nothing.

"You didn't actually review *any* portion of the manuscript!" the government attorney asked him, unable to believe Stafford had had no contact with me for well over a year.

"No, I never saw the manuscript," he replied. "And I have not read the book." A theatrical shrug. "I've been busy."

"Do you still consider yourself to be a friend of Frank Snepp?"

"An *acquaintance.*"

"You no longer have a friendship with him?"

Stafford lifted his unlit pipe and sniffed at it. "I no longer have the close relationship we formerly had."

On the afternoon he was dragged under subpoena to the grungy offices of the U.S. Attorney in Manhattan, he was alone. John Sims showed up to monitor the inquisition on my behalf, but nobody sat in the consulting attorney's chair at Stafford's elbow.

"Did you ever discuss with Mr. Snepp his options under the secrecy agreement?" asked Glenn Whitaker, Sally's unctuous husband, who likewise was an attorney for the Justice Department. Because of her alleged exasperation with the defense, it had fallen to him to handle today's deposition.

"We discussed he had three options," acknowledged Stafford. "He could clear the manuscript. He could clear the galleys, or not clear."

With a touch of petulance he added: "They were *his* decisions. I was not involved."

Down the table, the only other government lawyer present, Mayerfeld's corpulent deputy, Chris Winkle, scribbled notes.

A half hour into the questioning, Whitaker cut to the marrow. Poking through a pile of documents, he extracted Exhibit Number 3, a copy of my Random House contract.

"Mr. Stafford, understand: I am not trying to trip you up," he said as he nudged the contract toward him. "I am just curious. Exhibit 3 bears, I think, your signature."

Stafford tipped his bifocals forward. Whitaker tapped the document delicately. "When did you give that to Random House?"

"Early January," said Stafford, referring to the month I'd quit the Agency. Whitaker opened his mouth to respond, but the witness was too fast.

"I should not at the time have forwarded the contract," Stafford continued. "I misunderstood a phone conversation with Frank saying—what he said was, 'I am *going* to resign.' "

Whitaker grew still. This wasn't what he'd wanted to hear.

He tried again, asking if any money had changed hands at the time. Stafford said yes, he'd received an eleven-thousand-dollar check from Random House, made out to him, representing the first half of my advance.

"Was that *prior* to Mr. Snepp's resignation?"

"It may have been—only because I forwarded the contract before I should have."

"Did you *tell* Mr. Snepp about the check?"

"No."

Whitaker's eyes narrowed. "Didn't he have any *interest* in how much money he was going to get!"

"He did know. It's right here." Stafford thumped the contract with a knuckle. "He did *not* know when Random House had signed it because I'd jumped the gun."

With this line of inquiry going nowhere, Whitaker abruptly chose another. Hoping to divide and conquer, he challenged Stafford to explain why our friendship had ended.

It was a question Stafford feared. The last thing he wanted to admit was that he'd tried to steal from me.

So, he lied—bald-facedly, shamelessly—claiming that we'd parted ways because of the interview I'd given *The Washington Post* about "Saigon's Secrets Seized" five months after my resignation.

"In the article was the mention that he was working on a book," grumped Stafford. "You don't crack something like that until you're ready. It's a waste of space—public relations."

Detecting a note of asperity, Whitaker tried again to drive a wedge, pushing him to concede that he'd introduced me to Random House shortly after my return from Vietnam—long before I'd admitted.

"When you spoke to Mr. Snepp," he posed, "did you tell him you would take some action to find a publisher?"

A puzzled look from the witness. "He wasn't interested at that point in doing a book," replied Stafford warily. "He wanted to stay inside the Agency and wanted to do it for the Agency."

"He talked about doing some sort of writing *for* the Agency?" asked Whitaker.

Stafford nodded. "I think they call it an after-action, or something."

"Did he express what sort of concerns motivated him?"

"Moral concerns," said Stafford softly. "Concern for the people who had been left behind."

"*That* was his concern! About the people who were left?" Whitaker refused to believe it.

"Yes," said Stafford, his voice almost a whisper now.

— —

With only four names on their deposition list—Snepp, Stafford, Loomis, and Bernstein—the government's attorneys were able to breeze through discovery in a wink.

Not so, the defense. Frustrated in our interrogatories and forced to rely on direct questioning for what we needed to know, we soon found ourselves locked in round-the-clock depositions with nearly every spook I'd danced with—sixteen in all, including Norm Jones, the inspector general's representative who'd interviewed me; Polgar; and Stansfield Turner himself.

As a courtesy, we allowed Hedge and the Whitakers to pick the venue for these depositions. To my dismay, they invariably favored CIA headquarters itself. Not only did the prospect of returning to the place fill me with a kind of primordial dread; I genuinely expected to be met with hostile demonstrations in every corridor.

To make sure we didn't attempt any demonstrations of our own, Sally marshaled out her own troops in force, and finally enlisted her own husband, Glenn, to spell her.

Already known irreverently around the Justice Department as "Ken and Barbie," the two Whitakers came dressed each morning as if for a country-club mixer, in tasseled Guccis and impeccable button-downs, their very preppiness making schoolmarmish Brook Hedge seem all the more drab by comparison.

The CIA's own contingent was a bit more ecumenical, its array of eccentrics ranging from a cadaverous house lawyer who did little more than cough incessantly to the omnipresent Ernie Mayerfeld himself.

A portrait of middle-aged seed in half-rim glasses and suits straight off the bargain racks, Mayerfeld bore himself with an aggressive arrogance I knew all too well, for he'd once been an accomplished field operative. Of all the CIA representatives present, he seemed by far the most likely to whip out a nine millimeter and put a bullet through my head.

— —

"Are you aware of any investigation, or any investigation by the inspector general's office, concerning the evacuation from Vietnam?"

"I know of no investigations."

When John Sims put that question to the inspector general's deputy, Norm Jones, on April 24, we were only two days into our deposition schedule and already numbingly exhausted.

"Do you remember if Mr. Snepp stated something such as: 'Now I would like to talk about the problems with the evacuation'?"

"I honestly don't."

This deposition was among our most important, for in attempting to justify myself, I'd made much of Jones's refusal to hear me out about the evacuation.

"Do you think it is possible that Mr. Snepp raised this issue and that you did not take note of it?" Sims persisted.

"As with anything," the witness replied peevishly, "it is possible. It is certain I didn't make a note of it."

When I'd arrived at CIA headquarters that morning, a uniformed guard had saluted me smartly and directed me to a reserved parking spot in front of the main entrance within easy range of pivoting surveillance cameras. A titter of excitement had greeted me as I entered the visitor's lounge. To my surprise, no picketers had materialized. Instead, the awestruck chief receptionist had congratulated me on my gumption and slipped me a copy of *Decent Interval* to be autographed.

"Did you take notes during the interview?"

The witness considered Sims's question impassively.

"Yes, I did," replied Jones, nibbling at a fingernail.

"Are those notes still in existence?"

An embarrassed pause. "No."

"When were they destroyed?"

"Six months after the investigation."

Abruptly, Sims flung a subpoenaed document on the table, a copy of the final report Jones had written about our interview. Highlighted was a passage in which he'd dismissed my criticism of Polgar's reporting practices as psychologically twisted, the product of "a classic father-son relationship."

"Did it ever *occur* to you," asked Sims, "that this might be perhaps too important an interview to engage in speculation about someone else's psyche?"

"Oh, I don't feel that way even now," said Jones, cheeks billowing. "Too important? That is a value judgment."

Shuffling through other documents, Sims spotted a reference to a CIA security investigation of one Carla Christiansen.

My stomach turned over. It was the first time Carla's name had appeared in any of the discovery material.

"Do you think it likely that there exists a file relating to *that* investigation?" Sims asked the witness.

Sally immediately interrupted, "What pertinence would that have!"

With extraordinary restraint, Sims explained that any report bearing on someone's alleged cooperation with me "is clearly a file that relates to Mr. Snepp."

"I don't believe it is, counsel!" she rejoined.

Turning back to the documents, Sims found another provocative reference, this one to a CIA file labeled "John Stockwell," which likewise had been withheld from us.

He appraised Jones cooly. "Was any effort made to look for documents relating to Mr. Snepp that might have been included in a file maintained under Mr. Stockwell's name?" he inquired.

"I made no such effort," replied the witness.

"Are you suggesting," Sally cut in, "that any document in the inspector general's office which has the words 'Frank Snepp' in it you are entitled to? Is *that* your reading of the subpoena?"

Sims nodded. "I would ask that those files be searched."

"I am willing to be helpful," she spat back, "but I am not going to ask somebody to spend the next three days reading every sheet of paper maintained in the inspector general's office files."

Sims glanced at me and saw I was about to blow. "Could we take a short recess?" he put in hastily.

Trailed by Security personnel, I retreated to a nearby rest room.

Withdrawing into a toilet stall, I took a moment to compose myself.

Only as I was about to unlock the door did I notice a line of graffiti on the wall: "Down with Turner! Snepp for Director!"

The tension snapped.

— —

Day Six.

"Mr. Layton, do CIA regulations prohibit the disclosure of classified information to individuals who are not cleared to receive it?"

"I am not that familiar with the regulations in detail."

Within a week of Jones's unburdening, Mark homed in on Bob Layton, the CIA officer who'd been assigned to bird-dog me. This, too, was a critical deposition. In answering our interrogatories, Mayerfeld had included Layton among the CIA officials who'd allegedly received "assurances" from me that I would submit to censorship.

Ten minutes into the deposition, Layton, smoking obsessively, pegged Mayerfeld as a liar by insisting I'd never promised anything. "I never came round to the conclusion," he added, "that Mr. Snepp was willing to submit his manuscript."

For the remainder of the grilling, Mayerfeld sat glowering down the table at him, furious at having been called out by one of his own.

"Did Mr. Snepp ever offer to show you portions of his manuscript?" Mark inquired midway through the morning of the second day of the deposition.

Layton tipped his head and recalled "vaguely" my having made such an offer to him. "If that came up," he added quickly, "I would have refused."

Such candor might have become another witness, might even have prompted some sympathy from me. But as I studied Layton across the expanse of documents spread between us, I couldn't help wondering how he dared to testify against me at all. He'd worked in Saigon, lived with the Vietnamese, and of all people knew how desperate I'd been in the fall of 1975 to draw official attention to their plight.

Mark asked him about that.

Cupping a match with his hand, Layton lit another cigarette and conceded that I had voiced concern "that no postmortem or after-action report was being prepared."

"What was your response?"

"I would suspect that I told Mr. Snepp that I too was somewhat surprised by this."

"Did you take any steps yourself to stimulate a postmortem?" Mark continued.

A blush rose in Layton's cheeks. "I did not."

I stared at him in consternation.

Sally caught my look.

"Mr. Lynch," she barked, "I believe Mr. Snepp has been smirking at the witness's responses!"

Mark leaned over, exchanged a few whispered words with me, then, drawing himself up, delivered a most lawyerly rebuttal.

"During our off-the-record consultation," he announced to the room, "my client informed me he was not smirking. In any event, I cautioned him that smirking is inappropriate at depositions, and I am sorry Mrs. Whitaker was unnerved."

— —

Over the next few days, the deponent's chair was occupied in turn by Ted Shackley, George Carver, and Paul Walsh, each of whom endeavored to keep a straight face and civil tongue as my lawyers heaped on the impertinences.

"Did the East Asia division compile a damage assessment in order to learn the lessons of the fall of Saigon?" Mark importuned onetime division chief Shackley.

"No!" snapped the witness.

"Did Mr. Snepp express his feeling that the Saigon station reporting could have been better?" Mark posed *this* to Carver, the director's erstwhile principal adviser on the war.

"Yes, I recall he did," Carver acknowledged. He then looked at me and vouchsafed a condescending smile. "I reminded Mr. Snepp, when we discussed these matters, that it was an imperfect world, composed of imperfect human beings, and things could always be better."

Again Mark to Shackley: "Did you have occasion to meet with Mr. Snepp on his return?"

"I may have seen him on the way to the men's room."

"Can you recall substantive discussions?"

"No."

Though Shackley refused to admit any communion with me, Assistant Deputy Director Paul Walsh was only too happy to pretend he'd borne my angst gamely.

"I can't say that Frank said these words," he told John Sims under questioning, "but I was left with the impression that he had been through a great wrenching emotional experience."

"How did you form that impression?" Sims asked.

"He seemed to me pretty uptight. As you know, a lot of people, if not all the people who had gone through the evacuation, were pretty emotionally upset about it."

"Did you suggest to anyone that a formal investigation would be appropriate?"

A slight hesitation from Walsh. "I did not."

— —

As one witness after another copped to the indifference that had nearly driven me mad, Mark himself grew indignant, and by the time he had Shackley in his sights he'd lost all patience. What triggered the inevitable blowup was Shackley's inability to recall a memo somebody else had written about me. Carefully placing a copy of the document on the table, Mark leaned forward and in a voice tight with anger demanded, "Why?" Such an easy thing. Why couldn't the witness remember?

Shackley's sallow skin paled into translucence. "My concept of the modern man as a manager," he hissed, "is the guy who can take paper from the in-box and move it to the out-box and never put a piece of paper down because it accumulates."

He grabbed the memo and crumpled it.

"I read something, I call somebody, I go to a meeting, I call somebody. If he's not there, I send a memo. You know—*finished*! Because today's crisis is tomorrow's dead file."

He slammed a finger to his forehead. *"I don't carry it up in the cranial file!"*

Ice crystals hung in the air. Quickly, Mark changed the subject. Later, he would confide to me that of all our witnesses, Shackley seemed the one most capable of locking a troublesome ACLU attorney in a car and running in a hose from the exhaust.

— —

For all the evasions and the acid exchanges, though, none of the early depositions was a waste. Layton confirmed that the CIA *had* leaked classified documents to Bernard Kalb. Shackley admitted that he'd never been obliged to clear any of his own press statements. Carver acknowledged that I *had* sought permission to do a book under Agency auspices, and Walsh agreed that he and his deputy, William Parmenter, had vetoed it.

Separately, in his own deposition, Parmenter conceded that neither he nor Walsh had ever informed me that I had to submit even *non*secrets for clearance.

Sims asked him why.

"Because," said Parmenter, "it never arose."

Useful as these admissions were, however, much of the information we uncovered was like a dagger to the heart. Through interrogation and subpoena, the contempt in which I'd been held took on the names and faces of people I'd considered friends.

One of our most shocking discoveries came three days into our deposition schedule, when Sally released the record of an interview which Skip Dunn of Security and John Greaney of the general counsel's office had conducted with one Daphne Miller, just before my resignation from the CIA.

To judge from the document, the marvelously loquacious Ms. Miller had flayed me, betrayed me, and identified Random House as my only known contact in the publishing world.

At first, I couldn't even put a face to her name. But gradually, as I picked through the interview notes, I remembered the young woman from the CIA map department with whom I'd had a brief fling. But why had she reacted so vengefully?

Mark swatted me across the shoulder and reminded me that hell hath no fury. But he saw nothing funny in the implications of Daphne's treachery. If, as the interview documents suggested, she'd blown Random House's identity two years before, how could the CIA claim to have been stymied by my "duplicity"? Indeed, as he saw it, Daphne might actually have done me a backhanded favor.

I wasn't comforted.

Nor was there any comfort in discovering that hers wasn't the worst betrayal. Two days later, Sally handed over a memo Bob Layton had written months before about helpful tips he'd picked up from—Pat and Bill Johnson.

"Is the information in paragraph two," Mark asked Layton under deposition, "information which was provided to you by Mr. and Mrs. Bill Johnson?"

"It is," he acknowledged.

When Mark first showed me the note, I refused to accept its implications. "Everybody knew they were friends of mine," I protested. "Why shouldn't Layton have contacted them?"

Later I dashed off a telegram to the Johnsons at their home in Colorado, asking them to testify on my behalf. For days I waited for a reply. None came.

In the meantime, the CIA released another series of memos, these written by John Greaney about the help he'd received from my "two good friends."

As a small child, I had learned to escape pain by withdrawing into myself, by burrowing so far below the surface that no emotion could touch me. With the revelations about the Johnsons, I found I had no deeper to go.

CHAPTER 18

The Admiral's Unburdening

Duringour second week of depositions, Brook Hedge announced that my attorneys had finally been granted limited security clearances. For the first time, they were allowed to know the identities of operatives whose testimony might save my hide.

It was too little, far too late.

By now, the government's stinginess, its niggling responses to our interrogatories, had thrown us so off stride that we'd be hard-pressed to complete our depositions within Lewis's standing three-week deadline.

On Friday morning, April 28, Mark trudged into the judge's courtroom to beg for more time. His Honor opened with his usual tact. "You can ask for an extension," he bellowed, "but you know it's going to be denied!"

Sally strode to the lectern to accuse us of having dragged our feet during discovery even though she'd systematically thwarted our interrogatories and subpoenas. Demonstrating admirable restraint, Mark responded coolly by offering to wrap everything up in two weeks' time if the court would just cut us the slack. After a few more barbed exchanges, Lewis agreed. But he was adamant: A deposition a day! Otherwise—straight to trial!

— —

Day Fifteen.

"Can you tell us, Mr. Greaney, when you first became aware of the Snepp matter?"

"The closest I can say is the first week in January 1976."

I hadn't laid eyes on CIA attorney John Greaney in two years, not since that winter's day in 1976 when he and Skip Dunn of Security had precipitated my resignation from the Agency by demanding an affidavit that would have made *anything* I wrote forfeit to the censors. The gaunt face under the tousle of gray hair hadn't changed much in the interim.

Mark asked Greaney what had prompted that final confrontation with me, and was told of the interview he and Dunn had previously conducted with Daphne Miller.

"Did you believe the information which Miss Miller provided was credible?" continued Mark, handing the witness a memo Dunn had written about the interview.

Greaney pushed a finger at one part of the document. "I didn't believe the third sentence."

Mark smiled faintly and read the sentence back. It was a paraphrase of Daphne's revelatory assertion that I was "dealing with Random House in New York."

"Why didn't you believe that?" asked Mark.

Greaney plucked nervously at his lower lip. "I didn't believe Miss Miller's statement, period!"

Mark paused to let that sink in. Glenn Whitaker shot the witness an irritated look, and for a moment I almost pitied this dilapidated CIA attorney who'd done so much to thwart me. Obviously, he'd fumbled badly.

With a hint of gloating, Mark ventured on, asking Greaney if he'd considered taking legal action against me after our set-to on the eve of my resignation. The witness said he had.

Mark picked up Dunn's memo of that encounter and quoted from it: " 'The Subject was specifically queried as to whether he would sign an affidavit to the effect that he would submit the manuscript to the agency.' "

Mark looked up. "Did you think the secrecy agreement was insufficient in itself?"

"No," said Greaney gruffly.

Mark read on: " 'Subject was very firm in his response by saying that he would sign no such document and he has no intention of extending his legal obligation beyond the original EOD secrecy agreement.' "

Again a glance at the witness. "Does EOD refer to the entrance-on-duty?"

"Yes."

Whitaker cast his eyes skyward as if invoking divine help. Much as the government might want to paint me as a cynical rule-breaker, the memo made clear that the moment I'd left the Agency, I'd been convinced my original secrecy agreement, which I hadn't seen in eight years, was limited in scope.

"Did you believe that the thrust of the book was to be the fall of Vietnam?" Mark continued to Greaney.

"I had the impression it was an inflated view of Mr. Snepp's activities in Vietnam."

As the deposition wore on, Greaney acknowledged that his initial reluctance to sue me had been due to uncertainty over whether a manuscript existed: Sometimes he'd been convinced; sometimes not.

"When did you *again* become convinced?" Mark persisted.

"After talking to Mr. and Mrs. William Johnson."

I felt a chill along my spine.

Bestowing a mirthless smile on the witness, Mark asked what services the Johnsons had performed for him. Greaney conceded that they'd provided an affidavit for use against me in court and tapes of conversations with me. But, he added hastily, he'd never listened to the recordings or seen any transcript of their contents.

I snatched up a pen and jotted a note to Mark. The tapes were key, I wrote. The tapes showed the Johnsons sharing secrets with me. If Greaney could be made to admit that he'd heard them, he'd have to admit that his informants were tainted.

Mark scanned the note quickly, then shifted his gaze to Glenn Whitaker. Why hadn't the tapes been turned over to us? he demanded.

"No relevance!" rejoined the government lawyer.

A frown creased the sudden blush on Mark's face. Such objections were too vague, he protested. We deserved more precision.

Whitaker sniffed contemptuously. "I don't intend to give you any other response today or at any time for that matter."

"Is it your position," Mark replied carefully, "that I am not entitled to a *specific* objection?"

"You have gotten it."

Mark grasped the edge of the table, knuckles white. "I would recommend a refresher course in the English language for you!" he stammered.

Insult wasted. Whitaker refused to budge.

— —

Rough and tumble though it was, Greaney's deposition was merely a warm-up for the main event, the interrogation of his erstwhile informants, Pat and Bill Johnson.

Just before their arrival from Colorado, the government released Bill's latest memo about me, eight pages of single-spaced vitriol he'd composed shortly after my *60 Minutes* interview.

"Snepp never intended to make intelligence his career," declared the man I'd thought my friend. *"His ambition, probably from a time before he joined the Agency, was to publish books. Not particularly to write books. But to make a splash with books."*

The actual morning of the depositions, I first glimpsed "my two good friends" across the main-floor corridor at CIA headquarters.

"Snepp's opportunism was, or is, mixed with self-doubt, a sense of guilt that is disarming in his dealings with older people who try, for the good of the Service, to make the best out of the younger generation."

Pat, red-eyed and puffy-cheeked, approached me tentatively and bestowed an unenthusiastic hug. Bill, in bow tie and long face, grasped my hand briefly and greeted me facetiously as "son."

"Snepp always sought the easy simplification, the rhetorical twist, the adman's gimmick."

My lawyers quickly closed round me and hustled me away toward the elevators.

"This tendency affected the quality of his prose, or rather, made it impossible for him to understand what is meant by such critical terms as 'prose.' "

A security man unlocked the door to Room 6E49 and ushered us in.

". . . he was a lousy interrogator and a dishonest reporter . . ."

Mark asked me to help lay out the exhibits, the various journal entries and memos Bill had secretly written about me over the past two and a half years. As I shuffled through them, a nausea rose in me like the first intimation of poison.

"He has also stolen and used for his own enrichment property belonging to his employer . . ."

Settling himself at the end of the table, Bill gazed at me with such hatred, I was sure he would have shot me dead if he'd had a pistol handy.

"Snepp compounded his breach of trust with the government by deceiving the individuals he was interviewing . . ."

Mark smiled as he turned to the witness.

"Did there come a time," he asked, "when you began to furnish information concerning Mr. Snepp to officers of the Central Intelligence Agency?"

"I considered that all my contacts with Frank Snepp, as with other officers of the Agency, was Agency property," Bill answered briskly. "I usually recorded what contacts I had to record."

"Would you report these contacts?"

"I kept and do keep people informed of my contacts and the contents thereof, according to my judgment of who has use for the information, both orally and by memo."

I listened transfixed. He sounded robotic, inexorable.

Later, Mark asked Pat if she, too, had had occasion to report on me to the CIA.

"I don't think there was a beginning, middle, or an end," she replied, sipping diffidently at her water glass. "I think it was sort of in the natural course of events."

— —

Throughout the daylong ordeal, both witnesses tried to discredit my reasons for avoiding the censors. Pat insisted that, as briefers in Saigon, we'd never had the discretion to speak publicly without clearance. Bill averred stoutly that the Agency *had* prepared a postmortem on the evacuation, Shackley's Vietnam questionnaire, though he couldn't be sure, he admitted, that a final report had ever been written. "I presume it was," he muttered uneasily.

As in his memos to Greaney, Bill also tried to minimize the help he'd given me, insisting he'd read only two chapters of my manuscript.

Pat couldn't lie so easily. She confirmed that Bill had seen "other materials" and had served as a kind of "literary consultant" to me.

Both witnesses acknowledged having given Greaney the tapes of our conversations. Asked if the CIA attorney had discussed a possible lawsuit against me, Bill said no. "I am not a lawyer. He probably thought I wouldn't understand." But again, Pat was more candid. "There probably was discussion of legal action," she conceded.

On an even more delicate issue—whether they'd given me classified information—both admitted having discussed secrets with me that we'd known from our days together in the Agency, and both claimed to have shut me out after realizing I wasn't going to clear my manuscript. But, try as they might, they could not recall when that had been.

Nor could they be any more certain that I'd deceived them about my intentions. Pat acknowledged that she'd always thought it "possible" that I would not submit to censorship. Bill insisted he'd repeatedly urged me to do so, but when asked how I'd responded, he could only yammer embarrassedly, "I don't recall. I think I never heard Mr. Snepp say he would *not* clear the book."

It was a giant step backward. Though he'd accused me in the safety of the CIA's bosom of misleading him and others, he could not now bring himself to repeat the lie under oath.

— —

It was shortly after four that afternoon when Mark posed his final question. Pat was in the deponent's chair, and as Glenn Whitaker and Ernie Mayerfeld began gathering up papers and briefcases, she rose and came round the table to me. "I can't wish you good luck," she said, leaning to kiss me on the cheek, "but I can wish you God's speed." She then dipped her head mockingly and retreated into the hallway where Bill was waiting.

As she threaded her arm through his, he shot me one last murderous glance, then turned and swept her triumphantly toward the elevators.

That night, as I sifted through my emotions, trying not to succumb to them, I kept harkening to Bill's remark about routinely keeping book on friends and contacts. It was the clearest articulation I'd ever heard of the mind-set of the inveterate spy, and perhaps the best explanation I would ever have for what they'd done. Nurtured for thirty years on the voyeuristic psychology of espionage, they probably couldn't have resisted intruding on the lives of others if their own lives had depended on it.

— —

The Johnsons had been a surprise, their hostility unforeseen, but when I arrived at CIA headquarters on the fourth Monday of our deposition derby for the questioning of Tom Polgar, I had no illusions about what was in store. Long ago, I'd reconciled myself to the enduring emnity of this man.

Beneath the crown of newly cropped peach fuzz, Polgar's face looked thinner than I'd remembered, and the button nose commensurately larger. As the questioning got under way, he adopted a benign, almost casual air. But there was no mistaking the emotions seething underneath. Immediately challenging my claim that I'd had discretion in conducting briefings in Saigon, he dismissed me as "a relatively low-level employee of the station," as if I could never have borne such responsibility.

Mark instantly called him out, confronting him with official personnel documents, many of them over his own signature, describing me variously as "senior analyst . . . the most able briefer in Vietnam . . . uniquely essential . . . a thoroughly effective interrogator . . . the principal drafter of station appraisals, presenting the views of the senior officer"—Polgar himself—"on political and strategic questions."

Polgar listened with grim resignation. He could no more dispute any of this than he could deny having repeatedly promoted me. All he could do was avoid my eyes.

Mark asked him if I'd attempted to prompt an official inquiry into the evacuation.

A shaft of light sliced across the panes of Polgar's thick glasses. "He told me he would like to write such a postmortem."

"What was your response?"

"I had no problem with that."

"Did you know whether the Agency was either conducting or preparing to conduct such a postmortem?

Polgar clasped his hands like a man trying to pray. "I had no knowledge of it."

Mark hauled out a letter Polgar had recently sent to a reporter complaining at length and in detail about *Decent Interval.* "Did you obtain approval from anyone in the CIA before sending this letter?" he asked.

"I object!" Sally Whitaker cried, "and advise the witness not to answer on the grounds of relevancy!"

Mark flicked the letter with a well-gnawed thumbnail. "I would like to note that this line of questioning is highly relevant to our defense of selective enforcement. This letter discusses some of the events which were discussed in *Decent Interval.*" He leaned forward and peered at Sally over the rim of his glasses. "We would like to ask if you would reconsider your objection and instruct the witness to answer."

"I *will* reconsider our position," she replied—then, after a beat, added, "and having done so, advise you that we do not intend to change it."

— —

For pure obduracy Sally's performance that morning surpassed anything we'd seen before. Time and again, she refused to produce documents we'd requested, claiming that some were duplicative of previously released items and others protected as "attorney work-product," since Polgar had helped her prepare for the lawsuit. At one point, she simply rattled off a series of diverse and unrelated objections without settling on any one of them.

Mark's face reddened. "Can you identify the documents that fall within the objections you just asserted?"

"I believe I have described them sufficiently enough."

"How many documents are there?"

Sally gave him a pitying look as if he were beyond help. "No, I won't."

Even Polgar gaped in astonishment.

Mark was practically levitating. "Are you going to tell me what your ground for the objection is!"

"Same ground as previously stated."

"You have stated so many," he roared, "I can't possibly know which ones you are referring to!"

A dismissive shrug. "You have such an excellent memory, I'm sure you can!"

Mark wasn't one to suffer any insult gladly, and moments later, after Sally made the mistake of asking a question that had previously been answered, he lashed back at her. "I am beginning to wonder," he snorted, "if you pay attention to the conversations that take place in these depositions."

Her lip quivered. "I will not dignify your comment with a response!"

— —

The antagonisms of that morning carried over in spades to our next deposition, for the testimony being sought there was so critical to both sides that neither could afford to give an inch. Indeed, whatever we might drag out of Admiral Stansfield Turner could well determine the very outcome of the case.

To handicap us in advance, Sally refused to grant us any more than an hour with the witness on the excuse that top-ranking government officials should be immune to the rigors of civil suits. Then, on the assigned afternoon, she hobbled us further by having Turner show up twenty minutes late, thus forcing Mark to jettison several critical questions. Malignly, she refused to grant us a follow-up session without a court order, which she knew Lewis would never grant.

Before being sworn in, Turner circuited the room to shake hands with all present, giving me a particularly warm squeeze. Even to my ever-suspicious eye, he appeared the very portrait of probity, the iron-gray hair and square jaw setting off a complexion so flawless that it might have been dusted with makeup.

Mark was so impressed that he took care to punctuate even the most pointed questions with a deferential "sir."

Still, throughout the interrogation, the witness himself seemed ill at ease, flicking nervous glances around the room even as he fidgeted with a fountain pen, the studs in his French cuffs clicking disconcertingly across the tabletop. Only when commenting on my integrity—"I simply took this gentleman at his word. . . . I felt he was sincere"—did he let his eyes settle on me.

From the outset, Mark's tactic was to recall Turner's public comments about me and ask him to confirm, explain, or deny them. To my amazement, the witness stumbled repeatedly, particularly when quizzed about his favorite topic: my "duplicitous" performance during our get-together the previous summer.

Mark set up the key question carefully: "I believe you stated that you recollect Mr. Snepp assuring you that he would submit his manuscript."

Turner gave Glenn Whitaker an uneasy look.

"Can you recall," Mark continued with studied precision, "how he made that statement?"

"I think he made it in terms of saying that he was going to live up to his agreement," Turner replied hesitantly, the cuff links beating their tattoo. "I think his response to my query was, 'I am going to live up to my agreement.' Something to that effect."

I felt a prickle of exhilaration. This was a far cry from what Turner had peddled publicly, with his incessant claim that I'd explicitly promised him my manuscript.

Mark gently nudged the admiral again: "He said he would *live up to his agreement*? Is that your testimony?"

"That is my best recollection," said Turner with a hint of defensiveness. "There was no question in my mind when he left that he had made a commitment."

"To do what?" Mark retorted.

"To submit the manuscript to the Central Intelligence Agency for security review."

Mark tried to suppress a smile. "Was that the *impression* that you derived from his statement, that he would live up to his agreement?"

Sally and Glenn Whitaker seemed to shrink into their Guccis.

"That is correct," Turner answered sheepishly. "I took action based on that assumption."

Assumption!

The word exploded in my ear. I tried to catch Turner's eye. He looked away, embarrassed.

Mark pressed on, asking Turner what action he'd taken based on his "assumption" that I'd turn over the manuscript.

For the next several minutes, the befuddled witness again sounded like one of his press releases, claiming that, in light of my "pledge," he'd decided against seeking an injunction; that his general counsel, Tony Lapham, had taken no further action to prompt one; that the next time I'd come to his attention was the day *Decent Interval* had first made headlines.

Mark listened politely, then less politely presented Turner with evidence, in the form of subpoenaed documents, that he was lying.

Slap! Exhibit Number 1 hit the table with gratifying resonance. It was the letter I'd sent to Lapham's deputy, John Morrison, right after my meeting with Turner—the one in which I'd demanded why I was being asked to sign a new secrecy agreement if my original one was valid.

Slap! On top of this landed Exhibit Number 2: a follow-up memo Morrison had sent to Turner, describing my letter as "coy or evasive" and suggesting yet another overture to the Justice Department to determine if legal action could be taken against me.

Confronted with these documents, Turner raised his well-manicured hands in a gesture of resignation. "Clearly the answer that I gave"—he was stammering now—"was incorrect."

"Right," Mark shot back. Then, adopting a most innocent tone, he added: "I certainly wasn't meaning to trip you up."

Turner flushed, struggling to keep his temper. "No, I'm not complaining," he bumbled on. "I am not ashamed that I don't remember these things."

Not ashamed! I clenched my jaw and willed myself not to blurt out something imprudent. The Director of Central Intelligence had spent the last four months smearing me with wonderfully honed untruths. And now he was ready to plead—*poor memory!*

Pursuing the thread, Mark forced Turner to admit that, far from trusting in any "promise" from me, he had agreed with Morrison that I was being coy and evasive, and had approved another query to the Justice Department to see if I could legally be barred from publishing. Glenn Whitaker invoked attorney-client privilege to keep us from learning the Justice Department's response, but enough had been said already to give the lie to Turner's oft repeated assertion that he'd been tricked by my "false promises" into calling off legal action against me.

As the allotted hour drew to a close, Mark stepped up the pressure. Whipping out a copy of the CIA's press release, "Answers to Inquiries," he demanded to know how Turner could reconcile my letter to Morrison with the line, "The director had no further word from Mr. Snepp"—following the May 17 meeting—"until he read descriptions of the book in today's newspapers."

Squirming, Turner answered lamely, "What I intended in saying this was that Mr. Snepp did not communicate with me in any way about his intent to publish his book."

By now, the Whitakers were tapping their watches impatiently, but Mark managed to slip in one last zinger. Producing a letter that Turner had recently sent to the Senate Intelligence Committee, he gestured to a passage in which the admiral had bragged about having generously "provided Mr. Snepp with unclassified information which he requested." It was a reference to the highly classified briefing package Colby had allowed to be shown to the Kalbs and which Turner had subsequently released to me.

Mark gave Turner an appraising look. "Were these documents classified at the time Mr. Snepp requested them from you?"

"Yes," he answered stoutly. "But I arranged to have them declassified for his purposes."

"Had you been able to determine, Admiral, whether those documents had been shown to the Kalbs before they were declassified?"

"No."

I tried again to catch Turner's eye—he knew the Kalbs had been shown secrets—but he was too busy scrambling to his feet to give me a second glance.

Despite this last bit of prevarication, Mark danced out of the deposition convinced that the witness had badly hurt the government's case. In answering our interrogatories, Mayerfeld had put the admiral at the top of the list of CIA officials I'd supposedly misled about my intentions. But as Turner had admitted, I'd not so much misled him as he'd misled himself.

Mayerfeld had also declared in his representations that the Agency had been so taken in by my deceit that it had been cheated out of the opportunity to stop me. But again, Turner's testimony told a different tale, leaving the government's sleaziest charge against me—that I'd lied my way into print—empty and moribund.

— —

For the balance of the depositions, Hedge and the two Whitakers simply tried to stall us off, often stretching their "not relevant" claim to absurd lengths to keep us away from key evidence. The biggest stretch came during our questioning of a representative of Turner's *Decent Interval* task force, specifically when we asked about the group's contention that I'd never attempted to prompt a postmortem of the evacuation. Since this "finding" reflected badly on my credibility, John Sims wanted to know how it had been reached.

Instantly, Sally objected: "Lack of relevance!"

Sims's eyes widened. "Are you taking the position that Mr. Snepp's credibility is not an issue in this litigation?"

"Only to the extent that you put it in issue," she replied breezily.

He tried again, but was immediately cut off. "I am not going to argue with you," she snapped. "You ask the questions, get your answers, and get out of here!" After another flurry she added acerbically, "These depositions are nothing but harassment, clearly, and we are not going to put up with it."

The cynicism and recalcitrance of the government's lawyers prompted the same in many of the witnesses we called, and even encouraged one of them, Skip Dunn of CIA Security, to feign amnesia to avoid leveling with us. Midway through our session with him, John Sims produced a subpoenaed CIA memo that likened me to Philip Agee, Sam Adams, and Victor Marchetti, and asked what inference was to be drawn from the comparison, the obvious one being that critics of the Agency share a disproportionate susceptibility to official persecution.

Dunn studied the document with exaggerated intensity, determined not to be drawn out. "I couldn't really accurately describe the qualities they have in common," he answered at last.

Sims pressed him: "To your knowledge, has Mr. Marchetti ever been *critical* of the Agency?"

"I don't recall," Dunn replied with mock innocence. "I am not that familiar with Mr. Marchetti."

Questioned about Sam Adams, he proved equally dodgy, and when challenged about the Agency's archenemy, Philip Agee, this deputy chief of Security pretended to be positively brain-dead. He couldn't "remember" enough about "Mr. Agee or his book," he said, to be able to "analyze" one or the other.

Sims rolled his eyes. "Do you remember whether the book is critical of the Agency?"

"I will object!" cried Brook Hedge, thus shutting off any further inquiry into whether only critics of the CIA were getting the short end of justice.

— —

So excessive was the government's stonewalling that it finally, inevitably, backfired. Sally herself set up the moment by refusing in one of the later depositions to surrender a document that she'd given us in censored form in an earlier one.

"Mrs. Whitaker," Mark injected chidingly, "would you please explain for the record why we are getting objections to documents which you've already produced?"

Her large eyes moistened. "It's just not humanly possible," she stammered, "to check and double-check everything."

"I frankly interpret this as dilatory and obfuscatory," he retorted, reminding her that she'd used the same rationale she was citing now—attorney-client privilege—to justify withholding only *parts* of the document before. Such inconsistency made a mockery of the privilege.

"Counsel, you have the document!" she wailed. "And I resent that accusation. If you don't like my explanation, I am sorry. That's just too bad." She dabbed her nose with a tissue. "And you can do whatever you want about it now. You can go to court. I don't care."

Mark countered with a better idea, arguing that because of her inconsistency, she'd forfeited the right to withhold any part of the memo and should release it in its entirety.

Her snuffling reached a crescendo. Ernie Mayerfeld cupped a hand to her ear and whispered encouragement. Nodding pathetically, she choked back her tears and held firm against any concession.

But she couldn't help looking the fool. From then on, her husband, Glenn, did most of the heavy lifting for the government.

CHAPTER 19

Spoiler

B Y THE TIME the depositions were over, the shock of betrayal and the pain of having to confront so many wrenching memories had given way to the kind of bizarre euphoria that comes from having dodged a bullet and survived. I could also content myself with having scored a major coup by blowing a hole in the CIA's very rationale for censorship. Over the past four weeks, Sally had repeatedly left classified information intact in supposedly "sanitized" documents released to us under subpoena. Each time, I'd spotted her error and urged her to correct it, and each time, she'd refused for fear of embarrassing the prosecution. The public record of the case thus remained speckled with secrets, the only ones ever compromised as a result of the publication of *Decent Interval.* Still, no one could now honestly claim that I didn't know how to recognize and protect secrets on my own.

Of all the testimony we elicited during discovery, the most immediately valuable gave proof to what we'd always assumed. In an otherwise dull, gray deposition, deputy CIA general counsel John Morrison had confirmed that a manuscript with no confidential data in it, one like my own, would not be subject to clearance under the terms of my final secrecy agreement.

For Mark, that cinched it, delivering the case for us in a neat, tidy package. Believing that even myopic Judge Lewis would now have to see the light, he dashed off a brief asking him to rule in my favor summarily. A hearing was set for May 12.

Had it come sooner, I might have walked away vindicated. But sadly, the lag time between the filing and the court date was just long enough to allow an unforeseen catastrophe to obliterate my chances for easy exoneration. During this fateful seven-day interval, my old rabble-rousing friend, John Stockwell, stepped from the shadows and flung an uncleared memoir of his own onto front pages and television screens across the country. Nothing would ever be the same again.

The book, a scathing indictment of CIA activities in Angola, caught me broadside. The first I learned of its publication was on the day it happened. Bernie and I were out for a stroll in her West Side neighborhood when our friend, Gloria Emerson, came rushing up in a dither. "Have you heard!" she shrieked. "John's going to be on *60 Minutes* tonight!"

Bernie slumped against me. My own legs buckled. You didn't have to be a cynic to know that Stockwell's born-again extremism would do me no good.

As I would learn only later, he'd been planning his surprise for months. After *Decent Interval* had come out, he'd gone to ground, snagged a publisher, and written as fast as he could, completing his manuscript without a nod to the CIA. Like my own book, his *In Search of Enemies* had been edited and printed secretly and distributed by a sales force innocent of its contents and authorship. The *60 Minutes* broadcast was merely one more leaf snatched from my own playbook.

But oh, the timing was lousy.

"CIA Ex-Agent Follows Snepp, Writes of Secret Angola War," cried *The Washington Post*. In a stroke, Stockwell had given the government all the proof it needed that I was some sort of wayward Pied Piper beckoning disgruntled former colleagues off to the printing presses.

— —

If Stockwell had stuck to the facts, his antics might have been redeemed. The CIA's secret war in Angola *had* been an abomination. To circumvent congressional restrictions, the Agency had disguised combat advisers as "intelligence-gatherers," forked out millions for mercenaries, colluded with the despicable South African security service, and misled lawmakers about the extent of its involvement in the conflict. These truths needed telling, and there were no secrets among them, for it wasn't the Angolans who'd been kept in the dark, but Congress and the American people.

But Stockwell wasn't content to play messenger. He wanted to be an avenging angel, too. "I would like to close the CIA down," he declaimed to *The Washington Star.* The CIA had done things, he told Mike Wallace, "that stretch the bounds of conscience."

Well, yes; true enough.

But for all his moral indignation, Stockwell hadn't quite mastered the script he'd borrowed from his new liberal friends, and an incongruous pragmatism kept leaching through. "Obviously, when you do things that are illegal and bad," he told the *Star,* "it would be nice to have them win, to succeed—to be able to say, 'Well, it was kind of a bad thing we did, but at least it worked.' But when you don't have the integrity, discipline, and competence to win, there isn't anything to pin a rationale on."

Such ambivalence didn't play well with the press. "If we grasp what he has been saying these past few days—and this isn't always easy—" editorialized the *Star,* "he initially came to condemn the operations of which he had knowledge because they failed. His objections are reminiscent of the double-whammy barrage of congressional investigators: that what the CIA did was often illegal and unconscionable and besides it didn't work."

Even more troubling, especially to me, was Stockwell's somewhat casual way with secrets. While declining to expose agents' names as Philip Agee had done—"I don't have the stomach for it," he told one reporter—he seemed constantly to be playing chicken with himself. On *60 Minutes* he punctuated a sober discussion of Angola by announcing gratuitously that the CIA had a dozen undercover operatives working at the United Nations. The following morning, at a press conference, he admitted having salted his book with secrets.

Logically, none of this should have redounded on me, since Stockwell and I were as different as night and day. When asked, for instance, why he hadn't reacted as I had to our Vietnam misadventures, he responded blithely, "Vietnam to me was in effect a break in my African series of tours. I wasn't in the mood to blow the whistle then. I was just in the mood to ride this tour out." It was an appalling declaration, and if the media and the CIA had been listening closely, they would have realized that we weren't speaking from the same page at all.

But unfortunately, the many differences between us were soon lost to view. On *60 Minutes,* Stockwell smudged the lines himself by announcing grandly that if the Agency hadn't been so corrupt, "it probably wouldn't have occurred to myself and Snepp and Marchetti and Agee and others to speak out." *The Washington Post* was moved to portray the CIA's two latest turncoats as twin peas from the same poisonous pod, and *The Wash-*

ington Star decried "the recruitment policies that have made such callow and incontinent people privy to sensitive operations."

In view of this easy lumping together of the faithless, my bid for summary judgment quickly became a sick joke.

— —

On the morning of the hearing itself, the Alexandria courthouse was overflowing with reporters, most of them on hand for the *Truong-Humphrey* proceedings. A few did break away, however, to watch Mark perform in a chamber down the hall.

Speaking from scrawled notes, he sketched out his main arguments, insisting that since I'd published no secrets, I'd violated neither my termination pact nor any implicit fiduciary obligation of trust. "We believe the government has no cause of action against Mr. Snepp, and this case should be dismissed," he declared bravely.

"Well, that is denied without going further," Lewis retorted, clucking impatiently under his breath. "I disagree with you in the beginning. The question is not whether it"—he meant *Decent Interval*—"is classified or nonclassified. The question is whether that contract can be enforced, if he will submit what he is going to publish before he publishes it."

Ernie Mayerfeld, seated a few rows away from me, smiled serenely. Lewis had just summed up the government's case in a nutshell.

Wearily, Mark fought back, pressing Lewis for a consolation prize, imploring him to help salvage our discriminatory-enforcement defense by forcing the Agency to identify *all* the scofflaws it had allowed to go unpunished. Even before he'd finished, Lewis was wagging his head disapprovingly. If we wanted such a list, he snorted, we'd have to put it together ourselves.

Over the next two days, Mark tried to make the best of this bad decision by compiling a two-page inventory of books and articles by suspected rule-breakers. When he handed it over to Ernie Mayerfeld for inspection, only one name on it prompted a nod. In a written response, Mayerfeld acknowledged that ex-agent E. Howard Hunt's autobiography, *Give Us This Day,* had not been "formally cleared for publication."

He would not, however, confirm any other possible breach, and refused to comment at all on the most egregious clearance violation Mark had uncovered, the fact that a magazine called *Periscope,* written and edited by a group of "loyalist" CIA alumni, had never been submitted for clearance and never sanctioned. Mayerfeld declared loftily that any question about *Periscope* was beyond the scope of Lewis's latest order, though he didn't bother to explain how or why.

— —

Meanwhile, the hysteria Stockwell had unleashed spread like some poisonous spill. "There's more leaks here than there are in the men's room at Anheuser-Busch," grumbled right-wing patriarch Senator Barry Goldwater in a speech soon after Stockwell's *60 Minutes* appearance, and former CIA director Helms warned a Senate panel that the Agency, already weakened by congressional investigations, was now "hemorrhaging" secrets through "books and newspapers."

"If it continues," he added, "this country is going to be at a serious disadvantage."

A few days later, the presiding judge in *Truong-Humphrey,* picking up the vibrations, doomed the two defendants by framing the larceny charge against them in the most prejudicial way possible, and two days after that, the jury found both men guilty of larceny and espionage, rendering a verdict that was stunning in its implications. From now on, the leaking of government information by anyone—whistle-blower or spy—could be prosecuted and punished as an act of theft.

Though I'd never been given to easy communion with my ideological opposites, the drift of things made any company seem welcome. So when a liberal Washington think tank, the Institute for Policy Studies, invited me in late May to participate in a conference on whistle-blowing, I shelved my conservative biases and showed up.

Mort Halperin, one of my ACLU advisers, keynoted the gathering, pointing out that Carter had now succeeded where Nixon had failed, winning judicial support for legal theories that could be used to silence whistle-blowers. Senator James Abourezk expanded the theme. "Snepp and Stockwell did not sign away their First Amendment rights!" he bellowed. "The Agency is not the master, nor the employee the slave."

Seated alone in a corner, boozed-up, bleary-eyed Victor Marchetti cheered the polemic with a case of hiccups.

During a break, Dan Ellsberg, leaker of the Pentagon Papers, pulled me aside to sympathize. A small, wiry man with the distracted air of a fugitive on the run, he seemed a millennium away from the gun-toting true believer he'd once been in Vietnam, *before* his conversion. This particular evening, he was campaigning against commercial nuclear reactors, with the same Old Testament zeal he'd once reserved for Washington's warmongers. Listening to him, I was reminded of those figures out of Sartre who seek to define themselves by the glint in someone else's eye, and couldn't help wondering, fearfully, if I was succumbing to the same temptation.

Of all those who paraded their consciences that night, none sobered me more than Stockwell. When I first strode in, he broke away from a group of reporters and scurried over, as if we were still comrades-in-spirit. "Boy, you've got to win your case," he boomed. *"For all of us."* It didn't seem to occur to him that his theatrics had diminished my chances of winning anything for anybody.

A short while later, a crowd gathered at one end of the hall to watch a film underwritten by the Institute to document Stockwell's own private war against the CIA. As the reel played out, the principal's two faces came into jarring focus: the moralist decrying the Agency's immorality, the odd pragmatist lamenting the paucity of helicopter gunships to turn the tide in Angola.

As the lights came up, many in the audience were gazing at one another embarrassedly, and near the front row, I could see CIA lawyer Chris Winkle, who'd been sent to play watchbird, frantically jotting notes as usual.

Afterward, in a brief speech of my own, I suggested that the best way to prompt reform of the intelligence community was through responsible criticism devoid of secrets.

The applause was depressingly spare.

— —

Given the intensity of the backlash against Stockwell, the thought of going back to court filled me with trepidation. But one morning in late May, Judge Lewis set the machinery inexorably in motion by announcing that my trial was just three weeks away. He also summoned both sides to his chambers at once to sort out the issues at bar.

During the first moments of this awkward encounter, as Mark bantered with Hedge and the Whitakers, Lewis studied me skeptically across his uncluttered desk, a huge portrait of Eisenhower looming at his shoulder. The old judge's visage seemed as battlewise and uncompromising as the one on the canvas, and I had a sense that I'd become for him something of a beachhead to be conquered and secured. Indeed, once he brought the meeting to order, he made no pretense of impartiality. At every opportunity he mispronounced my name, calling me "Mr. Shepp," and only one of our demands seemed even remotely reasonable to him. Over Sally's strenuous objections, he agreed to let us interview one last deponent, the CIA officer who'd presided at my induction into the Agency in September 1968.

As Sally began outlining her own trial strategy, Lewis relaxed into a paternal glow, brightening perceptibly when she let on that former director George Bush might testify in Turner's place. "Mr. Bush is an old friend of mine!" he exclaimed gaily. "I'd be glad to see him."

Brook Hedge then took the floor to explain the most difficult issue facing the prosecution, its theory—or nontheory—of damage. Lewis quickly grew fidgety, telegraphing his impatience by groaning whenever she paused for breath. Trying to keep her cool, she trundled on doggedly, arguing that even though I'd broken a contractual obligation, it was the same obligation embodied in my fiduciary duty, so a penalty appropriate to a breach of trust could be assessed, despite this being a contract case.

Lewis rolled his eyes and moaned again. Instantly, Sally jumped in. Since a fiduciary cannot be allowed to retain his ill-gotten gains, she said, the government was entitled to all my profits without any showing of concrete damage, even though such a showing is normal in contract cases.

Lewis jerked forward, a scowl spreading across his rumpled features. "How could the Agency's unproven injuries automatically equal all the defendant's revenues?" he demanded. Brook stole a glance at Sally and started in again. But Lewis wouldn't have it. He ordered them to come up with something coherent in writing or forget the whole thing.

It took Hedge and the Whitakers several days to fill the order, and though what they threw together was little more than a Chinese menu of mismatched law, at least it wasn't still alive and twitching. Declaring me to be a fiduciary or "trustee" of the government by virtue of my having been exposed to sensitive information, they argued that the case was still "contractual," since my obligations, including my "fiduciary" ones, were "governed" by my secrecy agreement. And yet, because of the gravity of my offense, the traditional remedies for breach of contract simply wouldn't do.

"The defendant's actions," they maintained, "severely hamper the Central Intelligence Agency's ability to gather intelligence, which in turn adversely affects the United States' ability to maintain an effective defense." Such damage, they said, is unquantifiable, and therefore impervious to jury determination. The only appropriate remedy was for the court to decide the issue on its own.

Under common law, they argued, when "money damages are not determinable," the court may grant "equitable relief," impounding all the offender's profits, without impaneling a jury to assess the extent of his depredations.

It was this solution they urged on Lewis, even though, they acknowledged, it would require some "judicial inventiveness."

To make all this seem reasonable, they argued further that my original secrecy agreement was "unambiguous" and subject to no interpretation but their own. That meant there was no "factual issue" in dispute, and thus no need for a jury trial.

Plowing through this potpourri of illogic, Mark could only marvel at the government's audacity in serving it up, and I could only wonder what the hell I was being tried for. I didn't understand any of it. Sally's serpentine legal theory, snaking from contract law to fiduciary law and back again without ever embracing one or the other, called for much more than "judicial inventiveness"; it demanded a trip to Fantasyland.

In a hasty counterbrief, Mark accused the Justice Department of trying to deny me the amenities due any defendant in a contract suit, and urged Lewis not to be taken in.

— —

Meantime, we took advantage of the only dispensation His Honor had granted us. One early June morning, Mark and I traipsed out to Langley to confront the CIA officer who'd handled my induction ten years before.

The Agency didn't make it easy. Rather than field one candidate, it presented three. Only if I picked the right one could I hope to substantiate my claim that I'd been misled at my induction about my secrecy obligations. Otherwise—kiss that argument good-bye.

Sadly, all three candidates looked familiar, and I couldn't decide which one had briefed me on that morning so long ago. Mark understood, but slung a fist at the wall in frustration.

— —

Anticipating a hard and bitter trial, Mark decided to snatch a week of badly needed vacation before launching into final preparations, and suggested I use the interval to brush up on my facts. I took the advice too literally, and by the time he returned, I'd burned the candle to the wick.

Even so, I refused, typically, to admit exhaustion and allowed Mark's colleague Geoff Vitt to begin putting me through mock cross-examinations, pummeling me day after day with questions to prepare me for the onslaught. My fatigue quickly assumed apocalyptic proportions, and I began to doubt I could even survive the trial.

In the midst of all this, my prospects brightened unexpectedly. Within the past two weeks, William Colby had finally published his long-awaited memoir, and as he was launched on the inevitable publicity tour, he was barraged with questions about everything from CIA kill plots to my own impending trial. At one point, a *Washington Star* reporter asked him if he approved of the lawsuit against me. "No, quite the contrary," he replied. "Mr. Snepp's case, frankly, I find a rather ambiguous one, and I confess I'm not quite sure what the government is trying to do here. The government is now proceeding on a civil action based on a contract, the same contract that I made. But the object of the contract is to keep secrets, and in this case, I gather, the government does not contend that any secrets were exposed. If that's the case, I'm not sure what the rationale is."

Mark showed the statement to Vitt and Sims and offered a daring suggestion: If Colby truly felt this way, why not call him as a defense witness? Never mind that I'd accused him of bungling our Vietnam withdrawal and letting slip self-serving secrets to the Kalbs. Mark felt the former director would be an ideal counterpoise to Turner.

The idea was batted about for twenty-four hours. No one was sanguine about Colby, but since no one was sanguine about Lewis either, Vitt and Sims finally agreed to take the gamble, and Dershowitz fell into line after learning Colby had once known my father.

Only John Shattuck, the bushy-haired head of the ACLU's legislative liaison office, remained skeptical. Colby, he warned, was talking out of both sides of his mouth. Despite his sympathetic noises to *The Washington Star,* he'd also told *People* magazine recently: "Snepp and Stockwell have written books discussing subjects they promised in writing not to discuss without express approval of the Agency."

So which Colby to believe? Shattuck felt the guy was too slippery to be believed at all.

At Shattuck's suggestion, Mark contacted Colby to see if we could question him informally prior to trial. The answer came back: no.

Had I been on better terms with my father, I might have prevailed on him to talk to his old school chum. But my father and I hadn't spoken in months. So, with time running out, I was faced with a daunting choice: embrace Colby sight unseen, or go to court with no one to speak for me.

Taking a deep breath, I agreed to have Colby subpoenaed.

— —

The day before the trial, my lawyers spent hours dragging me through practice questions and clipping deposition excerpts to be introduced as evidence. Across the Ellipse, at the Justice Department, Sally and her own cohorts heatedly debated whether to alter the Complaint against me to include a breach-of-secrecy charge, so as to strengthen their hand. They knew that if Colby's own clearance violation emerged in court, they'd need all the help they could muster. Ultimately, they decided to stick with the case as conceived.

At the end of the day, I called Bernie for some last-minute encouragement. The rigors of the past two weeks had kept me so distracted that I had the eerie sense of talking with a stranger. She felt the same way. "I was reeling from all the shocks with nothing to hold on to," she confessed to me years later. "Every setback seemed worse, because I felt so detached. I knew I couldn't bother you. So I crept into myself."

An old boyfriend of hers, sensing far more than I did, had recently drifted back into her life, and now Bernie, my closest companion and confidante, was withdrawing from my madness. It is indicative of how lost I was that I didn't even begin to realize, this last night before trial, I was now totally alone.

CHAPTER 20

Reckoning

THE THIRTY-FIVE MINUTES it took me to navigate the rush-hour crawl from my Arlington apartment to the redbrick courthouse in Alexandria seemed to stretch on to infinity. So taut were my nerves, so heightened the senses, I registered snippets of the passing scene that had eluded me before: the bedraggled weeping willow far across the rugby field near the Potomac; the dazzling blue-green of the patches of woods through which wound the joggers' path; a nondescript blackbird, so dazed by the roar of jets from nearby National Airport, he mechanically dive-bombed each passing motorist as if, thereby, to vent his rage at the unrelenting sonic torment.

It was the morning of June 20, the day of trial.

My ramshackle Ford, much the worse for wear and neglect, rattled forlornly over the railroad tracks just this side of Alexandria's city limits. Pulling up at a stoplight, I nervously thrummed the steering wheel, tried to steady my breathing, and gave up silent thanks that Bernie, fidgeting by her phone in New York, was there, not here.

Far from being a burden just now, the solitude afforded an unaccustomed luxury, a moment's freedom to delve into my feelings as I hadn't done for weeks.

What was it that lay off the plumb line: Fear? Confidence? Or was I simply too numb to be able to tell one from the other?

That was it. Too numb.

The light changed. I threw the car hard into gear and roared into the center of Alexandria at twice the posted speed, as if daring the law to take me. Foolish challenge, that. The law would have its way with me soon enough with half the provocation.

As I swung into a parking lot a block from the courthouse, I found myself trying to sort out the odds. Among the sure negatives was Lewis himself; on the plus side, a solid legal defense and energetic defenders; and among the many "imponderables," my star witness, William Colby.

If he was truly as skeptical of the government's case as he'd seemed in his *Washington Star* interview, he might turn Lewis around. If not . . .

On the corner across from the courthouse, I bought a newspaper, flicked a glance at a superficial preview of the trial, then stood toeing the curbing impatiently, as I waited for a "walk" signal.

Briefly, my eyes shifted to the statue of the Confederate soldier in the center plot, his head bowed in mourning over lost comrades and a lost cause. Another beaten cavalier like my headstrong forebear Colonel John White Gulley, who had charged the guns once too often at Gettysburg. Crossing under the soldier's lifeless gaze, I had an awful feeling that I was launched on an equally fatal passage.

The courthouse steps were bristling with reporters. I waded in, fending off microphones, weaving lenses, banal questions.

In an anteroom off a crowded second-floor corridor, my small army was assembling when I arrived. Dershowitz and Geoff Vitt showed up in the obligatory uniform of the prosperous trial attorney, right down to vest and pinstripes, while my other two defenders, Mark Lynch and John Sims, trudged in looking typically themselves, all rumpled intellectuality verging on seed. The always considerate Sims asked if I had any last-minute questions. Had he known what lay ahead, he might more properly have asked if I had any final requests.

Inside the spacious, soberly appointed courtroom, artists were skittering crablike along the aisles, scratching instant portraits for the nightly newscasts. Shrinking before them in the spectators' gallery were Turner, Mayerfeld, Lapham, Winkle, and a host of CIA spear-carriers. Barbara Babcock of the Justice Department's Civil Division had plunked herself conspicuously in a front row, by way of demonstrating support, she told a reporter, for the staff lawyers who'd concocted the case against me. In one of the minor ironies of the morning, several of the courtroom Picassos mistook her for a member of my family—"Maybe his wife," one of them muttered—and began furiously sketching her chipmunk features.

At the prosecutors' table, Brook Hedge and Glenn and Sally Whitaker were whispering noisily to one another as a newcomer, the assistant U.S. attorney for Alexandria, looked on impassively. As Dershowitz and I wound our way to our own cockpit, I glimpsed among the spectators Bob Bernstein and Bob Loomis, and (of all people) Daphne Miller's parents.

Before joining us, Mark, Vitt, and Sims strode over to their opposite numbers for perfunctory handshakes.

Suddenly, amid some commotion, Colby materialized at the main doorway and scanned the packed benches for space. Catching his eye, Turner waved and smiled. An icy draft brushed my soul. Could the two be in collusion?

I was still shuddering when the court clerk blurted out, "Oyez, oyez, oyez!" and formally called the court into session.

The entire assemblage rose as Judge Lewis, looking like the Lord High Undertaker in his flowing black robes, swept in and mounted his pedestal.

Owl-eyed behind thick, square glasses, he passed a hand through plastered locks and ground his jaw like a man trying to keep his false teeth in place. After a seemingly interminable pause, he invited both sides to introduce themselves. "Ready for the defendant!" Vitt proclaimed solemnly.

No sooner had Lewis disposed of these formalities than he proceeded to dispose of us. First, he denied Vitt's request for a set of ancient CIA secrecy agreements which, we were certain, would show that the CIA had altered its prepublication review requirements many times. ("Irrelevant!" intoned His Honor.) He then refused to let us exclude from the jury list the names of Justice Department and Pentagon officials who, we feared, could not be impartial. "Since when did we strike government employees?" drawled the man in black. "We don't disqualify people because they have responsible positions."

Dismaying as these pronouncements were, however, they were merely the playful exertions of a cat toying with a mouse. Ten minutes later, before hearing a scintilla of evidence, Lewis delivered his first big swipe. "I am certain you're already en route to Richmond," he told Mark. "I won't disappoint you. I'll tell you the route if you don't know how to get down there. I-95, go south."

Mark went pale. Richmond was the home of the Appeals Court of the Fourth Circuit, and I-95 the highway that led there. If we were already on our way, clearly this trial was over before it had begun.

But Lewis wasn't about to send us packing just yet. Lest the case be thrown right back at him, he knew he'd have to make a show of resolving the key issues, the most important of which was: What kind of case was this anyway? A contract action? A breach of fiduciary duty? A First Amendment dispute?

He was typically forthright. "This is not a First Amendment case!" he proclaimed loudly, not once but many times as Mark continued sparring with him.

At one point, to justify himself, Lewis deftly misquoted *Marchetti,* declaring that the court had ruled in that case that the defendant had voluntarily signed away his First Amendment rights on joining the CIA.

As Mark bit back a protest, Lewis then attempted to make me worthy of Marchetti's punishment by turning me into a faithless fiduciary who'd been caught stealing trade secrets. "Does he have the right to take the job, get all the information, then resign and divulge to the whole world everything the CIA does?" he demanded, voice keening.

"He is free to use whatever information he gains to write a book after he resigns," said Mark carefully, "as long as he does not publish classified information."

"I don't think he is," Lewis replied.

I listened amazed.

Mark realized what Lewis was up to—a faithless fiduciary can be punished without any proof of damage—and challenged him on it. "I am surprised, Your Honor, that you will not let a jury determine whether the injury the CIA claims to have suffered flowed from the fact Mr. Snepp published the book."

Lewis retorted: "Every fiduciary case I've read, where a person breaches a trust, a fiduciary relationship, he is not allowed to keep his so-called ill-gotten gains at the expense of his employer."

Only twenty-five minutes into the trial, Lewis clearly had bought the government's theory of the entire case.

"We're not talking about an automobile accident or anything else," he added emphatically. "We're talking about *this* case, *this CIA case!*"

Mark tried another tack, reminding Lewis that if I'd published something truly dangerous, the government could have relied on any number of criminal statutes to punish me. Trying to gag and impoverish someone for what I'd done violated the First Amendment, he insisted.

Lewis looked profoundly shocked. "What you are saying"—his voice rose suddenly—"is all I have to do is steal the latest neutron bomb secret and give it away!" He patted a handkerchief to his lips. "The First Amendment says I can tell it. My, my."

Mark tried to stammer out an objection, but Lewis rudely cut him off. "Nobody has the right to divulge classified information!"

With estimable equanimity Mark again reminded him that nobody had accused me of betraying any secrets. But Lewis countered that he was just dealing in semantics.

Gesturing angrily at me, he continued: "Now, this man was employed by the government. He was put in the most secret of secret positions . . ."

Mark tried to break in, but Lewis sailed on.

"As a result of what he learned while he was there functioning as a CIA agent for the benefit of the public, he came out and did what? He published everything—I won't say everything he may have learned, but a whole lot."

Finally, Mark interrupted: "We asked the government, 'Do you contend that there is any information in this book which is classified?' "

Lewis: "I don't want to get any further into your term classified, because I disagree!"

Mark: "Let me complete what I asked them: 'Or information not made public by the CIA?' They said, 'No, for the purposes of this litigation, we do not contend that.' "

The clarification zinged right past His Honor.

As I listened, I could hear my defenses toppling like dominoes. For if I was indeed a security violator, it followed that I'd betrayed a fiduciary's obligation and all my secrecy agreements. The First Amendment *wouldn't* protect me.

Mark tried desperately to refocus Lewis's attention by reminding him that my final contract differed from my first one, and that contract law made me liable only for the last one. But Lewis waved this subtlety aside, proclaiming exuberantly that my original contract, covering even unclassified information, was the only binding one. The final agreement, he declared arbitrarily, was a mere "release document."

Dershowitz put a comforting hand on my shoulder. Vitt shifted forward in his chair. For a moment I thought he might launch himself at the bench.

Unfair as these preliminary rulings were, they were within Lewis's prerogatives as a judge. Since all involved *legal,* not factual issues, none deserved to be submitted to a jury.

But there were others that did, including, as Mark struggled to point out, the purely factual question of whether my original agreement was enforceable under the circumstances of this case. He was prepared, of course, to argue it wasn't, that it had been obtained "fraudulently" by the lying induction officer, that the Agency itself had breached its provisions by refusing to countenance my grievances.

Quickly, Mark ticked off these points and urged Lewis to summon the jury to consider them. And just as quickly, Lewis dismissed them as unworthy. Declaring my original agreement to be "not ambiguous"—shades of the government's pretrial brief—he refused to let us introduce any evidence that I'd been misled by anyone. Nor would he accept that the CIA had a duty to entertain any employee complaints beyond simple personnel gripes. Referring to my original agreement, he intoned majestically that there was nothing in it that said "he's entitled to be heard if he wants to write a book about what ought to have been done in the evacuation of Hanoi."

"*Saigon,* Your Honor," Mark offered with a poker face.

"Well, Saigon," conceded Lewis. "They didn't get to Hanoi. I forgot that."

Not content merely to rewrite the Agency's grievance rules, Lewis went on to suggest that I'd been well served by them. "Specifically," he posed to Mark, "do you claim that your client filed a grievance with somebody under paragraph six that the jury—forget the jury!" Again, the handkerchief fluttered to his lips. "What grievance do you say he filed that was not heard?"

Mark: "The evacuation from Saigon was mishandled."

Lewis: "How did he file such a grievance?"

Mark: "He went and talked to his superiors, his chain of command. He wrote a paper which he submitted to the Center for the Study of Intelligence. He did have a meeting with the inspector general and raised it. He was told it was too controversial and complicated. They weren't interested."

A smile flickered across Lewis's furrowed visage as he heard how my concerns had been brushed aside. "You say he brought them and they heard them," he said teasingly, "but they didn't do anything about it, is that right?"

"That's right, Your Honor."

"Therefore, because they didn't do anything about it, that breaches his agreement?"

Mark hesitated, sensing the steel trap closing. Delicately, he backtracked, emphasizing that he wasn't saying that at all. "Every time he raised this issue," he explained carefully, "people cut him off."

A few white strands loosed themselves from the pomade as Lewis switched his head disapprovingly. "Let's get it specific," he rasped. "Do you claim that Mr. Snepp under this grievance committee formally filed any kind of grievance?"

I tried to catch Mark's eye. No use. "Yes, we do," he replied.

"Was this before or after the fall of Saigon?" Lewis shot back mockingly. "This was *after,*" answered Mark.

Lewis ran a finger down the edge of his glasses and assumed a solicitous air, as if he'd miraculously grasped what the defense counsel was driving at. "They wouldn't listen to his complaint? It was too hot. They wouldn't listen."

"Too hot to handle," Mark acknowledged, hoping to fix the idea in Lewis's brain.

If he succeeded, it was small consolation. Lewis quickly went on to argue that even if that *had* happened, the Agency had broken no compact with me. "Nothing in this agreement," he insisted in hopelessly muddled syntax, "would relieve him from divulging it publicly if they wouldn't listen to his story, and the court so rules."

"We're cutting down our jury issues," Mark groaned.

"Down to zero," Lewis agreed cheerily.

That much Mark wasn't ready to concede. "We would also like to present to the jury," he declared bravely, "the question of whether the CIA is going after Mr. Snepp for some purpose, against a pattern of allowing other CIA officials to publish and give speeches without getting advance clearance."

Lewis wheeled his eyes skyward. "You're not serious!"

"We would like to take it to a jury."

"I said you are not serious on that, really." Lewis's voice cracked into a higher octave.

Mark smiled weakly. "I understand where Your Honor stands on this argument."

"I have already ruled on this selective prosecution." He shook his head in disgust. "You are saying because they didn't sue somebody else, or let somebody else make a CIA speech, either with or without approval, they cannot enforce this agreement."

Mark tried to interject, but Lewis rolled over him.

"Selective prosecution applies basically to criminal law," he continued. "Of course, the court is not going to allow the government to be tried in this case. We don't have invidious prosecution. It is not a prosecution. It is a civil suit."

"There are a host of cases," Mark objected, his own voice rising, "that hold the government cannot enforce licensing or regulatory schemes in the First Amendment area for invidious purposes."

"The answer is, it's already been ruled!" Lewis seemed on the verge of apoplexy. "I will rule again: *This is not a First Amendment case!*"

Desperate now, Mark turned to the question of damages. "If they are pleading breach of contract, then they are obliged to show how the breach of contract injured," he insisted. "That is a matter for a jury."

Lewis disagreed. For him it was a foregone conclusion that I'd done grievous harm. "I would have no difficulty in determining that the American people suffered a loss," he snorted, "if someone was allowed to divulge any information that was detrimental to their best interests. It is a loss. You don't have to give away an atomic secret."

Nor did he see any reason for a jury to try to quantify the pain I'd allegedly caused.

"I don't think the government has to show it lost two dollars!" he exclaimed. "The real issue is whether they can enforce the written agreement. If they can't, then any employee of the CIA can go and get all the secrets and go into the novel business." He peered at Mark intently. "That is the real issue, isn't it?"

Mark tried to explain that Lewis was mixing apples and oranges, that only the law of equity, involving breaches of trust, would relieve the government of the burden of proving injury to a jury. Contract law wouldn't, he emphasized. And since the government had argued that my fiduciary obligation was "governed" by my secrecy agreement, the case was still a contract action and should be handled accordingly, with a jury in the box.

Lewis let this dervish of legal logic spin itself into oblivion. What was at issue, he retorted, echoing his favorite argument, was not a breach of contract. "It is a breach of fiduciary relationship, the same kind of case where an employee took a corporate inner secret, modus operandum, and used it to his advantage and exposed it to Ford." He pushed his chin at me. "The court will rule he has a fiduciary agreement absent the agreement."

Sally and her comrades cast wary looks at one another. This was the very argument Griffin Bell had forbidden them to make, lest they put every "fiduciary" in the government under liability for writing without official approval. And yet, here was Lewis doing it for them. Should they risk offending him by objecting?

There was whispered consultation. Finally, Glenn Whitaker rose to announce the consensus.

"I think Your Honor is correct," he said. "Even if he hadn't signed the secrecy agreement, he would still have a fiduciary duty with respect to confidential information he was given access to."

It was a sly explication. Whitaker knew I hadn't exposed any confidential information even if Lewis didn't.

For good measure, the tassel-toed attorney reminded the old judge that the established penalty for a breach of trust was automatic confiscation of all ill-gotten gains. "We would ask for a constructive trust to be imposed, and an accounting," he said.

Wearily, Mark fought back, pointing out that traditionally, a fiduciary is obligated only to keep secrets, and that I'd done that. Lewis responded predictably. He simply wouldn't accept that my writings were secrets-free.

"I don't want any further argument or we will be here until tomorrow," he grumbled.

Mark bowed his head. "Then I guess the case is over," he murmured half to himself.

Summoning the prospective jurors who'd been waiting outside the courtroom, Lewis explained to them why they wouldn't be needed—"There is no factual issue for you to determine"—and then, as an afterthought, invited them to stay around as spectators to witness the final goring. Only two of them had the stomach for it.

— —

With all factual and legal issues now supposedly resolved, Lewis could have wrapped things up at once. But he didn't. Despite having just pronounced all facts to be beyond dispute, he stunned everyone by announcing that he would now conduct a bench trial, without a jury, to determine what the facts were.

Mark's face darkened. Clearly, Lewis was out to sabotage my appeal. Allegations that hadn't been debated, much less proven, would now, in the cold type of a court transcript, take on the aura of fact.

Before proceeding, Lewis let the government introduce a copy of *Decent Interval* into evidence. "The court of appeals might have more interest in reading it than I will," he said, pursing his lips as if he'd just tasted something sour. "They might not want to buy the book, so I'll let them have a copy to read."

He flicked some lint off his sleeve.

"*I* am not going to read it," he continued. "And it's certainly understood that it is not being admitted as the truth, anything in there."

What he did intend to admit as truth, however, was anything that seemed likely to bolster the government's case. He made that clear enough by immediately consenting to let the government call its star witness, Admiral Turner, who, Glenn Whitaker explained, would have important things to say about my "false promises" to the Agency and the question of damages.

Mark quickly objected. "They started as a contract, and then make it a fiduciary case! Now they are trying to get us on breach of promise!"

Lewis, however, found nothing objectionable in this, and promptly beckoned Turner to the stand.

Over the next hour, he allowed the admiral the greatest latitude in setting out the government's entire case, not merely its theory of damage and complaints about my "duplicity," but *everything*.

Under Glenn Whitaker's gentle questioning, Turner began by recycling the CIA's "they're-too-dumb-to-tango" argument, claiming that no lowly ex-agent is smart enough to keep secrets out of print on his own. Determining what's classified, he said, requires "someone with a broad perspective" and a good "corporate memory" who "can separate information he's received in newspapers from information he has received from classified sources."

The secrecy agreement, with its clearance rule, he added, is a way for the "experts" to "ensure that an employee is not inadvertently releasing" what he shouldn't.

What's more, said Turner, the agreement is a "visible means of control," without which the Agency could never persuade sources that their confidences and identities would be protected.

Whitaker asked him, "Admiral Turner, has there been an adverse effect on the CIA, or on you as director of the CIA, resulting from Mr. Snepp's refusal to submit his book for prepublication review?"

"There clearly has," replied Turner, laying it on thick. "Over the last six to nine months, we have had a number of sources discontinue work with us. We have had more sources tell us that they were very nervous about continuing work with us. We have had very strong complaints from a number of foreign intelligence services with whom we conduct liaison, who have questioned whether they should continue exchanging information with us, for fear it will not remain secret.

"I am not attributing these exclusively to Mr. Snepp," he emphasized. "I am saying that his is one, and a very serious one, of a number of incidents that have diminished this worldwide confidence in our ability.

"His, in particular, because it has flaunted the basic system of control that we have. If he is able to get away with this, it will appear to all those other people that we have no control, we have no way of enforcing the guarantee which we attempt to give them when we go to work with them."

Glenn Whitaker smiled obsequiously and said he had no further questions.

On cross-examination, Mark tried to pin Turner down, demanding to know if indeed it was my conduct and not the other "incidents" he'd mentioned that had sent such tremors through the intelligence community.

"Admiral Turner, you have testified that the CIA had sources discontinue their willingness to cooperate."

A quick acknowledgment from the witness.

"You have also testified you can't attribute this phenomenon exclusively to Mr. Snepp. What else do you attribute this to?"

Turner suddenly seemed uncomfortable. "There have been other leaks, other books written without authorization."

"What other sorts of leaks have there been?"

"Objection sustained!" roared Lewis even before prosecutors could squeak out an objection. "We are not going to get into that. I could name half a dozen things that have been publicly stated, that have been public news about everything the CIA has done wrong."

In an even voice, Mark explained that he was merely trying to determine if I was truly responsible for the damage attributed to me. But Lewis stood his ground. "We're not going to make the CIA expose more than they've already exposed."

Squaring his shoulders, Mark turned back to Turner and asked if he could think of anything besides my book that might have weakened confidence in the Agency's security procedures. Despite Glenn Whitaker's instant objection, Lewis gave an inch.

"I am going to let him answer," he told Whitaker, "because the answer obviously has to be yes. He doesn't control the world. He would like to. But I don't think he does. Do you, Admiral?" Lewis's square panes swung on the witness. "You don't control everything that goes on in the world?"

"No sir," Turner replied in an awed whisper.

"You would like to find out and control everything the Russians do, wouldn't you?" Lewis continued airily—then, without suffering a response, abruptly added: "Let's get on with the case!"

Mark nodded agreeably and tried again.

"Admiral Turner, do you know any sources that discontinued their cooperation with the CIA because Frank Snepp published *Decent Interval*?"

"Objection!" barked Glenn Whitaker.

"Sustained!" chimed Lewis.

His glasses caught a glint of light as he turned to Mark. "I'm surprised at you," he said reproachfully. "Why do you want the CIA to divulge everything? This is no place to disclose that kind of information."

Mark: "I'm not asking him—"

Lewis: "You asked him who it was."

Mark: "No, I didn't. I asked: Has there been any source which has discontinued its cooperation with the CIA because of *Decent Interval*?"

Lewis: "He said, in his opinion, quite a few. You wanted to know who they were. I will not allow him."

Still determined, Mark took another run at the windmill, this time with slightly greater success. Through deft questioning, he maneuvered Turner into admitting that it was not so much the publication of *Decent Interval* as the attendant *publicity* that had caused the damage he rued.

Turner: "The way the book was published was contrived to put emphasis on the fact that it was published without authorization. That was played up as a marketing gimmick. In my opinion, that has particularly made this a grievous problem for us."

Mark (incredulous): "Your testimony is: the way this book has been *marketed* is a factor that has injured the CIA!"

Turner: "Because it emphasized the fact it didn't go through the clearance process. It therefore helped to tear down the visible form of control that we have in the secrecy agreement."

Mark: "You're testifying that the statement Mr. Snepp made, and the publicity Random House gave it, the fact it was on *60 Minutes*—those things damaged the CIA? *Is that your testimony?*"

Turner: "I'm saying those are some of the things that damaged the CIA, and the way those things were done was particularly damaging."

A wry smile dimpled Mark's lean cheeks. Turner had just given us far more than he realized. If it was the hoopla over *Decent Interval* that had triggered this lawsuit, here was proof positive I was being singled out for an invidious purpose with no relation to any measurable damage.

Again Mark prodded the witness, asking him to explain if any of these things "which you call publicity gimmicks involve the disclosure of secrets." But Lewis squelched an answer. "Objection sustained!" he bawled.

Mark (to Turner): "Do you want to answer that?"

Lewis: "Objection sustained. How can he?"

Mark: "His mouth was opening."

Lewis: "They still can't answer questions I ruled they can't answer."

Politely but firmly, Mark responded that he was merely trying to establish *some* "causative link" between what I'd done and the damage Turner decried.

For a moment, Lewis seemed contrite. "I wouldn't object to him answering a lot of questions"—his hands fluttered about him like tethered birds—"if we weren't going to open this Pandora's box and let you try the fall of Saigon. I am determined you shall not do that in this case."

Mark ignored the remark. "I want to ask him whether any source has discontinued its cooperation with the CIA on the grounds *Decent Interval* was published!" he exclaimed.

Lewis bucked forward, chin yawing. "Objection was sustained!" he said tightly, "because now you're asking him to divulge what I would call confidential information." He snatched off his glasses and squinted hard at Mark. "I am sure a lot of foreign governments," he continued, "would like to know there's been a lot of sources cut off to the CIA. But I don't think he is going to tell that. I am not going to require him to tell that."

And he didn't. With that, Lewis foreclosed any further inquiry into whether *Decent Interval,* the publicity surrounding it, or even its publication had anything to do with the devastation ascribed to me. As usual, the government was being allowed to toss around the most outrageous allegations without having to produce a shred of evidence.

Even so, Mark scored a few hits off Turner.

As in his deposition, Turner conceded that I'd never actually promised him my manuscript.

"Did Mr. Snepp say he was going to submit the manuscript in other words?" Mark asked him.

"I don't recall that, no," grumbled the witness. "I believe he told me he was going to adhere, conform to his secrecy agreement."

Mark continued: "Did you know Mr. Snepp signed two secrecy agreements?"

"I don't know what his status was."

"Have you read any secrecy agreement Mr. Snepp was likely to have signed?"

"I don't know."

"Mr. Snepp's agreement?"

"No."

All this Turner admitted without a hint of contrition, even though he'd repeatedly accused me in public of having broken a written oath and a promise.

Sally and her colleagues cringed. If Turner was so ill-informed, how could they possibly argue that I'd *deliberately* misled him with "false promises"?

Lewis, realizing the witness was in trouble, tried to rescue him by refusing to admit into evidence excerpts from his deposition in which he'd admitted having "assumed" much more than I'd actually promised.

Still, Mark managed to twist the blade. Whipping out a copy of my exit agreement, he asked Turner why, if it was so important for the Agency to have a "visible means of control" over everything in its files, this document required only the screening of secrets. Hardly had Glenn Whitaker screamed "Objection!" before Lewis yelled "Sustained!"

The witness himself sat mute, nervously tinkering with his cuff links.

In another part of his testimony, Turner fudged the truth about two other issues he'd also lied about during his deposition. Claiming that he'd been unable to ascertain if the leaks to the Kalbs had compromised classified information, he denied knowledge of any early attempt by the Agency to prompt a lawsuit against me.

Mark let the first fib pass, but not the second. Just as he'd done in the deposition itself, he produced a memo written by Tony Lapham that proved the director had been made aware of all attempts to gag me.

"At the time you met with Mr. Snepp," Mark said, holding up the memo, "you did know the Agency had asked to file a lawsuit."

"Apparently," Turner conceded tartly.

At another point, Mark tripped Turner up again by asking if I'd ever filed any written complaints about the Agency. Turner claimed he couldn't remember. Mark immediately hauled out a copy of the complaints-strewn letter I'd given to Turner at our meeting the previous summer. Scowling, the witness tried to weasel his way out by claiming never to have read it. "I put a note on it, or sent it out and said, 'Somebody look at this.' I didn't read it," he declared archly.

After attempting a few more passes, all of which were parried by Lewis himself, Mark threw in his sword. "I think I have no further questions," he told the judge bleakly. "I have a lot, but no further I can ask."

— —

The other government witnesses who paraded to the stand were even less effective than Turner.

Herbert Hetu, the CIA's chief public affairs flack, who had so often assured the press that I'd broken my secrecy agreement, admitted under oath that he'd never seen any of the agreements I'd signed. Nor was he sure whether every new recruit was required to submit to censorship, even though in his alternate capacity as head of the Prepublication Review Board he was responsible for administering the clearance rules. "I have only been in the Agency since last March," he whined defensively.

Robert Gambino, the CIA's security chief, proved equally ill-informed. When John Sims asked him if CIA secrecy agreements had always required prepublication review of everything, Gambino replied, "Yes." Patiently, Sims advised him he was wrong, that the entry agreement used between 1971 and 1974, a copy of which we'd obtained during discovery, focused only on secrets.

In view of this, Sims wondered if Gambino might like to "reconsider" a claim he'd made earlier in his testimony that prepublication review had long been an integral part of the CIA's security system. Instantly, Sally screeched, "Objection!" Lewis responded, "Sustained!"

During her own questioning of Gambino, Sally asked him to explain the circumstances under which secrecy agreements were signed. Lewis didn't like the question; he didn't want to hear that they were signed upon resignation as well as at the time of recruitment, since that would validate my final contract. So he immediately leapt in. "What was that question!" he bawled before Gambino could answer. "Clarify that. I don't want to open a Pandora's box."

"Nor do I," Sally murmured apologetically.

"I almost let the door open," Lewis warned her.

"I withdraw that question," she replied in a choked voice.

— —

During the lunch recess, my lawyers and I retired to Vitt's office around the corner to pick over some deli sandwiches and my prospects. Neither were very appetizing. Mark was convinced we ought simply to cancel Colby's testimony and my own and pray for relief in Richmond. I objected. The record was so strewn with distortion that my character and chances for vindication on appeal seemed in danger of being hopelessly compromised. At least we ought to air my side of the story. Dershowitz agreed. The vote carried: Colby and I would be the next paper targets.

I put through a quick call to Bernie and told her of the morning's agonies. She offered to catch a shuttle within the hour to be on hand to stanch the bleeding. I told her no. I was fit company only for rats. Her abrupt hangup signaled more than momentary exasperation.

On the courthouse steps, I bumped into Bob Bernstein and Loomis, who'd just lunched with columnist Mary McGrory. "She's going to do a helluva column on this," Bernstein assured me, resting a hand on my shoulder.

"I never thought we'd see anything like this outside the Soviet Union," said Loomis glumly with a twitch of his mustache.

Back inside, half the spectators who'd jammed the benches only two hours earlier had decamped, knowing full well how this circus would end.

Winding my way back to the defendant's table, I brushed past Bob Layton and Bill Christison, and nodded politely. Both shrank away as if before a leper.

Behind them, already seated, was Colby, my last best hope, typically poker-faced, seeming to catch the eye of someone far over my shoulder.

The usual courtroom rituals followed quickly upon Lewis's theatrical reemergence, and within moments, Colby was called as "a witness by and on behalf of the defendant."

Looking fit and suntanned, this now private attorney and registered lobbyist for Japan strode forward with the confidence of one who'd often made such treks before.

Duly sworn, he briefly outlined his awesome career in intelligence, and seized on one of Mark's questions to indulge in some self-promotion. "I have written a book," he crowed—then paused and added: "But *it* has been approved by the Agency."

Whether that remark made him a perjurer, I can't say. But it was the first sign that he wasn't the witness we needed.

Confirmation came quickly. Asked about the effects of nonclassified disclosures, Colby launched into a spiel that demolished what was left of my case. While conceding that the release of certain intelligence might not be harmful, he argued passionately that a disclosure need not compromise secrets to have an adverse impact.

It need only be *unauthorized.*

"A reputation for an agency unable to exert discipline over its members and protect its sources," he declared gravely, "would hurt the Agency."

"If its agents were allowed to be the judge themselves for what they published?" Lewis put in. "Do you understand the question?"

"I understand," Colby replied. "And my own performance in submitting my book to the Agency—"

"You submitted yours, you say?"

Colby nodded. "Because I believe—"

"You are not the judge of what ought to be published?" Lewis couldn't resist leading the witness.

"That's right."

Lewis sat back and fluffed his robes. "Therefore," he continued, "if one were allowed, as you would have it, to be the judge of printing what he wanted to print, that *could* be damaging, and would be?"

Colby's face remained impassive. "That would be damaging to the Agency and its reputation abroad. Yes, Your Honor."

"*Would* be?" Mark echoed, trying to wrest himself from shock.

"Could, and would be with respect to other nations who felt the Agency could not protect secrets," said Colby, nodding.

"Not in *every* event?" Mark was groping for straws.

"Not in every event," agreed Colby, "but in general, it is a possibility."

Though he denied that an "authorized" book, like his own, could do any damage, he insisted that perfectly legitimate congressional investigations might.

More helpfully, Colby admitted that secrecy agreements *are* signed on leaving the Agency, that the grievance system is meant to handle political as well as personnel gripes, that "a number" of CIA memoirs had been published without clearance.

"Have any of those books failed to cause problems for the CIA?" Mark put in quickly.

Not quickly enough.

Lewis immediately jumped in. "He just clearly told me, regardless of what he said"—the old man's words tumbled over one another in a cascade of illogic—"an uncleared book would be frowned upon, to say the least, by corresponding agencies."

He turned to Colby challengingly. "Isn't that right?"

The witness agreed.

And so it went, to the bitter end.

If Colby's testimony wasn't the perfect double-cross, it was close.

And of course, nowhere in it was there even a whiff of his own failure to abide "by the rules"—not a hint of the fact that he'd cleared his own book only belatedly, after having submitted it to his publisher.

"Call your next witness!" snapped Lewis.

Mark beckoned me forward.

Raising my hand for the oath, I could feel Lewis's eyes crawling all over me.

Over the next hour, as he and Sally took turns hammering me, Lewis remained in a high rage. Even my background seemed to vex him. "You're a college graduate, well versed in the English language!" he screamed when I tried to explain that my original secrecy agreement had been variously interpreted to me.

He swung to the audience. "I'll treat this case entirely different than if he were a backwoods boy who didn't know anything."

At no point would he let Mark quote from any of the documents we'd introduced into evidence. And when, on one occasion, he learned that the prosecution had been too forthcoming during discovery, handing over a document he considered too helpful to me, he lectured Sally sternly, "I never required you to give him secret information. . . .

"Next time, don't give him things you are not required to. They'll take advantage of you, whatever you do, lady or man."

Despite the hopelessness of it all, Mark put me through the paces, coaxing me to make clear that I hadn't knavishly thumbed my nose at the rules, but had genuinely believed that agents and ex-agents *need* not have their every utterance cleared.

"We were not ventriloquists' dummies," I testified, echoing a line from our briefs. "We didn't have the right to declassify anything. But we did develop a discretionary capacity to distinguish what was classified and what wasn't."

Lewis wanted proof that this view had been officially sanctioned. I reminded him of my induction officer's assurances that clearance was not required of nonsecrets.

"I am not going to let you talk about a phantom," he warned me. "If you cannot identify the person you're charging with having told you something, then I won't let you say it."

He demanded that I do what I hadn't been able to before trial: select from among the CIA's three candidates the precise briefer who'd given me this advice.

"You're an expert agent," he snorted. "You're trained in this field."

Mark looked hard at me, pleading silently. Taking a quick breath, I turned back to the judge and asked him to let me have another look at the three candidates, all of whom were waiting outside the court-room.

The trio trotted in. I studied each one, looking for a face to match a ten-year-old memory. Finally, I simply guessed, pointing to a slender man who identified himself as Robert Griffin.

Lewis ordered Griffin to stand by for questioning, and bade Mark continue with me.

Attempting to make the most of the opening, Mark inquired earnestly, "Mr. Snepp, would you have signed the secrecy agreement if you understood it to require preclearance of all information?"

I was about to boom out an emphatic "No!" when Lewis swung abruptly to the prosecutors and demanded preemptively, "Any objection?"

"Yes, Your Honor," Sally replied hastily. But before she could even muster the word "Objection!" Lewis shouted "Sustained!"

Later, on cross-examination, Sally assailed my story about the briefing officer. If he'd actually told me my clearance obligations were limited, she said, why hadn't I made some notation to this effect?

I told her I had.

"Where?" she replied derisively.

"On the termination agreement."

Her face paled.

"I signed my name to the termination agreement and took that as—"

"That's not the question!" Lewis snapped, cutting me off.

In his own direct questioning, Mark asked me about another reason I'd had for interpreting my obligations loosely—the fact I'd been allowed to interrogate sources in Vietnam without any script or supervision.

"What kind of sources?" said Lewis, breaking in.

"Defectors and prisoners."

The old man's face contorted. "I am not going to allow you!" he exploded, so carried away he couldn't even finish the thought. "That is so far beyond the point. Next question!"

He paused to catch his breath, then: "I mean if you're contending that you thought you had to get clearance before you interrogated anybody in connection with CIA activities."

"Sir, with all due respect, that's the reading of one particular clause in that agreement. That is why—"

"That's your reading!" roared Lewis.

"No, sir," I replied softly. "My reading is different."

"Don't argue the case!"

Immediately, Mark interposed himself, asking me to recall other events that had "confirmed to you your understanding that the 1968 secrecy agreement only applied to classified information."

Despite a torrent of objections, I groped my way through a well-rehearsed litany: the Marchetti ruling, the Agency's failure to prosecute other unapproved memoirists like Miles Copeland and Joe Smith and the exit agreement itself.

Mark bore in: "Did the signing of this document give you a belief as to your obligations under the—"

"Objection sustained!" howled Lewis.

Sally Whitaker flushed. "Thank you, Your Honor."

Turning to a related issue, Mark asked if my understanding of the clearance rules had been affected by the fact that so many CIA officers had given me freewheeling, obviously unapproved interviews for my book. I started to answer, "Yes," but Lewis cut me off. Nor did he see any significance in the fact that CIA supergrades, like Ted Shackley, routinely gave press interviews without clearance or reprimand. Could that have influenced my view of the rules? Lewis wouldn't let me say.

Nor was he impressed that the CIA had taken no action to punish me for the unapproved interview I'd given *The Washington Post* months before my book was published. "I'm an old newspaperman," he added dreamily, as if we were discussing mutual life experiences.

"I was quoted directly," I interjected, determined to keep him focused.

"I've been quoted and misquoted so many times," he went on, his voice fluting, "I wouldn't know how it would be otherwise. Next question."

"I want to get this testimony in," Mark objected, "because it demonstrates that the CIA knew Mr. Snepp was writing a book. They didn't take any action at this time to tell him that he was—"

"Objection sustained!"

Mark pressed on: "Why did you conclude that you would have to write the book outside the CIA?"

"Because the Agency told me it wouldn't approve of my writing it on the inside."

"Sustained!" shouted Lewis without waiting for the government attorneys to stir. He glowered at me. "You signed an agreement not to write it is one reason among others."

I started to protest since there was, of course, no such agreement. But Glenn Whitaker interrupted. "Thank you," he said to Lewis.

"Your Honor," Mark injected, "we haven't been into this before."

"I think we have," said Lewis. "Let's get on with it."

Still determined to prove me blameless, Mark bore in on another key issue. "Mr. Snepp, while you were in the CIA, did anyone ever tell you that you had a fiduciary obligation—"

"Objection sustained!" Lewis snarled. He looked at Mark contemptuously. "That's just a trifle leading, isn't it?"

With no prospect of demonstrating why I might not have interpreted my obligations as the CIA had, Mark moved on to the Agency's apparent indifference to my complaints. Lewis defended the Agency every step of the way, first by mocking me, asking if I'd protested the evacuation before or after it happened ("all after, not before," he quipped), then by insisting there was no legal reason to believe I'd been deprived of any rights just "because the CIA wouldn't entertain" my grievances. At this, he caught himself, realizing he'd said too much, imputing bad faith to Langley. He turned to apologize to the glowering prosecuting attorneys.

"He got it in the record that he wanted to discuss it in depth," he exclaimed, raising his hands in a gesture of resignation. "They wouldn't talk to him, wouldn't discuss it."

"As part of the grievance procedure," I put in to underscore the point. Furiously Lewis wheeled on me.

"We wouldn't be here if you were going to decide the case! You answer questions when you're asked," he raged. "I've been broad-minded in letting this be open, but I'm not going to let it get completely out of hand."

— —

Pursuing her own questioning, Sally tried to repair the damage Lewis had done by having me acknowledge that I'd never gone to the inspector general's office on my own, but only after being summoned. Lewis considered this nit-picking and politely invited her to move on.

Hauling out my "admissions," the compendium of my garbled press statements, she had me read the ones that suggested I'd misled Turner, and then demanded if I *had*. "Only by omission," I confessed wearily, puzzled that this was even an issue in light of Turner's own testimony.

Later, in rebuttal, Mark had me recall how, after meeting with Turner, I'd specifically refused to sign an affidavit pledging my manuscript to the Agency. But Lewis quickly grew impatient.

"What difference does it make?" he grumped to Mark. "I've given him undue latitude in expressing his views."

What difference does it make? Was Lewis suggesting that my testimony was *useless*?

As Sally continued cross-examining me, she gave Lewis something else to carp at: the date on my Random House contract. Cutting in, he asked me to explain why it predated my resignation from the CIA. Carefully, I ticked off the misunderstandings that had led Stafford to turn the contract over before I'd told him to.

With a wave of the hand, Lewis dismissed this as a "quibble" and warned me, "We'll get along faster if you'll answer the question."

"I agree with Your Honor," Sally put in malignly.

In an instant, Mark, shaking with rage, was on his feet. "Your Honor, that's wholly objectionable, that kind of editorial comment!" he shouted. "It's very improper for her to comment on the quality of Mr. Snepp's testimony."

"It won't impress me at all—I mean, her comments," replied Lewis.

Mark held the floor. "She shouldn't be permitted to insult and harass—"

"I don't believe she's been like that," said Lewis, cutting him off. "I don't want any further comment. I don't want you to accuse her of harassing this CIA agent. She's been very polite with him."

Indeed, as Lewis saw it, she'd been too polite, letting me wriggle around too many questions, and to make sure it didn't continue, he promptly took over the questioning himself.

Picking up a copy of my original agreement, he turned to me and asked sneeringly if I'd actually believed that a mere briefing officer like the newly remembered Robert Griffin could "verbally modify" a solemn legal document like this.

I nodded. "I accepted this man at his word," I said, adding that I would never have signed the entry agreement otherwise. "You must understand, I was very naive, going into the CIA."

"You must have been," sniffed Lewis, "if you signed such a document."

"Naive about the intelligence business," I persisted. "I was willing to accept anything they told me as being the way it was."

Tossing the document aside, Lewis asked me to explain what I thought was meant by the term "position of trust." I replied that it signified a relationship of trust, one in which "you rely on the other officer's word, and he on yours."

Lewis didn't like that answer and pressed for another. "In other words," he put in, "you did not understand that a position of trust meant that you would not divulge any secrets or information that you got from the CIA?"

"It meant," I countered, "that I would not divulge secrets without clearance. I would never violate that trust."

Frustrated, Lewis tried again. "If it was left to you to decide what was classified and what wasn't," he posed carefully, "and you determined that Number One Secret was not classified, that would end it, wouldn't it?"

I disagreed as gracefully as my own seething rage allowed. "Sir, a secret has a stamp on it. I wouldn't take the document and take the stamp off."

He sighed loudly.

"I would never release material in a document that was classified."

This time he seemed defeated.

— —

Before wrapping up my testimony, Mark attempted to have me clarify for Lewis that I'd been flying blind upon leaving the Agency, that at the time of my resignation no one had bothered to tell me that I'd have to submit all my writings for review.

I responded by pointing out that it wasn't until months later, not until John Greaney sent me a copy of my original agreement and a formal request for my manuscript, that I'd realized I was being held to obligations beyond my termination agreement.

Lewis shook his head incredulously.

Mark then asked if I had "concurred" in the way my obligations had been explained to me during or after my meeting with Turner.

Lewis broke in. "What difference does it make!" he snapped—*what difference does it make?*—and gave me leave to step down.

As I dragged myself back to the defense table, Sally announced that she would like to call four rebuttal witnesses: Norm Jones, John Greaney, Robert Griffin, and—Bill Johnson.

Lewis seemed perturbed. "I'm getting a little old," he grumbled. "How long do you want to go?"

"I was hoping to get all the evidence in," she replied warily.

"It won't make any difference," he muttered.

It won't make any difference?

But he agreed to proceed anyway.

First up on the rebuttal list was Griffin, my erstwhile induction officer. Even under Sally's questioning he managed to embarrass himself by maintaining, incongruously, that despite having no recollection of me, he was certain he hadn't told me what I claimed. On cross-examination, Geoff Vitt seized on this inconsistency to demolish his credibility.

So complete was the humiliation, that Mark felt emboldened to ask Lewis again for a jury trial. "There are facts here," he declared, "that clearly should be determined before a jury."

"There are *no* facts!" Lewis responded irritably. "Just impeaching. There are no facts here."

"Impeachment is a fact," Mark objected. "Whether something happened or didn't happen is a fact."

"I've *ruled*," said Lewis preemptorily, bringing the argument to a close.

Next, Norm Jones, the inspector general's representative, shuffled forward to assert that I'd never attempted to prod him into conducting an evacuation study.

This time it was Mark who wielded the scalpel, reminding Jones that he'd told us at his deposition that he couldn't really say for sure whether he'd discussed the evacuation with me. Jones stared at his trembling hands and tried to double-talk his way clear. But Lewis grew impatient and conceded to Mark, "That's what the deposition shows."

When Bill Johnson climbed into the witness stand, Glenn Whitaker immediately asked him if he'd urged me to submit my manuscript to the Agency for security reasons. Bill said yes. But on cross-examination Mark reminded him of the memo he'd written to Greaney, in which he'd boasted of having told me to seek clearance for a different reason. "Did you in fact recommend to Mr. Snepp that he try to get a 'sympathetic reading,' so that what came out would be 'favorable' to the Agency?"

"Objection!" yelled Whitaker. But Lewis wouldn't let him dispute the printed word. "Obviously, if it's in there," he told Whitaker brusquely, "it's in there."

He wasn't so willing, however, to let Mark embarrass the witness on a more critical question: whether he'd given me classified information. Although Bill had conceded as much during his deposition, Lewis sustained the government's objection to revisiting this issue. "It is well beyond rebuttal," he advised Mark. "Even if it wasn't, it wouldn't be admissible."

The government's last rebuttal witness, John Greaney, should have fared well, being a lawyer himself. But when he tried to argue that I'd promised him my manuscript during an obscure phone conversation in the summer of 1976, Geoff Vitt took him apart. Forcing him to admit that what I'd really promised was that I'd live up to my secrecy agreement, he then asked the CIA lawyer if he'd bothered to ask me which agreement I was referring to.

"No," replied Greaney tartly. "I had a copy of his secrecy agreement."

Vitt held up a copy of my termination pact. "Here is a secrecy agreement he signed when he left the Agency."

Greaney wrinkled his nose, denied it qualified as a true secrecy agreement, but acknowledged he'd had a copy of it, too, at the time of our conversation.

Vitt pressed him again: "Did you ask Mr. Snepp which one he was referring to?"

"No," replied Greaney with a resigned sigh.

"Nothing further," said Vitt.

With Greaney's testimony done, a clearly exhausted Judge Lewis pulled the curtain on the day's proceedings. Noting the lateness of the hour, five P.M., he declared a recess until ten the following morning, and then repaired to his private chamber.

As the few remaining spectators filed out, my attorneys and I gathered up our papers and tried to reassure ourselves that things could have been worse. Dershowitz congratulated me on holding up under Lewis's battering—"I've seen hardened criminals break under less pressure"—and assured me that the old man's misbehavior put us in the best possible position for the inevitable appeal.

Outside the courthouse, we dodged reporters, Mark warning me to reserve comment on Lewis until the verdict was in.

The next several hours blur in memory. I recall vaguely watching TV reports on the trial, grieving over the line to Bernie, and finally drinking myself into a dead sleep.

— —

The following morning, *The New York Times* and *The Washington Post* front-paged blistering reports on the trial. The *Post*'s Fred Barbash gave special prominence to Lewis's myriad pronouncements of "objection sustained!"—he'd offered twenty-seven of them even before the government attorneys had uttered a word—and his intimations that the evidence would "make no difference." He also quoted nameless sources as speculating that Lewis had had his Opinion written even before the trial.

None of this, of course, made Lewis any friendlier toward me as the court reconvened. From the moment he mounted the bench at ten A.M., his flat, pug-dog features were draped in a massive scowl.

So predictable now was the outcome of the trial that even the few observers who'd suffered through the previous afternoon's deliberations had opted for entertainment elsewhere. The gallery was almost empty, save for a handful of reporters and a clutch of CIA men and fellow travelers, including Polgar and Bill Johnson, who were sitting elbow to elbow, smoldering. Polgar, in fact, looked capable of murder, and I pulled Sims aside and asked him to keep him under watch. Sims nodded indulgently, though he must have thought I'd finally gone bonkers.

Leading off the summations, Glenn Whitaker pooh-poohed my fraud claims by suggesting I was too savvy to have been fooled by any briefing officer, and then took a swipe at my integrity by misquoting Turner to the effect that I *had* promised him my manuscript. He also accused me, predictably, of opening the floodgates to massive leaks.

"Mr. Snepp's actions have established a precedent for further breaches," he told Lewis, "because they are a public announcement that the CIA cannot maintain control."

He noted approvingly Colby's mendacious claim that he'd cleared his own book, and added primly: "Certainly Mr. Snepp cannot be held to any lesser obligation than the obligation Mr. Colby acknowledged."

He then moved on to defend the Agency against my charges of bad faith, claiming that the CIA never had any obligation to hear my grievances and that I'd never taken them to the inspector general anyway. "We believe the inference from that is," he declared, "that he didn't want to process a complaint. He *never had a complaint!*"

Sims whipped a hand on my arm to keep me from leaping up. Mark shook his head in warning. Reluctantly I settled back, my face aflame. How dare this Justice Department flunky who'd sat out the war in law school say I had no complaint about the betrayal of the Vietnamese!

By the time I'd regained my composure, Whitaker had brushed aside my termination agreement as irrelevant and was rambling on about why the government deserved all my profits without any proof of damage. "We can't measure with any certainty the amount of damages, the amount of money that we have lost as a result of Mr. Snepp's actions," he told Lewis. "We do know our reputation in the intelligence community has been severely injured. The courts are clear: When damages are not determinable with any reasonable degree of certainty, the court may and should turn to equity. Your Honor, the equity that we are seeking in this case is a constructive trust and an accounting."

Lewis beetled an eyebrow. "You've asked for an injunction. What do you want the court to enjoin?"

"We would ask that Mr. Snepp be enjoined from publishing anything concerning intelligence activities generally, the CIA, or his activities in the CIA, unless he first submits that to the CIA for its review."

Lewis snapped his head in approval, dismissed Whitaker, and promptly invited the defense to respond.

Striding briskly to the lectern, Mark bade Lewis a curt "good morning," and launched in.

"I think I know where we're going with this, and I don't want to take too much time. But I do want to make a few comments—"

Lewis jerked forward. "What are you inferring!" he growled, then, fling-ing a hand at the assembled reporters, "See, they might draw the wrong in-ference when you tell me, to start with, you already know where you are going."

"I assume we are going to Richmond," replied Mark dryly.

Lewis's head swung from side to side. "I want to make it understood: I didn't direct you to go to Richmond."

Mark frowned, debating whether to call Lewis down. Wisely he chose not to, and moved on to substance.

Knowing me to be incensed at the attacks on my integrity, he reminded Lewis that I had not promised Turner or anyone else my manuscript. Nor had I published surreptitiously, he added, pointing out that the Agency had kept so fully abreast of my intentions that it had twice sought an injunction to stop me.

Equally fallacious, he went on, was Whitaker's contention that I hadn't attempted to raise the evacuation issue with the inspector general's repre-sentative. Even the representative himself couldn't be certain one way or another.

Lewis seemed to become increasingly agitated during this outpouring, and at one point he interrupted to congratulate himself for having permit-ted all this "evidence" to be aired—"even though again," he added peev-ishly, "the *Post* said I didn't admit any evidence, and I did it all day. They said I didn't admit any."

Mark hesitated, then responded quietly, "Your Honor, I'm here to de-fend Frank Snepp."

There was a titter in the courtroom. Lewis stiffened, but for once re-strained himself. After some self-conscious paper shuffling, he veered back to Mark's last point and insisted the Agency had no obligation to give me "a public hearing or any other kind of hearing."

To this, Mark responded that the grievance system was so material a part of the bargain I'd struck with the CIA—my discretion in exchange for the Agency's ear—that the bargain couldn't hold without it.

"You say 'so material,' " Lewis replied, "but the court says it just doesn't fit that."

"That's a fact issue," snapped Mark.

"I don't think it is."

"Well, you're making a factual ruling, Your Honor."

"I don't agree with you."

Undeterred, Mark went on to chide Lewis for not recognizing my termination agreement as a contract. Since both parties had benefited from it, it was this document that defined my contractual obligations.

And that being so, I'd been relieved of the duty to clear anything but secrets.

Lewis seemed perplexed. "Where does it in any degree relieve him of submitting anything?"

Mark blinked his eyes in amazement. "The second agreement couldn't be plainer. It applies only to classified information!" he cried, stressing for the umpteenth time that I hadn't been accused of releasing any such material.

He took a breath, then continued in a more subdued voice. "Your Honor, both Admiral Turner and Mr. Colby testified that the Agency has no problem if unclassified information, or information which has already been made public, is released. They would like to have a first look at it before it's released, but they didn't incorporate that requirement into this termination agreement.

"Now, as a matter of policy, maybe they are right. I am not here to fight that policy issue. But I respectfully suggest Your Honor has adopted a policy argument. I would again respectfully submit you are adopting that policy argument and ignoring the language of the agreement that Mr. Snepp actually signed and was actually obligated to."

Lewis seemed to recede into the collar of his black robe, only two eyes peering out.

"And while Admiral Turner and Mr. Colby may have made a persuasive policy argument," Mark added, "they should take that testimony to Congress and get a law to require what they want to do here."

In the meantime, he said, it would be "grossly unfair" to hold me to a commitment I hadn't made in my final contract.

Still no response from Lewis.

There was another reason for holding me blameless, Mark continued. The injury which the CIA claimed to have suffered "is simply too speculative and too tenuous" to be attributed to *Decent Interval.*

At this, Lewis finally roused himself. "You want the CIA to expose with specificity the sources they lost!" he exclaimed indignantly.

Mark replied sharply: "We were prevented, Your Honor, under your ruling, from asking any questions as to whether there are other reasons why foreign intelligence services and intelligence sources may be declining to cooperate with the United States!"

But Lewis didn't care. He was tired of the whole subject. "I won't allow it."

Nor would he allow any interpretation but his own of my First Amendment rights. Indeed, he mischievously tried to rephrase Mark's own argument so as to make it seem indefensible. As "counsel" would have it, he warbled, "he"—a finger jabbed at me—"has the right to expose anything he wants."

"I'm sorry, Your Honor," Mark protested, "you have loaded it in a way I cannot accept."

"I haven't loaded it. You are the one that loaded it."

"I don't say the First Amendment protects his right to disclose classified information," Mark insisted. Indeed, any disclosures truly harmful to the country, he reminded Lewis once again, could bring criminal penalties or an injunction.

"Suppose they don't!" Lewis retorted. "Can he go ahead and release it just because he says it's not classified?"

Mark bowed his head, struggling to rein in his fury. At last: "All I am saying, Your Honor, the First Amendment prohibits a system of prior restraint with respect to unclassified information or information which has already been made public by the United States."

Even if it didn't, he continued, such momentous questions ought to be decided by Congress, not the courts. In fact, the Supreme Court itself had made clear, he said, that "if the government is going to burden the constitutional rights of its employees, it has to have solid congressional or presidential authorization."

Lewis pressed his hand to his chest in a gesture of surprise. "You're bringing up something new!" he protested. "That contention has never been made by you before."

Now Mark lost it. *"It was in our Opposition to Summary Judgment!"* he shouted. "If it's the first time you have heard it, you haven't read our papers. That argument has been made in this court since March 30."

Lewis's jaw tightened. Mark realized he'd gone too far, apologized, and quickly slid into his final argument, a coolly reasoned assault on the impossibly muddled theory under which the Justice Department was trying to impoverish me.

"This has been a fascinating spectacle to behold," said Mark, referring to the evolution of the government's case. And it had also been inevitable, he went on, since without considerable tinkering, the case wouldn't have amounted to a hill of beans. Under contract law, the government couldn't have collected any more than a nominal fine without proving that I'd damaged the CIA. Which it couldn't do, he emphasized. So, it had pursued an argument that required no such proof, portraying me as a disloyal "fiduciary" whose "ill-gotten gains" could be seized through outright confiscation, or as Whitaker had put it so delicately, the imposition of a "constructive trust."

But that hadn't worked either, Mark continued. Legally, fiduciaries are responsible only for protecting an employer's secrets. That's why, as he saw it, the prosecution had finally fallen back on the novel theory that "equity will not suffer any wrong to go without remedy"—"that when money damages for a violation of a contract are insufficient, equity will impose an adequate remedy."

"By this totally arbitrary formula"—Mark had slipped into his pulpit pose, hands folded discreetly in front of him—"the government has taken a case in which they cannot prove more than a dollar's damage or nominal damage and managed to escalate it to the point where they can recover in excess of sixty thousand dollars"—the defendant's royalties to date. "That is punitive."

Lewis rolled his shoulders and smiled faintly, perhaps impressed. But impressed or not, he wouldn't budge, and tried to cajole Mark into conceding that the government wasn't demanding anything so unique after all. Under the classic theory of fiduciary obligation, he ventured, wouldn't the court be entitled to confiscate a fiduciary's ill-gotten gains?

Mark gave a quick nod, but just as quickly reminded Lewis that the classic theory didn't apply here, since this fiduciary had betrayed no confidences.

"In order to prove a breach of fiduciary trust," he explained, "the breaching party has to take away something that was held in confidence. They haven't proved that here, Your Honor."

Before Lewis could object, Mark plunged on, switching course so rapidly that the old man was left sputtering in frustration.

Noting that the CIA performed services no more vital to the nation's security than the State or Defense Departments or the National Security Agency, Mark argued that if "position" and "responsibility" alone had conferred on me an implicit obligation to clear all my writings, then tens of thousands of other government employees were similarly constrained. "I know of no way you can distinguish the CIA from these other national defense agencies," he wound up. "If Mr. Snepp has breached his fiduciary duty, he joins the company of very distinguished Americans, starting with Henry Stimson and Dean Acheson. . . .

"They have written books telling about how their government operated. They didn't do anything wrong. And neither has Mr. Snepp."

Mark stared at Lewis a moment, then withdrew to his chair. A lump rose in my throat as I nodded to him in appreciation.

Not deigning to answer Mark's arguments, Lewis responded by harking to his own fixation of the day, the malignancy of the press that had so recently criticized him. "Let's don't beat questions to death," he began nervously, his eyes darting to the reporters in the gallery and then back again.

"You know you have an absolute right to go to the court of appeals. I have specifically said on occasion that the best route is I-95. I have no qualms about saying that. If it offends anybody so be it.

"Newspapers love to distort things. You gentlemen"—he blinked hard at the reporters, then without completing his thought, turned back to Mark. "I'm an old newspaperman," he went on. "I learned this art long before most of these reporters were born. I used to work for the *Times Herald-Record*—they don't know it—way back in the twenties. I love the press and respect their right to say what they want to at any time."

For the benefit of the press, he then proceeded to defend his handling of the case, especially his refusal to grant me a jury trial, which, he said, had hinged on his decision that there were no factual issues open to dispute. Granted, he'd given serious consideration to my claim that I'd been misled by my induction officer, but had decided it didn't wash because—and here he completely misstated the facts—the defendant had been unable to identify *any* of the three CIA officers who ordinarily handled inductions.

What's more, Lewis continued, "the law does not permit some written agreement to be varied or altered by some less solemn agreement, to wit: by any oral statement or ex-parte statement, even in writing." That's why, he said, my claims of fraud warranted no jury consideration—and why, too, he'd decided that my termination pact, a less "solemn" document by his arbitrary reckoning, didn't release me from the terms of my original one.

It was a judge's prerogative alone as a matter of law, he said, to figure out which of the two agreements was binding.

"Therefore there was nothing for a jury to decide," he repeated, eyeing the reporters suspiciously. "That is why we conducted this trial in the manner in which we did, notwithstanding again, as I say, that some of the press indicated that the court had arbitrarily indicated that the evidence didn't make any difference."

He paused and ran a hand though his hair. "It just goes to show they don't know all of it, or report it correctly."

As for the way he'd handled the witnesses themselves, in particular me, he had no apologies about that either. "I went not one step, but five steps, as far as I am concerned, farther than I had to go," he declared self-righteously. "I wanted to give this defendant every opportunity to state what he wanted to say about why he did what he did."

His eyes were careening wildly. "I let him say it"—his voice rising—"heard his statement, much of which was not relevant to the real issue in this case."

And what was the real issue?

"It is so plain and obvious to me!" he bellowed, pounding the bench for emphasis. "If all agents were allowed to tell what they want to tell, when they want to tell it, without any clearance except themselves, anything they learned, whether it be from English intelligence or French or any others"— he was gasping for breath—"the United States wouldn't get much information."

Glenn Whitaker gave a satisfied smile.

After a pause to compose himself, Lewis went on to lament the fact that higher courts had left such decisions to him. "Now I don't know why they like to impose all this authority upon a poor, innocent district judge who does everything from run schools to penitentiaries," he observed ruefully. "And now I am apparently going to have to run the CIA."

With both law and national policy, as he saw it, demanding my head, Lewis had only one other issue to consider: what penalty to mete out. Fearing that he might disappoint the prosecution, he explained to Glenn and Sally apologetically: "If he had the money and I fined him ten million dollars, it wouldn't reduce our budget one penny per person."

The answer, he concluded, "may be relieving him of all the 'ill-gotten gains,' so everyone might know—providing, of course, the court of appeals upholds it—you can't breach this type of secrecy agreement and expect to make a profit off of it."

Professing himself in a quandary, he said he would reserve final judgment for a few days. Yet he left no doubt he considered me to be the type of scoundrel who deserved the harshest punishment. Pointing a shaking finger at me, he thundered, "He knew full well that he had no right . . . to release that information without submitting it for clearance. . . . There is no question in this court's mind he did it willfully and deliberately. . . . He did it surreptitiously, secretly, behind everybody's back."

It was this, he added, more than anything else that convinced him I'd known I was breaking the law. "You don't write sixty-thousand-dollar contracts in public parks," he sniffed, confusing both facts and figures, "if you want anybody to know about it. . . .

"He doesn't deny"—again the finger stabbing—"that all those negotiations were done surreptitiously. He doesn't deny it was done for the deliberate purpose, for the willful purpose of keeping the alleged world's greatest intelligence-gathering force from finding out he was printing a book. . . .

"Why he published it, he doesn't say, at least he didn't say on the witness stand. I haven't read this book, so I don't know what he purportedly said in there, or whether he subscribed to everything that is quoted in there."

He brushed a stray lock off his forehead. "I would be surprised, I have no evidence of it, if some of this book wasn't edited at least by some pro-

fessional editors. Most books are. But he never said he was doing it, à la—
I call it the Pentagon Papers—to save the United States from some great
crime that was being perpetrated or to let the American public know all
these things."

He cocked his head as if daring anyone to disagree, then abruptly
whapped the bench with his hand. "He did it for money! There is no question he did it for money." Eyes shifting to the reporters in the gallery: "So
you can publish what you will in the press!"

While again reserving final judgment, he reassured the prosecutors that
he saw my offense as they did. "Under the circumstances of the case," he
told them, "I think it was a willful, deliberate breach of contract and a willful, deliberate breach of the highest trust that you can have, to divulge
information"—eyes settling on me—"and particularly to do it for money."

And with that, the gavel descended, ending it.

As Lewis came off the bench, rage swept through me like a malarial
fever. I could barely bring myself to walk over and congratulate the smirking federal attorneys for a job well done.

In the center aisle, Bill Johnson touched me on the shoulder, causing me
to turn abruptly into his dead eyes. "I do hope they don't take all your
money," he remarked, before moving on.

PART IV

NO QUARTER

CHAPTER 21

Ill-Gotten Gains

IF YOU SQUINTED into the light of the thumbnail moon, you could almost imagine away the wreckage sliding past in the mud-stoked Potomac.

I'm Mr. Han, the translator. I'm Loc, the Nung guard.

The night the trial ended, I went down to the river's edge near my Arlington apartment and stood there, benumbed, staring out over the water, trying to imagine away the wreckage—and the desperate voices that still clawed through the static over the CIA radios in Saigon.

I'm Tran, the driver. Please do not forget me!

How desperately I wanted to believe, despite the savaging I'd suffered, that the messenger had not disgraced the memory. But the Cheshire-cat smile of a moon mocked the pretension.

You've betrayed them again, I kept admonishing myself—betrayed them by playing the perfect elder son, never showing emotion, enduring the denigration as if there were honor in that.

Which there wasn't.

Honor would have demanded hurling the insults back, howling Lewis down for belittling my one pure act. An Ellsberg would have known what to do, would have swapped propriety for contempt and risked jail for it.

But not this son of the South, this dead soul of rectitude still yearning to be welcomed back into a world that had now banished him forever.

I would have expected better of you, Mai Ly whispered across the wastes of memory. *I would have expected better of you.*

— —

The morning after, Carla called from St. Thomas to offer condolences, having seen reports of the trial on TV. Bernie was holed up somewhere in Brooklyn and so missed the initial coverage. She later scoured the stands for back copies of various bad-news chronicles—and despaired.

"Judge Lewis's treatment of Mr. Snepp's motives was perhaps too harsh," *The Washington Star* noted stiffly. "We suspect zeal more than hope of profit stimulated his authorship, and that complicates the question of fidelity."

"If the law is a ass, as Dickens wrote of another judicial proceeding," observed columnist Mary McGrory, "the law is a bully in the Alexandria court of federal judge Oren R. Lewis."

"I cannot remember," remarked columnist Gary Wills, "another judge since the worst racial trials of the South who would say what Judge Lewis did when Snepp's lawyers tried to introduce evidence. He muttered that it 'won't make any difference.' "

"One need not wonder why the Justice Department filed the case in his district in the first place," commented *The New York Times,* "but the problem is not the judge. It is the case. We thought it a crude business when the government filed it last winter. It now appears cruder still."

So hostile was press reaction to the government's performance that Griffin Bell felt compelled to remind everybody he was just noodling. "I'm testing a method of securing the intelligence system," he told *Newsweek.* "I have nothing against Snepp."

To reassure the public that open government was still alive and kicking, the White House promptly issued a new executive order liberalizing procedures for classifying documents. But few of Carter's more liberal constituents were fooled. As they saw it, what Carter, the quintessential liberal, had done was to put the archenemy beyond criticism. "During Watergate," Marchetti's coauthor, John Marks, told *The Christian Science Monitor,* "there was one kind of perception of the CIA. But there is a new perception now, and that is, we've gone too far against the CIA."

The tensions growing out of the trial were greatly aggravated by Lewis's delay in putting a lid on it. Two weeks later, on July 4, he still hadn't issued a formal ruling, and my nerves were close to unraveling. "They've taken away my honor!" I shrieked to my journalist friend Laura Palmer, and at an Independence Day brunch, I told Mark flatly that I'd defy any gag. "There've been too many trade-offs already!"

He fixed me with a killer's eye and warned that defiance would sabotage my appeal and probably land me behind bars to boot. "This isn't some fucking Antigone act!" he snapped.

Oh, but I couldn't help but wonder if I wasn't prey to the same fatal hubris.

— —

Three days later, on the morning of July 7, the curtain rang down on a bona fide Greek tragedy. A stern-faced Judge Albert Bryan hauled convicted spies Truong and Humphrey back to the Alexandria courthouse and socked them both with fifteen-year prison sentences.

It was an appalling end to an unconscionable injustice. The secrets they'd compromised were garbage, the damage done minimal, and Hanoi was yesterday's enemy.

But whatever pity I felt for the defendants was decidedly short-lived, for out of some warped sense of mischief, Judge Lewis chose the same morning to unveil his long-delayed judgment against me, as if the spies and the penitent were brethren under the skin. By ten A.M., Mark had summoned me to the courthouse to read it.

We convened in a cloister just off the courtroom where Lewis had heard my case. As Vitt and John Sims hovered at my shoulder, Mark and I picked through the draft. It was infinitely worse than we'd expected.

"The publication of Snepp's book, absent CIA prepublication review, has caused the United States irreparable harm and loss," Lewis proclaimed. "It has impaired the CIA's ability to gather and protect intelligence . . . [and] demonstrates, unless redressed, the potential vulnerability of all information provided to the CIA on a confidential basis." He offered this diagnosis unequivocally, even though Turner's ambiguous testimony was the only proof of damage the government had presented.

Though Lewis had forbidden me even to utter the word "Vietnam" in his courtroom, he had no trouble interpreting my motives. "Mr. Snepp published the book *Decent Interval* for personal financial gain," he insisted. "He admits he has already received some sixty thousand dollars in advance." In fact, I'd admitted no such thing, my advance having been barely a third of that amount.

As at trial, Lewis overrode my constitutional and contractual arguments by ignoring or crassly misstating them. Nor did he even tip his hat to what made my case so unique—the government's stipulation that I'd published neither classified nor even nonpublic intelligence data.

This omission enabled him to treat the case as a mere replay of *Marchetti,* a down and dirty breach-of-secrecy contract suit. Claiming that we'd "misread *Marchetti*," he insisted that that "case does not invalidate the CIA's secrecy agreement"—even though we'd never argued it did. Our position had always been that *Marchetti* merely put nonsecrets beyond the censors' reach.

As for my final secrecy agreement, which we'd claimed likewise limited my clearance duties, Lewis twisted it beyond all recognition.

"Snepp's agreements are clear and unambiguous," he began familiarly. Then: "His 1976 secrecy termination agreement is not limited to classified information as he would have it—it reads classified information or any information concerning intelligence or the CIA that has not been made public."

Since the government hadn't accused me of publishing either type of forbidden data, Lewis's objection was pure red herring. But it served him and the government well, allowing him to argue I'd violated even my final contract by compromising unclassified confidences not previously made public by the CIA.

"Both secrecy agreements require submission of all such material," he observed. In short, he found me guilty of an offense I'd never been charged with.

Nor did he confine himself to the one "fact" in the case he'd claimed to be both decisive and indisputable: the unapproved publication of my book. Instead, as Mark had feared, Lewis quick-scythed his way through a whole range of contested factual issues, disposing of each as if it had been carefully considered and resolved at trial.

He claimed I'd "read and fully understood the duties" prescribed by my original secrecy agreement despite everything my lawyers had argued to the contrary. He asserted, in distortion of my own testimony, that I'd *admitted* not having taken my grievances to the CIA's inspector general. And, despite Turner's demurrals under oath, he held that I'd "assured or at least had led both Admiral Turner and Mr. Morrison of the CIA legal staff to believe" that I'd submit my book for screening.

On top of this, "Snepp admits he did everything he could to keep the CIA from knowing about it prior to publication," declared Lewis. Accordingly, he found that the defendant had "willfully, deliberately, and surreptitiously breached his position of trust with the CIA, and the secrecy agreement dated September 16, 1968."

Because he considered the injury I'd inflicted to be so great, Lewis decided harsh penalties were in order, above and beyond nominal damages, which he felt "would be nothing more than a license to continue doing what the law forbids." Instead, as Sally and her colleagues had demanded, he imposed a constructive trust over all my royalties, in effect confiscating them for the government.

"One who breaches his trust and secrecy agreements," he thundered, "ought not to be permitted to retain his ill-gotten gains."

On the matter of the prospective gag, he found it equally justified and ordered that it be imposed permanently to prevent "any further violation" of my contract. Casting his diktat in the most sweeping terms, he barred me from ever publishing without official approval "information or material relating to the CIA, its methods and activities generally . . . which the defendant gained during the course of, or as result of his employment with the CIA."

Since everything I knew about intelligence could be fit into this fat basket—what did "as result of" mean anyway?—the gag seemed to stretch on forever. Virtually any writing I did in the future about my Vietnam experiences and their effects on me was potentially subject to clearance.

Lewis then invoked a passage from *Marchetti* to suggest that I would have deserved to be restrained this way even if I hadn't signed anything. "Confidentiality inheres in the situation and relationship of the parties," ran his chosen quote. "The law would probably imply a secrecy agreement had there been no formally expressed agreement."

With this, Lewis gave his ruling the global reach both Mark and Griffin Bell had feared, since any bureaucrat could be said to be in a relationship with the government that *implied* a secrecy agreement.

In closing, Lewis instructed Hedge and the Whitakers to "prepare an appropriate judgment and injunction in accordance with this Memorandum Opinion."

By the time I'd finished reading, I was livid. "No way I'll obey this thing!" I howled. Mark thumped the table with his fist. "You don't, you go to jail!"

Sims peered at me anxiously and explained that it would be in my interest to keep the case clean, not to muck it up with contempt citations. Vitt thrust his hands in his pockets and paced. "We don't even have the final language of the injunction. Let's wait for the final language, Frank."

I stared into Sims's eyes but saw no flicker of sympathy. "I'm not promising anything," I replied.

— —

As my lawyers and I emerged onto the courthouse steps, scores of reporters crowded round. "The government is seeking all the book's royalties and it's welcome to them," I spat out. "But the royalties won't buy back the honor the CIA lost during the final days of the Vietnam War. And it won't purchase the Agency immunity from responsible criticism. I thought this kind of gag order was reserved for countries the CIA was working against!"

A reporter asked if I'd abide by it. I willed myself not to look at Mark. "I'll wait to see the final language of the injunction before deciding if I can, in conscience."

Mark broke in: "We'll appeal on grounds that Frank didn't violate the second agreement, and on the constitutional grounds that a person cannot sign away his First Amendment rights."

A short distance away, one of Sally's flunkies was telling another journalist that my money would go to the national treasury if I lost on appeal.

As I hurried through the courthouse parking lot, a stringer from the Associated Press ambushed me. "C'mon, you really gonna clam up for the government?" he trilled.

"Wait and see," I shot back.

Barely an hour later, the phone in my living room was jangling off the hook. One caller who got through was Mark. "What the hell did you tell the AP!" he bellowed. "They're running a story saying you're gonna defy the injunction." I assured him brusquely that I was being misquoted, and hung up.

I leaned back and stared at a cobweb swinging lazily in a corner of the ceiling. Dust had collected on the filaments. That's how neglected my life had become. I picked up the phone again and dialed Dershowitz in Boston. "I'm having trouble with Mark," I told him. "You have to talk to him. I'm not sure I can live with this gag order." Dershowitz promised to do what he could.

Moments later, Bernie punched through the incoming calls. "How bad is it?" she demanded, her voice choking. I told her how bad, and she broke down. She was feeling so isolated, so cut off, she sobbed. Why hadn't I called her right away? Wearily, I tried to make excuses, tried to blame my thoughtlessness on the pressures of the moment.

Later that night, sitting in my darkened room, I took a call from my father. He was the only member of my family who'd managed to reach me this day, and though we hadn't spoken since December, what he had to say was strangely comforting. "These fool federal judges don't know a goddamn thing," he told me. "You'll pull through in the end." I thanked him for the vote of confidence and tried to think of something else to fill the silence between us. I couldn't. He grumbled good-bye and rang off.

The following morning, Bob Bernstein of Random House publicly denounced Lewis's ruling as a "bad joke."

"The net impression was not of American justice at its most judicious," agreed *The Christian Science Monitor.*

"Beyond the legal issues of this particular case," noted *The Washington Post,* "are some real issues of public policy. Should some but not all former government employees be allowed to write about their experiences so long as they do not disclose classified information? Should some but not all of these employees be able to determine for themselves what is and is not classified? Should some but not all employees have to submit their manuscripts for review to the very agency they are criticizing or embarrassing?"

Meanwhile, the one voice I had expected to hear keening hot and defiant remained conspicuously mute. Not once in the days following the judgment did John Stockwell vouchsafe a word to me. Heartened by the positive response he'd received at a recent congressional hearing, he felt impervious to Lewis's brand of justice. Mark agreed he probably was. "The government won't go after him," he remarked to me dryly, "unless you crash and burn on appeal."

I am ashamed to say I experienced a touch of bitterness at this. Not that I wished John ill. It's just that he'd done so much to poison the air, it seemed a bit arbitrary that I should suffer the vapors alone.

The immunity Stockwell seemed to enjoy did not extend very far, however. Two days after the ruling, a House judiciary subcommittee reported that uncounted thousands of federal employees in agencies as disparate as the Treasury and Energy Departments routinely sign agreements not to reveal information they pick up on the job.

Given this fact, observed *The Nation* magazine, "the administration's civil suit against Mr. Snepp represents a significant increase in the power of government to suppress dissent."

— —

As Sally set to work on drawing up the final Order, Mark fenced with her constantly, endeavoring to persuade her to go easy. It was wasted effort. By the time she handed us her draft on Friday morning, July 14, vengefulness had supplanted all reason.

Making the most of the latitude Lewis had given her, she demanded that I hand over a money order for $60,000 within a week—*one week*—even though my earnings to date amounted to only $42,000, over half of which, my $22,000 advance, had already been spent. She also recast Lewis's proposed injunction to make it applicable to any of my "servants" and "assigns." Random House was thus put on notice that if it helped me breach my contractual and fiduciary duties again, it would share in the consequences.

When a copy of the draft dropped through the mail chute, I couldn't reach Mark and called Dershowitz instead. His reaction was an awed "Wow!" I was not encouraged.

I brought up the gag and asked if he'd talked to Mark about the possibility of my defying it. "I think we all see eye to eye," he replied delicately, "about the most appropriate manner for you to act." I got the message: no defiance.

I was about to throw the phone against the wall when an unaccustomed impulse toward self-preservation gave me pause. "What if I test the gag by writing a commentary on my case?" I asked testily.

"Unapproved?"

"*Newsweek*'s got a guest column. Would it put me in contempt?"

Dershowitz thought a moment, then ventured it probably wouldn't, since I'd learned nothing about the case itself "during or as a result of" my CIA employment.

That made me feel better. So did something else he told me. Bob Bernstein, it seemed, was now so worried about me that he was trying to persuade the American Association of Book Publishers to join him in hiring Dershowitz as Mark's full-time cocounsel.

"I'm totally in favor," I replied shamelessly.

"A group of newspaper publishers will also file a brief," said Dershowitz. "What they can do that your lawyer can't is talk about how the press sees the case. I think it's important because judges read editorials."

— —

The following Monday, Mark rendered his own verdict on Sally's draft. "My plan is to write back and tell her to shove this up her ass," he advised me. "Then I suppose she'll submit it to the judge, and we'll have an opportunity to file objections. That could keep him from signing this thing for two or three weeks."

I asked about the sixty thousand dollars. He said he and John Sims had been discussing how to handle this, and had decided—"subject to your approval, of course"—to seek a "stay" of payment until after the appeal. But, he added, he wouldn't ask for such relief from the gag itself. "It would look like we were trying to get you off the hook."

I tried to choke back a sob.

"Now, we could shorten the time considerably by filing a notice of appeal at once. But"—a slight hesitation—"I've got a lot to do. I'd prefer to wait."

I took a deep breath. "How long?"

"There's a good chance of getting the case argued next spring."

Next *spring*! Six months of being unable to write except at CIA sufferance? The earth seemed to be falling away beneath me.

"I really want to move ahead quickly," I said tightly.

Mark gave a sigh.

Meantime, I continued, I had this *Newsweek* piece I intended to write. Another sigh.

I promised to send him a copy to look over—and slowly replaced the receiver.

Feeling at wit's end, I called Dershowitz and told him Mark wanted to go slow. Dershowitz was amazed. "We can certainly move for an expedited appeal," he snapped. "It's not in your interest to delay the appeal. The case could lose the media attention we've all worked so hard to obtain."

Eight hours later, worn-out and desolate, I grabbed a plane to New York. On the chance Mark couldn't arrange a stay and the sixty thousand dollars came due in a week, I knew I'd have to call in some favors I wasn't even owed.

When I shuffled into Loomis's office, I didn't have anything concrete to propose, just a muzzy vision. What if I were to write another book? What if we continued our collaboration?

He chuckled, lit a small cigar, and suggested I retain an agent to make the best deal for me. He ticked off several candidates. I quickly settled on a waiflike dynamo at International Creative Management named Lynn Nesbit.

What she urged me to take back to Loomis was a proposal for *two* books: a spy novel, whose particulars would later be worked out, and an account of my case to be completed within three months to capitalize on my notoriety. Unwilling to admit to her or myself that I barely had enough energy to write a postcard, I agreed.

Had Bernie and I been on better terms, she might have warned me off this ill-conceived piece of audacity. But I didn't even contact her. I didn't want her to see how pathetic I'd become.

At one point during my stay in New York, Dershowitz breezed in on other business and, despite a busy schedule, agreed to meet me at the Hilton bar. After treating him to a beer and some forced bonhomie, I asked point-blank if he'd take on my case full-time. He replied uncomfortably that he couldn't be sure; the publishers' group Bernstein had asked to hire him hadn't been willing to do so. But, he added quickly, Random House might pick up the tab itself, and if that happened, he'd be able to give me his undivided attention.

Exhibiting my usual lack of judgment, I passed this along to Mark. He'd been up all night drafting a response to Sally's proposed order without

Dershowitz's help and didn't take kindly to the idea of being upstaged. Offering a few choice words about Dershowitz, which I'm sure he didn't mean, he threatened to resign on the spot.

Staggered, I phoned Dershowitz and begged him to help damp down the crisis I'd precipitated. He quickly arranged a conference call to assure Mark he wasn't trying to cop anybody's glory.

Mark took the assurance gracefully and then, just as gracefully, asked Dershowitz how we might proceed from here. I listened astonished. Had I missed something? Hadn't a rocket just screamed through the rigging? Or had this all been an act on Mark's part to soften up both Dershowitz and me for a hard sell?

Act or not, hard sell is what we got. Though still committed to seeking postponement of the financial penalties, Mark remained adamant that we *not* petition Lewis or the Fourth Circuit to hold off the gag. "We'd be asking the court to say Turner's position is wrong," he argued, "and that's not a question we want resolved hastily. I think I know how it'd go."

With exquisite tact, Dershowitz suggested a middle way. What if he approached Sally's boss, Barbara Babcock, and asked her informally not to enforce the gag or money judgment until after the appeal? If she agreed, we'd get what we wanted without having to risk anything in court. She was an old friend of his. She might buy in.

Mark seemed reconciled.

— —

"Turner claims he needs this precedent to enforce discipline in the CIA and to ensure secrets are kept."

My guest column appeared in *Newsweek,* Monday, July 24.

"But if the higher courts agree with him, the chill will be felt far beyond CIA ranks . . ."

The article was didactic, defiant, and unapproved. Would Sally cry "Contempt!" and call for jail time?

Ominously, late Monday afternoon she advised Mark she wanted to see us in court the following Friday.

— —

"I spoke to Babcock and she seemed agreeable."

Dershowitz phoned barely twenty-four hours later to tell me he'd reached Sally's boss and found her open to bargaining.

I felt a cowardly sense of relief.

"Her words were, 'Alan, don't ask me stuff that's not doable. Give me stuff that's doable and I'll do it if I can.' I'll be getting back to her to try to firm this up."

Though Dershowitz seemed impatient to ring off—he was always in a hurry—I was desperate to find out what he'd heard from Random House. Had Bernstein agreed to hire him?

With a sigh he said no. Bernstein had been advised that if he paid any of my lawyers, he might be prosecuted for trying to slip book profits to me under the table.

"That means," Dershowitz added apologetically, "I can't . . ."

I cut him off, thanking him for his generosity, not wanting to hear how he could tend to my fate only part-time, not wanting to acknowledge that my sole best hope was still the infuriatingly wise Mark Lynch.

That afternoon, as I was going through my ritual laps at a neighborhood swim club, I tried to sort out my conflicted feelings toward Mark. He'd done his damnedest for me and provided the best defense I could have asked for. And yet I resented his caution. It was as if we were gradually switching places, my high-minded ACLU attorney trading me his radical-ism for my instinctive circumspection.

— —

"Are you going to seek a stay?"

Sally called Mark the following morning and asked what he meant to do at the Friday hearing, two days away, when Lewis was to finalize his Order.

"We'll see what the old boy signs, then decide," Mark told her.

At no point did she mention my *Newsweek* article or hint at retaliation. Dershowitz's overture to her boss apparently had had the desired effect.

Later, Mark confided to me that Sally had also shown some flexibility on the money issue, offering to let us defer payment if we posted a bond to insure that the government could collect if it won on appeal.

"I'd keep my profits?"

"For now." He paused to let that sink in, then: "If she agrees to a stay on the money, but not the gag, will you take it?"

The tempter—tap, tap, tapping at my resolve.

I told him I'd just put twenty thousand dollars in the bank representing the first slice of my paperback advance and had another slice on the way, but if it all went to the government now—I could feel a rationale build-ing—"there won't be a pot to piss in."

Mark remained silent, waiting for me to punctuate this poor-man's tale with a paean to my First Amendment rights.

I bit my tongue. "Let's see what Lewis signs."

— —

I showed up outside the courtroom early Friday morning before Mark had arrived and found myself gazing across the corridor at Sally, Brook Hedge, and Ernie Mayerfeld. After a moment, Ernie strode over and invited me to join them for a cup of coffee. "On my dime!" he quipped.

Not willing to appear graceless—at least I still had that over them—I followed him and the two women to the coffee machine. As we all sipped and eyed one another suspiciously, I couldn't help slipping in, "Didn't realize you guys were trying to bankrupt me."

Sally sniffed at the steam rising from her cup. "Oh, Frank, we know you have millions squirreled away," she replied without a hint of sarcasm.

When I entered the courtroom a few minutes later, I fully expected Judge Lewis himself to be lying in wait. But to my surprise, he ignored me and immediately launched in against his other hobgoblin, the hated press. Why were the reporters treating him so unfairly? Why did they think his preliminary ruling was meant to stifle criticism of the CIA?

"I made it quite clear therein," he whined to Sally, "that Mr. Snepp retained his right to speak about the CIA, and the press didn't say a word about that! And he retains his right to criticize as any other citizen might, and he can get up and make a speech about it, as far as I'm concerned."

Sally drummed her fingers idly.

"I clearly said I was not stifling any criticism of the CIA. He can criticize all he wants to."

She nodded sympathetically, as if Lewis had every right to feel victimized. The old man's face softened. He bade her come forward and proffer her arguments.

Despite her recent conciliatory noises, she gave nothing. The government wanted all my royalties at once, plus an expanded version of the gag order reaching my "servants" and "assigns."

The softness in Lewis's face gave way to perturbed impatience. He hadn't expected her to want to *improve* on his handiwork.

Mark stood to answer. With more deference than I could have managed, he urged Lewis to hold off all money judgments for sixty days and allow me to deduct what I'd paid in taxes and expenses over the past two years. The government, he said, was being "patently unfair" in demanding money I'd already spent.

Lewis listened intently, eyes compressed, as Sally wagged her head, implicitly inviting him to shrug all this off.

But for once he didn't. "Well, I'll give him thirty days to make an accounting," he said suddenly.

Her jaw dropped.

He raised a copy of his opinion and shook it at her like a sandlot preacher commending the Holy Word. "That order was entered when—July seventh?"

She spread her hands.

"It's almost been thirty days," he continued. "When I was trying cases, do you know how long it would take to get an order in?"

Her face froze in trepidation.

"About an hour and a half," he purred. "If it was in my favor, I'd write the judgment up immediately and take it over and give it to the judge for fear he might change his mind within the statutory period."

She started to object, voice tremulous.

"I'm just being *facetious,*" he assured her soothingly. He then looked at Mark and waved a hand vaguely at the federal attorneys.

"It doesn't take thirty days to write a judgment, but I know they've got to clear it with everybody, including my *friend,* Griffin Bell." His eyes shifted back to Sally. "Isn't that right?"

"Correct," she said guardedly.

Suddenly Lewis paused, as if realizing he'd said too much, and shot a glance at a lone journalist doodling in the spectators' gallery. What would the loathsome media make of such familiarity toward the attorney general? *From familiarity they'll assume partisanship and bias . . .*

You could almost hear the thought ticking over.

Frowning, Lewis held the reporter's gaze a moment, then hitched his shoulders fatalistically and slid off into something none of us had seen in him before—ambivalence. While agreeing with Sally that I'd broken a trust, he declined to accept her wording of his Order and directed her to come up with something better.

Afterward, over lunch, Mark declared we'd won a minor victory. I disagreed. Gagged and effectively bankrupt—money pledged was as good as gone—I could see little to be celebrated.

Wrenching a bite from his sandwich, Mark retorted archly that a simple thank-you might be in order. It hadn't been an easy morning, any more than any morning had been during this case, and unless we were all a little more *considerate* of one another—he fairly spat out the word—things could get a lot worse.

"Thank you," I said meekly.

"You've gotta realize you're not the easiest client to deal with."

I nodded.

"There're even some people around town who think you're still on the Agency's payroll, and I'm being had."

I was too shocked even to murmur a protest.

— —

All through the following weekend, I wrote as fast as I could on the assumption that, come Monday or Tuesday, Lewis would slap on his gag and I'd have no latitude to write anything without clearance. Once that happened, there'd be no writing at all, for I was determined not to give the censors the satisfaction. Do it once, and they'd have a precedent. I could almost hear Sally crooning, "Now see, Your Honor, no blood on the carpet. No harm done to his First Amendment rights. Let Snepp stay gagged a lifetime."

By Monday morning, I'd dredged enough debris from my imagination to fill one book proposal, a prospectus for a novel about an affair I'd had with a French woman in Vietnam. I called Loomis shortly after ten and waited anxiously as his line rang and rang. Finally, his secretary picked up. No, Mr. Loomis is not in town. No, Mr. Loomis can't be disturbed. His first vacation in months. Your name, please?

I clicked off and sat staring dumbly at the proposal. No Loomis, no sale. And the clock was ticking.

Meanwhile, Sally advised Mark she would no longer haggle with him over her draft Order. She was certain Lewis already had his own version worked out and would give her everything she wanted.

The stall paid off. By midafternoon on Tuesday, Lewis had filed a draft with the court clerk that sewed up the case for the government. Not only did he affirm Sally's expanded gag proposal; he also directed me to hand over to the court, by August 28, three weeks away, an accounting of what I'd earned from *Decent Interval* and a *check* for the same, "payable to the Treasurer of the United States."

Mark waited on his end of the line as I tried to steady my breathing.

The only concessions Lewis had granted were borrowings from *Marchetti*. The Agency could excise nothing from any manuscript except classified information and had to complete each clearance procedure within thirty days.

"So what do I do?" I asked, feeling utterly bereft.

"Submit your writings under protest," said Mark, "or get a job."

When Dershowitz learned of the Order, he was so incensed that he urged me to arrange a conference call with Mark to see if we could launch an appeal at once.

An hour or so later, Loomis, all suntanned and refreshed after his brief vacation, listened dismayed as I described our mutual predicament: nothing could be shown to him. No notes. No outlines.

"*And* they want my advance plus everything else I've made thus far," I told him.

"Could be $116,000 pretty soon," he volunteered.

"Whatever's available to me."

He suddenly grew quiet. "But it *isn't* available," he said after a long pause. "Don't you remember? Stafford wrote a cap into your contract. You don't get paid more than forty thousand dollars a year, whatever you earn. To spread out the tax burden."

Giddy, I called Mark to let him know. It was the best news we'd received since the trial. The cap meant that the government couldn't immediately flay me alive.

— —

"Where are we?"

Dershowitz opened the scheduled conference call the following morning with his usual imperial aplomb.

"You got a copy of the Order in the mail yet?" Mark asked from his office near the Capitol.

"No," replied Dershowitz from Cambridge.

"Me neither," I affirmed, sitting hunched over my battered desk in Arlington with financial papers spread out before me and a tape recorder patched into the receiver to provide a verbatim record of the conversation. Let it never be said that I'd forgotten how to play spy.

"After all the hoopla," Mark continued, "it's still not clear they're gonna give us credit for taxes or expenses."

"It can't be legal to make Frank pay what he's already forked over in taxes," Dershowitz objected indignantly.

Already, I was beginning to feel like a spectator at my own hanging.

Dershowitz asked if the government was still open to negotiation on finances. Mark ventured that Sally might accept a bond in place of immediate payment pending appeal. The only question was: who would underwrite it?

A poignant silence settled over the conversation. Somewhere my frazzled imagination picked up the faint Thump! Thump! Thump! of the ball being bounced into my court.

"I'll talk to Loomis on Monday," I said after a long pause.

Murmurs of satisfaction all round.

"Now for the injunction," said Mark. "The immediate problem is what to do about the circulation of outlines for books or articles."

"Have you spoken to Sally?" asked Dershowitz.

Mark chuckled. "Her response is, 'Well, just have Frank submit everything.' "

Great. Clearance for the sake of determining what has to be cleared.

"You could read the Order loosely," suggested Dershowitz, ever the devil's advocate.

"That's what Loomis thinks," I put in. Both lawyers waited. Pained indulgence. I continued timidly, "He wonders if he can't see outlines on an informal basis."

"A plausible interpretation," Dershowitz affirmed. "Prepublication isn't a settled concept."

"On the other hand"—Mark's voice was tightening—"given the judge's hostility toward Frank, I think if the issue ever came before him, he'd really try to nail him."

"What about speeches?" I asked.

Dershowitz exhaled slowly as if reluctant to respond. "I imagine the CIA contract can reasonably be interpreted to include oral disclosures."

"Just be sure to keep your notes rough," suggested Mark.

I could feel the blood drain from my face.

"I guess we still have to grapple with the hardest issue," continued Dershowitz. "What to do about staying the injunction?"

"The government is not willing to discuss it!" snapped Mark.

Dershowitz sailed on serenely. "One way of approaching this is by going up to the court of appeals and saying, 'Frank hopes to continue his career as a writer . . .' "

If Mark was going to draw the line, he'd do it now.

"What if Frank were to write an article and arrange for a publisher to take it?" he shot back.

I sat bolt upright, surprised. This wasn't what I'd expected.

"Interesting," mused Dershowitz.

"We'd have a concrete and immediate issue, like in the Pentagon Papers case," Mark continued. "Something to publish. A ban on it. A clear case of prior restraint."

"But I'm already under a gag order," I protested.

"But it's a gag on hypothetical *future* writings," said Mark. "We need something real, an actual article. Then we'd go to court to seek a stay of the injunction to let you publish it."

"Frank, is there any good short article on the horizon?" asked Dershowitz.

Trying to sound positive, I said I might be able to crank out a truncated version of the love story I'd envisaged for my novel. Or an essay about how to become a moral collaborator in the Agency.

"Nothing classified?" inquired Dershowitz.

"Not even close."

"Sounds good," said Mark.

"How do I sell these articles?" I asked skeptically.

"You don't," Mark replied. "All we need is an affidavit from a magazine editor saying, 'Mr. Snepp has explained he has a romantic short story to sell, and we'd be happy to consider it.' That would be enough to take to court."

Dershowitz pressed, "How fast could you knock these things out?"

"Three weeks, maybe," I said, pretending I actually could.

"And if we get our brief on the merits finished in September," Mark interjected, "we could take a pass at the district court on this stay at the same time."

I practically fainted. A brief on the merits in September—an appeal of the entire case!

Dershowitz gave no sign of having heard the bombshell.

"We can plead that they expedite the proceedings," Mark went on. "I'm pretty sure we can get a hearing date by the end of the year."

I bowed my head in thanksgiving.

"We await your articles with interest," Dershowitz said to me. "Being one of only two people in the United States who'll be able to read them, I feel privileged."

I drove into Georgetown an hour later to buy a six-pack and mull over what I'd heard. No, Mark wasn't being fickle. Like any good lawyer, he'd simply decided that by slathering some familiarity on this case, making it feel like "Pentagon Papers II," he could cut the risks. And who could blame him? Wasn't the law all about familiarity, precedent?

Not that the risks weren't still pretty daunting. In asking the appeals court to lift the injunction enough to allow me to publish my articles, we might indeed provoke an adverse ruling that could prejudice the entire appeal, expedited or not.

Still, better sudden death than a slow garroting.

— —

On the flight to New York the following Monday, I kept trying to convince myself that since Random House was still cashing in on *Decent Interval,* its profits having been left untouched, Loomis shouldn't feel put upon. But it didn't work. Going back and asking him now to float a bond I might never be able to repay—only days after having asked him to buy two books I might never be able to write—*that* was putting a lot of freight on friendship.

Still, what choice did I have?

As usual, Loomis greeted me as if I were a favored nephew and made me feel completely at ease in my beggar's role. He did urge me, however, to have Dershowitz call Bernstein and explain the bond to him. The two were close friends, and generosity was always best oiled by friendship.

But how much generosity would be needed?

Sadly, much more than I thought.

Two days later, Sally told Mark that since I was considered a "flight risk," any bond we came up with would have to be sufficient to cover my likely profits over the next three years, which she arbitrarily set at $175,000.

Otherwise, pay up now in cash.

I was dumfounded. Given the annual forty-thousand-dollar cap on my earnings, I couldn't have pocketed anything close to $175,000 in three years. What was Sally hedging against? A blockbuster movie deal?

— —

"So how ya holding up?"

The night I returned from New York, Vic Marchetti put in a surprise call to me at home.

"Wanna come over for a few belts?"

He clearly was sucking at his third or fourth set of ice cubes of the evening. "I've been savin' the premium stuff for you," he assured me jauntily.

I told him thanks, that I was up to my elbows in lawyers and didn't have a moment to breathe, that I was wrecked financially and saddled with an injunction that made no sense. So I just wasn't feeling very sociable.

"Aw, you're taking all this too seriously."

"Really?" Trying not to sound brittle.

"You know what I do with my injunction?" he continued. "Ignore it. Refuse to clear anything. And I write all the time. My attitude is: if you think I'm violating the injunction, sue me! They tried it once. Judge said they were full of shit."

Frazzled as I was, I vaguely remembered: Marchetti hauled back into court for saying too much in a TV interview, the Agency calling for a contempt citation. But by then, the judge had lost patience with the CIA's security claims. He let Marchetti walk.

"You got a break," I muttered.

"You, too! Ole Roarin' Oren did you a favor making such an ass of himself."

"Not the way it feels."

"He'll get dinged on appeal, for sure."

Marchetti fell silent for a moment, and I could hear him refilling his glass. Then: "Stockwell talked to you?"

I told him not for a while.

"Well, it's gotta be tough being Jesus Christ."

I let that pass.

"Agee was that way too, you know. We were contemporaries like you and Stockwell. And he lost me for the same reason. I kept saying, 'No, no, no, it's not about fucking the Agency over. It's about reform.' But then he'd go off on some messianic toot and send me a letter with lots of gibberish scribbled in the margins. Stockwell's your Agee."

"And he'll walk."

"Naw. The feds just want you first. Cleaner shot. But they'll nail 'im. Wait and see. There's a pattern to all this. First they ping me for revealing secrets, whatever the hell they are; then take you down for unclassified stuff. Next, they'll just grab Stockwell and put him in jail. Make him a martyr."

"Nobody will give a damn."

Marchetti snickered. "We found that out, didn't we?"

"No matter how clean you are, the Agency starts screaming 'national security!' and everybody just assumes you've sold out the country."

"Oh, you'll beat that rap, Frank. Nobody's gonna mistake you for a flag-burner. At worst, you'll get a slap on the wrist, maybe a ten-thousand-dollar fine. And you'll be stuck with an injunction on the grounds you're untrustworthy. Not being an apologist means you're untrustworthy. But my gut feeling is, you're gonna come out okay." He snickered again. "Even if you aren't the most lovable guy. You know, if you'd written, 'It was just one big fuckup in Vietnam,' you wouldn't be so cut off. All the bleeding hearts would be falling all over you."

"You write what you believe."

"Yeah. But the trick is to win. That's what you and I never understood."

— —

It took Random House lawyer Gerald Hollingsworth several minutes to explain the mechanics. "The bond will be issued in your name," he told me in a call the following morning. "You sign it, but we pay the premium and provide the indemnity agreement, which insures that the bondsman can turn to us if he can't collect from you."

Random House had again come through, agreeing to underwrite Sally's new $175,000 levy.

Loomis then got on the line to broach the most delicate issue of all. "Just as a legal matter," he said gently, "we'll have to make sure there's a way we can get some money back if you lose. I hope there'll be enough money somewhere so we won't have to take it out of the profits of your next book."

Suddenly I could hear the chains of indentured servitude jangling in my ear. Already I was hocked to the gills with no real prospect of income *except* my next book.

The rest of the day I brooded. If I let Random House float the bond, I'd survive the present but mortgage the future. Win or lose, I'd eventually have to repay Random House, and if I lost and forfeited all my profits, they'd be left holding the bag, a very empty one.

I couldn't let that happen.

I called Mark and told him I'd decided to create an escrow account of my own. Whatever I could scrape together would go into it to secure the bond so Random House would never risk being caught up short.

"How will you survive?" he asked in a troubled voice.

"By praying for a big advance."

He hesitated, his breathing clearly audible on the line. Finally he asked, "You holding up okay?"

It was so unlike him to embarrass me with personal questions—and so unlike me to reveal anything—that I could think of nothing to say.

He cleared his throat and filled the silence for me. "I'm sorry I haven't been able to do more for you, Frank. I really am."

— —

Knowing that he'd have his hands full with the appeals briefs, Mark left the bond negotiations to John Sims and Gerald Hollingsworth. The two of them kept things humming along nicely up until Wednesday, August 23, five days before the actual payment deadline. But then suddenly a snag developed, a very big one.

Sims called that afternoon to tell me about it. Aetna Insurance, he said, had declined to cosign the indemnity agreement out of distaste for my "negative notoriety," and several other insurers, upon learning of Aetna's objection, had instantly pulled back as well. "We're in trouble," he moaned. "I don't know if we can fix it in time."

He was considerate enough not to spell out the implications, but he didn't have to. Given Judge Lewis's biases, I knew full well that if I failed to comply with his Order in any way, he would toss me in jail for contempt.

Immediately, I called Hollingsworth to see if he had any ideas. He said he was looking into the possibility of having Random House's own underwriter, Federal Insurance, serve as guarantor.

For the rest of the day and much of the night, he worked feverishly to bring this about, but the following morning, Federal jinxed the negotiations by insisting that Random House's parent company, RCA, cosign the indemnity agreement. "That would be like trying to awaken a sleeping giant," Hollingsworth advised me sadly. "There's no way RCA's board of directors can assemble and reach a decision before Monday's deadline."

I packed an overnight bag and called Loomis to say I'd be in New York within hours to throw myself on his mercy.

No sooner had I hung up than I was socked with another dose of bad news. A friend called to tell me about an item he'd just spotted in the press: "Publisher Lyle Stuart is braced for shocks as he prepares to bring out a new book by Philip Agee called *Dirty Work.*"

I had to grip the phone with both hands to keep from dropping it.

The article went on to say that Agee and other anti-CIA activists had recently met in Havana to launch a new tell-all magazine dedicated to exposing the identities of American operatives around the world. It was perfect corroboration for Sally's direst alarms and the best advertisement for CIA censorship I'd seen since the start of my case.

As I dragged myself onto the Eastern shuttle to New York, I couldn't help wondering: Was some malign god toying with me?

Whatever the source of my bad luck, however, this time I was spared. The moment I arrived, Loomis jammed a check for $15,000 into my hands, the first installment of a new two-book advance amounting to $55,000. Combined with my accumulated royalties, this would give me enough ready cash to cover what I would have to pay over to the government on Monday. Random House had rescued me just in time.

With the immediate crisis averted, I urged Hollingsworth not to bother with the bond any longer. But he couldn't let go. Through the weekend he badgered and begged Federal Insurance to reconsider, and early Monday morning he and Bob Bernstein finally persuaded the insurer to settle for Random House's own endorsement of the indemnity agreement, in lieu of RCA's.

Three hours later, I walked up to the clerk's window at the Alexandria courthouse and handed over a newly executed bond for $175,000, together with a tally of my book earnings to date ($61,590) and my taxes and expenses over the past two years ($24,187).

This should have done it, disposing of all my immediate liabilities. But Sally wasn't satisfied. When the accounting reached her desk, she accepted it only provisionally and warned that if I lost my appeal she would go back over my expense claims with a fine-tooth comb. Her intransigence left me in limbo with no way of charting the bottom line. Did I owe the government everything I'd earned from *Decent Interval* and was likely to earn, or something less? Gross versus net profits?

The immediate practical consequence of this uncertainty was quite simply financial devastation. For in setting up the escrow account that was meant to secure the Random House bond, I now had no choice but to dump in everything Sally could demand on a moment's notice, my total profits to date *plus* some approximation of my long-ago-exhausted advance of $22,000. The only money I had on hand to apply toward that last amount was the $15,000 I'd just received against my *new* book contract. That would have to go into the escrow too.

And yet, how *was* I to survive? Until I completed my new books and collected the remainder of the $55,000 advance, I was flat broke, writing for free.

If I had strength to write at all.

CHAPTER 22

Black Dog and Stephani

No one could quite figure him out. Was he simply a frustrated romantic playacting at being a spy? Or worse, a bargain-basement Benedict Arnold?

Either way, when the FBI arrested twenty-three-year-old William Kampiles just before I turned my bond and accounting over to Judge Lewis in late August, the CIA suddenly had far worse to worry about than my unforgiving memory. The Era of the Mole was now upon us: the true and the brave selling out Mother Agency for a few pieces of silver.

William Kampiles had labored only briefly in the traces, eight months as a lowly clerk in the CIA watch office. But on bailing out the previous fall, he'd set himself up for a major career change by pocketing a top-secret spy satellite manual and then offering to sell it to a Soviet diplomat for an astonishingly modest three thousand dollars.

Fortuitously, for reasons unknown, he'd suffered second thoughts after sealing the deal, and in a follow-up penitential letter to the Agency had volunteered to spy on the Russian buyer. But alas, no one had taken him seriously, and over the next several months, with both the CIA and Justice Department panting after me, the letter had lain unopened and unread in a senior CIA operative's briefcase.

Had Langley's elite been less fixed on yours truly, would they have tumbled to Kampiles sooner? Probably not. But they might have realized, as they eventually did, that not one, but thirteen of the ultrasensitive satellite manuals had disappeared in recent months, the majority having been lost through sheer negligence. And that might have trivialized—even for them—the inconvenience I'd caused.

But no, it couldn't and *didn't* happen: finding fault had always come more easily to them than admitting it.

And when at last Kampiles did get the attention he so richly deserved, the coincidental looming threat of Philip Agee's newest exposé afforded them a perverse consolation—a fresh excuse to play victim and turn up the heat on me.

Moles in the hole! Make an example! Off with Snepp's head!

The payoff was immediate.

Two weeks after Kampiles's arrest, six weeks after the judgment against me, just days before Agee's reemergence in print, a Senate subcommittee unveiled a new proposal to outlaw the disclosure of CIA agents' names, even previously published ones. The bill's putative target was Agee, but so toxic were its implications for anyone remotely vulnerable that even some of my detractors began to fear for me.

Daphne Miller's German-born mother, who'd sat stoically through my trial, sent word through her equally chastened husband that she now saw that I was no traitor. The trial, she added hyperbolically, was unlike anything she'd witnessed since Nazi Germany.

— —

Had I been less dispirited, such hot-air inversions might have afforded some comic relief. But the very paucity of emotional support, so often traceable to my own self-absorption, made any glad hand seem welcome, and I found myself groping pathetically after every one.

The more so after Bernie's final letter to me.

"How are you?"

So anodyne, so deceptively breezy in its preamble.

The letter reached me the first week in September, just after Kampiles's arrest. Bernie had taken off for her native Antigua two weeks before, to "come down," as she put it, from the rigors of recent months. She'd also taken up with a newly rediscovered former boyfriend, though somehow I'd managed to shut that out, even while remaining subliminally aware.

Former boyfriend, indeed.

But then, what claim did I have anyway? Emotionally bankrupt as I was, not having wanted her at the trial for fear of the bias she might inspire in the judge.

So I pretended to be glad (or reconciled at least) that she'd gone to the islands to come down. She deserved it, certainly. And much more.

Much, much more—from me.

But I was not prepared for the revelation she'd buried several paragraphs in.

"He's asked me to marry him. What do you think?"

I glared at the letter as if defiance might defeat its meaning, then crumpled it, stuffed it away, and drank heavily that night, long after Clyde's final call.

Still my favorite Georgetown hangout, Clyde's. The resident gin slingers all knew me well by now, ignominy having made me a prized decoration. "Hi, Frank. Gonna beat the bastards?"

Marry him!

Nor had she offered any qualifier to take the edge off, no scribbled marginalia soliciting my disapproval.

What do I think?

Shortly before daybreak, despite heavy inebriation, I threw on some sweats and staggered onto the jogging path along the C and O canal, hoping not to disturb the water moccasins. Staggered for who knows how far. Retching along the way. And trying to convince myself I could have done nothing different.

But I knew better.

Bernie—light of my life, who'd nurtured me through it all.

Bernie, who'd asked for nothing except, jokingly, my cooperation in making her the proud owner of a blue-eyed baby.

Jokingly is the way she'd posed it, but not the way she'd meant it. That I knew. She'd loved me and had wanted my love, and I'd backhanded her as easily as I'd backhanded Carla and Mai Ly and another baby too many dreary memories ago.

Staggering. Terrified of the snakes.

Then, slumped on the muddy bank, ill and despairing.

And all the while, trying to frame in my mind the beginnings of a letter back to her.

I was too caught up, don't you see?

"Just call back in an hour," is how I'd put it to Mai Ly. Same alibi, only costlier then, writ in blood. But essentially, no different. Always some higher purpose beckoning. Always too caught up to do the right thing.

Duty, honor, truth-telling, redemption. What a wretched litany of higher purposes! What a flimsy alibi for a compromised conscience.

I never wrote that letter back, my selfishness needing no explication. And soon after returning from the islands, Bernie announced she was pregnant by her former boyfriend and would marry him, and the last of my emotional tethers snapped, leaving me adrift in the thickening mists of self-justification.

"Did you ever intend to marry her?" asked Loomis in a moment of consideration.

"Dunno"—and feeling the creeping chill of my own cynicism as never before.

"I had a friend once," he replied uneasily, "whose lover wound up betraying him. So I understand how you feel."

But he did not understand at all. Not because he couldn't, but because I dared not let him. Not him or anyone else. Whoever stared into these mists might glimpse the monster ungraced by any higher purpose, and that, my fragile ego would not allow.

— —

I said nothing to my lawyers about what had happened, and the distance between us served as a kind of shield, keeping them from seeing enough of my frailties to dampen their own enthusiasm for my case. I should have leveled, of course, should have told them I no longer felt worthy of anyone's commitment.

But my ego wasn't up to that, either.

So I let them go on believing I still believed too, and by the end of the second week in September, Mark had completed a written plea to Judge Lewis to stay the injunction pending resolution of my appeal. Somehow, I'd also managed to pull together outlines of the articles I'd promised him as pretexts for this initiative (the romantic love story and the essay on bureaucratic compromise), and my agent, Lynn Nesbit, had coaxed letters from *Esquire* and *The Atlantic Monthly* expressing interest in publishing them should they be liberated from Lewis's gag.

The intended purpose of all this, Mark persisted in reminding me, was to position us, legally, where *The New York Times* had been on the eve of the Pentagon Papers decision.

Remember: in early summer 1971, this and other newspapers had received and begun publishing bootleg copies of the Pentagon's secret history of our early involvement in Vietnam. The Nixon administration had cried "Havoc!" and preliminary injunctions had ensued. But the Supreme Court, on reviewing the jeremiads, had found them wanting and had lifted the gags, allowing publication to continue.

Mark felt the same consideration should be extended to me, and with better justification. The newspapers, after all, had wanted to air secrets; my prospective offerings were as harmless as you could get.

In his initial brief, Mark neatly summarized the arguments that would propel us up the appeals ladder. Drawing on a battery of U.S. Supreme Court decisions, he began by reminding Lewis of the constitutional bias, the array of legal precedents, against the kind of gag that bound me. He then launched into a survey of the Pentagon Papers ruling itself, noting that the Supreme Court had refused to uphold the gags in that case despite the government's claims of grave, impending peril to the national security.

Why, then, the gag against me? he demanded. Indeed, why *any* sanction at all since "the government has not even attempted to demonstrate, nor has the court found, that publication will surely result in direct, immediate, and irreparable damage?"

If such a threat existed, he went on, the government would have obtained a gag order against me prior to my trial. Which it hadn't.

Ironically, no sooner had Mark finished his brief than the Justice Department embraced a new prosecutorial policy that seemed to repudiate the very logic of its case against me. On September 10, the chief of the criminal division ordered subordinates no longer to go after leakers who tattled for "constructive" reasons, unless they'd stolen secret documents in the process.

The directive's ostensible purpose was to reassure the public in the wake of the *Truong-Humphrey* verdict that government whistle-blowers wouldn't be routinely strung up on larceny charges. But couldn't its protections be extended a little further—to me?

Mark thought so and dashed off a solicitous letter to Griffin Bell himself. Reminding him that I'd stolen nothing, leaked no secret, and had written only to alert the public to the "inadequacies of the United States withdrawal from Vietnam," he called on him to drop the case against me.

Two days passed. Nothing happened. Then on Tuesday, September 13, we discovered something that helped explain why. A reporter from *The Washington Star* called to tell me that months before, just prior to my being sued, the FBI had caught newly retired ambassador Graham Martin in a security breach that made *Decent Interval* look like a Sunday school hymnal—and had let him walk. Martin, it seemed, had not only lifted sensitive documents from the State Department, as had long been known, but had let them fall into the hands of car thieves.

It was my first glimmering of the squalid little scandal the government had carefully kept hidden throughout its suit against me. And it gave a sinister gloss to the new "whistle-blower" directive. If Martin's transgression ever became public, as now seemed likely, the Justice Department could always rationalize not prosecuting him by dubbing his "misappropriation" a permissible act of whistle-blowing or executive discretion.

The reporter who alerted me to the story was reluctant to publish it because Martin was even then recuperating from cancer surgery. But no such qualms afflicted me. I quickly tipped off *The Washington Post* to what I'd learned, then floated word back to the *Star* that its competition was about to score a scoop.

The following day, both newspapers front-paged lengthy reports about the purloined files, which, as the *Post* reported, "cover the entire span of major U.S. involvement in the Vietnam conflict from 1963 to 1975." The *Post* quoted Martin himself as saying he'd intended to turn the documents over to the Lyndon B. Johnson Library in Austin, Texas. But, noted *Newsweek* in a follow-up story of its own, he hadn't bothered to tell the library of these plans until seven weeks *after* the documents had been heisted from his car.

Other sources insisted that the Justice Department was still considering whether to prosecute Martin under a seldom-used statute dealing with misuse of classified documents. But nobody expected this to happen. *Newsweek* cited official concern that "a trial could expose any secrets" that hadn't been compromised already, and *Time* reported that federal officials were "satisfied" that "Martin had no intention to write a book," though in fact he'd been quoted in earlier press accounts as saying he might.

Whatever the reason for his being spared, my staunchest defenders were infuriated. Random House president Bob Bernstein whipped off a letter to the *Post* challenging its reporters to "question Griffin Bell about what seems to me to be another example of discriminatory enforcement by the CIA.

"Obviously, the CIA knew about this situation when they chose to go after Frank Snepp in federal court," he snapped. "I don't have to wonder what would have happened if they had found those documents in Mr. Snepp's car."

— —

Given Oren Lewis's own chronic indifference to the discrimination issue, it would have taken a bolt from heaven to persuade him I deserved any consideration because of what Martin had done. Still, he was unusually civil toward me when we showed up in his court the following Friday to plead for a lifting of the gag to permit publication of my two articles.

"I'm not questioning this man's loyalty to the United States," Lewis muttered, letting his eyes slide over me. "I'm not impugning his personal loyalty and integrity, because I think he's a fine gentleman."

I glanced at Mark, astonished.

Whatever had tempered Lewis's mood, however, didn't make him receptive to our arguments. "If he's got a right to print those two articles," he retorted after Mark had summarized his brief, "he's got a right to print book number two, book number three, and anything he wants to."

He added: "I can't believe that the CIA, if he has a fictional story, they wouldn't clear it in the proverbial fifteen minutes."

Mark insisted that wasn't good enough, that under constitutional principle even a moment's delay in publication burdened me impermissibly.

"I don't buy this First Amendment argument!" Lewis replied, voice rising. "He didn't have to take that job with the CIA. Nobody put him in a straitjacket and forced him to go into the Agency."

And so—it was decided. No stay. No nothing.

— —

Somehow I found myself in New York the following weekend. There, to talk to Loomis?

Don't quite remember.

Or to see Bernie?

She was affianced now. A million miles beyond reach.

Or maybe to give a speech. That's how I was supporting myself these days. Speaking off the cuff. No cue cards, no notes, lest the Agency demand I clear those, too.

Rotary clubs and college students were among those who paid to hear me, their curiosity always seeming slightly prurient, like a spectator's curiosity at a hanging. How will the condemned hold up? Eager eyes raking me for some symptom of a crack-up.

Still, I accepted such invitations gratefully, for otherwise I would have been dirt-poor, all my other earnings now bleeding away into the escrow I'd established against the threat of total confiscation.

So yes, it was probably a speech that had brought me in. And now, done with it, at the end of the day, I was taking a jog around Central Park and feeling less besieged, when suddenly, just after veering into Sheep's Meadow, I spotted the balloons.

Then her.

Much, much thinner than I'd remembered her from college, more fragile than the aspiring young model who'd been the Barnard roommate to my soon-to-be first wife—less remote than the doe-eyed seductress who'd dominated the covers of *Seventeen* and other fashion mags during my two years in graduate school and first years in the Agency.

Indeed there was something about her that evoked a quality I'd first encountered in the Vietnamese: a hint of unspeakable suffering.

Stephani Cook, is that you?

She was standing at the edge of the meadow, clutching the strings of the balloons in one hand and the grubby paw of her second-born in the other. She recognized me immediately from the news photos, she would later say, and embraced me as if I'd brought hope for the bereft.

She'd been thinking of me a lot, she said, following my travails in the press, and wondering if our paths would ever cross again. In her eyes, it was providential that they had.

After introducing her son, Zachary, and assuring me that she was happily divorced, she invited me to dinner at her East Side apartment. Blessedly, she was so thoroughly immersed in my case, thanks to the media coverage, that I didn't have to tell her what I'd been going through, didn't have to pretend to be whole. In fact, from the first moment we spoke, she seemed to be so intuitively in touch with the black dog within me that I felt I had no need to explain very much at all.

Over dinner, I began to understand why. That intimation of suffering was no illusion on my part. She wore it in every filigree of her being, in the emaciated hands and sunken cheeks, the eerily silken hair and the hideous scar that peeked just above the neckline of her dress.

She caught my eye on the scar and stood up suddenly, pulling her dress open to reveal a zipper of stitched and tortured skin that extended to the very top of her pubic bone. The gesture and the wound it revealed were so profoundly shocking that it barely registered she was exposing her body to me. All I saw were the ravages of a war that made mine seem insignificant by comparison.

Slowly she closed the dress and brushed her eyes with the back of her hand, and I could tell from the tremors she was weeping.

But not from sorrow, she assured me after a long while. From relief. She, likewise, was in need of someone to whom nothing had to be explained.

The evening then metamorphosed into a hundred and one nights, as she spun out the chapters of her own horror story. The first unexplained chest pains and fainting spells . . . the doctors pooh-poohing them all as the vapors of a neurotic beauty . . . then the exploratory surgery . . . the misdiagnoses . . . the hysterectomy . . . the open-heart surgery . . . doctors dipping again and again into her body, systematically dismantling it in search of an ailment they could not diagnose.

For months, the savaging had continued, until finally someone had thought to question her about Zachary's birth. She'd delivered in her kitchen, having been unable to get to the hospital on time, and there'd been no placenta in the afterbirth, and had she appreciated the significance of that omission, she was later told, she might have spared herself so much torment. For the body's failure to eject the placenta can denote a rare form of cancer.

Which, in fact, is what she had.

Chemotherapy had reduced her to a specter from Buchenwald and destroyed the long auburn hair that had cupped her face like a petal. But it had also obliterated the cancer and bought her a second life.

It was the experience of resurrection that gave us common bond, she told me as we clung to each other several nights later. Vietnam had been my cancer, and confession my deliverance.

Or so she thought.

I suspected her sanity, of course; was convinced her many near-passes with death had accustomed her to self-reflection beyond what anyone could safely endure. And yet, there was a familiarity to her madness that made me feel more comfortable with my own.

— —

Mark noticed the change in me at once, and was not pleased. Suddenly I was my old irascible self, second-guessing his every decision.

"Get laid less often," he admonished me curtly after my first night with Stephani, for he'd long ago lost patience with my attempts to play lawyer.

Had he been less a lawyer himself, I might have taken offense. But he was still delivering far more for me than I had any right to expect.

In just the past few days, since our bout with Lewis, he'd been reading and rereading case documents in search of a loophole we might have missed, and miraculously had found one. From the outset, Sally had tried to justify prepublication review by claiming that no mere middle-grade agent like me could recognize or protect a secret without the Agency's help. But in reviewing the text of my final secrecy agreement, Mark had discovered a passage that gave the lie to this nonsense. Buried deep in it was an admonition to the signatory to report to "appropriate" officials any attempt "by any authorized person to solicit classified information."

"How the hell can you do *that*," Mark exclaimed with rising excitement, "if you can't recognize secrets! This paragraph blows Sally's logic out of the water."

To be sure it did, he gave plenty of space to his new discovery in the brief he wrote and sent to the appeals court in Richmond on September 25. Urging the court to reconsider and reverse Lewis's recent decision not to lift the injunction, he argued that the CIA would face no risk if this happened, since like all Agency employees, I'd been trained to protect secrets and "entrusted" to do so.

Elsewhere in the brief, he slipped in a reference to Martin's recently exposed knavery. Recalling that Admiral Turner, in his trial testimony, had declined to blame me exclusively for the Agency's security problems, he suggested that Martin and William Kampiles might bear a larger responsibility. Their misdeeds, he reasoned crisply, "appear on their face much more likely to be the cause of a loss of confidence in the CIA than does Mr. Snepp's publication of unclassified, public information."

The government fired back immediately, eight federal attorneys, including Brook Hedge and the CIA's Tony Lapham, signing off on its opposition brief.

"It's the same old Mau-Mau job," Mark grumbled as he reviewed it with me.

And indeed it was. Up top was what appeared to be a major concession, an acknowledgment that my final secrecy agreement was a contract, not merely a "reminder" or "release document," as the government had previously claimed. But having given us an inch, Hedge and company then tried to snatch it back. Insisting that my final agreement "resembled" Marchetti's first one, they argued tortuously that since he'd been forced under his court-ordered injunction to clear everything, my final agreement implicitly carried the same requirement.

— —

Since judicial rules permitted a written response, Mark and John Sims quickly cranked one out. Before mailing it off, they sent me a copy, and though I liked what I saw, I wanted more, especially a more forceful answer to a suggestion by the government that CIA secrecy agreements were entirely reasonable.

To my chagrin, both of them said no. "The case is already too abstract," Sims explained soothingly. "Let's not throw any more dust in the judges' eyes."

He had a point, of course. The case had become so abstract that almost nothing that mattered to me personally figured in it any longer. Vietnam had been reduced to an occasional footnote, and no one who'd been closest to me and who best knew my motives warranted even *that* much recognition. Bernie might as well have been exiled to the moon. Carla too.

What kind of law loses sight of the truth this way?

— —

Carla.

So far was *she* removed from any immediate relevancy that her arrival back in Washington the second week of October came as a shock. I'd imagined she would stay away forever, to avoid being further tainted by association with me. And in fact, there was an element of escapism in her return.

She'd come back, she told me, to let the Agency know she was ending her sabbatical and her CIA career as well.

I managed to reiterate how sorry I was about what I'd done to her. She lied and said, "No harm done." It wasn't my behavior, or even the Agency's, that had brought her to this turn, she emphasized, but merely a desire to put the past definitively behind her. Indeed she continued to believe in the Agency's basic mission, though—she added ruefully—the Security boys certainly hadn't treated her well.

"Do you make something of that in your case?" she inquired as she leaned to kiss my cheek.

"Too abstract," I told her.

It was the last conversation I would have with Carla for many years.

— —

A night or two later, I bound up my wounds and shuffled off to a party thrown by a prominent Vietnamese expatriate, former anti-Thieu conspirator Tran Van Don. It was a swank affair, like one of those soirées back in Saigon where everyone's shared agenda had been to spy on everyone else.

"All the biggies were there," I told Stephani in a call afterward.

"Walk down memory lane, huh?"

"Ambassador Bunker. Colby. General Westmoreland."

Some of the names struck only a faint chord with her. *Colby?* Sure. *Ellsworth Bunker?* A former Saigon ambassador, Martin's predecessor, I told her.

And *William Westmoreland?* Once U.S. commander in chief in Vietnam.

"I knew that," she objected mildly.

"They flocked around. Everybody with a kind word. 'We're with you. Curious to know who you are—*what* you are.' "

"Any good-looking women?" she asked, for Stephani couldn't imagine my having any other motive for suffering such indignities.

"Mrs. Colby came up and said, 'We're very sorry the judge treated you this way.' "

"Why didn't you take me along?"

"You wouldn't have recognized me. With these types, I'm very 'Yes sir, No ma'am.' "

"Southern gentleman all the way."

"Several CIA men pulled me aside to say, 'We support you.' "

"Did you ask: Why not openly?" There was a touch of impatience in Stephani's voice.

"You have to be genteel at these sorts of dos."

"Even when they're tearing out your throat?"

I closed my eyes, trying not to be provoked. "There was this old professor of political science from Georgetown," I continued evenly. "A survivor of the Nazi camps. He said, 'You know, young man. You're a man of honor.' "

"Poor Frankie. You need that, don't you?"

I felt the sting but let it pass. "Mrs. Bunker, who's an ambassador in her own right, told me how sad she was about the Vietnamese left behind."

"She know any of them by first name?"

"I had my picture taken with Westmoreland."

"And yes-sir'd him, too, I bet."

Very carefully, I answered: "He said he thought every day about those who died under his command."

"Did *he* have any first names?"

I was now gripping the phone so tightly I could barely feel my fingers. "The one thing I have that the average protester doesn't is compassion for those in power. The agony they feel."

"You're generous tonight."

"It was a strange evening."

"I believe it. Because they're all your enemies."

CHAPTER 23

Road to Richmond

CONSIDERING THE PLAGUE of bad luck I'd suffered since the start of the lawsuit, it would have been refreshing if the appeals process had played out more congenially. It didn't. Three days after Mark had sent our brief to Richmond, Philip Agee was back in the headlines and at the heart of my case. *Seven hundred CIA officials identified!* shrieked *Time* about the security implications of Agee's latest book. *Many in danger for their lives!*

Relying on the alarmist quotes from anonymous CIA officials, the magazine intimated that the Agency was now hard-pressed to stop such secrecy breaches except through civil suits like the one against me. It might as well have said "Hang Snepp to silence Agee."

By startling coincidence, barely eighteen hours later the appeals panel in Richmond rejected my plea for relief from Lewis's gag and directed all parties to be ready to argue the *entire* case within six weeks.

My final reckoning had just been jump-started.

"I think it's a positive sign," Mark assured me, trying to put the best face on the news. "The court obviously considers the case important."

"It's certainly not a bad sign," Dershowitz volunteered with no greater conviction. "It's neutral. There is no way it's a bad signal."

— —

As word spread of the impending appeal, several media organizations offered to file amicus briefs for me, and PEN, the international writers' lobby, quickly organized a symposium to highlight the First Amendment issues. Norman Dorsen of the ACLU agreed to moderate, with Benno Schmidt of Columbia Law School and Floyd Abrams, First Amendment counsel *extraordinaire,* volunteering for the panel.

David Atlee Phillips, who upon retirement from the CIA had launched the slavishly apologetic Association of Former Intelligence Officers, was invited to represent the opposing viewpoint, which promised to be provocative indeed, since the group's newsletter, *Periscope,* which he edited, had never been submitted to the CIA for censorship (and never prosecuted à la *Snepp*).

Talk about discriminatory enforcement.

I was asked to deliver the keynote.

— —

PEN's headquarters, a converted townhouse in lower Manhattan, had all the charm of an inquisition chamber in Salem, Massachusetts. Cracks around the sagging doors and windows admitted the chill of early winter, and there was a chill indeed, for this was October 23, only three weeks before my date in Richmond.

Fired up as I was, I couldn't warm myself against the chill.

The crowd was sparse but impressively bouillabaisse, predictable haranguers from the professional left blending uneasily with sleek midtown litigators, civil liberties fanatics, a grande dame or two, and a dozen or so threadbare scriveners freighted with practiced angst.

Scattered through the audience was a handful of box suits straight off the rack at Langley. One held a tape recorder aloft, the better to catch my every word.

As I began my peroration, I scanned the upturned faces for some sign of old Victor Marchetti. In a call the night before, he'd promised to fly in to lend moral support, but he'd also remarked wryly, over the familiar clack of ice cubes, that a marinated fruitcake never travels well. So—

Stockwell, too, had taken a rain check. Dear old John, still stewing over the fact that my infamy had so far exceeded his. Only briefly had his book vied with Colby's on the lower edge of the bestseller lists. Agee's latest hadn't registered at all.

Kurt Vonnegut, a late arrival, waved enthusiastically as he took a back-row seat. Days before, he and fellow novelist E. L. Doctorow had approached me privately and denounced the suit against me as a throwback to the excesses of Joe McCarthy. I was too callow to be shamed by their attaching such misplaced importance to me.

Autograph seekers flitted from one spare seat to another, trying to cozy up to Vonnegut.

My defiantly liberal friend Gloria Emerson sat hunched in a middle row vibrating like Mother Fury and jabbing angrily at her notepad. Occasionally, she glowered up at the CIA's mouthpiece, David Phillips, as if searching for just the right place to deliver a head shot.

Rangy and sunbaked with a Southern accent thick enough to curdle grits, Phillips seemed merely bemused as he gazed out from the dais, the liver spots on his temple pulsing evenly. At no point during my presentation did he look at me, and I wondered if he might be embarrassed at having to play the scold here. He was, after all, an alumnus of the old school—Guatemala, Lebanon, Bay of Pigs—and much as he might have detested loose-lipped malcontents like me, the tradition he embodied, battered as it was, detested even more the idea of leaving bodies on the battlefield.

Photographs preserved from the evening show the keynoter himself hollow-cheeked and rail-thin, an unraveling blue polyester suit drooping from slumped shoulders, the hard set of the jaw conveying neither strength nor determination but merely the contrived earnestness of one who dares not admit, even to himself, that he is lost.

Midway through my speech, I began searching the audience for some glimpse of Stephani. I needed her contempt for those who'd survived nothing. But she'd stayed away, fearful, as she would later explain, that Bernie might show up to demand her place at court.

Near the front row, a Hollywood filmmaker hung his head dejectedly as I wound up. He'd approached me weeks before about writing a screenplay about my experiences. But his lawyers had since convinced him it might be subject to censorship too.

The applause that followed me back to my seat was polite but grudging. The firebrands in attendance clearly would have preferred more fire from me. Moderator Dorsen quickly summoned CIA apologist Phillips to the battlements.

Struggling to be as nonconfrontational as possible, having realized he was dangerously outnumbered, he focused his plaints on the fact that I'd kept a diary in Vietnam, and implied that this in itself might have been a serious security breach. There wasn't even enough applause to qualify as polite.

Dorsen then invited Columbia's boyish professor, Benno Schmidt, to the microphone.

Smiling shyly, Schmidt slipped off his large black-framed glasses and huffed on one of the lenses. "When you listen to Mr. Snepp describe his case, I think one's natural reaction is to say, 'How can this be?'" Presuming to answer his own question, he pointed out that because Congress had repeatedly refused to pass broad secrecy legislation, the government had been obliged to improvise whenever attempting to curb serious leaks.

In the Pentagon Papers case, he said, the government had tried to frighten the courts into clamping down by howling about irreparable harm. That hadn't worked, so next it had tried contract law, and that had. "In the Marchetti case," he explained, "the government was successful in persuading a federal court that, in effect, the secrecy agreement could take the place of a statute . . . that a contract of that kind authorizes a court to enjoin publication of classified information.

"Now, can *Marchetti* justify the decision in *Snepp*?" he posed challengingly. "I don't think so.

"This case," he observed, "is an example of what happens when the law is in terrible disarray. Pentagon Papers and *Marchetti*—those are the only precedents. Imagine that! On a subject of this importance, only two judicial precedents in our history. . . .

"And so the courts feel a little bit at sea, rudderless. The result is decisions that are, in an important sense, lawless."

This time, thunderous applause. Moderator Dorsen abruptly cut in to introduce Floyd Abrams, whom he described as a man of "unusual objectivity," notwithstanding his role as defense counsel in both the Pentagon Papers and Marchetti cases. Abrams nodded politely as he assumed the floor.

"I come to you plunged in gloom," he announced with an apologetic glance at Schmidt. The reason, he confided, was the unpredictable way in which judges had lately disposed of prior restraint issues. In the Pentagon Papers case, he said, the original trial judge had first questioned the patriotism of *The New York Times,* then challenged the government to demonstrate the damage it had suffered.

Even more quixotic, he continued, was *Marchetti II.* After being gagged, Marchetti had turned his manuscript over to the Agency, and then, upon suffering massive deletions, had challenged the CIA to defend them in court. Abrams had represented Marchetti's publisher, Knopf. Miraculously, the judge, Albert Bryan, who'd been so hostile toward Marchetti at his first trial, had softened in the aftermath. "Judge Bryan came to the conclusion that almost nothing in the Marchetti book was classified," Abrams told the audience.

But later on appeal, he went on, the Fourth Circuit had reversed Bryan and issued a new opinion, allowing the CIA to retain its deletions if it could show that the disputed information *could* have been "classified," or *should* or *might* have been "classified."

This display of judicial caprice was deeply troubling, said Abrams, all the more since the government seemed determined in my case to take the Marchetti ruling one step further. Think about it, he said: "The CIA comes to court and says, 'We understand this is not classified; nonetheless we have the right to suppress it as if it were, unless Mr. Snepp first submitted it to us on a simple contract basis.'

"I wish Mr. Lynch and Mr. Snepp well," he added, "but read your papers in a month"—again a baleful look at Schmidt—"and if what you read is that Mr. Snepp lost his case *because* there was a contract, or that Mr. Snepp lost his case *notwithstanding* the fact that the material was *not* classified, should I suggest that you think again about what's going on?"

What might be going on, he ventured, was a certain pandering to power and status. Indeed, he'd often wondered who would have won the Pentagon Papers case if the defendant had been *The Village Voice,* not *The New York Times.* "If I am right in thinking that the prestige of the *Times* made it possible to win that case," he wound up, "then we should all be concerned not just about the CIA but about another branch of government as well."

Amid a light patter of applause, Norm Dorsen snatched the microphone back and invited the panelists to question one another.

Immediately, I asked Phillips about the pro-CIA newsletter he edited: "Why don't you submit your *Periscope* for review?"

"It doesn't work," he replied.

"Why am I being sued and you're not?"

A flush crept up the suntan. "Since you've asked me this question," he replied, staring determinedly at the audience, "I find it curious, even astonishing, that they should have chosen Frank's book."

He shrugged as if to accentuate his bewilderment. "Why did they choose a book which I think most people agree—and I do—is a good one?"

He looked squarely at me for the first time. "Why Frank's book instead of say, Stockwell's book, when Stockwell has publicly said, 'Yes, I have revealed classified information.' "

Gloria Emerson sprang to her feet. "If you find that it is astonishing that the CIA is attempting to punish Mr. Snepp," she shouted, "why then have you not attempted to reach Stansfield Turner to protest the action!"

Phillips squared his shoulders. "I believe that the proper course would have been for Frank or his publishers to submit the book to the Agency."

Gloria: "And yet you say it's a good book."

"Let me explain."

"Please."

"A lot of the people who work for any intelligence organization are grubby little people—"

"Oh?" Gloria put in.

"—that you just hire for grubby little jobs. All of them aren't capable of the right kind of decision about the material that they have made available to them."

A hand shot up in the back row. Dorsen immediately recognized Bob Bernstein of Random House. Bernstein stood, patted down his pinstripes. "We know from rather recent experiences," he said to Phillips, "that there are a lot of grubby little people in the White House and a lot of grubby little people in the State Department. So I don't see why the grubby little people in the CIA should be discriminated against."

Cackles and guffaws.

"Let the Congress make the law and all grubby little people be subjected to that law."

He then laid into the CIA itself for not treating its own grubs equally. Witness how easily Richard Helms had beaten the rap for misleading Congress, he said. "It seems to me that for Mr. Helms to be fined two thousand dollars for lying, and for Mr. Snepp to be fined over one hundred thousand for telling the truth—something has to be wrong with that." This time the applause blew the lid off.

— —

The buzz generated by the symposium jostled loose some of the promised amicus briefs on my behalf, and Mark and his collaborators soon completed an appeals brief of their own. Much of it was given over to the myopia of the man who'd made such a shambles of my trial. Judge Lewis, they argued, had erred in failing to submit the financial issues to a jury, in misinterpreting and minimizing my final contract, in imposing a gag without forcing the government to justify it, and in declining to consider our discriminatory enforcement defense. Such mistakes, they concluded, warranted a judgment in my favor, or at least a retrial.

After reading over their draft, I had only one complaint: nowhere had my defenders attempted to head off a personal attack on me. Mark patiently explained that the government wouldn't dare, that appeals briefs were meant to explore *legal* not factual questions.

On Friday night, November 3, a CIA staff lawyer shuffled up to Mark's door with a copy of the government's answer to us. Exhausted from hours of brainstorming about my case, he accepted an invitation to sit and share a cocktail with us and soon let himself get thoroughly lubricated and lugubrious.

Because he chose to unwind in the privacy of Mark's home, Mark feels to this day that we should not hold him personally accountable, by name, for what he told us. So I merely report his remarks, not his identity.

Expatiating candidly on the problems he and his colleagues had had with my case and with one another, our guest raised a pinkie at one point and remarked acidly that the folks at the Justice Department had "pricks this big" when it came to taking bold action against me. John Greaney, the CIA lawyer who'd initially tried to stop me, was, in his eyes, "an asshole" who'd committed so many "fuckups" he should have been fired. And our visitor seemed equally contemptuous of my erstwhile friend Linley Stafford, whom he leeringly characterized as "a closet queer, AC/DC."

I couldn't help wondering what interest the CIA might have had in Stafford's sexuality. A little blackmail fodder, perhaps? At this point, nothing would have surprised me.

As alcohol dissolved the last of our guest's inhibitions, he let us in on what he described as the government's biggest disappointment. At the trial, he said, Sally had hoped to shore up her case through a carefully rehearsed piece of theater. She'd expected Mark to ask of Admiral Turner on the witness stand, "Has any source terminated his work with the CIA because of Snepp's book?" To which Turner was to have answered, "Yes." Mark was then expected to have demanded, "Who?" Whereupon Sally would have objected in order to shut off the questioning, thus leaving the impression, without giving away anything, that I'd irreparably damaged the national security by scaring off agents.

But, commented our guest sadly, Lewis had bollixed things by interrupting so often, Turner had never gotten to answer yes.

— —

The sleaziness of the CIA man's gin talk turned out to be emblematic of the government's appeals brief as a whole. Just as I'd feared, a large part of it *was* devoted to a blistering personal assault on me. Zeroing in on my alleged duplicity, the brief's authors, including Assistant Attorney General Barbara Babcock, quoted from my press interviews to try to suggest that I'd known all along I was breaching my original agreement. Obviously, they were hoping through such insinuations to distract the appeals judges from the flaws in their legal arguments.

Fearing that the judges might indeed be tempted, Mark decided at last to rally to my reputation. In a short reply brief, he devoted a massive footnote to parrying every one of the government's little digs. It was the first time he'd ever attempted so energetically to defend me from myself:

Whatever Mr. Snepp may have said under the glare of the television lights while promoting his book, CIA documents demonstrate that he did not "trick" or "fool" the Agency.

The fact that he was writing a book was no secret. . . . The contemporaneous records also demonstrate that Mr. Snepp was openly adamant in his refusal to submit his book for censorship. . . .

Mr. Snepp's consistent belief since the day he resigned from the CIA was that the 1968 agreement only prohibited the disclosure of classified information but did not require submission of unclassified information. Therefore, according to a contemporaneous Agency record, he stated on January 22, 1976, that he "had no intention of extending his legal obligation beyond the original [1968] Secrecy Agreement," and consequently refused to commit himself to submitting his manuscript prior to publication. The next day, however, he agreed to sign the termination secrecy agreement, because its requirement for prepublication review was limited to classified information and therefore was consistent with his understanding of the 1968 agreement. . . .

The only matter which Mr. Snepp did attempt to conceal from the CIA was the identity of his publisher, because he feared that the CIA might approach the publisher and interfere with the publication of his book, as it had attempted to do with other books, including another book published by Random House. His apprehension was therefore not unfounded.

The night before the appeals hearing, it was raining torrents, and the drive down to Richmond over the water-choked interstate was like chasing Moses through the Red Sea. Stephani had agreed to come along in order to ensure, as she put it, that I did not become "too preoccupied" with myself. It was, of course, a doomed effort.

Though my bank account was now as barren as a CIA promise, I'd managed to borrow enough cash to treat us both to dinner that night at a fairly respectable Richmond eatery. By the time the waiter had settled us at an upstairs table, I was deeply into unsavory ruminations about the compromises my lawyers had made in their search for a perfect case. What had happened to Vietnam along the way? Why only passing reference to the evacuation in their latest briefs? Where was their moral outrage? Where, indeed, my own?

Stephani pulled irritably at a bow tie at her throat as I railed on through cocktails and appetizers, but finally, over the main course, she yanked the knot loose and ripped into me for fixating on what she considered peripheral issues. You fight to survive with whatever it takes, she admonished me. And if the principles and the pain that had driven me from Langley weren't sufficient to do that, "then shut up and let the lawyers do their job!"

The tongue-lashing plunged me into a gloom so profound that not even an additional martini could lift me out. Stephani was talking about herself, of course: battling cancer demanded ruthless pragmatism. But how far could I go down that road without losing all of myself? At what point did the tactics *become* the case?

I slept not a wink that night, and the next morning, when Stephani and I stopped briefly at the TV cameras outside the courthouse, my eyes were swollen and her bow tie hung loose like an unraveling garrote.

My first glimpse of the courtroom did nothing to improve my mood, for the furnishings looked borrowed from a shantytown funeral parlor. The garish green rug and shoddy wood paneling merely parodied the storied majesty of the law, and above the dais, a long-stemmed clock swung its pendulum with portentous squeaks and moans, as if to remind all comers that time was never to be taken for granted here.

As chief defense counsel, Mark had the dubious prerogative of speaking on my behalf, though both Sims and the ACLU's Mort Halperin were on hand to whisper encouragement. Robert Kopp, an appellate litigator for the Justice Department, took the podium for the plaintiff, with an array of subalterns, including Sally Whitaker and Brook Hedge, looking on anxiously from the gallery.

After offering up formal arguments, the two opposing attorneys traded rebuttals and fielded questions from the three-man panel. Judges Harrison Winter and J. Dickson Phillips were thoroughly acquainted with the case and even took turns drawing Mark out on points he'd passed over too quickly (like my candor in dealing with the Agency). By contrast, the third cog in the triumvirate, Walter E. Hoffman, gazed upon me with ill-concealed contempt and largely kept his counsel. His steel-rimmed glasses and implacable scorn reminded me discomfitingly of Roarin' Oren.

As the most aggressive of the questioners, Phillips bore in hard on the government's failure to pin a security rap on me, which he saw as an impediment to its money demands. If there'd been a breach of fiduciary duty, he advised Kopp, then in order to clean out my bank account, the government needed to show that I'd stolen something of value from the CIA and profited from it. But with no secrets compromised, where was the CIA's loss? "What is it we're trying to get at here?" he mused.

Kopp plucked nervously at the seat of his pants. "It is irrelevant," he said, "that no classified information is in the book."

Phillips retorted that it didn't seem irrelevant to him. No secrets, no damage, is the way he saw it.

I glanced at Stephani. Score one for us.

Kopp struggled to rebound, arguing that I should be punished anyway, that I was no better than a Wall Street broker who'd deliberately mishandled funds and thereby exposed an investor to undue risk. In such a case, he said, it would be irrelevant whether the investor suffered any actual loss.

When Mark's turn came, he slammed Kopp for trivializing the issues this way. "This is not a securities case!" he snorted. "You don't award damages for activities protected by the First Amendment without a finding of harm or malice."

The hearing wound up around lunchtime, and Mark and the rest of my legal team bore Stephani and me off to a local pub for an instant postmortem. Based on what we'd heard, no one expected the judges to dismiss the case on constitutional grounds, since there'd been too little jousting in that direction. But Mort Halperin seemed to be speaking for most of those present when he predicted I'd be remanded for a retrial on two counts: the damage question and the ambiguity of my first and final contracts.

"Frankly, I don't see how we can lose," I said hopefully.

"Provided Judge Lewis drowns in his soup before he can get his hands on us again," grumped Mark.

— —

Having played our best hand, there was now nothing more for us to do but wait. Though the appeals court had granted us an expedited hearing in deference to our constitutional claims, the likelihood of an equally expeditious ruling seemed remote indeed, for the docket in Richmond was jammed with cases, and the judges clearly had found the First Amendment less compelling in oral argument than in written brief.

Still, any chance I might have had of relaxing into a fatalistic haze evaporated abruptly when a French journalist called two days later and asked to interview me about a story that was now making headlines in Paris. It had just been reported, she told me, that the newly published French edition of William Colby's book, *Honorable Men,* included secrets the CIA had deleted from the American version.

"What could this possibly mean?" she asked.

I didn't have a clue. Since no one in the CIA or the Justice Department had yet let on to us that Colby had played fast and loose with the censors months before, I couldn't imagine how any official secret could have survived in *any* edition of his book.

I immediately phoned Mark to let him know what I'd learned, and he in turn pressed *The Washington Post*'s Larry Stern to fish for details. Overnight, Stern pieced together a story that revealed what Justice Department officials had known for some time: William Colby had lied at my trial. Far from adhering to his secrecy contract, as he'd claimed, he'd slipped his manuscript to his publisher, Simon and Schuster, before letting the censors have a chop at it, and had been allowed to continue sidestepping them till the book was in final galleys and about to go to press.

As Stern reported in his article, this breach in protocol had led to the actual security breach that was now the talk of the Paris press. The previous winter, as the government was preparing to take me to trial, a small French publishing house had bought the rights to Colby's memoir and then asked for a copy of the page proofs so translation could begin at once. Colby had consented and then forgotten about them. By the time the censors' cuts had been incorporated into the English-language proofs, the unexpurgated French edition of the book was being set in type.

As a result, French readers were now privy to secrets too sensitive for American consumption, Stern pointed out. Among them: details of a highly classified CIA operation, the name of a CIA station chief, and the identity of an American newspaper publisher who'd cooperated with the Agency.

The CIA laid the blame for all this on Colby himself, claiming through a spokesman that it had "negotiated the deletions" with him and trusted him "to ensure that they were honored by his publishers." No one was willing to admit that the Agency had helped him break the rules.

The story so enraged me, I nearly succumbed to spontaneous combustion. The CIA's double standard was now apparent for all to see. So, too, were the cynicism and duplicity of my own prosecutors. Had we known of Colby's breach prior to my trial, we could have exposed him as a liar. Had we learned of it before the appeals hearing, we could have made a mockery of the CIA's security complaints. By denying us the truth, the government had crippled my defense.

"Is it too late? Can't we make something of this?" I asked Mark as we studied the *Post* article.

He pulled his glasses onto the bridge of his nose and shook his head sadly. "Once on appeal, you're stuck with the facts the trial judge gave you."

CHAPTER 24

Second Life

L IFE IN SAIGON three years after its fall and rebaptism as Ho Chi Minh City is marked by harsh misrule, political repression . . ."

For ten days in the winter of 1978–79, soon after my appeals hearing, four French journalists trekked through the cities and wilds of Vietnam, seeing more of both than any Western reporters had since the fall of Saigon. Their observations, extensively chronicled in *The Washington Post,* made me feel lucky that the only reckoning I faced was at the hands of a vindictive CIA.

"The former U.S. embassy has been converted into the central security headquarters. . . ."

I tried not to think about what that might mean—how the embassy's new tenants might be dispensing "security." But the images kept surging forth: informants trading bloodlists across the ambassador's desk, shackled south Vietnamese shuffling one by one into my old top-floor office to be bullied or beaten into giving up others we'd left behind.

Was there any secret now those walls had not known?

"The reporters were denied precise statistics, but they claim to have received information . . . that there are more political prisoners today than there were under the Thieu regime."

As I absorbed these revelations, I had to keep reminding myself that despair is divisible, that what I felt about these continuing aftershocks of defeat could and had to be kept separate from my deepening despondency over myself.

Otherwise, the combination might simply drive me over the edge.

"Thousands of south Vietnamese . . . continue to disappear . . . often without a trace, into reeducation camps. . . ."

How quaint that euphemism, "reeducation." You could break a man's will with it, if the body lasted long enough. The victors had long ago figured out the right quotient, the precise amount of pain and hopelessness you could inflict without destroying the body.

And chillingly, I discovered, they'd also made me complicit.

Oh, how I wanted to creep away and die when another visitor to Vietnam brought out word that *Decent Interval* had become an instrument of "reeducation," the victors having translated it and turned it into required reading in the camps. To be purified, it seemed, inmates were being obliged to study Snepp on the fall, Snepp on the American defeat, Snepp on how Saigon's allies had turned their backs on their friends.

For the first time, I felt profound regret at having written at all.

If there was any consolation to be had, it lay only along a relativist's slide rule. The horrors of the camps paled alongside the genocidal madness now ravaging Cambodia. By early winter 1979, Pol Pot had exterminated two million fellow Khmers whom he'd found insufficiently "agrarian" for his tastes.

Even the Vietnamese were repelled, though less for moral than political reasons: Pol Pot was pro-Chinese.

So, shortly after the turn of the year, they sent their own indomitable army storming into Phnom Penh to cast out the demon and to deny the Chinese a foothold at Saigon's side door. The Chinese retaliated by hurling forces into the northern border provinces of Vietnam. Instantly, Hanoi struck back at both invaders and potential fifth columnists, and by the time hostilities petered out a few weeks later, thousands upon thousands of expatriate Chinese were being rousted out of enclaves in Saigon and other major cities, herded onto requisitioned junks and tramp steamers, and forced out to sea.

Later, in Geneva, at a conference on refugees, a Vietnamese official told a reporter I was partly responsible for this exodus—that in view of my claim in *Decent Interval* that over a million pro-American Vietnamese had been left *out* of the evacuation, Hanoi had decided to let a comparable number "escape."

It was moonshine, of course. The latest refugees loved Mao far better than Jimmy Carter. But if the CIA could make me an alibi for its sins, why not Hanoi?

— —

Meanwhile, I made alibis for those who would judge me. The case was too complicated to be decided quickly, I told myself. A delayed verdict had to denote conscientious deliberation by the appeals court.

Whether this was true, I couldn't know. But the agonizing wait needed some rational gloss, for it, too, could break a man's will.

"You're turning into an emotional undertaker," Stephani remarked one evening. "If it's not apocalyptic, it doesn't touch you."

In an effort to change that, she footed the bill for a week's getaway in St. Thomas early in the year. Bad investment, that. After two days, I suffered a relapse of the dengue fever I'd picked up in Vietnam, and she had to pack me in ice to keep me from burning up.

Not a way to spend a holiday.

I did repay the consideration, though. The more she told of her own ordeal, the cancer and endless misdiagnoses, the more I became convinced there was a book in it. Loomis didn't like the outline we drew up, but when my agent, Lynn Nesbit, put it up for auction, Colby's publisher, Simon and Schuster, weighed in with $110,000, five times what I'd received as an advance for *Decent Interval,* and a startled Stephani suddenly found herself committed to playing undertaker to her own distress.

— —

From January onward, as she started writing, I was left increasingly to my own distractions, and often to dolorous effect, for desperation made me easy prey to poor bedfellows.

I remember with particularly bitter amusement a turn-of-the-year bash at the New York Yacht Club, a virtual Who's Who of big money and blue-blooded conservatism. The affair ought to have been off limits to anyone with ACLU allies and impoverished finances, but because William F. Buckley had extended the invitation personally—as thanks for my having consented to be pincushion on so many of his *Firing Line* TV shows—I accepted.

The receiving line buckled as I moved along it, several right-wing glitterati turning away as I offered my hand. Only Buckley seemed genuinely reconciled to my presence. He clapped me on the shoulder and suggested I head for the bar.

Which I did, making my way along the fringes so as not to taint, not to offend.

By now, I'd developed a knack for holding conversations with myself at such gatherings. So the isolation came easily.

But just as I was beginning to grow a little bored with it, a crumpled figure, all spider-veined and bourbon-tipsy, hurled himself upon me, and suddenly nothing seemed boring anymore.

Arms curling around my neck, the full furl of the dilapidated suit pressing against me insistently.

"They fucked you over, Frank!"—the cigarette scythed the air like a Jacobin's torch—"just like they did me."

A tear swelled and dropped.

Horrified, I *pushed,* and E. Howard Hunt stumbled away, the whiskey in his tumbler rooster-tailing onto a nearby mink.

E. Howard Hunt, ex–CIA agent, author of many an uncleared potboiler, ex–Plumber-in-chief of the Nixon White House, instigator of many of the Watergate excesses that had brought down a president.

He stood staring at me mournfully, murmuring about our mutual mistreatment at the hands of American justice, one misunderstood martyr to another. He'd paid dearly for his White House misdeeds. "Pray you're not railroaded too!" he wailed.

I willed away a surge of nausea. Had the government so eradicated my true self that this *perverter* of the law could mistake me for a fellow traveler?

Hunt started toward me again, hand outstretched in succor. But before the fingers could close around my lapel, a voice boomed across the room— "I'm gonna kill you, motherfucker!"—and reflexively, I bolted away as the crowd around us scattered. Over my shoulder, I glimpsed the tightly wound figure of G. Gordon Liddy, FBI renegade, bearing in on Hunt, howling him down for having fingered Liddy's own Watergate excesses to the law.

How that showdown ended, I never ascertained. But as I fled away into the night, I realized I'd finally disappeared into the looking glass the government had so deftly constructed for me.

Hunt's mirror image indeed!

Yet, ill-conceived though that comparison might be, if the appeals court bought in, I was dead . . . dead . . . dead.

— —

While I bided my time badly with such paranoid fantasies, Mark plied his trade and traded on the notoriety he'd gained from defending me. Even his government counterparts now regarded him as something of a guru on national security law, and in early winter, as they prepared to take the accused spy William Kampiles to trial, they sought out Mark's advice on how to put the guy away—safely.

Since Kampiles was entitled to confront the evidence against him, there was a danger that he'd pull a "Falcon and Snowman," threatening to air so many secrets in court that the trial couldn't go forward. To avoid being "graymailed" this way, administration officials asked Mark how to narrow the evidentiary requirements of the case. They also worked out procedures with the judge, obtaining a protective order from him that enabled them to challenge any of the defense's evidence before it was presented in open court.

In this way, they would score a conviction without having to let Kampiles turn the trial into a secrets roast.

This elegant finesse, coming as it did on the cusp of my appeals verdict, carried a certain irony. As Griffin Bell had repeatedly emphasized, it was fear of graymail—the exposure of secrets in court—that had led the government to explore alternate methods of pursuing national security cases, including the no-fault contracts approach used against me. If the Kampiles formula could now be codified, part of the rationale for *Snepp* might drop away even as the case was reaching climax.

— —

The day William Kampiles was sentenced—he got forty years, and was lucky—Mark began playing out another gambit that threatened to upstage me. He and John Sims filed a document in the federal court of Washington, D.C., announcing that another ex–CIA agent, a man named Ralph McGehee, had a memoir in the works that he wanted to publish without clearance. On January 29, they asked the court for a summary judgment allowing the petitioner to bypass the censors.

For weeks, the two had been tinkering with *McGehee,* seeing it as an opportunity to replay *Snepp* without Snepp—without all the problems I posed—and in a liberal federal district where the Marchetti precedent held no sway. If they could persuade the D.C. court to rule summarily in McGehee's favor, they could plead the classic rationale for Supreme Court intervention: Two neighboring federal districts had decided the same issue in different ways: *Snepp* for prepublication review, *McGehee* against. Then they'd take *McGehee* straight to the highest court in the land to resolve the contradiction.

Apoplectic doesn't begin to describe my reaction. If anybody ascended those heights, it had to be me.

"For chrissake, Mark! After all I've been through!"

We were striding furiously back and forth below the Capitol steps the morning after he'd filed the first *McGehee* brief.

"It's a clean case, Frank," he replied. "McGehee hasn't published anything, hasn't given any screwed-up interviews, hasn't shown his manuscript to anybody."

I stopped abruptly and rounded on him.

"But what *has* he done?"

"Nothing. That's the point. And if he wins, you walk away with your money. Think of the First Amendment implications."

I dared not open my mouth for fear I might start wailing.

All I'd been through. My reputation in shreds.

And who the hell was McGehee anyway? Twenty-five years in the Agency, he claimed. A veteran of the Indochina wars, he claimed, though I'd never known him, and I'd been at the center, goddammit. So *who* was he?

An invented renegade, I eventually discovered. An author inspired and nurtured by Agee's and Stockwell's pals. A man who wanted to destroy the Agency in order to save it.

A small Washington publisher had offered to bring his book out, a treatise on our foibles in Indochina. And a magazine editor had filed an affidavit avowing interest in publishing a companion article.

Sound familiar?

Oh yes, this was merely a reprise of the scenario Mark had concocted for me months before, when he'd pressed Lewis to lift the injunction and let me publish my love story and essay on bureaucratic compromise.

Remember the First Amendment implications, I kept telling myself.

It didn't help.

— —

In late February, as the D.C. court began pondering McGehee's arguments, I staggered off to Paris to help launch the French version of *Decent Interval.*

It was an excursion along the thin edge of sanity.

The Chinese had just invaded Vietnam. Refugees were drowning at sea. The new tenants of my old embassy office were demanding obeisance in blood.

I was so demoralized, I couldn't proceed. After only a day or so, I broke off the publicity tour and went searching for sanctuary in the past, scouring the city for a Frenchwoman I'd met in Saigon back in 1969, during my first months there.

She'd been mistress to a top Saigon official, and I'd thought she might help American intelligence seduce him. Instead, she'd seduced me: my first intoxicating brush with the moral ambivalence of a country at war.

I needed her reassuring aura of duplicity to know that the center still held.

She was the unlikeliest of Saigonese, this round-eyed beauty of pragmatic loyalty and inestimable sensuality, a thief of life cruising the graveyard, lusted after by every homesick Westerner and generous with more than a few. The first time I spotted Danielle Haller, she was crossing Nguyen Hue Boulevard heading for Givral's, and she not so much negotiated the careening traffic as commanded it, a Gauloise jutting from the center of her mouth, blond hair flouncing, the red bell-bottoms whipping the lean legs, tugging the hips, no panty line showing, and the black silk shirt clinging to her like wet tissue. She wore it all as if she were making an offer. Which of course she was. . . .

I'd conjured this description as the opening flourish of the love story I'd written the previous fall to support Mark's plea for injunctive relief. No one would see it now unless, of course, I consented to give it to the censors for "security review." Which I wouldn't.

I found Danielle living alone in one of the seedier sections of Paris, her estranged husband having decamped on some adventure, as he'd frequently done in Saigon. I barely recognized her at first, or barely remembered, the black silk having given way to scruffy fatigues that gripped the newly fulsome body a little too tightly. But still, there was the evocative aroma of the Gauloises about her, and a kind of defiant charm that made me wonder if the role of outlaw wasn't endurable after all.

The face I presented to her was certainly no kinder to memory. "Much too thin," she found me, "like someone on a death march." And when I confessed that I was so busted that I could barely afford a meal a day, she tossed her head and shoved me into the nearest bistro. We'd experienced some frissons that year in Saigon, she reminded me as she ordered for us both. And even if her life hadn't amounted to much since then, she could at least keep me from starving.

Shortly after I returned to Washington, little care packages began arriving from Paris, checks for two hundred or three hundred dollars. Where Danielle got the money I didn't know or want to ask, for in Saigon her connections had often been less than savory. But over the next few months, as the legal machinery continued to grind ever so slowly, her generosity indeed kept me from starving.

"I don't understand why I have such tenderness for you," she remarked at one point. "I guess what I like is your capacity for solitude."

I dared not tell her that this capacity was simply a horrid little legacy of the war we'd shared, a fear of ever again getting close to anyone I might not be able to rescue.

— —

Yet, if Danielle bought me survival, I was no closer to deliverance. The appeals judges were still cogitating in the wake of my Paris trip, and no one knew when to expect a ruling.

Even more discouraging, the political context in which they would decide my case was turning nasty, thanks to growing unrest in Iran. By late February, the Shah had bowed out, the Ayatollah Khomeini had bowed in, fundamentalist guerrillas had briefly invested the U.S. embassy in Tehran, and an evacuation of all nonessential embassy personnel was under way. At Langley, would-be whistle-blowers were crawling out of the woodwork to regale the press with stories of suppressed intelligence and myopic analyses, and a congressional committee had already joined the president in criticizing Stansfield Turner personally for having foreseen too little.

True to habit, the admiral responded to this crisis as he had to earlier ones by finding someone else to blame. In a freewheeling *Newsweek* interview, he hinted that American intelligence had been blinded to the coming storm in Iran because friendly spy services had refused to cooperate with us out of concern for indiscreet "books by former CIA agents Philip Agee, Frank Snepp, and John Stockwell. . . .

"The people in other countries," he fulminated, "just don't understand why we can't keep classified information out of the public domain."

Was the appeals court in Richmond listening? We soon got an answer.

Late Thursday afternoon, March 20, three weeks after the Turner interview, Mark informed me in a hurried phone call that a decision had come down.

"How bad?" I asked, heart racing.

"I've heard only that *part* of Lewis's decision was upheld, *part* of it reversed and *part* remanded for trial. Also, Judge Hoffman dissented in part."

Twelve more hours passed before anything else was known, twelve hours with my head under the guillotine, and now no hope of reprieve for, whatever the shadings, it was clear we hadn't won. By the time Mark and John Sims arranged a conference call with me late the following morning, I was in deep shock.

— —

"Well, they tore your skin off," Mark began colorfully, "but left you a few Band-Aids."

"What about the gag?" I asked, immediately concerned about what mattered most.

"Stays on."

"If they'd found you more sympathetic"—John sounded desolate—"it wouldn't have gone this way."

"As for the money," Mark continued, "they won't let the government just snatch it. Not without proof of a security breach. But don't count your chickens. Remember how Sally asked for punitive damages in the original complaint?"

I remembered all right: punitive damages for breach of contract, massive fines beyond any compensation for provable injury to the CIA.

"Well, the court says they're back on the table. The government can have 'em just by proving you're a deceitful bastard."

"So where are the Band-Aids?" I asked bitterly.

"Oh, to get any money out of you, Sally has to take you back to court," said Mark. "And she may figure: why bother? She's got the precedent she wanted. That may be enough."

Somehow, I couldn't imagine Sally ever letting me die a quick and easy death.

— —

The written decision was even worse than Mark had described. In its meandering twenty-one pages, the judges endorsed all of Judge Lewis's ugly "factual" findings and dumbed down the Pentagon Papers standard for prior restraint to justify keeping me gagged. Far from requiring a "heavy burden of proof" from the government, they reasoned: "the danger to national security arising from an unauthorized publication of classified material is so great . . . that we think little proof of a probable future violation is required to justify injunctive relief."

On the financial issues, the court indeed split. The dissenter, Judge Hoffman, favored enforcing Lewis's constructive trust, the automatic lien on my profits, since he felt any other remedy might force the CIA to reveal its injuries in court. The two other judges, Winter and Phillips, whose view prevailed, ruled this out in the absence of any provable security breach, but left the door open to punitive fines if the government could convince a jury that I'd hoodwinked the CIA. Apparently, they didn't think this would be too difficult. "From the evidence," they declared, "a trier of fact could well conclude that defendant's actions . . . amounted to deceit."

— —

How could it all have gone so wrong?

Sims felt Hoffman had poisoned the well by hanging a charge on me that the government had never made. "Assuredly," the dissenter had written,

"Snepp made use of confidential information in this case, whether classified or not."

There were other errors of fact, errors that galled, errors that might have driven me mad if I weren't so far gone already.

In finding the Agency generally blameless, all three judges insisted I'd never been denied a hearing about the evacuation. They also refused to believe I could ever have been unclear about my obligations, and noted that I'd been told explicitly, on the day I'd resigned, that my exit agreement imposed the same clearance duties as my original one. What they didn't understand was that the only agreement I'd been shown that last day was the exit one, which made my obligations seem limited indeed.

— —

The government's chief appeals counsel, Robert Kopp, immediately took to the media hustings and claimed victory.

We didn't disagree.

Mark told *The New York Times* that he and his client "were terribly disappointed" with the court's cursory First Amendment analysis, particularly its holding that no proof of future violations was needed to justify the injunction.

The following weekend, he set up a conference call with my other defenders to pick through the rubble. I joined him in his office to listen in.

Everybody had an eminently sensible explanation for the debacle.

The CIA still exerted a magical influence on the courts, John Sims opined.

The Fourth Circuit itself was unnaturally conservative, said Dershowitz.

Though no one wanted to tempt my vindictive soul by admitting we'd made mistakes ourselves, there was general agreement that we might have made more of Oren Lewis's own misconduct. Our concern had always been that in criticizing the old man, we might alienate his brethren in Richmond. But clearly the soft-soap hadn't worked any better.

Our worst blunder, though, had been our failure to slather on enough beauty cream to cover the dirt the government had smudged on me. To the extent that we'd tried, we'd done so only peripherally, in footnotes to our legal arguments. But the government's lawyers had better understood the power of character assassination, literally prefacing their briefs with allegations of deceit. Their audaciousness had had the effect of Goebbels's Big Lie.

Not that I hadn't given them plenty of help. My clumsy press interviews, my outrageous remarks about having fooled Turner and the Agency, had so reinforced these unflattering impressions that it would probably have taken a Goebbels to undo them.

Still, I had a niggling feeling, as my lawyers and I reviewed our tortuous journey to Richmond, that somewhere along the way they'd come to view me too charitably, not as an imperfect soul who needed defending, but as an abstract cause that deserved it—and had skimped on the blarney.

— —

"So how do we repair the damage?" Dershowitz posed after we'd all digested our mea culpas.

Sims jumped in and ticked off the options: apply for an expedited rehearing in Richmond to correct the factual errors; sit back and wait for the government to try me again for punitive damages or on trumped up security charges; or head straight to the Supreme Court by filing for "cert."

With that, a new and mysterious word entered my vocabulary: "cert."— short for "certiorari," Latin for "certification." As Mark explained to my blank stare, if the Supreme Court decides to grant an appeal, it issues a writ of certiorari, commanding the lower courts to certify, or surrender, case records for review. To get heard by the Supreme Court, you have to apply for such a writ, for cert. It's like asking for a ticket of admission.

Sims, for one, didn't think this was the way to go. "We'd be better off letting Sally play out her hand and take us back to court," he insisted. "Another trial would give us more issues to appeal."

He paused and added pointedly, "And there's always McGehee."

"Forget McGehee!" I shot back.

Sims ignored me. "With a conflicting ruling out of his case, we'd be assured of cert.," he continued.

"Another trial could be messy," objected Dershowitz.

"Agreed," said Mark.

He then turned and peered into my eyes like a priest searching out the soul of a sinner. "It's your choice," he said, "but remember, an appeal could be risky. Right now, you've got your money, and you'll keep it if Sally decides not to go back to trial. But if we take this thing to the Supreme Court, you could lose everything. Money. Speech. The whole ball of wax."

— —

Alone, on a flight to New York that night, I tried to sort out the bidding. Mark was right: the safest choice would be to sit on my hands and hope Sally gave up. That way, I might wind up a rich man. But rich in what? Money maybe. But in what else?

The more I thought about that, the more I harkened to what I'd originally meant to accomplish, but hadn't. Writing *Decent Interval* had been an act of contrition and a challenge to official Washington to do right by those we'd abandoned. But Sally had turned it into an offense of her own devising and recast me in an image that fit the crime. Unless I was now willing to risk everything, the rulings she'd won against me would define both my past and my intentions, and I might very well remain locked forever in that room on the top floor of the embassy with the radios crackling and the voices screaming over the channels and Mai Ly making that last unheeded call for help.

I stared at my elusive reflection in the cabin window and wondered if I had the courage to try again to rescue myself.

Shortly after I landed, I advised Mark of my decision: I wanted to take the case forward.

In a matter of days he petitioned the appeals court to put off enforcing its judgment against me so he could apply to the Supreme Court for a writ of certiorari on my behalf, for permission to argue my case. He asked for ninety days to prepare the cert. request. On April 5, the appeals panel responded pettily by granting us only a third of the time.

— —

Even if I hadn't had worries enough, my complicated friend Stephani would doubtless have made up any deficit, for there was a part of her that couldn't abide playing second fiddle to anyone else's crisis. If she wasn't at the vortex, she wasn't in her element. So I shouldn't have been surprised when, soon after the appeals judgment, she drew me aside in New York to give me some bad news of her own.

A few weeks before, she told me, she'd been caught in a lurid bedroom tryst with a prominent man-about-town. The scandal would soon surface in the tabloids, but she wanted me to hear it from her first.

Now, you may wonder: what conceivable import could this sordid little revelation have had against the backdrop of my legal problems? Stephani had never pretended to be bound by polite convention any more than I had, and as far as I was concerned, her ghastly experiences had earned her dispensation for almost any excess.

And yet, coming now, amidst the devastation of the appeals ruling, this garden-variety betrayal left me feeling as bereft and isolated as a spacewalker with his umbilical cut. Stunned at my own vulnerability, I lay for days in my shuttered apartment back in Arlington, staring into the darkness and wondering if I could bear being so alone.

By the third day, I was so weak from not eating that I was beginning to experience weird visions, nothing whole cloth, just snatches of a face at the embassy wall, a hand clinging to the barbed wire atop the back gate, an old man in square-framed glasses shrieking, "Objection sustained!"

At some point amidst this swirling chaff, a blimp floated over the horizon and metamorphosed improbably into the rotund figure of Victor Marchetti, lying on his couch, a tumbler propped on his gut, his undershorts speckled with Top Secret labels and his pants hanging, as usual, on a nearby breakfront to defeat those costly wrinkles—and I started giggling, uncontrollably at first, then, as I came down, with a flush of genuine amusement that I knew was my bridge back.

Oh, Victor, how crazy they'd made you. Alcoholic. Bitter. A caricature of rebellion. Yet, in essence, the very picture of the inescapable ambivalence all of us brought away from Langley, that most exclusive of insiders' clubs.

Isolated? Of course I was. What, more or less, could you expect from the habit of secrecy? What was secrecy, anyway, but an excuse to be cut off? Stephani had actually done me a favor by reminding me that isolation was not an aberration, but my natural condition.

That night, I tried repeatedly to reach Victor by phone, but nobody picked up. Maybe he was lying there in his own cocoon, drinking himself into an easy escape, anesthetizing the pain that inevitably came from separating oneself from the one place where isolation seemed perfectly normal.

I remembered what he'd said about his own initial response to that pain, that he stayed in bed for days, not bathing, not speaking to anyone, not eating . . .

On the fifth day, I called Stephani.

— —

When I saw her back in New York soon afterward, she railed at me for having been incommunicado and complained, without irony, that I'd probably been holed up with a new romantic interest. But her true disquiet, I could see, arose from something closer to her own tangled passions. Dejected to a degree I'd never seen before, she confessed that she'd been paralyzed for days, unable to add a word to her manuscript.

I can't remember how long it took her to acknowledge what was troubling her, for she seemed to float through nights and days of trying to figure it out herself. Finally, one morning, she asked if I'd ever heard of Susan Sontag, and I said yes, I knew her to be a noted essayist and intellectual. She nodded as if relieved, and confided that she'd lately been mulling over a thought she'd picked up from Sontag, the idea that illness is metaphor, a kind of symptom of spiritual malaise, and had decided that it helped elucidate why she'd developed cancer of the placenta.

I wanted to stop her, to ask to be spared any more details of her active sex life, for I could see where this was going. Cancer of the womb. Illness as metaphorical punishment.

But what Stephani said next so shocked me, I could think of no response at all. Throughout her childhood, she explained hesitantly, she'd suffered sexual abuse at the hands of her father.

"It's the story I feel I have to tell," she added. "But I'm terrified."

I stood up and left her apartment, and spent a long while gazing dumbly out over the tattered grandeur of Central Park. Voices on the radios? Abandoned allies? Small betrayals by comparison.

When I finally returned, she was still sitting on the edge of the bed where I'd left her.

I told her that candor is cathartic, that she should tell her story, all of it, and set herself free of it. Only on one condition, though: that she alert her father beforehand. No ambushes. They could cost too much, as I well knew.

Eventually, she contacted her father and did as I'd suggested. Afterward, I saw little of her. She became so caught up in her suddenly prolific writing that she had no time for anything else.

I told myself I didn't mind, that she'd left me with something precious, a perspective that shamed me out of my own self-pity. Nothing I'd experienced, no loss or perceived injustice, would ever begin to approximate the monster she'd confronted and vanquished. To that extent, Stephani gave me my own second life.

— —

For serious discourse and casual libation, Mark and I had come to favor a small café on Capitol Hill where a bartender with the profile of a Serbian princess slung the best Bloody Marys in town. One afternoon in late April, a month after the appeals verdict, Mark invited me to a one-on-one under the lady's attentive gaze, for he had news that might end my legal troubles forever.

"Sally's offering a deal," he began without preamble. "You agree not to go to the Supreme Court. The government agrees to let you off with a fine. More than ten thousand but less than sixty thousand dollars."

"No punitive damages?" Pulse quickening.

"My guess is she doesn't want to take you to trial—*ever.* Too risky for her."

"What about the gag?" It was always the gag that worried.

He shook his head.

I took a gulp of Bloody Mary as he watched my eyes over the rim of the glass.

"I told her you probably wouldn't accept," he said after a long moment. By now he understood me instinctively.

"Not if the gag's left on."

He kept gazing at me as if searching for some sign of ambivalence. The D.C. District Court hadn't yet ruled on McGehee's plea for summary judgment. So, I was still the only game in town.

"Why this offer now?" I asked.

"The window on the Supreme Court is closing. They want to know what our next move will be."

— —

My refusal to bargain forced the government into an exquisite dilemma. With an overture to the Supreme Court now inevitable, the solicitor general, the Justice Department's chief advocate, had to decide whether to seek review of any part of the *government's* case. Since the appeals court had refused to grant a constructive trust, he could ask for consideration of that issue. But if he did, he might lend enough weight to my own appeal to assure me a hearing.

What to do?

Weeks passed without a decision. Finally, on June 8, Wade McCree, who occupied the solicitor general's post, asked the Supreme Court to give him until mid-August to make up his mind. He needed the additional time, he said, to determine what we would do, and how to respond. Noting that the government had already won everything it wanted *except* a constructive trust, he indicated that he might challenge this part of the appeals decision if I were to challenge the gag order. In other words, he wouldn't act unless I did, but if I did, he would demand restoration of Judge Lewis's entire ruling against me.

In effect, he was offering me a chance to reconsider Sally's proffered bribe. Griffin Bell later admitted that if I had bailed out at this point, the government wouldn't have sought *any* money from me.

Mark asked me again if I wanted to go forward.

But he knew the answer already.

Ten days later, he delivered our own cert. request, our formal application for a hearing, to the Supreme Court's headquarters just across the street from the ACLU offices on Capitol Hill. The fifteen-page document, which he'd coauthored with Sims, Dershowitz, and Alan Morrison of Ralph Nader's Public Citizen Litigation Group, was not a detailed legal brief. Typically, the only purpose of such pleadings is to persuade the justices that a case is worthy of their attention. If the tease works, the opposing sides are invited to file full written arguments, and finally to defend them orally before a sitting panel of the Nine.

This ritualized procedure is meant to ensure that every important nuance of a case is aired and understood.

Mark and his colleagues therefore tripped only lightly over the profound legal questions at the center of *U.S. v Snepp.*

Can the courts impose prior restraint based on secrecy agreements without explicit congressional authorization?

No!, they argued, citing all the precedents that had become rote for us.

Can a bureaucrat's commitment not to publish secrets be construed to require clearance of nonsecrets as well?

No again!, they insisted, pointing to the Pentagon Papers case and the "heavy burden of proof" the Court itself had prescribed for prior restraint.

May a court award punitive damages against the alleged violator of a secrecy agreement who publishes no secrets?

Here, Mark and his coauthors waxed a bit more elaborate, reminding the Court that in two famous libel cases it had limited the use of punitive damages lest juries exercise "their discretion selectively to punish expressions of unpopular views." Mark and his colleagues thought the same reasoning ought to insulate me.

Immediately after they filed the petition, the American Association of Book Publishers and The Reporter's Committee for Freedom of the Press posted amicus briefs on my behalf, thus adding to the pressure on the government to come out swinging. Would Sally and her cohorts demand restoration of the constructive trust? "Their deadline is August 17," Mark advised Bob Bernstein in mid-July. "If they do cross-petition, the chances of the case being taken are substantially greater."

Four weeks later, on the day of the deadline itself, Solicitor General McCree finally made his move. It wasn't what we'd expected. In answering our cert. request, he sent not one written response to the Supreme Court, but two.

The first brief portrayed me as a mendacious cheat who'd lied to the Agency and thus deserved no consideration at all.

Had McCree stopped here, he would have been solidly on record as favoring the status quo: no cert., no Supreme Court hearing—end of case.

But he went further. In the second document, he asked the Court to review the constructive trust issue *if* it chose to grant my petition. While claiming to be satisfied with the appeals ruling, he argued that a constructive trust would be a better deterrent to future violations than punitive damages, since it would allow the government to seize profits with no need for a jury trial. Thus, he said, if the Court reviewed any part of the case, it should also consider the propriety of reinstating the constructive trust remedy.

It was a weaselly position, but ingenious, too. Without actually seconding our cert. request, McCree was keeping his oar in the water.

"Mark thinks this only marginally enhances our chances of getting a hearing," I wrote to Loomis. "But others believe it will tip us in."

Soon afterward, Mark sent a reply to the Supreme Court in which he protested McCree's attempt to prejudice the case by casting me as one who'd made false promises to the Agency. "This is not a fact, but an allegation," he insisted, "which Mr. Snepp has vigorously disputed."

— —

Each year, some three thousand petitioners apply to be heard by the Supreme Court, often on issues of great constitutional import. Only a few are chosen, and the alchemy by which the justices finally exercise their discretion is known only to themselves and their clerks. Until a decision is reached at one of the Court's private Friday conferences, the supplicants can only pray and wait.

Which is what everybody connected with *Snepp* began doing in late August 1979.

— —

In the meantime, another First Amendment case, one with great relevance for me, began competing for public attention and for Mark's own legal skills.

The previous spring, a young researcher named Howard Morland had written a controversial article about the hydrogen bomb for a liberal Wisconsin monthly, *The Progressive*. His purpose: to quicken debate over nuclear proliferation by showing that too many vital secrets about the bomb had already become public.

In conducting his research, Morland had relied solely on unclassified materials. But when the government found out what he was up to, it panicked. Justice Department officials raced into federal court to demand a restraining order. Not only did they warn of impending irreparable harm, they noted pointedly there was an actual law on the books that authorized what they were seeking: the Atomic Energy Act explicitly allows the government to bar the publication of restricted nuclear data.

The judge, Robert Warren of the U.S. District Court in western Wisconsin, succumbed to the overkill and issued a preliminary injunction on March 26, two weeks after the appeals judgment against me. As Mark and the ACLU later pointed out, it was "the first preliminary injunction against press publication of political speech in the history of our country." (The Pentagon Papers case had involved temporary restraining orders, and the ruling against me was not press-related, at least not directly.)

Like Oren Lewis, Judge Warren rewrote precedent. Though the government had cried irreparable harm, he rationalized the injunction in looser terms, claiming that if the article were published, it would likely reduce the time that some nations might need to achieve nuclear capability. It was not a judgment based on rock-solid fact.

Soon afterward, the case took a truly bizarre turn. Another private researcher discovered that the government had accidentally declassified and placed on open library shelves at the Los Alamos laboratory "how-to" articles about the bomb that were infinitely more revealing than Morland's piece. Morland and the magazine promptly asked the ACLU to intervene, and Mark was enlisted to help write an appeals brief challenging the injunction.

The document he coauthored with the ACLU's Bruce Ennis recycled many of the arguments honed and polished in my case. Insisting that the government hadn't come close to meeting the irreparable harm test set out in Supreme Court rulings on prior restraint, Mark and his cocounsel denounced the injunction as unconstitutional, especially since the information it was meant to suppress had already become public.

"There is no secret, there is no danger," Ennis argued at the appeals hearing itself in early September.

In rebuttal, federal attorney Thomas Martin, who'd helped author the appeals documents in my case, offered an Orwellian argument that rivaled any made against me. Even if private citizens had once had access to the disputed material in a public library, he said, "we still say no more people should."

The appeals court began considering these arguments within days of our filing for cert. But events quickly overtook the deliberations. The second week in September, a third private researcher sent open letters to two California newspapers expanding on the disclosures in the Morland article. On September 15, shocked government officials obtained a gag order against one of the dailies, but they couldn't act fast enough to keep the other from ramming the letter into print.

Once that happened, further resistance was pointless. The government asked that the gags be vacated, as they no longer served any purpose.

"A great victory!" columnist Anthony Lewis proclaimed in *The New York Times*. Theoretically he was right; an unprecedented challenge to free speech in this country had been blunted. But in practical terms, the case wouldn't and didn't go away. The Justice Department immediately hired Tony Lapham, who'd just left his CIA post, to help hunt down and prosecute any bureaucrat who'd assisted Morland, and legal scholars noted that though the gag orders had been dropped, dangerous new precedents had been left strewn behind. Unclassified public information had been suppressed for months, the protections of the Pentagon Papers case had been flouted, damage had been assumed where there was no proof of any, and supposedly independent federal judges had bent over backward to accommodate *all* the government's national security claims—this in a case where the press, not some disgruntled ex–government employee, was the offender.

If the courts were now so unsafe for scriveners like Morland, what hope could they offer me?

CHAPTER 25

Auguries

A T SOME POINT IN THE *Progressive* case, Howard Morland called to seek comradely support. Bewildered by what was happening to him, he said he was beginning to feel like a lamb being led to slaughter.

Which, of course, he was, though I was too considerate to tell him so.

As author of the offending article, he could have been prosecuted on felony charges if the government had moved beyond prior restraint to the criminal sanctions envisioned in the Atomic Energy Act. And yet, time and again, there was old Howard out front and defiant, spouting off about the magazine's First Amendment rights, even though every word he uttered could have been turned against him in court.

Nor did he seem to understand how the law works anyway. His boundless idealism had led him to imagine that jurisprudence merely mirrors what is morally right. It was a misconception that had afflicted me at the start of my own legal travails, and I could only hope that he was disabused of it before being forced to learn the hard way, as I had, that noble intentions sit only lightly on the scales of justice.

Not that I knew it all, mind you. Oh sure, I'd taken an active interest in my case and had absorbed enough to be able to ask pointed questions. (My lawyers all had bruises to prove that.) But if someone had challenged me to explain why I felt so ill-used by the courts, I could have done little more than parrot Mark's latest briefs.

Such ignorance was inexcusable after two years of nonstop litigation, and as I listened to Morland muddle his way through legal principles that were his only salvation, I decided that self-respect demanded more of me.

So, beginning in late summer, I did what my lawyers had feared all along. I tried to become one of them, or more accurately, to put myself inside their gestalt by devouring every text on First Amendment and national security law I could lay hands on.

It was not a heartening experience, for I quickly discovered that the constitutional protections about which Mark had written so confidently were as flimsy as gossamer—and had been ever thus. Though the nation's founders had dreamed up the First Amendment to ensure against press controls of the sort once favored by colonial authorities, politics, war, and prudishness had quickly compromised the ideal. A federalist Congress had passed the Alien and Sedition Acts in 1798 to limit criticism of a federalist president, and during the Civil War, generals and postmasters on both sides had censored mail and newspaper dispatches from the trenches. Later, bluenoses in former pilgrim country banned books they considered obscene, and by the end of World War I, a malcontent could be jailed as a spy for simply criticizing the American war effort. Only much later were the espionage laws narrowed in scope to rule out such overkill.

In the meantime, Franklin Roosevelt wrote the first presidential decree on secrecy, and Harry Truman later adapted military classifications to civilian agencies like the CIA. At no point did Congress mandate any of this. Official secrecy was, and has remained, the stepchild of presidential prerogative alone.

Typically, Top Secret labels are reserved for information whose disclosure can do maximum damage to the nation's security, and lesser classifications for less volatile stuff. But any president can expand or contract the underlying definitions with the stroke of a pen.

For anyone who's signed a secrecy agreement, the very elasticity of the classification system means that, theoretically, nothing's beyond censorship. What's disclosable one day may wind up a censorable secret the next because of a new presidential directive. This arbitrariness should have made CIA prepublication review unconstitutional from the start.

— —

As I burrowed into the law books, I was surprised to discover that the Supreme Court had come to the censorship issue only fairly recently. The ruling that had established the first firebreak dated back to the early 1930s. A muckraking journalist named Jay Near had riled the city fathers of Minneapolis by publishing scurrilous tales about them, and they'd retaliated by shutting him down under a local nuisance law. The Supreme Court took up his appeal in *Near v Minnesota*—and came out ringingly in his favor. Writing for the Court, Chief Justice Charles Evans Hughes declared that "it is the chief purpose of the [First Amendment] guaranty to prevent previous restraints on publication."

Hughes was no absolutist, however, and went on to say that censorship might be justified in rare circumstances, as when a publication threatens to outrage public morals, incite violence or panic, or harm the nation's security. That last exception is why I was now facing a gag order. But as Hughes originally conceived it, its scope extended no further than extreme wartime emergencies.

In a series of follow-up decisions, the Court tightened the leash further by placing "a heavy burden" on the government in justifying censorship under any circumstances. This principle survived and flourished down through the years, and found its apotheosis in the seminal Pentagon Papers case of 1971. Despite pleas of impending irreparable harm by Nixon officials, the Supreme Court found they had not met their heavy burden of proof, and lifted the temporary gag orders they had sought against the press.

The unsigned per curiam opinion didn't explain how the government's lawyers had fallen short, but three justices provided clues in concurring opinions. Byron White and Potter Stewart, backed by William Brennan, argued that in order to justify such gags in the future, the government would have to show that publication "will surely result in direct, immediate and irreparable damage to our nation and its people."

Two other members of the majority, William O. Douglas and Hugo Black, ruled out prior restraint under virtually any conditions, and the sixth majority voice, Thurgood Marshall, disallowed it because Congress had passed no law permitting it. Both White and Stewart endorsed this view.

The Pentagon Papers decision thus erected what seemed to be a formidable barrier against censorship: no law, no censorship; no proof of harm, no censorship.

Five years later, in an equally important case, the Court added filigree. Ruling on an appeal from the Nebraska Press Association, it declared that whenever the government seeks to gag the press (this time, in the interests of a fair trial), it must show a "high degree of certainty" of harm.

Since the government had shown no certainty of any harm in my case, this ruling, plus the Pentagon Papers one, ought to have kept the wolves at bay.

Ought to—but so far, hadn't.

Why?

Consistency, or the lack thereof, in the Supreme Court's own canon. Indeed, for every encouraging precedent I could find, there seemed to be three or four others that weren't.

Dershowitz uncovered a particularly troubling one. Back in the free-wheeling 1960s, he told me, the Maryland legislature had made a stab at recouping public morals by creating a board of censors to prescreen potentially obscene movies. One distributor, a man named Freedman, had balked, denouncing the system as unconstitutional prior restraint, since the censors could sideline any film until the exhibitor had successfully appealed in court.

The Supreme Court agreed with him, but only conditionally. Justice Brennan, writing for the majority, held that such censorship might be okay if coupled with speedy and internally consistent appeals procedures.

I needed no prompting to see the danger this ruling posed for me. If the Supreme Court could be persuaded that the CIA's clearance program contained such safeguards, it might well pass constitutional muster under *Freedman v Maryland.*

Beyond the substance of *Freedman,* I was disturbed, too, by its authorship. Justice Brennan was normally one of the Court's staunchest defenders of the First Amendment. If he could split hairs, who couldn't?

As I continued my research, the precariousness of my situation became all the more apparent. In particular, the Pentagon Papers decision began to look like a false beacon in the night. Two of the strongest majority voices in that case, Black and Douglas, had since retired. So had one of the dissenters, Justice Marshall Harlan. No great loss there. But two of the other dissenters, Harry Blackmun and Warren Burger, were still on the bench and unlikely to be any more sympathetic toward me than they had been toward *The New York Times.*

Even more disturbing, there were nits and tats in the concurring opinions of Stewart and White that made me wonder if I could even count on them. Stewart had argued, for instance, that the government was justified in trying to suppress publication of some of the Pentagon Papers in the name of national security, and Byron White had indicated that he "would have no difficulty sustaining convictions" if any of the offending newspapers were prosecuted under the espionage statutes.

Given these considerations, I figured only one holdover from Pentagon Papers was a sure bet for me: Thurgood Marshall, with the possible addition of Justice Brennan.

Of the newcomers to the Court, none even came close to being sure bets. William Rehnquist, as assistant attorney general in the Nixon administration, had defended its closed-door policies and helped to prosecute its leakers, including Ellsberg and Russo. Even less congenial was Lewis Powell, a Virginia squire and longtime colleague of the Fourth Circuit zealots who'd sent me up the river. Indeed, his impeccable conservative credentials were matched by a special affinity for the constituency that hated me most. During World War II, he'd served as a military intelligence officer and had been attached to the hugely sensitive British eavesdropping operation that had cracked the German military code. If any of the justices had reason to be overly protective of official secrecy, it was Lewis Powell.

The Court's latest recruit, John Paul Stevens, was harder to read. A moderate appointed by President Ford, he was known for idiosyncratic theories and his expertise in antitrust law. Since joining the Court, he'd rendered only one opinion on the First Amendment: a less than enlightening acknowledgment in the Nebraska press case that he agreed with "most of what Justice Brennan" said about the ruling.

— —

By early October, I'd learned enough to be truly despondent. Not only did existing precedent and the predilections of the sitting justices offer little hope; it had become apparent that there is a catch-22 built into First Amendment law itself that can make its application a crapshoot. Since the First Amendment implicitly discourages Congress from legislating about censorship, judges are left with considerable freedom to write the rules themselves. And as I'd discovered from painful experience, some judges can run rampant.

Oh sure, legal scholars use lofty terms like "reasonableness test" or "balancing test" to try to dignify such judicial inventiveness, but they might as well call it lawmaking-by-the-seat-of-your-pants. Justice Potter Stewart once cautioned his own brethren about this practice. "So long as members of this court," he wrote, "view the First Amendment as no more than a set of values to be balanced against other values, that Amendment will remain in grave jeopardy."

Sage counsel, that. Too bad Stewart himself didn't cleave to it. The very "test" he applied in the Pentagon Papers case to define the limits of prior restraint—will publication "surely result in direct, immediate and irreparable damage?"—was itself an invitation to subjective spitballing. What does "surely" mean? Or "direct," or "irreparable"? The answer could depend on what His Honor had for lunch, or on his political prejudices.

Even worse, I discovered, public servants of any sort, including CIA agents, are automatically assumed by law to warrant less First Amendment protection than anyone else. The defining case, decided long ago by the

Supreme Court, involved an Illinois teacher named Pickering who'd gotten himself fired for publicly criticizing the local school board. He appealed his dismissal as a violation of his First Amendment rights, and though the Supreme Court agreed, it warned that a judge is entitled in such cases to strike a balance between the "interests" of the public servant "in commenting upon matters of public concern, and the interest of the state, as an employer, in promoting the efficiency of the public services it performs through its employees."

Though I was no longer a public employee, Sally had cited this ruling in some of her own pleadings, and no wonder. If she could make it stick, my actions would be judged not against any irreparable-harm standard but simply in terms of whether they diminished the CIA's efficiency.

Oh boy.

— —

The first day of October, Mark received word from a reporter that my case had finally penetrated the cloud layer on Mount Olympus. According to this informant, my cert. request, my application for a hearing, would be considered at the Court's private Friday conference four days away. Since Mark was not optimistic about my chances, he warned me and the rest of the defense team that we might be back in Lewis's courtroom battling Sally over punitive damages in the not too distant future.

That possibility was almost as daunting as the prospect of outright defeat at the hands of the Supreme Court. Mark was exhausted. I was worse, and the consensus among my lawyers was that if there was an honorable way to avoid a return match with Lewis, we should seriously consider it.

Mark hatched a plan. The moment our appeals request was denied, he told me, he would send a letter to the Justice Department aimed at shutting the case down. He showed me a copy of his draft and asked me to look it over with as little prejudice as I could.

It wasn't easy.

Combining pathos and cold logic, the letter counseled the prospective reader at Justice (1) that taking me back to court would be patently unfair, since Colby hadn't been sued for his sins; (2) that the government had already won through my case a powerful deterrent to future violations; and (3) that my life was pretty much wrecked anyway, insofar as I was proscribed from being a writer unless I agreed to submit to censorship. Which I would not.

"The government has thus succeeded," Mark wrote, "in imposing severe restrictions on Mr. Snepp's ability to pursue the profession of his choice, and further proceedings against him would only be gratuitous."

So far, so good.

But then Mark turned nasty. He wanted the Justice Department to know, he continued, that in the event of retrial, "all the evidence"—and implicitly all CIA secrets relating to me—"will have to be submitted for a jury determination."

To rebut Turner's contention that I'd frightened off intelligence sources, "we will have to elicit the identity of the sources to whom Admiral Turner referred and what they have expressed to the CIA."

To defend my motivation for writing, he said, "it will be necessary to recount a great deal about the final days in Vietnam and the aftermath at CIA headquarters."

Indeed, to convince the jury that I hadn't written for personal gain, "it would be highly relevant" to show what secrets I might have included in the book "to make it more sensational and more marketable."

"The pursuit of this defense would require Mr. Snepp to do what he has thus far refused to do and what he does not wish to do—reveal sensitive intelligence matters."

It was as bald an attempt at graymail as Mark could have conceived, and as I read through the draft, I couldn't help marveling at the irony. In order to dissuade Sally from taking me back to court for publishing *no* secrets, he would have me threaten to blow every secret I knew. What a sorry choice I'd been reduced to.

But I knew it was no choice at all.

I told him to spike the letter and forget it.

— —

The Supreme Court's Friday, October 5 conference came and went without producing any headlines about my case. A week passed, then another, and another—and still no word. Meanwhile, with each passing day, a malign outside influence, the deepening crisis in Iran, added to the political winds blowing ill for me.

Finally, in early November came the deluge. A ragtag band of Iranian fanatics overran the American embassy and seized fifty-two Americans, including three CIA officers and a huge stash of secret documents identifying local spies and collaborators. It was a disaster achingly reminiscent of the one I'd lived through in Saigon, and though Turner had once dismissed *that* debacle as "a piece of history that is not particularly relevant," had he taken the lessons to heart, CIA operatives in Tehran might not have been caught with their guard down, their files intact, and their agents stranded beyond reach.

The humiliation plunged the American people into a paroxysm of rage that would last over four hundred days and admit little sympathy for heretics like me. Suddenly, I was no longer in demand on talk-show circuits. Suddenly, the imperatives of national security were no longer mere ashes in the mouths of unreconstructed Cold Warriors.

The Supreme Court itself ought to have been impervious and above it all, but as Dershowitz was quick to remind me, the justices read newspapers just like the rest of us.

Nor was Iran the only shock therapy that would test their neutrality. In early December, after weeks of fevered speculation in the media, Watergate reporter Bob Woodward and his researcher Scott Armstrong put the Court itself in the hot seat with a newly published, highly controversial book called *The Brethren*.

Nothing could have been more certain to sour the Court on exposés. Not only did the authors trash several of the title characters, particularly Chief Justice Burger, whom they portrayed as a pompous, disengaged lightweight; they made a mockery of the Court's own pretensions to secrecy by bragging publicly about how their juiciest revelations had been leaked by the justices' own law clerks.

If Burger and his sympathizers had ever needed instruction on the dangers posed by disloyal fiduciaries, they had it now. And if they were looking to deliver an object lesson to their own faithless, the pending case against me provided just the ticket. As reporter Lyle Denniston of *The Washington Star* pointed out, the very principles under which I'd been sued could conceivably be turned against Woodward and Armstrong and the leakers who'd serviced them.

My own lawyers saw *The Brethren* as the last nail in the coffin. If it didn't actually kill my chances of appeal, it destroyed any hope of dispassionate consideration.

— —

During the first week in December, as *The Brethren* scaled the bestseller lists, new rumblings about my case echoed across Capitol Hill. Mark learned from press contacts that the justices had been juggling my cert. request like a hot potato and would take no action on it until after Christmas. It was Justice Lewis Powell, the Fourth Circuit patrician and erstwhile intelligence officer, who'd apparently caused the delay by repeatedly asking for additional time to consider the petition. The Court's newest member,

John Paul Stevens, reportedly had also taken a keen interest and had asked the appeals court in Richmond for the entire case record.

Normally, such requests aren't made until after a cert. request is granted and the justices are writing opinions. What Stevens was up to, Mark couldn't guess.

"Maybe they're haggling over the issues," I posed hopefully.

"Too early," Mark replied. "That comes after briefs. All they've got now are the bare bones."

The following Sunday, the *Star*'s Denniston recycled these rumors in a front-page story. "The Supreme Court is having trouble making up its mind on a key case on the rights of a former CIA agent," he reported.

"Only members of the Court and their staffs know what problem any justice is having with the case.

"But legal experts have begun to speculate that one significant factor could be the government's potentially sweeping claim that it has the right to collect all the money that Snepp has made or will make from his book."

CHAPTER 26

--- ---

Judgment Day

As CHRISTMAS APPROACHED and the Brethren haggled over my cert. request, I tried to relax but couldn't. The stress of anticipation kept me awake at night and on edge by day. Mark tried to cheer me up by inviting me to join in his family's holiday revelries, but his own obvious anxiety merely intensified my own. I tried to forge ahead with the book I owed Bob Loomis, but each time I looked at the pitiable manuscript, the emotional overload shut me down.

Despite being anything but religious, I damned the gods and prayed for a miracle.

But alas, the only vision that materialized was one wholly unwelcome. Two days before Christmas, the inimitable Philip Agee came back to haunt like one of Scrooge's yuletide visitations.

What occasioned his resurrection was his usual excessive zeal. Determined to needle the CIA at every opportunity, he'd allowed himself to be wooed by the Ayatollah's fanatics and reportedly was on his way to Tehran to take part in a show trial for the CIA agents held hostage. Agency officials thought this was too much. On December 23, at their behest, the secretary of state pulled Agee's passport.

Immediately after Christmas, his ACLU lawyer bustled into D.C. District Court to protest the revocation on grounds that it violated his client's First Amendment right to speak and travel freely as a "journalist." Sally Whitaker's husband, Glenn, fought back, warning that it was Agee's "stated intention to go about disrupting the intelligence activities of the United States."

The judge ultimately agreed with the defense that fundamental First Amendment issues were at stake, and declared that the secretary of state had exceeded his authority. But the Circuit Court of Appeals immediately granted the government a stay on the ruling, thus leaving Agee without a valid U.S. passport.

The decision was a bellwether, sobering proof that an international crisis could turn even liberal jurists into willing adherents of dubious national security claims.

But if Iran tilted the scales, it was a last spasm of Cold War hysteria that sent them crashing.

Flashpoint: Afghanistan. Two days after Christmas, Soviet forces invaded en masse to exploit regional instabilities unleashed by the Iranian revolution, and suddenly the American spy establishment was again everybody's last best hope. The CIA began girding for counterinsurgency operations unparalleled since Vietnam, and even the staunchest proponents of intelligence reform realized this was not the time to ply their cause. Proposals for a new restrictive charter for the intelligence community soon dropped off the congressional agenda, and liberal activists dropped into a discreet silence.

It was scarcely a propitious moment to be a "renegade" ex–CIA agent caught in the tendrils of American justice.

— —

Three weeks later, as the clock ticked on, retired Supreme Court justice William O. Douglas died, adding to my sense of impending catastrophe. A near-absolutist on free-speech issues, the old champion's passing seemed to signal the end of an era when one might dare to assume that the First Amendment really meant what it said: "Congress shall make no law . . . abridging freedom of speech"—and implicitly, no one else either.

Then, a few days later came the first real premonition of the worst I could imagine. On Tuesday morning, January 29, Mark called to say the Court had just issued a decision that spoke closely to the issues of my case, and had decided them all wrong.

The ruling involved a set of Navy and Air Force regulations that barred men in uniform from circulating public petitions without approval of higher authority. Justice Powell, the old intelligence officer, had written the Opinion and disposed of all constitutional objections in a stroke, with the support of Burger, Blackmun, Rehnquist, and disturbingly, Justice White, who'd been such a force for moderation in the Pentagon Papers case.

"Without the opportunity to review materials before they are dispersed," Powell decreed, "a military commander could not avert possible disruptions among his troops."

In a note to me, Mark spelled out the inescapable implications. "Although this is a military case," he remarked, "I'm afraid some of the justices might readily liken the CIA to the military and be willing to approve burdens on the First Amendment rights of CIA employees."

As it turned out, he'd hit the nail right on the head.

— —

I was sitting at my desk, trying desperately to make my pen move across a blank page, when the call came through.

"Are you sitting down?" Mark's voice was pulled tight as a slingshot.

"They've taken your case—"

My heart lurched.

"—and decided it."

I felt as though I were falling through space.

"A summary judgment. All in the government's favor. The gag. The constructive trust. The dirt."

It was the morning of February 19, 1980.

I could barely choke out a word. "But *how*—with no briefs or arguments?"

"That's what a summary judgment is. Very rare. They must have decided this case from reading the newspapers."

He said the six-to-three ruling was unsigned—a per curiam decision—but that the likely author was Powell, who was joined in the majority by Blackmun, Rehnquist, Burger, White, and Stewart.

Stewart too!

Justice Stevens, backed by Marshall and Brennan, had written a stinging dissent.

"But it won't make any difference," Mark added wearily. "It's over."

I sleepwalked through most of the rest of the day, too devastated to feel much of anything. At one point, my father called to try to comfort me with the fact that the Court had committed an egregious excess. "Some president is going to realize the power he's been granted by this decision," he told me, "and impose censorship throughout the government. This is infamous."

Whether anyone else phoned to offer sympathy, I can't recall. Griffin Bell later wrote in his memoirs that Admiral Turner threw a champagne bash for all the government lawyers to celebrate their splendid victory.

Around twilight, I arrived at Mark's ACLU offices across the street from the Supreme Court building. A press conference was under way, and the overflow had spilled out onto the lawn below his window. A constitutional expert who'd helped with my defense brushed past me without registering any recognition.

None of the countless reporters on hand asked me anything more than "How do you feel?" Already, I'd become a nonperson, an italicized metaphor for a very bad First Amendment case.

Maybe that's all I'd ever been destined to be. From the moment Judge Lewis had discouraged any mention of Vietnam in his courtroom, this case had been about someone I barely recognized.

Too upset to endure even small talk, I soon left and walked over to the steps of the Supreme Court itself. The lamps at the bottom of the ascent cast a baleful glow over me as I stood gazing up at the sweeping arches of the portico, searching the inscription there—"Equal Justice Under Law"— for something other than irony.

After a few moments, as I was turning to leave, a young tourist approached and asked if I would snap a flash-photo of him on the steps.

"Great-looking place," he remarked jauntily as I lifted the camera. "Ever been inside?"

I tried to steady my hand. "No. Never inside."

— —

The ruling against me was summary in every sense of the word. No legal precedents were cited in its nine pages of text and only a few in its eleven footnotes. First Amendment issues were reduced to a single footnote. Still, the government got everything it had asked for: immediate and automatic ownership of all my profits and a lifetime injunction requiring me to seek CIA approval for even unclassified writings about anything remotely related to intelligence work.

As one journalist pointed out, "It was the first time the Supreme Court had approved prior restraint on writing or speaking about matters of government policy."

On the facts, the six justices who'd ruled against me echoed the unsubstantiated assumptions of the lower courts that the uncleared publication of *Decent Interval* had "caused the United States irreparable harm and loss" by exposing classified information to "the risk of disclosure." They also suggested in a footnote that, whatever the merits of the case, the CIA deserved special deference anyway. Taking "judicial notice" of journalist Thomas Powers's recently published *The Man Who Kept the Secrets,* a biography of Richard Helms that included many uncleared quotes from ex-agents, they declared the Agency to be "essential to the security of the

United States and, in a sense, the free world . . . whatever fairly may be said about some of its past activities."

On contractual matters, the majority refused to acknowledge any difference between my first and final agreements and decreed peremptorily that *the* secrecy agreement is a "reasonable" restriction on employee activities "that in other contexts might be prohibited by the First Amendment."

They were unconcerned that Congress had passed no law authorizing CIA censorship and found simply that the director of Central Intelligence can impose prepublication review as part of his vague statutory authority to protect intelligence sources and methods.

Nor did they bother to try to justify the gag order against me in terms of any threat of harm, irreparable or otherwise. Indeed, in a footnote, they intimated that the government might seek such injunctions in the future, not merely to protect secrets but also to preserve the *appearance* of airtight official security. The government, they said, has "a compelling interest in protecting both the secrecy of information important to our national security and the appearance of confidentiality so essential to the effective operation of our foreign intelligence service."

Even more excessively, they expanded on the government's theory of fiduciary duty and held that clearance requirements might be imposed without any secrecy contract. "Quite apart from the plain language of the agreement, the nature of Snepp's duties and his conceded access to confidential sources and materials could establish a trust relationship," they reasoned.

In a signal to the Court's own leakers, they also made clear that this theory could justify censorship throughout the government. "Without a dependable prepublication procedure," they declaimed, "no intelligence agency *or responsible government official* [italics added] could be assured that an employee privy to sensitive information might not conclude on his own—innocently or otherwise—that it should be disclosed to the world."

Much of the remainder of the ruling was given over to rationalizing the preferred financial penalty. CIA employment involves an "extremely high degree of trust," the majority argued. Snepp understood this, but "deliberately" and "surreptitiously" broke the rules. Requiring the government to go back to court to sue for punitive damages "would subject the CIA and its officials to probing discovery into the Agency's highly confidential affairs." Thus, a constructive trust is the only logical answer—a solution "swift and sure"—and a fair shake for the transgressor himself, requiring him only "to disgorge the benefits of his faithlessness."

Nowhere in this stream of judicial consciousness was there any careful balancing of competing values, any recognition that the remedy imposed might threaten free speech. The scales were skewed entirely to the government's advantage.

In trying so hard to accommodate the CIA, the majority mangled both facts and law. They wrongly claimed, for instance, that the alleged harm I'd done was "undisputed," and mistakenly treated as "fact" Lewis's gratuitous assertion that I'd deliberately misled CIA officials into believing I'd submit to clearance.

Their most serious error, however, was a misinterpretation of law growing out of a convoluted attempt to sugarcoat CIA censorship itself. In one of their notorious footnotes, they insisted that if I'd submitted my manuscript to the censors and disagreed with any cuts, the courts could always have stepped in to arbitrate. They cited the Marchetti ruling to support this, and argued that in any dispute over deletions, the Agency would have "borne the burden" of going to court to try to justify and enforce them through an injunction.

The trouble is, that's not the way the Marchetti ruling read at all. It stated that in any such censorship dispute, it was the author's responsibility to take the matter to court. Otherwise, he was stuck with the deletions.

This wasn't merely a detail for Talmudic scholars. The confusion left open a critical question: If the CIA gets heavy-handed, how do you get to court? The majority's garbled explanation suggested that your only option was to thumb your nose at the censors and hope they'd sue for an injunction. Otherwise—no access to judicial review.

As the Court had long ago held in its ruling on the Maryland film censorship board, the only saving grace for any system of prior restraint is a set of orderly safeguards against abuse. By botching the judicial review issue, the majority had left me with no sure safeguards at all.

— —

Compared to the majority opinion, Justice John Paul Stevens's dissent was positively enlightened. Most important, he recognized that CIA secrecy agreements burden one's constitutional right to criticize the government.

"The mere fact that the agency has the authority to review the text of a critical book in search of classified information before it is published is bound to have an inhibiting effect on the author's writing," he maintained. "Moreover, the right to delay publication until the review is completed is itself a form of prior restraint that would not be tolerated in other contexts."

On the contractual issue, Stevens proceeded from the premise that CIA secrecy agreements are designed to protect secrets, not stifle critical speech. Since the government had pinned no security breach on *Decent Interval,* he reasoned, there was no ground for damages.

Nor did he feel that the Court was right in enforcing a constructive trust or charging a breach of fiduciary duty in such circumstances. Indeed, he argued, it wasn't the author who was being "unjustly enriched" here, but the government.

With the concurrence of fellow dissenters Brennan and Marshall, Stevens would have preferred to see this case deliberated more carefully, particularly in view of its uniqueness. While allowing that "the government may regulate certain activities of its employees that would be protected in other contexts," he reminded the majority that no court had ever considered "the enforceability of this kind of prior restraint" reaching even unclassified material, "or the remedy that should be imposed in the event of a breach." Thus, at the very least, "the issue surely should not be resolved in the absence of full briefing and argument."

It wasn't exactly a ringing endorsement of First Amendment values— but still far better than what the majority offered up.

— —

Critical reaction to the ruling was swift and unsparing. "An unprecedented vote for censorship," editorialized the *Los Angeles Times*.

"No court decision in history," exclaimed columnist Nat Hentoff, "has so imperiled whistle-blowers, and thereby, the ability of all citizens to find out about rampant ineptitude and corruption in the agencies purportedly serving them."

The Washington Post chided the Brethren for disposing of the case in "a casual, even cavalier manner."

Nathan Lewin complained in *The New Republic* that they'd "approved a procedure under which, no matter how harmless the article or book, its publication is unlawful if the government does not approve it."

"The government may act not only to protect classified data," observed Bob Lewis of the Society of Professional Journalists, "but also information that has 'the appearance of confidentiality.' "

Columnist Anthony Lewis noted that none of the Pentagon Papers requirements for prior restraint had been applied in *Snepp*. "[T]here was no finding that his book would result in 'direct, immediate, irreparable,' or any other kind of harm to the nation," he remarked in one of his many commentaries on the case. "The Court did not even mention *Near v Minnesota*, the presumption against prior restraint, or any First Amendment law."

"No case," wrote Alan Dershowitz in a commentary of his own, "better illustrates the hypocrisy of 'conservative' judges who claim to be adherents of 'judicial restraint' and opponents of 'judicial activism.' The Snepp case is a paradigm of judicial activism: Congress had declined to enact a statute prohibiting the kind of disclosure at issue in the Snepp case or granting the government the power to seize the earnings of an author who made such disclosures."

Henry Kauffman of the American Association of Book Publishers called the Opinion "an unadulterated disaster" and predicted "enforcement actions" against employees of the thirty other federal agencies that deal in classified information.

"In addition," he observed, "the broad injunction remedy could, in theory, form the basis for a contempt action or fresh injunctive relief against any publisher who knowingly acts in concert with a government employee who violates his contract or fiduciary duty toward the government."

Why had the Court overreached so drastically? Bruce Fein, a court expert for the American Enterprise Institute, saw the decision as "a reaction to the confidences improperly breached" in *The Brethren.*

Professor Archibald Cox of Harvard had a simpler explanation. "Because *Decent Interval* contained no classified material," he wrote, "the rejection of Snepp's First Amendment defense must have been based partly upon the reprehensible character of his conduct and the need to deter such conduct in the future."

Anthony Lewis agreed, but added: "Moral disapproval of Mr. Snepp for breaking his promise comes ill from a Court that, in this case, showed contempt for the law."

— —

If First Amendment purists were stunned by the ruling, Washington's secrecy lobby hastened to capitalize on it. CIA deputy director Frank Carlucci immediately called on Congress to exempt the Agency from all disclosure provisions of the Freedom of Information Act, and Senator Barry Goldwater urged the Justice Department to bring a charge of treason against anyone who publishes sensitive information.

Agency apologists, meanwhile, acted to head off a backlash to the ruling by embellishing the libels against me. Turner forgot having testified that he'd merely "assumed" he had a promise from me to submit my manuscript, and incessantly repeated the claim that the promise had been explicit and duplicitous. Conservative columnist James J. Kilpatrick insisted that the ruling had "nothing on earth to do with a 'citizen's right to criticize the government,' " as Stevens had maintained, and everything to do with faithlessness.

"A man should keep his word," Kilpatrick remonstrated. "Simply as a matter of honor and never mind the law, Snepp's conduct was indefensible."

In early March, as the House Intelligence Committee launched secret hearings on the implications of the ruling, CIA officials made my "faithlessness" an excuse for their own selective enforcement of the rules. Asked why others like William Colby hadn't been sued for sins surpassing my own, CIA lawyer Ernie Mayerfeld replied, "We have greater concern about people like Snepp who, after having repeatedly promised the director to submit his book for prepublication review, went ahead and surreptitiously published."

There was also a determined effort by CIA witnesses to make censorship seem pain-free and as all-American as apple pie. The chief of the prepublication review board announced proudly that only three manuscripts had been suppressed in their entirety in the past two years, and added with a hint of noblesse oblige that *Decent Interval* would have passed muster with only "a few changes."

Privately, a CIA lawyer named John Peyton confided something a bit more disturbing to Mark. He said that if the censors had gotten hold of my manuscript, they would have ripped it to shreds on any pretext.

— —

By the time the House committee wound up its hearings (I was not invited to testify), the CIA was feeling so cocky that it summarily rejected the panel's call for an independent censorship board to ensure against abuse. In explaining why, Mayerfeld described intelligence as a "somewhat arcane business, a skill or craft" that would be difficult "for someone else to make determinations about." He intimated that the Agency would oppose interference by the courts ("judicial review") for the same reason.

Not that he had anything to fear in this regard. Within two weeks of its ruling against me, the Supreme Court again deferred to privilege by handing down a decision that favored Henry Kissinger over the First Amendment. Several press organs had sued for access to phone logs Kissinger had maintained at public expense during his years as presidential security adviser and secretary of state. Upon retirement, he'd spirited them away and then slipped them to the Library of Congress with the understanding that he would control access until his death. The press argued that the documents should be available to everybody under the Freedom of Information Act. But Justice Rehnquist, writing for the majority, declared, in effect, that the Court could not force the government to produce what it did not control. In short, thievery insulated the thief.

"Impeccable chop logic thus lets the Court construe strictly—against the citizen—laws whose very purpose was to increase public access to official information," groused *The New York Times*. "Contrast this with the Court's much more inventive response, just two weeks ago, to the case of Frank Snepp."

Columnist Mary McGrory put it more bluntly. "In other words," she said, "if you are rich and powerful and have rich and powerful friends, the law is on your side."

— —

It is routine for a petitioner stiffed by the Supreme Court to request a re-hearing, and just as routine for the Court to refuse. But when Mark went through the motions of filing such a request in late March, he couldn't re-sist admonishing the Court that "this is, in fact, a petition for an opportu-nity to file a brief and to be heard" in the first place.

In his plea, he accused the Court of having overstepped its authority by approving a system of prior restraint unsupported by law, and by imposing a financial penalty, the constructive trust, which the government had wanted "only if the Court granted Mr. Snepp's petition for review." Which it hadn't.

He also blasted the majority for failing to recognize that my final secrecy agreement required clearance of only classified and nonpublic CIA data. "Indeed," he wrote, "since Mr. Snepp abided by the terms of his second agreement, there is no ground for the Court's finding of 'faithlessness' or a willful, deliberate, and surreptitious breach of either contractual or fidu-ciary duties."

Two weeks later, the Court rejected the "rehearing" petition without comment.

Long afterward, one justice continued to worry about what had been done to me. In a speech to a lawyers' conference in 1982, John Paul Stevens picked up where he'd left off in his dissent, denouncing the decision as "to-tally unnecessary" and as "an exercise of lawmaking power" by the Court.

— —

Normally, Supreme Court deliberations remain swathed in as much secrecy as any covert CIA operation. Thus, for a long while, the internal logic that had produced the ruling against me could only be guessed at. One glim-mering came years later when Justice Harry Blackmun complained to an audience in Princeton that I was the guy who'd leaked secrets and blown agents' names. One of those present suggested he might be mistaking me for Philip Agee.

Whether this misapprehension figured in Blackmun's actual vote against me cannot be determined, for he and the three other justices who'd retired but were still alive when this book was completed—White, Brennan, and Powell—refused to be interviewed for it.

It was only after a fifth retiree, Justice Thurgood Marshall, died in 1993 that any private Court records were thrown open to the public. Marshall had deeded to the Library of Congress the detritus of his twenty-odd years on the Court, including confidential memos and conference notes from his brethren.

Seventeen years after the *Snepp* ruling, I visited the library to search these papers for insights into how and why I'd been clobbered. It was like opening the grave of some creature long dead. I was terrified that I might discover in the sarcophagus a perfect image of myself, proof that the Court had not misjudged me after all.

No mention of *United States v Snepp* appeared in the computerized index of Marshall's papers or in the folders containing "bench memoranda" and other scholarly dissertations on rulings during the 1979–1980 term. My case apparently had passed through the justices' in-boxes without accreting anything like a learned gloss on its merits or implications. For a while, it seemed I might have left no trace at all.

But then, near the end of my visit, I discovered a small packet of revelatory conference schedules from Chief Justice Burger himself, and finally, in a folder labeled "Per Curiam Opinions," a collection of draft rulings on *Snepp*.

Not long afterward, retired Justice Brennan gave me permission to examine his own private records of the case. Together with the Marshall files, they provided as complete an insider's perspective as I could have wished for.

— —

The conference schedules bear out what Mark learned long before the final decision: On October 5, 1979, the justices considered for the first time my request for cert. and the government's conditional cross-petition. But contrary to what we'd all assumed, the Court didn't merely consider these applications but rejected both outright. Handwritten notes from the Marshall-Brennan collection indicate that all but one of the justices voted not to accept my case and to leave in place the appeals judgment against me.

The holdout was former intelligence officer Lewis Powell.

A note scribbled into the October 5 schedule by Chief Justice Burger himself reads: "Relisted—JLP," meaning that Powell persuaded his colleagues on this date to postpone final disposition of the case. Another notation, this one made by Brennan in his own copy of the schedule, reveals that the delay was granted so that Powell could write a brief protesting his colleagues' decision to reject my request for a hearing.

Far from wanting to see my case deep-sixed, he hoped to convince his brethren to take another look at it and to rule against me brutally. The proof of this is to be found in a document he circulated among them six weeks later. Bearing the title "Mr. Justice Powell Dissenting," it calls on the Court to take up my appeal for the sole purpose of destroying me financially.

"I would grant the petitions for certiorari in order to reimpose the constructive trust found by the District Court," he wrote in the opening paragraph.

In explaining why, he said he'd been impressed with the arguments of the dissenting appeals judge, Walter E. Hoffman, who'd "recognized that Snepp had assumed two distinct obligations, one to protect classified information and the other to submit all manuscripts for prepublication review." Powell agreed with Hoffman "that both obligations derived from the same trust relationship" and "that Snepp breached a fiduciary obligation." Accordingly, he felt that all the proceeds from *Decent Interval* ought to be "impressed by a constructive trust."

Except for some minor word changes and a few footnotes, the rest of Powell's draft contained virtually everything that would wind up in the final judgment against me, every innuendo, every mistake, and every over-the-top secrecy theory save one that would be added later.

It was in this initial draft, for instance, that Powell first attempted to persuade his colleagues that my first and final agreements were the same, that I'd "willfully, deliberately, and surreptitiously" breached them, and that I'd "misled" the Agency into believing I wouldn't. It was here, too, that the Court was first encouraged to believe that *"undisputed"* evidence proved that my actions had "irreparably harmed the United States government.

"If former agents may rely on their own judgment about what information is harmful," Powell declared, sounding more like a CIA flack than a judge, "the intelligence services of friendly nations and the agents recruited by the CIA cannot be assured of the secrecy upon which their cooperation depends."

The effect of this Sermon on the Mount was catalytic. Burger and the onetime Pentagon Papers moderate, Potter Stewart, immediately sent Powell notes imploring him to add their names to his dissent, by which they meant they favored granting me cert. for the punitive reasons he'd outlined. Three days later, after Powell had produced a second draft, Justice Blackmun advised him, "You have written a persuasive dissent and I am happy to join it." The following day, November 20, Justice Rehnquist likewise fell into line, bringing to five the number of justices who thought my appeal worth hearing on the most prejudicial grounds possible.

Duly encouraged, Powell circulated another document seven days later under the title, "First Draft—Per Curiam Opinion." Virtually indistinguishable from the foregoing dissent, it had an equally galvanizing effect. Everybody who'd favored the one—Blackmun, Stewart, Burger, and Rehnquist—quickly endorsed the other by signed letter.

In addition, on November 29, Byron White, onetime champion of the First Amendment in the Pentagon Papers case, signaled his willingness to climb aboard. "Although I voted to deny rather than give plenary consideration to this case," he wrote to Powell, "now that your per curiam suggests a summary reversal, I join."

"Summary reversal"—that phrase says it all. In effect, by November 29, Powell had stampeded five of his colleagues into accepting my case and deciding it against me without any written or oral briefs from either side. He'd done so with a polemical attack on me and an almost apostolic defense of official secrecy and the CIA. The only "authorities" he'd had to draw upon were his own experiences as a World War II intelligence officer, the government's often inaccurate conditional cross-petition, and the original trial and appeals rulings that had been attached to our petition.

No one in the newly forged majority had bothered to examine the raw case files from Richmond, the trial transcripts, or any key depositions to see if Powell's interpretation of the facts matched reality. The first evidence that anyone even *asked* for these files appears in an internal memo dated November 29, the same day White threw his support behind Powell to round out the anti-Snepp majority. In it, the clerk of the Court ordered the justices' secretaries to strike all references to my case from the upcoming Friday conference list, since "the record has been requested."

— —

Weeks before the final ruling, Mark had heard from reporters that it was Justice Stevens who'd asked for the trial records. The Brennan-Marshall papers confirm this. Among them, I found a first draft of Stevens's dissent brief that includes specific mention of these case documents.

John Paul Stevens, heretofore a cipher on First Amendment issues, wasted no time in throttling the majority for caving in so easily to Powell's arguments. Immediately after the Christmas holidays, on January 4, he distributed his first proposed dissent to the committed majority and to Brennan and Marshall, who had not yet spoken.

In his only immediate concession to Powell, Stevens agreed that my first and final agreements imposed identical clearance requirements, extending even to nonsecrets. But he was equally adamant that since I'd exposed no secrets, the government had no basis for charging a breach of fiduciary duty or demanding a constructive trust.

"The interest that the agreement was designed to protect—the confidentiality of classified information—has not been offended by what Snepp did," he wrote.

From first draft to last, he also belabored the majority for deciding the case summarily, on the basis of the government's cross-petition. Even on January 4, he was willing to denounce this procedure as "uninhibited" and at odds with "a more conservative approach to this case."

Where his original draft differed most dramatically from later ones was on First Amendment issues. Initially, Stevens was wonderfully outspoken about the evils of secrecy agreements. In his original January 4 draft, he found that clearance obligations extending to nonsecrets were "doubtful" under "the rule of reason," particularly since "the commitment was of indefinite duration and scope," and he declared resolutely that "the agreement is contrary to public interest in the unrestricted dissemination of classified information."

He was also more aggressive in attacking Stansfield Turner's contention that my book and "others like it" had frightened off foreign intelligence sources by making them unsure of CIA security procedures.

"Admiral Turner's truncated testimony," he wrote on January 4, "does not explain whether these unidentified 'other' books actually contained classified information (unlike Snepp's) or whether foreign agencies fear the publication of unclassified information which Snepp and other CIA employees have a First Amendment right to disseminate. . . . If the latter is true, then the reluctance of foreign governments to work with our government must be accepted as an inevitable by-product of the exercise of First Amendment rights by government employees."

Persuasive reasoning, to be sure, and Brennan and Marshall were so impressed that they quickly agreed to join the dissent. On January 11, Stevens passed around his second draft with their names attached.

But Lewis Powell was not one to be steamrollered. Over the next four weeks, he pummeled Stevens with successive drafts of his per curiam opinion, including ever-expanding footnotes that seemed designed to reduce the First Amendment to an article of convenience for the CIA.

On January 15, in his second proposed per curiam, he slammed Stevens for daring to suggest that "damage to our nation's ability to cooperate with foreign intelligence sources must be accepted as an inevitable by-product" of the First Amendment.

Relying on suspect "factual" findings, he also disputed Stevens's assumption about the benign effects of my actions. "Both the District Court and the Court of Appeals," he retorted, "found that a former intelligence agent's publication of unreviewed material relating to intelligence activities can be detrimental to vital interests even if the information is unclassified."

Four days later, in his third draft dissent, Stevens again attacked Admiral Turner's "sketchy" claim that I'd damaged the Agency, and speculated that the CIA itself might have contributed to the unease of friendly intelligence agencies by leaving too many secrets unclassified. He also worried that Powell was trying to give the CIA "carte blanche" to censor even unclassified information simply on the basis that it might be "detrimental to vital interests."

Roaring back in a new draft of his own, Powell dismissed Stevens's view as "a misapprehension of the concern reflected in Admiral Turner's testimony. . . .

"The problem," he continued patronizingly, "is to ensure in advance and by proper procedures that information detrimental to the national interest is not published."

As for giving censors "carte blanche," he insisted that all he was proposing was preclearance "subject to judicial review." In explaining his point in a footnote, he misquoted *Marchetti* and thus injected into his burgeoning majority opinion the confusion that would finally make it impossible to know what safeguards were available against censor abuse.

On January 23, an exasperated Stevens, in a fourth proposed dissent, chided Powell for arguing, as he had throughout, that there were plenty of Supreme Court precedents to justify curbing the First Amendment rights of CIA employees. None of the cases Powell had cited, said Stevens, "involved a requirement that an employee submit a proposed public statement for prerelease censorship or approval."

Yet, brave though this sally was, the debate was taking its toll. Nowhere in this fourth draft did Stevens return to his "carte blanche" theme; his critique of Turner's testimony was now divided between text and a footnote that took the edge off; and his condemnation of secrecy agreements under the "rule of reason" had given way to a fog of hedged judgments.

Picking through the wreckage, one almost feels sorry for Stevens. Here was a proponent of sober-minded jurisprudence, or (as he put it) "a more conservative approach to this case," mud-wrestling a former intelligence officer who had no qualms about flogging personal dogma as fact and law. What's more, in attempting to answer Powell blow for blow, Stevens had forced his adversary into ever more extreme judgments about the appropriate scope of officially sanctioned censorship. As Stevens observed in each of his drafts, there was truly an "uninhibited character" to this "exercise in lawmaking."

In early February, both protagonists submitted additional drafts (Powell's fourth, Stevens's fifth), though without breaking any new ground. At the Court's customary Friday conference on February 15, Stevens asked to have the final decision on my cert. request delayed (Burger noted: "Relisted—JPS"), possibly to let everyone absorb his closing arguments. But when the vote came four days later, the outcome was exactly as the majority had preordained it the previous November, before seeing even a scrap of the raw case files.

— —

Since late-breaking news is seldom discussed in formal Supreme Court documents, it is impossible to tell from the Brennan-Marshall papers whether the hostage crisis in Iran or the Soviet depredations in Afghanistan influenced the majority's deliberations of my case. Theoretically, they shouldn't have. But neither should Turner's unproven puffery about the alleged trauma inflicted on anonymous intelligence agencies by my book and "others" like it.

The impact of Woodward and Armstrong's exposé, *The Brethren,* likewise remains indeterminable, though the Marshall papers do reflect growing agitation over it. In one folder, I found a television interviewer's letter to Chief Justice Burger inviting him to participate in a broadcast about this "dangerous book" and warning him that it "will surely alter the public's perception of the highest court in our land unless it is met openly by a member of the Court." On January 3, the day before Stevens circulated his first proposed dissent, Burger sent the interviewer a note declining to appear on his show but assuring him, "I am not insensitive to the concerns which you set forth in your stimulating letter."

— —

Given the crucial role Justice Powell played in the decision against me, I felt compelled, after studying the Brennan-Marshall files, to try to understand him better, as if the condemned might profit from knowing his executioner. Was this simply a case of one unrepentant ex-spook delivering a blow for the constituency? Or was Powell, seventy-two years of age when he wrote the per curiam opinion, so viscerally antagonistic toward me and all I stood for that he couldn't possibly have voted any other way?

The Brennan-Marshall papers provide no clue beyond the draft per curiams themselves. But as I combed back through Powell's past, I happened upon an extraordinary document he'd written for the United States Chamber of Commerce in 1971, the year before he'd joined the Court. Somehow, Powell had neglected to mention this confidential memo, titled "Attack on the American Free Enterprise System," at his confirmation hearings. The omission may well have been self-protective, for had he brought the document to light, it would surely have raised questions about his suitability as a justice.

"No thoughtful person can question that the American economic system is under broad attack," he remarked in the memo's opening paragraphs. "The American political system of democracy under the rule of law is also under attack, often by the same individuals and organizations who seek to undermine the enterprise system."

He named the culprits: "the Communists, New Leftists [he singled out Herbert Marcuse], and other revolutionaries who would destroy the entire system, both political and economic." Among his most hated bugbears were Ralph Nader, whose consumer advocate group was the professional home of two of my lawyers, John Sims and Alan Morrison, and Mark's own American Civil Liberties Union, which Powell complained had exploited the judicial system to advance its liberal agenda. "It initiates or intervenes in scores of cases each year," he griped, "and it files briefs amicus curiae in the Supreme Court in a number of cases during each term of that court. . . .

"Moreover, much of the media," he continued, "either voluntarily accords unique publicity to these 'attackers,' or at least allows them to exploit the media for their purposes. . . .

"The newsstands—at airports, drugstores, and elsewhere—are filled with paperbacks and pamphlets advocating everything from revolution to erotic free love."

He also condemned television as an offender and called for heavy policing. "The national television networks should be monitored in the same way that textbooks should be kept under constant surveillance," he said.

"There should be no hesitation to attack the Naders, the Marcuses, and others who openly seek destruction of the system. . . . Nor should there be reluctance to penalize politically those who oppose it."

And what was his preferred arena of combat? "Under our constitutional system, especially with an activist-minded Supreme Court," Powell argued, "the judiciary may be the most important instrument for social, economic, and political change."

To a man of these sensibilities, the Frank Snepp case must have seemed the payback opportunity of a lifetime.

POSTSCRIPT:
SETTLING ACCOUNTS

"I live a very reclusive life," I told the *Chicago Tribune* in the summer of 1980, five months after the Supreme Court had lowered the boom. "I don't socialize a lot because if I do, the writing doesn't get done."

And the writing now was everything, the only way out. Two books owed to Random House—one about the case and the other a newly conceived novel about the Kennedy assassination—and debts beyond measure.

Nor was there any avoiding the censors, not if I was to write at all. Bolstered by the Supreme Court's solicitude, the CIA had recently circulated a new set of guidelines extending the clearance requirement to novels, speeches, and just about everything else, with the possible stated exception of "a manuscript of a cookbook" or "a treatise on gardening." The censors also were claiming the right to delete not merely properly designated secrets but anything they deemed "classifiable." Whatever that meant.

"My sister is a graduate student in psychology and considers me sort of a lab rat," I remarked to a group of concerned publishers soon after the guidelines went into effect. "She wants to see how long I can take this without cracking."

Stockwell and Agee Get Theirs

"An atrocious, un-American decision. Truly, truly tragic," John Stockwell declared upon learning of the Court's peremptory disposal of my case. Two weeks later, the Justice Department moved to dispose of him by suing him under *Snepp* for his own unauthorized book.

Philip Agee, that other errant author, was already facing a similar reckoning. The previous fall, he'd made the mistake of filing a Freedom of Information suit in the federal court in Washington, D.C. The government promptly countersued, claiming that by going to court he'd put himself within reach of American law and the sanctions of *U.S. v Snepp,* even though he was still holed up in Germany.

Both Agee and Stockwell quickly retained Mark Lynch to represent them, and quickly profited from his expertise. In negotiating an out-of-court settlement for Stockwell, Mark claimed that his client had already spent his book profits and would be wrecked financially and unable to support his family if he were obliged to fork over a commensurate amount. This sob story persuaded Justice Department officials not to demand any past royalties from Stockwell but only future ones, though they did oblige him to submit to prepublication review from now on.

Agee fared even better.

Shortly before his trial date, a young woman contacted me and gave me a copy of an official reading list she'd recently picked up at a public CIA recruitment seminar. Included in the rundown were the titles of five books explicitly labeled "critical" of the CIA, four of them by ex-agents who'd been sued for breach of contract—Stockwell, Marchetti, Agee, and me. The rest of the bibliography was given over to books and employee memoirs less hostile to the Agency, some published without clearance, none ever subjected to legal action.

Hosannah! Here at last was what Mark and I had been looking for all along—proof from the Agency's own cupboard that its rules were being enforced only against its critics.

Mark attached the list to his brief for Agee and urged dismissal of the case. The judge declined to go that far and put Agee under a lifetime gag, requiring him to submit to censorship. But in view of the bibliography and the discrimination it reflected, he refused to let the government seize any of Agee's book profits.

Thus, both Agee and Stockwell walked away from their legal battles with money in hand, even though both had admitted breaching official secrecy.

My own financial reckoning for publishing *no* secrets was to be a bit more severe.

Snepp Gets His

Four months after the Supreme Court had spoken, Sally Whitaker announced that I would be required to surrender all my royalties minus only federal income taxes within forty-five days. She would not forgive state taxes, the advance I'd spent long ago, or the expenses I'd incurred while writing. Her inflexibility meant that I owed the United States Treasury $144,931.85—far in excess of the $106,629.60 that had pooled into the escrow I'd set up for my profits.

The decision had come from on high. Attorney General Benjamin Civiletti, Bell's successor, was convinced, as he explained to Random House's Bob Bernstein, that I'd lied my way into print and deserved to be crushed for it. He didn't seem to care that other far more notable "fiduciaries" were thumbing their noses at their own clearance obligations. George Bush, soon to be a vice-presidential contender, had declined to clear any of his speeches on defense or intelligence policy, and the White House acknowledged that Henry Kissinger had "vastly overstated" the classification review he'd received for his own recently published memoirs.

Bernstein, citing these examples of privileged dispensation, urged clemency for me and persuaded authors John Hersey, Bernard Malamud, and Robert Penn Warren to do likewise. Civiletti brushed them off. Accordingly, on August 12, I was obliged to hand over the first of two scheduled payments to the United States Treasury, a cashier's check for $116,658.15.

This drained my escrow, leaving me penniless and unable to cover the second installment due in two weeks. To spare me a contempt citation and jail time, Bob Bernstein dipped into Random House's coffers and loaned me the amount outstanding—$23,921.50.

Because of the novelty of the financial judgment, the Internal Revenue Service eventually launched an audit of my 1980 tax returns and, only after an extensive investigation, declared me "clean." The state of Virginia refused to remit any of the taxes I'd paid on the money the federal government had seized.

To keep me in bare essentials, the Authors League loaned me five thousand dollars in the summer of 1980, and my French friend, Danielle Haller, sent me another care package. But effectively, I was destitute, my personal debts having risen to well over forty thousand dollars.

Someone older and more sophisticated than I might have been broken by these reverses. But at age thirty-seven, I still had youthful illusions of immortality and no sense of the enormity of the crisis I faced. Nor did I have any time for self-pity. From the moment the ruling was announced, I knew I would have to write as fast as I could or drown in red ink.

By Herculean effort, I completed my projected novel in early June and turned it over to the censors, though with a plea that they renounce any claim to such works of fiction. They ignored me and ordered me to strike from the manuscript the name of an actual CIA operative which they'd previously cleared for publication in a book by a more favored ex-spook. When I objected that the name had already slipped out, they admitted their "mistake" but asked me to delete it anyway, since further publicity, they argued, could place the identified agent in jeopardy.

Indignant though I was, I couldn't endanger the operative. I removed the name.

Still, if the Agency had been careless, so had I. My novel was a mess. Loomis declared it unpublishable. For the first time, I glimpsed the abyss yawning before me.

"Once you shoot your load as a critic of the Agency, there's nowhere else to go," Vic Marchetti told a reporter who asked how I could possibly survive. "Your only alternatives are articles or fiction or consulting, because you can't get a job after that. You become completely ostracized. Oh, you can go to the extremes of the Far Right and the Far Left. But who wants to live in the Bowery and write for the *Yipster Times*?"

What Was the Point, Anyway?

Ironically, even as catastrophe loomed, the government's reasons for taking me to court began to split at the seams. Though I'd been prosecuted to shore up CIA security, CIA security disintegrated anyway. Seven traitors were uncovered among the ranks of past and present employees in the next six years, and several more in the next decade. Obviously, *Snepp* had had no deterrent effect where it mattered most.

Equally transient was the fear of leaks that had figured so prominently in the case against me. Three years after leaving office, Jimmy Carter himself admitted that the unauthorized disclosures he'd once agonized about "weren't devastating to our country or particularly embarrassing to me."

As for suggestions that *Decent Interval* itself might have compromised some vital security interest, a former deputy director of the CIA, Robert Amory, publicly declared otherwise soon after I'd been reduced to penury. By his reckoning, my book "reflected a totally responsible concern for security and told a tale of incompetence at low and high levels in Saigon-Washington that demanded airing."

The Censorship Virus Spreads

Benjamin Civiletti, who'd done so much to finish me off, immediately recognized the awesome powers conferred by *Snepp* and tried to put a lid on them. In December 1980, he issued a staff directive ruling out *Snepp*-type suits except against violators who'd actually signed secrecy agreements or publishers who'd actively solicited security violations. He also urged the incoming Reagan administration to be similarly constrained.

But Ronald Reagan was even less enamored of open government than his predecessor. After only a year in office, he threw out Civiletti's guidelines and launched the most concerted security crackdown ever undertaken by a modern American president.

First target: William Colby.

The Justice Department's complaint against the former CIA director, filed in the fall of 1981, accused him of having breached his secrecy agreement by allowing Simon and Schuster to see his memoir before the censors had had their say. Legal authority cited: *U.S. v Snepp.*

Colby's lawyers fought back vigorously, and in December, wrangled an out-of-court settlement that limited his liability to a ten-thousand-dollar fine and a promise not to violate his obligations again. Compared to my punishment, it was a slap on the wrist.

But the shock of seeing one of their own caught out sobered many of my other former detractors. Griffin Bell quickly consented to have portions of his own memoirs blue-penciled by Reagan officials, and ex–CIA director Turner dutifully submitted *all* his writings to the Agency for prepublication review.

He also discovered what Marchetti and I had known all along: CIA censorship can be devilishly capricious.

Hoisted on His Own Petard

Obtaining clearance for his memoirs—which were highly critical of Reagan intelligence policies—proved particularly difficult for Turner. The censors demanded over a hundred deletions ranging, in his words, "from borderline issues to the ridiculous." After interminable negotiations, he asked Tony Lapham, now in private practice, to mount a court challenge on his behalf. But on rereading the *Snepp* decision, they discovered that the garbled footnote about the appeals process left them hobbled: To get to court, they would have to provoke the Agency into taking the first step.

Accordingly, Turner sent a letter to Langley threatening to publish the disputed material unless the government obtained a restraining order to keep him from doing so. "My objective," he explained, "was to gain the intercession of a third party to arbitrate the dispute, namely the court." But Justice Department officials outfoxed him. Instead of seeking an injunction, they hinted that if he defied them he would be sued as I had been.

"This was the most irresponsible position they could possibly have taken," Turner groused. "The threat to take me to court after the fact could not have retrieved the secrets. It could only have exacted retribution. . . ."

Ultimately, he caved in, out of concern that even a hint of defiance "could encourage less responsible individuals to be cavalier about releasing secret information." But in later congressional testimony, he complained of the "gross abuse" of his constitutional rights and acknowledged that secrecy contracts "are useful but not critical" to the national security.

"As long as there is almost no check on the arbitrariness of the CIA," he wrote in his memoirs, "it is likely that there will be further abuses of the public's right to knowledge about its government."

Reagan "Snepps" the Entire Government

As Turner chafed, President Reagan fulfilled his bleak prediction, issuing a new secrecy directive that enabled bureaucrats to reclassify what was already in the public domain. Administration lobbyists also rammed through Congress an "Agee bill," making it illegal for anyone to publish the name of a covert American intelligence operative, even one lifted from a library book.

On March 11, 1983, the White House unveiled something even more outrageous, an Orwellian edict, aptly titled Directive 84, that put nearly the entire executive branch, scores of federal agencies, under a regime of secrecy agreements—with *Snepp* as its authority.

Congressional outrage was instantaneous, and Reagan moved quickly to damp it down by canceling one set of contracts he'd imposed. But cagily, he left another batch in place that were equally restrictive.

His successor, George Bush, tightened the vise, and by early 1990 over 140,000 employees of forty-eight federal agencies and one million government contractors were bound by some sort of secrecy pact. Several congressional committees imposed similar agreements on their members and staff, and at least one Supreme Court justice, newcomer Sandra Day O'Connor, required her law clerks to sign *Snepp*-type covenants.

In the meantime, as many had feared, overzealous public servants began using *Snepp* to muzzle mere critics of official policy. What hastened the trend was a law passed in the mid-1980s known as the False Claims Act. Designed to encourage exposure of waste and fraud in government, it allowed whistle-blowers to pocket up to 30 percent of any proceeds recovered. But the Bush administration tried to keep federal workers from jumping on the bandwagon by denying them awards for any scoop picked up on the job. "A government employee has a fiduciary obligation to protect confidential information," Justice Department officials argued in one court action. Their rationale, of course, was *Snepp*.

Nor were the Republicans alone in abusing the blunderbuss bequeathed by my case. When a former FBI agent published an account of President Clinton's romantic dalliances, the Justice Department threatened to sue for the author's royalties on grounds he'd violated his "secrecy oath."

Echoes of the Imperial Presidency

On a more cosmic level, the ripple effects from *Snepp* helped reshape the powers of the presidency itself.

Traditionally, federal courts had been reluctant to endorse any presidential initiative not specifically authorized by Congress. But after the ruling against me, judges became increasingly solicitous of the president in national security cases, and increasingly willing to let him stretch his authority, even in constitutionally dubious ways, without any law to justify it.

The first whiff of change came in 1981, when the Supreme Court took up the Agee passport case on appeal. In deciding whether Agee could be prevented from traveling abroad to rail against the CIA, the Court harkened to its finding in *Snepp* that the government has a "compelling interest" in preserving the "appearance of confidentiality"—and brusquely dismissed the defendant's free-speech arguments.

The dissenters, Brennan and Marshall, complained that the Court was permitting the executive branch to tamper with a citizen's constitutional rights with no authority from Congress.

Four years later, *Snepp* was applied even more expansively in a Freedom of Information case brought by my own erstwhile lawyer, John Sims. He'd sued the CIA for access to unclassified records pertaining to people and institutions involved in its mind-control experiments. The Supreme Court, on appeal, refused to liberate these documents because, once again, it was loath to compromise the "appearance of confidentiality." *Snepp* thus became a weapon with which the government could eviscerate the Freedom of Information Act.

In subsequent rulings, the Supreme Court built on *Snepp* to reinforce the idea that government employees and contractors are in a world apart when it comes to constitutional rights. In one judgment, the Court emphasized that in my case and others, it had "recognized that Congress may impose restraints on the job-related speech of public employees that would be plainly unconstitutional if applied to the public at large."

Where Are They Now?

Even as reverberations from *Snepp* rolled through the courts, many of the original dramatis personae bowed out.

Graham Martin died unlauded in 1990. His obituary in *The New York Times* reminded readers that one ex–CIA agent named Frank Snepp had severely criticized his handling of the Saigon evacuation. Even in death he couldn't escape me.

Tom Polgar retired from the Agency in the early 1980s and later assisted Congress in its Iran-Contra probe. In our only face-to-face encounter, at a university seminar, he refused to acknowledge my presence.

William Colby died by drowning in 1995 after publishing a second book, this one fully cleared, about Vietnam. A reviewer for *The Washington Post* noted that his failure to rebut my allegations about the evacuation was a tacit admission I'd been right.

Bill Johnson, whose friendship had proved so false, tried to garner literary fame by cranking out manuscripts by the dozen, including a novel about the Roman spies who'd betrayed Christ. Except for some obscure articles on counterintelligence, none of his writings ever found a publisher.

John Stockwell wrote a novel about intelligence, decamped to Cuba for a while, tried his hand at screenwriting, and cozied up to maverick film director Oliver Stone. From time to time, he threatened obliquely to sue me for claiming he'd become radicalized.

The true radical, Philip Agee, continued to potshot the Agency from foreign shores. In late 1989, according to press reports, CIA operatives caught him trying to recruit a female CIA employee in Mexico City on behalf of Cuban intelligence. Agee escaped and later denied being a Cuban agent, though he did acknowledge that "for twenty-five years I have been one more American working in solidarity with activities in Cuba."

Victor Marchetti, my favorite functional alcoholic, gave up booze and veered to the political right, pumping out diatribes for a libertarian journal. In a plot twist worthy of a John le Carré novel, an Islamic terrorist working for a courier firm owned by Marchetti's son shot and killed two CIA employees outside the Langley headquarters in 1993. FBI and CIA agents later caught the murderer in Pakistan and brought him home for trial. Marchetti was not, of course, involved. Neither was his son.

Judge Roarin' Oren Lewis died in 1983 after officiating at the trial of Ted Shackley's onetime colleague Edwin Wilson, who'd taken to supplying CIA arms and expertise to Libyan terrorists. During his waning days, Lewis was twice sanctioned by the appeals court in Richmond for outrageous judicial conduct. His obituary in *The Washington Post* declared his most controversial ruling to be the one against me.

Lead prosecutor Sally Whitaker eventually left the Justice Department and lobbied in vain to become a judge. Her colleague Brook Hedge was more successful, ascending to the bench in Washington in October 1992.

The ever-formidable Mark Lynch crowned his ACLU career by successfully arguing a crucial national security case before the Supreme Court, one that strengthened the right of homosexuals to seek and hold government security clearances. Afterward, he went to work for the prestigious Washington law firm Covington and Burling to "make a little money" for his expanding family.

John Sims, my ever-indulgent second, achieved tenure at a law school in California and spends his days teaching constitutional law and bedeviling the national security community with brilliantly honed Freedom of Information requests. Geoffrey Vitt took his panache to the gentle climes of Vermont, and Alan Dershowitz made media manipulation a familiar handmaiden of American justice by playing the highly visible, wonderfully articulate defender of Claus von Bülow and O. J. Simpson.

Bob Loomis was elevated to a vice president's slot at Random House and continued to nurture me despite my false promise as an author. The company's president, Bob Bernstein, retired to devote himself to the Helsinki Watch Committee on Human Rights.

My beloved CIA friend, Carla Christiansen, married soon after the Supreme Court ruling against me and eventually launched a new and highly successful career in official Washington. Her brilliance had overcome the stigma of our intimacy.

Bernie, dearest Bernie, left the man she'd married in the wake of my trial, raised their daughter, and helped launch her on a promising ballet career. Our friendship resumed as Bernie moved up the corporate ladder at ABC, and continues as she battles the terrible vagaries of cancer. The bravest of the brave.

Stephani Cook, the quintessential cancer survivor, published the autobiography of her disease in 1983. It was an international bestseller. She now advises New York advertising firms on how to seduce the public.

Danielle Haller, the French seductress who saved me with her "gifts," came to New York in 1981 to rescue me from bachelorhood. I cared too much for her to force her to share my misery. For a long while afterward, we tried to meet periodically at a rendezvous of her choosing, though often I was too impoverished to be able to afford the fare.

Indeed, for me, recovery remained as slow and torturous as Sisyphus's uphill journey.

The Climb

"Sometimes I think I'm living out a Kafka story," I told *The New York Times* two years after the Supreme Court decision. "Or maybe it's *1984*."

Initially, I'd hoped to eke out a living as a writer and lecturer, but the venom of the Court's ruling made potential patrons wary. Loomis continued to press me to complete my projected book on the case, but fear of antagonizing the CIA and winding up in jail for contempt overwhelmed inspiration.

By early 1983, I was out of money and all hope. Only the timely intervention of Jack Langguth, a journalism professor at the University of Southern California who'd once been Saigon bureau chief for *The New York Times,* kept me from leaping from a very high window. He asked me to come to USC to participate in a conference on Vietnam and then arranged to have me teach courses on investigative journalism, secrecy, and First Amendment law. For the next two years, I lectured from brief course notes or memory so as avoid having to let the CIA censors into the classroom. Later, Ben Cunningham, a journalism professor at California State University, arranged a similar appointment for me at that institution. The trust he and Langguth bestowed helped deliver me from the ignominy I'd earned in court.

In the meantime, I'd begun to do consulting and producing work for ABC News and to dabble in Hollywood, though always under the CIA's scrutiny. One night, after I'd appeared as a guest on ABC's *Nightline,* the legendary actor Marlon Brando called and asked me to help prepare a film script on the CIA and drug trafficking. He was astonished, but did not object when I told him that all my contributions would have to be cleared by the CIA. In due course, all of them were, marking the first time that a fictional Hollywood script had ever been subject to CIA vetting.

Not long afterward, the producers of a dramatic ABC television series, *Undercover,* picked me up as technical adviser and staff writer. The hour-long episodes I wrote, though wholly fictional, were submitted for censorship. It was the first time the CIA had ever ridden herd on a regularly scheduled television series.

Occasionally, during this period, I supplemented my television income by hiring myself out as defense consultant in national security cases. One such assignment required a government security clearance. The CIA and

State Department shrieked bloody murder when I applied for one. But the FBI could find nothing to disqualify me—I'd never breached official secrecy, after all—and gave me the nod. Only the breadth of the prescribed secrecy agreement, even more comprehensive than my original CIA one, ultimately kept me from taking the job.

I'd been that way before. No thanks!

Snepp II

Not that my troubles were behind me. On the contrary, by the time the *Undercover* TV series went off the air, I was embroiled in a new legal battle with the Agency, this one involving an abuse of the power it held over me. Several years before, I'd managed to sell two program proposals of my own to CBS, one for a miniseries about my case and the other for a fictional dramatic series about spies. To overcome the network's reticence, I'd assured CBS's lawyers that the Agency would have to clear any manuscript within thirty days, as Judge Lewis had prescribed. Based on that guarantee, CBS paid me twenty thousand dollars to write story treatments for both projects.

Within months, the Agency's censors cleared the draft for the series. It was the eighteenth manuscript I'd turned over to them, and except for their "request" years before that I not republicize the name of a previously exposed CIA operative, I'd never been pressed to change a word in any of my writings.

But when I submitted the draft for the miniseries, my luck ran out. A week after the thirty-day clearance deadline had expired, the censors handed me a massive set of deletions that extended even to material they'd allowed me to publish in an earlier manuscript. In effect, they were reclassifying what they'd green-lighted before.

CBS executives barely waited for me to protest to Langley before canceling both the miniseries and the series. A month later, the censors added outrage to injury by announcing they were replacing the initial deletions with new ones. Though more modest, these likewise applied to previously cleared or benign information. For example, in laying out one scene, I'd written: "In the customs area, Frank Snepp hands over his diplomatic passport." The censors had struck out the word "diplomatic." In another scene, I'd had my character drive up to the U.S. embassy gate in Bangkok and stop at a Marine checkpoint. The censors had eliminated the words "Bangkok" and "Marine."

Enraged and under pressure from CBS to repay the development money, I went searching for a lawyer to sue the CIA on my behalf. Having missed the thirty-day deadline, the censors clearly were in contempt of Lewis's original order.

Ultimately, the Washington office of a venerable law firm, Morrison and Foerster, agreed to represent me free of charge. The two attorneys assigned to the case, Henry Levine and Debra LaGapa, were experts in administrative law and insisted on trying to resolve the deletion issues through an appeal to the Agency.

What followed was a year of excruciating negotiations, unduly prolonged by the Agency's insistence on running security checks on Levine and LaGapa. Finally, in March 1987, the CIA's deputy director agreed to drop all the demanded deletions save one, on grounds that the disputed material had previously been approved for publication in an earlier manuscript—exactly the argument I'd been making all along.

Levine and LaGapa took the Agency to court in January 1989, three years after the original thirty-day clearance deadline had elapsed. They asked the federal judge in Alexandria to cite the Agency for contempt, restore the remaining deletion, and reaffirm the thirty-day rule.

It was not to be. The judge found that the CIA had "made substantial and diligent efforts to comply" with the deadline, and that the original court order imposing it was "open to reasonable interpretation."

I felt poleaxed. The thirty-day clearance rule was my only protection. Without it, how could I ever persuade any editor or filmmaker that I could deliver a manuscript on time?

Despair engulfed me. I considered giving up writing altogether. Finally, out of sympathy, Mark Lynch agreed to appeal the decision for me.

To simplify the case, he decided to ignore the remaining deletion and concentrate on getting the original court order clarified to shore up the clearance deadline and judicial review procedures.

The streamlining didn't help. The appeals judges of the Fourth Circuit rejected all his arguments and made clear that if an author's appeal does reach court, it should be viewed skeptically. "The courts must avoid second-guessing the CIA's decision to classify information," they decreed as if that were the argument here.

On the opening day of its 1990 term, the Supreme Court announced it would not grant me a hearing and thereby let the lower court's ruling stand.

A lawyer for the Society of Professional Journalists pronounced *Snepp II* even more injurious to First Amendment values than the Court's original decision against me, since it abandoned authors to the eccentricities of censorship with little hope of judicial succor.

Never in my life had I felt so helpless.
And yet, the trauma still wasn't over.

Return to the Beginning

Five months later, in early 1991, my mother died of emphysema, leaving her drawings in *Decent Interval* as poignant testament to her artistic promise. A week later, a British TV crew took me back to Vietnam to participate in the filming of a documentary about past CIA activities there. Coming so hard upon my mother's death, this pilgrimage tested my sanity as nothing else had. I felt like the mourner at a funeral who is asked to open the casket of an old friend.

Part of the journey, ironically the easiest part, was given over to excursions behind what had once been enemy lines. Flying into gray, bleak Hanoi itself, I had an eerie sense of having seen it all before through the eyes of secret informants I'd debriefed during the war. Peace had brought the victors little comfort, for the ongoing American trade embargo, prompted by *their* failure to account for *our* MIAs, had preserved and exacerbated the devastation of the past.

Everywhere you looked, the north Vietnamese bore their pride on stooped shoulders draped in tattered uniforms, standard fare for both civilian and soldier alike, and even in the city's great plaza, where socialist realism had achieved a kind of apotheosis in the hideous mausoleum that preserved Ho Chi Minh's remains, no one knew how to smile.

At Hanoi's vaunted military museum, the body of a MiG jet lay obscenely atop the blasted hull of an American B-52 as if consummating a rape, and old men in pith helmets and fading fatigues sat brooding over a shabby diorama depicting the Viet Minh victory over the French at Dien Bien Phu in 1954. Only a corner display of yellowing Western photographs celebrated the American disgrace of the evacuation, which, after all, was but a brief moment in Vietnam's long struggle against foreign sway. I stared at the drawn face of Graham Martin in one of the photos and was glad he'd never known what a demeaningly small space he occupied in the enemy's gallery of war. For me, though, the implicit insult—the insinuated inexorability of our defeat—was subtly comforting, for it made the betrayals we'd committed seem inevitable, and therefore less damning.

At another point in the journey, I traveled with the British TV crew south to the most notorious former outposts of the Communist revolution. In Tay Ninh Province, just northwest of Saigon, we trekked to a mountaintop cave that had often served as headquarters for the transient Communist command during the war, a unit known to American intelligence as the Central Office for South Vietnam, COSVN. How often had I attempted to pinpoint its location for American intelligence, and how I'd struggled to imagine its vulnerabilities. But it was no more than an indentation in the jungle with a small Buddhist altar to honor Communist dead, its very insignificance a mocking reminder of how little American might had counted in the balance. I declined to light a joss stick in memory of my fallen enemy, and contented myself that I had no business here.

Later, as I explored a labyrinth of tunnels stretching toward Saigon from the former Communist redoubt in the district of Cu Chi, I experienced the first of several epiphanies. Until the early seventies, entire Viet Cong battalions had hidden in these subterranean cloisters, emerging periodically to launch attacks toward the South Vietnamese capital. The afternoon of my visit, as I stood at the entrance to one of them, marveling at the endurance of those who'd dwelt within, I suddenly glimpsed ghostly figures in black pyjamas flitting among nearby trees and felt the adrenaline shock that had always come with the first scent of Viet Cong. But this time the phantoms coalesced into a gaggle of boisterous Vietnamese kids at play among the rat holes of the tunnels, their peasant garb and stick rifles terrifying evocations of an enemy that was no more. They giggled and pointed at the startled American and then grabbed my hand and urged me to come play with them, and as I gave myself over to their innocence, to the gaiety of these children who knew nothing of the ancient war that had pitted me against their fathers, I realized for the first time that the past was truly receding.

It was a revelation dramatically driven home in Saigon itself, now known as Ho Chi Minh City.

As the Russian-made Tupolev jet banked in over what had been Saigon's Tan Son Nhut airbase, a dusty red haze drifted over the network of arrow-straight highways long ago gouged into the earth by efficiency-minded American engineers to speed American might to war. The vista was achingly familiar and, in its familiarity, vaguely reassuring, despite my dread at having to confront the land of so many of my failures. But gazing out of the cabin window, I immediately sensed a change from what I had known before. Nowhere along the horizon did flyspeck choppers natter after hidden prey, and the once tortured landscape of memory with its bomb craters and lightning gashes of defoliation had given way to a patchwork of lush jungle broken only by the meandering seam of the Saigon river.

When I stepped onto the tarmac, plainclothes security cadre quickly closed round me, though I could glimpse beyond them, along the edges of the runway, rows of rusting American aircraft peeking from behind crumbling revetments like shy witnesses to the American humiliation. Mr. Nguyen, a security man too young to have been my wartime foe, demanded my passport and handed me a visa form that forbade me to come armed with any "coded messages" or to attempt to communicate with old friends, on pain of being ejected forthwith.

On the drive into the city, the ramshackle security van bucked and weaved through traffic every bit as homicidal as I remembered, though bicycles predominated in place of the once omnipresent motorbikes. Ads for Hondas and Japanese electronics winked and beckoned from decrepit roadside billboards once given over to French toothpaste and Bastos cigarettes, and immediately I began to suspect that Tokyo, not Hanoi, had won the subtlest of victories here. Only moldering heaps of concrete memorialized the location of the huge American military headquarters that had stood on the edge of Tan Son Nhut until departing U.S. officials had dynamited it into oblivion the last night of the war.

My hosts put me up at an old American billet in the center of Saigon that had since been converted into a socialist parody of luxury but still bore its former name, Rex Hotel, in noodling Christmas lights over the entrance. I had gambled at the rooftop bar in the old days and during periodic shellings had taken refuge in various of the building's reinforced windowless rooms. Mr. Nguyen had reserved just such a bunker for me, and each night I lay in the claustrophobic darkness, listening to the skittering of rats and feeling like one of my own former prisoners in a hermetically sealed cell.

The first morning I stepped into the halogen glare of Saigon's dry season, the shock of familiarity momentarily routed all other emotions. It was the season of the Tet holidays, and the streets were jammed as they had been in the days I remembered so fondly, with entire families straddling flimsy motorbikes and zipping maniacally through the crush of traffic, and wizened old cyclo drivers hawking discreet diversions, and beggars young and old grappling at the sleeves and pockets of passersby. Firecrackers set up a constant stutter like machine-gun fire, and flowers of every color exploded from kiosks along old Nguyen Hue Boulevard, where I'd taken my first apartment in this city back in 1969.

Only as I stood at the intersection of Le Loi and Nguyen Hue Boulevard, savoring the mingled aromas of diesel, fresh-baked pastry, and rot—all so redolent of the past I loved—did the security men reappear and a sense of inalterable change banish my impulsive euphoria. Oh, there were differences all right, too many to be imagined away. Gone were the flowing *áo dài* tunic dresses Saigon women had favored of old—too reminiscent of the south's decadence, the new masters had decreed—and few of the strollers brandished books, for over one hundred intellectuals had been jailed only six months before. The historic veranda of the Continental Hotel, where Graham Greene had once sipped aperitifs and jotted the first draft of *The Quiet American,* had been enclosed as if to discourage such bourgeois indulgences, and a Christlike replica of a seated Ho Chi Minh, beckoning the little children unto him, now dominated the park in front of the Rex movie theater.

As I stood studying the statue and musing on its seeming incongruity, a schoolgirl approached, handed me a flower to place at Ho's feet, and astonished me by asking in perfect English what I thought of Vietnam's patriarch. Perfect *English*?

I told her vaguely that Ho had fought bravely for the cause he believed in, then pushed a dollar into her hand and stuck the flower in my buttonhole. She retrieved it, and still smiling, placed it alongside Ho's sandals. So charming was the gesture I couldn't bring myself to object, and in my acquiescence I felt a slight easing of a long familiar burden on my soul.

That night, all the city's populace seemed to converge on the now abandoned presidential palace of the old regime, graveyard of so many American hopes, to partake of a spectacular Tet fireworks display. Just before nine o'clock, a brace of rockets screamed over the building, etching fiery traceries in the darkened windows, and sorties of roman candles ruptured into splinters of color, and bombs exploded, and the rattle of firecrackers drove my imagination back to that last night before the evacuation when Communist shelling and small-arms fire had rent the darkness over Saigon—and our final illusions. Reeling under the phosphorous trails and thundering cacophony, I clamped my hands to my ears and wondered if my heart might split apart like a pinwheel of fire.

Then, abruptly, the bombardment ceased as if someone had turned a switch. Raggedly, a Vietnamese rock band whined to life atop a platform near the gate that Communist tanks had burst asunder on liberation day, and shy young couples disengaged from the shadows, the girls in Western crinolines and the guys in Levi's, and began to grind and wriggle to a poor imitation of Madonna's latest. Two years before, Saigon's new masters had outlawed dancing. Clearly, youth had won out, a new generation flexing muscles never tested in war. Again the burden seemed to lighten.

My third or fourth morning in the city, Mr. Nguyen allowed me to tour the downtown area, though with his now familiar admonition not to contact old friends. With the security cadre following by car, a grizzled cyclo driver with broken teeth and a sardonic smile peddled me lazily into the chaos of the waterfront, and I began to realize that the new masters had repaired this city the way Potemkin had built his villages: one block beyond central Saigon's gaudy facades stretched a proscenium of decay and desolation.

As the cyclo approached the old sailing club where I had often supped while watching the war rage on the other side of the river, the driver leaned forward and in halting English welcomed me back. He'd worked for the Americans during the war, he said, and had spent eight years in reeducation camps for his trouble. He wasn't bitter at being abandoned, only curious why his former ally had invested so much and then disappeared. I murmured that the investment had counted for little against miasmic geopolitical stakes. He nodded as if he understood, though I could see he didn't. I prayed that time would eventually make the answer irrelevant to him.

On the pretext of inspecting an amusement park that had newly risen on an old garbage dump, I asked to be delivered to a three-story tenement where Mai Ly had once lived with the child I believed to have been my own. I desperately wanted to go inside, to ask the denizens if they remembered her, if there was any chance I had misapprehended her death and the child's. But Mr. Nguyen's warnings constrained me. The last thing I would do was imperil anyone with my curiosity. After tossing a handful of flower petals on the sidewalk as if discarding refuse, I bade the driver continue on, even as I scanned the passing faces for some semblance of a youthful mirror of my own. Had my son lived, he would be eighteen by now.

Farther along, as we drifted past the old naval yards, I spotted the forbidding compound where I'd interrogated some of our most important prisoners, including the magnificently disciplined Nguyen Van Thai. Hanoi's own Ministry of the Interior now occupied the cells behind the deceptively benign green shutters and slime-burnished walls, but no guards were in evidence, and just beyond a bracelet of razor wire out front a young boy sat at a noodle stand, dolloping up breakfast and surveying the world contentedly from beneath a baseball cap with "NFL" emblazoned across it. Catching my eye, he grinned and held out the bowl as if in offering. Reflexively I shied away, remembering how street urchins had offered hand grenades concealed as home cooking in the old days. He looked perplexed as I struggled to remind myself that the only real enemy here now was my memory.

Moving up old Tu Do Street with its still fragrant gutters and shabby bars, the driver pulled abreast of a forlorn bookstall, and I asked him to stop to let me peruse the offerings. To my astonishment, several pirated copies of *Decent Interval,* in English and Vietnamese, nestled among translations of Karl Marx, and the proprietor, a brusque old Vietnamese woman, asked me in French if I'd ever read it. I smiled and nodded, and quite without prompting she informed me that the author had been persecuted by the American imperialists and was now dead or in prison. I nodded again and bought a copy and walked back to Mr. Nguyen's car, which was idling just down the block, and handed him the book through the window. For the first time, he evinced something like a smile. Timidly, he asked me to autograph the title page and seemed touched when I wrote "To a new friend." He confessed he'd never had much contact with Americans or much use for them since his brother had died at their hands during some long-ago campaign in Quang Tri Province. As I walked back to the cyclo, he was avidly flipping the pages.

Near the former American embassy stood an open-air temple where Mai Ly had often gone to offer alms for the poor, and I asked the driver to drop me there. The scene within might have been lifted from some Vietnamese vision of hell. Beneath the stone eyes of a huge laughing Buddha, scrofulous beggars in ragged South Vietnamese uniforms scrabbled after me, dragging mangled limbs across broken terra-cotta tile already laced with blood tracks. I emptied my pockets at them in some misbegotten bid for forgiveness, and in the ensuing melee an armless boy was trampled and an old man fell into a quivering spasm that caused the mob to part in terror.

A saffron-cloaked bonze beckoned to me, and I followed him to a large stone urn where a bouquet of joss sticks awaited immolation. I lit one, then another, in memory of Mai Ly and my mother, and prayed to the depths of my soul that I would find no one I knew or loved here, for death would have been preferable.

Countless bruised and crippled fingers crept up my trouser legs, and suddenly Mr. Nguyen appeared alongside, kicking and shoving the beggars out of the way. His hands closed around my arm and he dragged me off, chiding me for trying to use this holy place as a screen for forbidden contacts with spies and lackeys of the old Saigon regime.

He did not deport me, though. Not his "new friend."

Later, above a treeline ravaged by the belching exhausts of too much modernity, the old embassy's rooftop helipad hove into view as the cyclo driver wheeled though the intersection of old Mac Dinh Chi and Thong Nhut. My heart sprang against my chest as the long shadow of my former home passed across us. The bomb shield, a crossword puzzle of small windows and concrete girding masking the face of the building, was peeling in long, dry husks, and out front, the concrete canopy that once led the powerful into this sanctum of illusion listed so precariously that I would have been wary of passing underneath. A small plaque tacked onto the outer wall told of the final merciless evacuation.

The driver deposited me at the side gate, and I walked through unchallenged, the guard booth being deserted, and picked my way warily through the imaginary masses that had howled and pleaded here twenty years before.

Chickens scrabbled through the flowerpots where the Viet Cong had set up sniper nests during the 1968 offensive that had penetrated the embassy walls, and a slight breeze whisked debris across Martin's parking space, still vaguely delineated by painted lines and the word "Ambassador." Nearby, a tree stump sprouted delicate tendrils, all that was left of the great tamarind that had once commanded the courtyard, a tree the ambassador had refused to have cut down for fear of signaling American defeat, even though its very presence had thwarted the landing of the evacuation choppers. Finally, Marine guards had brought out the buzz saw—and the choppers had come in.

Another tamarind still stood near the embassy's back doorway. Time and too many wet seasons had split open its trunk to expose a sinewy interior chillingly reminiscent of the musculature of a human body stripped of skin. During the latter stages of the evacuation, the downdraft from incoming choppers had ripped open abandoned bags of half-shredded classified documents and blown the contents high into the branches of this tree. Strips of top-secret material had remained lodged there until the Communists had arrived hours later. Meticulously, they'd pieced the documents together and used them to track down and identify Vietnamese we'd left behind. The tree's gutted old carcass seemed to bespeak the quality of American honor that day.

Soon, Mr. Nguyen arrived with other security cadre in tow and informed me the embassy's three bottom floors, including the ambassador's old office, were now occupied by a foreign oil consortium, though I suspected this was merely a euphemism for some sort of intelligence operation. The upper floors, however, remained abandoned, and no Western television crew had ever been granted access. But Mr. Nguyen was feeling expansive. He agreed to let me and the British crew tour the sixth floor where my own office and Polgar's had been located.

As I stepped out of the stairwell, the past slammed into me like heat from an open furnace. I had to steady myself as my imagination wheeled back to that last night when legions of terrified Vietnamese had lined this corridor, desperately waiting to be led up to rescue choppers on the roof. Again I heard them screaming, felt them pawing at my sleeve, clinging to me as if I were a surety to salvation.

Behind the door still marked "628" I found the shell of my old office and the CIA operations room. The place had been stripped of all furnishings, and someone had ripped out the light and electrical fixtures, apparently searching for bugs or surveillance cameras that we might have left behind but didn't. The pillaging had not banished the ghosts, though. Standing at the plastic-paned window, gazing numbly out at the front gate where panicked throngs had gathered on April 29, 1975, in hope of rescue, I could hear the hiss and crackle of CIA radios rising in my ear and detect again the static-filled cries for help from abandoned friends and agents. *I'm Mr. Han, the translator. I'm Loc, the Nung guard.* I apologized to my British companions for the tears I couldn't stanch.

On the stairwell leading to the rooftop pad, flak-jacketed Marine guards materialized out of memory to punch and shove Vietnamese out of the way so the last CIA contingent could make its own escape. I'd averted my face in shame that night, unable to look those in the eye who were being sacrificed to my own deliverance.

The shame still burned on my cheeks, and as I emerged onto the rooftop pad, now flaked and moldering, the remembered howl of the chopper's engine roared through my brain, overloading the already tortured circuitry, and suddenly I found myself teetering on the edge of the pad, like a diver preparing to plunge into the depths.

Startled, the camera crew crowded in on me, jostling me away from the brink, and as I stumbled back, I caught a brief glimpse of a very young child in the street six stories below, waving up at me gaily. Abruptly, the whap of the chopper blades ceased, and in its place the benign clatter of street noise wafted up at me, and lifting my eyes I saw a clutch of multihued holiday balloons drifting skyward over the steeple of Saigon's cathedral and felt as though I were being borne away by them from what I realized now I could never change.

Before leaving Saigon, I wrote a postcard to a friend: "I have spent much time sharing stories and rice bowls with former enemies and have joked with those I would have interrogated or killed. I have communed with the ghosts and stray chickens that have inherited the last bastion of American glory in Vietnam, and for the first time I have seen the children truly laughing."

Final Dispensation

Four years after I made my own peace with Vietnam, the United States followed suit, formally recognizing the Hanoi government after obtaining assurances of help in tracking down Americans still missing. Two years later, the first American ambassador to set foot in the country since Graham Martin's ignominious departure took up residence in Hanoi. I applauded both developments as likely to contribute to the welfare of our abandoned South Vietnamese allies. In a sense, recognition accomplished what I had long sought. That struggle was finally over.

In the meantime, though, I'd let more immediate moral obligations go wanting. Despite the many years since the Supreme Court ruling, I'd been unable to muster the strength to complete the book about my legal travails that I owed Random House. The rage for which the book was to have been an antidote had paralyzed me. Even more destructively, I'd refused to bury the hatchet with my father. Shame at having hurt him so had kept me from opening myself to him even as his health had steadily declined. By early 1997, cancer, emphysema, and heart failure had reduced him to the torments of Job, and our alienation was into its tenth year of mutual silence. He'd written me out of his will. I'd written him out of my consciousness. He was as good as dead.

But then, in January of that year, the elder of my younger sisters, Candy, who had her own problems with him, called to warn me that death might soon overtake any chance of reconciliation. Angrily, I decided that if he meant so little to me there would be no harm in seeing him one last time.

When Candy and I walked into his hospital room, he wore the ghastly pallor I'd last seen on the face of Graham Martin. His eyes fluttered open and erupted in tears. "I forgive you and you forgive me," he murmured. "Now let's get on with things." In that single utterance he rendered as irrelevant as the war the tensions that had existed between us.

My father survived his lapse that January, and soon after being released from the hospital, he summoned me and urged that I put aside everything, every TV production job, every other distraction, to finish the book on the case. He would even underwrite the endeavor, he said.

And he did. For the next eight months he footed the bills and encouraged me even as my will flagged. It was his inspiration and largesse that enabled me to uncover Justice Lewis Powell's role in my undoing. He paid for the research and endorsed my conclusions. He told me that I'd been betrayed by the law he himself had spent a lifetime upholding.

I wrote as fast as I could, knowing that my father was dying. I wanted him to know why I'd bloodied him, why I'd lashed out at the senator who'd controlled his appointment to the bench. By the following June, I was sharing the manuscript with him even though my gag order forbade it. Nothing had finally been cleared by the CIA, but still I gave manuscript pages to my father. He tried to read them, but by now he was legally blind. The CIA's first-look rights were preserved by a blind man's infirmity.

As I neared completion of the manuscript, I confided to a friend that I was fearful of finishing it, that I'd been haunted by the premonition that once the book was done, my father would die.

In mid-September, I wrapped up the final chapters. Five days later, I received a call from a hospital room in North Carolina. My father came on the line and gasped over the painkillers, "I'm dying. I love you."

I immediately flew to his bedside, and with my two sisters, my brother-in-law, and my brother I was with him when he passed away ten horrible days later.

My brother, David, told me my father had expressed only one regret: that he would not live to see this book published.

Shortly after his death, the CIA's prepublication review board reviewed the final chapter of this manuscript, as it had the entire work before, and in the words of its reply to me, posed "no security objection to its publication."

INDEX

ABOUT THE AUTHOR

FRANK SNEPP graduated from Columbia College in New York and later earned a master's degree from Columbia's School of International Affairs. In 1968, he was recruited into the CIA, where he worked for eight years as both an analyst and an operative responsible for interrogations and agent debriefings. During his second tour in Vietnam he became the Agency's principal in-country analyst of North Vietnamese political affairs. Awarded the CIA's Medal of Merit after Saigon's collapse, he soon resigned and spent the next eighteen months writing *Decent Interval,* a bestseller about the end of the war that would become the focus of the Agency's efforts to control all such publications in the future. Since that book, Frank Snepp has taught constitutional law, written for magazines and dramatic TV shows, coauthored screenplays, and worked as a television news reporter and producer, responsible for covering such stories as the Iran-Contra scandal and the Monica Lewinsky affair. A television documentary on drug trafficking, which he wrote and produced, has won numerous awards for investigative journalism, including an Emmy, and his advocacy of free-speech issues has landed him a J. Roderick MacArthur Foundation grant (to assist with this book), the Hugh M. Hefner First Amendment Award, and the National First Amendment Award of the Society of Professional Journalists. Twice divorced, he lives in California.

ABOUT THE TYPE

This book was set in Times Roman, designed by Stanley Morison specifically for *The Times* of London. The typeface was introduced in the newspaper in 1932. Times Roman had its greatest success in the United States as a book and commercial typeface, rather than one used in newspapers.